DYNAMICS IN PASTORING

by

JACOB FIRET

Professor of Practical Theology,
The Free University, Amsterdam

"Thou didst lead thy people like a flock
by the hand of Moses and Aaron."
Psalm 77:20

WILLIAM B. EERDMANS PUBLISHING COMPANY
GRAND RAPIDS, MICHIGAN

Translated from the Dutch edition, *Het agogisch Moment in het pastoraal Optreden*,
© Uitgeversmaatschappij J. H. Kok—Kampen 1982

Library of Congress Cataloging-in-Publication Data

Firet, Jacob.
  Dynamics in pastoring.

  Translation of: Het agogisch moment in het pastoraal optreden.
  Bibliography: p. 293
  Includes index.
  1. Pastoral theology—Reformed Church. 2. Reformed
Church—Clergy. I. Title.
BV4011.F513 1986   253   85-29381

ISBN 0-8028-0169-2

Contents

Translator's Note

The present translation is a complete version of Dr. Jacob Firet's book *Het agogisch Moment in het pastoraal Optreden* (lit. The Agogic Moment in Pastoral Role-Fulfilment). That title really covers the contents of the book. It needs no explanation here since entire chapters are devoted to a careful exposition of what is meant by "the agogic moment" and by "pastoral role-fulfilment." Only the word "agogic" tends to puzzle the person who first encounters it. Pivotal to Dr. Firet's position is that when God comes to people through the intermediary of pastoral role-fulfilment he aims at a change in their psycho-spiritual functioning. This change occurs through the intermediary of an interhuman relationship and is therefore open to some degree to analysis and reflection. The specifically agogic for Dr. Firet is located in the effort by which the minister of the gospel hopes to achieve this change in the way a human being functions and in the nature of this change.

I call the translation "complete" because nothing essential to the English reader has been left out. A few digressions in the book were condensed or omitted, but they are rare. My aim throughout was to make the book readable for people with a professional interest in the gospel ministry without losing the integrity of the original. Dr. Firet has followed the convention of distinguishing his main argument from excursus material—material that supplements and illuminates the central argument but that is not immediately necessary for it. I have translated these digressions and have maintained Dr. Firet's distinction by placing them within brackets. Where I could not lay my hands on existing translations of the Dutch or German poems quoted in the text, I tremblingly offer my own.

The book, which was first published as a doctoral dissertation in 1968, has gone through five printings and is required reading in a number of theological seminaries. And no wonder! It reestablishes the entire field of pastoral theology on its scriptural foundations while it freely and liberally, yet critically, uses insights from the social sciences wherever they open doorways for the practical theologian. One follows the author's argument with mounting excitement and marvels at the relentless thoroughness with which he arrives at his definitions and conclusions.

A problem which dogged me throughout relates to the use of inclusive language. I want the book to be as attractive to women as to men. The usual ways of avoiding generic words which have become objectionable strike me as grammatically or stylistically awkward. So, to give both sexes their due, I have chosen to use "he" as the inclusive pronoun in one section and "she" in the next, throwing the hobgoblin of consistency to the winds. On balance, I believe the translation tilts toward a predominant use of the inclusive "she."

Acknowledgments are in order to Professor Martin Bakker, Associate Professor of Germanic Languages at Calvin College, for his help in interpreting the long Nijhoff poem; to Dr. Barbara Carvill for her inexhaustible willingness to check my translation of the numerous quotations from German authors; to Professor Stanley Wiersma for his help in finding appropriate substitutes in English literature for a couple of didactic verses from the Dutch; to the Rev. Michael De Vries, Th.M., for his critical and enlightened reading of the entire manuscript; and to Ms. Sue Ebels for her tireless efforts in typing.

The defects which undoubtedly remain must be laid at my doorstep.

JOHN VRIEND

Author's Preface (1973)

Do I, five years after publication, still stand by what I have written, at least to the extent that it can be reprinted without alteration? That is certainly the case. Were I to write on the same subject today I would do it, in the main, as I did then. Increasingly I have become convinced that the approach to the problematics of practical theology which I discovered as I worked on this book is in principle correct. In many respects I can "find myself" in the conception of practical theology which H. D. Bastion has so vigorously defended. Especially his article "Vom Wort zu den Wörtern" (*Evangelische Theologie* 28 [1968]: 25ff.), which was published shortly after the appearance of the first printing of this book, struck me pleasurably with its similarity in intent.

This is not to say that I have not changed my point of view since the book was first published. A brief summary of the points in which my position *now* differs from my position *then* follows.

1. I am now inclined to view the praxis, which constitutes the concern of practical theology, less exclusively as the praxis of churchly functioning and pastoral role-fulfilment. The reason is not that I have less appreciation for the church; it derives more from a clearer insight into the possibility and reality of the coming of God in ways other than those of ecclesiastical institutions.

2. More than before, I am now convinced that it is desirable to bring about a "horizontal" arrangement of practical theology. I no longer speak of "churchly functioning" and "pastoral role-fulfilment," but of practical-theological communication and structures.

3. I am still convinced that our specialty of practical theology must be thoroughly theological. This implies, among other things, that it may consult other sciences after a careful methodological transposition of its questions. I now believe, however, that the drums of theology could be beaten with less vigor than I have done in this book.

4. The practical theologian cannot avoid entering into areas of theology other than his specialty. In this book I did this especially in the second part, with a view to constructing a model of pastoral role-fulfilment. There I ventured

especially into the terrain of biblical theology. More clearly than before, I now see that when a person tries to bring, e.g., Matthew, Luke, Paul, and John into one system, he is doing something which is problematic, to put it mildly. The effect of this would be, I think, greater caution in proceeding, but not much in the way of material change.

It has been a pleasure for me to notice that this book is useful to many who are interested in questions of pastoral praxis and pastoral theology. I hope that this edition—which was undertaken at the request of many who use it as a teaching manual—may serve the churches and clergy even more directly in their daily praxis.

August 1973   JACOB FIRET

Preface to the English Edition (1985)

For a long time the study of practical and pastoral theology in the Netherlands was characterized particularly by two realities. First, practical theology was strongly influenced by *German* works in the field (among others, F. D. E. Schleiermacher, E. C. Achelis, F. Niebergall, A. D. Müller, and E. Thurneysen). Second, in the area of theology it was viewed as an appendix, not as an independent field of study with a focus and method of its own.

After World War II, particularly toward the end of the sixties, there was a shift in emphasis. An important factor was the growth of contact between pastoral theologians in the Netherlands and a number of influential theologians in the United States, particularly those associated with the Clinical Pastoral Education Movement. In general, practical theology began to show a greater openness toward the social sciences. A plea was made for a more empirical approach and, as a consequence, the question arose how, with this emphasis, practical theology could nevertheless retain its *theological* character.

In this book I have made an attempt to pose and to open up for discussion a number of important theological questions relating to the pastoral ministry. In the process I have restricted myself to a biblical-theological approach which culminates in the construction of a theological model of ministry and ministerial role-fulfilment. Further, in my address to these questions, I have consulted the social sciences (especially psychology, social psychology, and pedagogics). A theological defense of this method occurs in the section "The Holy Spirit and Pastoral Role-Fulfilment" (pp. 116-34).

The title of the book is *Dynamics in Pastoring*. In setting forth a theory of pastoral role-fulfilment one can speak of the dynamics of ministry with a view to the different forces which exert an influence of some kind on the pastoral situation and on pastoral performance. In speaking of "dynamics in pastoring" I have in view the essential principles of ministry, the dynamics inherent in ministry without which *no* "ministry" occurs. I make a distinction between two sets of dynamics. In the model I call them the *hermeneutic* moment and the *agogic* moment, the former referring to the impetus toward understanding and the latter to the impetus toward change. In practice these two moments are bound up with each other; in fact they presuppose each other. But for the purpose of practical-theological analysis and research they are to be distinguished. The focus of this book is on the agogic moment.

Although originally it was not written for that purpose, this book now serves as a textbook for courses in pastoral theology in the Netherlands. From where I sit I cannot tell whether it will serve that function in other countries or in another language. I do hope that it will make a contribution to the discussions taking place in practical theology as well as to the formation of theory relating to the pastoral ministry.

I owe a large debt of thanks to Mr. John Vriend, who translated the book. I am grateful to my friend and pupil, the Reverend Michael De Vries, for standing ready to assist the translator. Finally, I wish to express my indebtedness to my friend and coworker, Jelle Van Nijen, who promoted the publication of this book in English.

JACOB FIRET

DYNAMICS IN PASTORING

I. Introduction: The Situation and Task of Practical Theology

1. THE UNCERTAIN POSITION OF PRACTICAL THEOLOGY

At the beginning of a study of the relationship of practical theology to the whole of the theological enterprise—even to science in general—W. Birnbaum remarks: "The discipline of practical theology still falters and flounders, being driven one way and another on the wide waters of the *universitas.*"[1] In Roman Catholic circles the situation is not very different. Says R. Füglister: Pastoral theology is the youngest of the family of theological disciplines; and theologians, at least in part, are not yet agreed "whether pastoral theology is only an introduction to pastoral care, or a scientific discipline about pastoral care and, if the latter, whether it may be credited with a theological character."[2]

In the main one encounters two virtually opposite conceptions of practical theology. One conception can perhaps best be described with words used in 1938 by L. J. van Holk—a position which still lingers though few would wish to be responsible for van Holk's formulation. According to him, practical theology is "a composite mixture of dogmatic definition and practical suggestions for the exercise of the preacher's office." It is a subject which can "hardly be called theological" and is "not strictly scientific." It covers "the practical-technical side" of the theological world.

Over against this conception is one which is possibly no more widespread these days but has found more forceful defenders. It can be expressed in the words of M. H. Bolkestein. Practical theology, says he, is "not the Cinderella of theology. It poses the theological question in a manner which differs from that of exegetical and dogmatic theology, but which is no less legitimate or

---

[1]W. Birnbaum, *Theologische Wandlungen von Schleiermacher bis Karl Barth,* an encyclopedic study of practical theology. Note: more completely bibliographical information is given in the List of Works Cited following the body of this work.
[2]R. Füglister, *Die Pastoraltheologie als Universitätsdisciplin.*

scientific."[3] In this line of thought practical theology is not an appendix of other theological disciplines and one even has to avoid calling it a part.[4]

[*A variety of proponents can be cited. Gerhard Ebeling states: "Theology is an indivisible whole because it has to do with one single fundamentally simple thing—the Word of God which is not many things but one." "The articulation of theology into different fields of study is meaningful only if each partial concern can be understood as of such a kind that the whole is latent in it."[5] Karl Barth offers his division of theology "as biblical theology . . . as practical theology . . . as dogmatic theology."[6] Entirely in keeping with this division, Eduard Thurneysen calls practical theology "the third form" of theology.[7] A. D. Müller and O. Haendler, the authors of the two most important handbooks on practical theology published in recent years, each of whom follows his own path, also in distinction from that of Barth *cum suis* and of Ebeling *cum suis,* wish to address the question What is practical theology? in a radically theological way. Müller describes practical theology as "the theological doctrine of the proper realization of the Kingdom of God in the church and through the church in the world."[8] According to O. Haendler, practical theology is "the theology of the structures of the contemporary church." Other theological disciplines "ought to acknowledge that the theological content and results of practical theology belong intensively, organically, and reciprocally to the organism of theology."[9] Practical theology has much more to do, and fundamentally something very different, than "showing how one does it." In this discipline one learns to understand "the essence and the life norms of the church."[10]]*

All these quotations may create the impression that practical theology has been totally accepted as a distinctive discipline in theology; even that theology in this specialty wishes to address itself to the concrete objectives and the actual existence of the church, its "realization" and its "present."

Before coming to this appraisal, however, one must call to mind the following considerations. First, whatever good things may be said about, and from the perspective of, practical theology, it does not yet really have a clear image of its own.

---

[3]M. H. Bolkestein, "Het Terrein der praktische Theologie," in *Nederlands theologische Tijdschrift* 15 (1960-61): 282ff.

[4]Even Abraham Kuyper expressed the view that it is not really correct to speak of "subjects" or "parts" in theology, since we are dealing with the "living members of a theological body" (*Encyclopaedie,* III, 1ff.).

[5]G. Ebeling, *Word and Faith,* p. 425.

[6]K. Barth, *The Doctrine of the Word of God,* p. 3.

[7]E. Thurneysen, *A Theology of Pastoral Care,* p. 12.

[8]A. D. Müller, *Grundriss der praktischen Theologie,* p. 13.

[9]O. Haendler, *Grundriss der praktischen Theologie,* pp. 1ff.

[10]Ibid., p. 13. W. Birnbaum, in his *Theologische Wandlungen,* pp. 233ff., falls into line behind Haendler. To him, practical theology is "the science of the concrete manifestation of the church of Jesus Christ in the present."

*The use of sectional brackets in this translation indicates excursus material.

Second, W. Jannasch remarks that practical theology as an independent discipline became necessary "when the other theological disciplines, as they grew more independent, threatened to distance themselves from their churchly task." According to him, the independent existence of practical theology is necessary even now, "because the church-relatedness of theology must ever be given new emphasis or regained."[11] One gets the impression, however, that that battle has been fought—and won. "Theology has to do with reality as a totality," says Ebeling.[12] Ever increasingly dogmatic theology is requiring of itself that it be functional. Ever more intensively ethics is busying itself with questions put to it by the church and the world. In the biblical sciences questions relating to the kerygma are central. The very practical questions concerning church structures and churchly modes of being are no longer the exclusive domain of any theological specialty. All of theology now seeks to be "a ministry" to the church,[13] and none of the other theological disciplines wishes to leave to practical theology the search for the real-life connections. All of theology "demands openness toward every kind of experience of reality."[14] Not just one, so-called "practical" specialty occupies itself with "Realization" (Müller) and "the Present" (Haendler, Birnbaum), but *theology* has this aim.

In view of this development one cannot a priori exclude the possibility that the "functionalization" of theology as a whole will overtake the "theologizing" of practical theology, and hence that theology—almost from the same motives which led it to give practical theology a place of dignity—will dismiss it as superfluous.

Third, in reflecting on the unity of theology in all its disciplines Karl Barth remarks that practical theology is in danger of degenerating into "the theory of a trade" (*Handwerkslehre*) "which is orientated by every conceivable practical consideration but not by Scripture, history, and dogma, and which is therefore theologically empty,"[15] "churchly instruction in practical skills." According to Birnbaum, practical theology had largely sunk to this questionable level around 1914.

But now something needs to be said on the other side. In practice it turns out that in many cases the professional skills of the theological graduate leave a few things to be desired. This becomes more obvious, and is felt more strongly by pastors and the like, to the extent that more helping professions make their appearance. In a variety of fields which resemble or border on the pastorate (e.g., social work, cultural activities, youth education, personal counseling) a process of increasing professionalization is taking place. In America, where this development began and is now most advanced, it seems that the traditional

---

[11]W. Jannasch, *Die Religion in Geschichte und Gegenwart*, V, col. 504.
[12]G. Ebeling, *Word and Faith*, p. 199.
[13]H. M. Kuitert, *De Mensvormigheid Gods*, p. 302.
[14]G. Ebeling, *Word and Faith*, p. 199.
[15]K. Barth, *Church Dogmatics*, IV/3-12, p. 88 (translation by G. W. Bromiley).

subjects of the theological curriculum are more and more overshadowed by courses which aim at the pastoral "vocation," such as "Christian Education, Pastoral Care and Counselling, and Church Administration."[16]

In light of all this—the unclear "image" of practical theology, the "practicalization" of theology as a whole, the pressure from the churches for a more professional training—one has to conclude that, contrary pronouncements notwithstanding, practical theology cannot really be sure of retaining its place of dignity as a genuine theological specialty in the midst of other theological disciplines. It could become another cemetery of past dreams.

2. PRACTICAL THEOLOGY — A THEOLOGICAL DISCIPLINE

It is a question whether this fate would be so serious. If theology as it is done at universities were really practical and functional, could not the churches take into their own hands the vocational training of their ministers, using seminaries as bridges between academic study and actual ministry?

It seems to us that there are at least two objections to a removal of practical theology from a theological curriculum.[17] The first objection derives from the situation of those who study theology, and the second is directly theological.

As for the first, theological students tend to have little sympathy for the popular conception that they are "studying to be pastors." H. Faber, in a public lecture presented when he assumed the position of lector in pastoral psychology, made clear that he is not averse to this popular conception.[18] He is increasingly impressed, as he listens to theological students and active ministers, with "their growing uncertainty about the pastorate." "This uncertainty," says Faber, "concerns the most vital aspects of the pastorate. I will mention a few: insight into the identification with one's own role and task; the relationship with parishioners; the integration of theological knowledge; preparing for the actual work of the pastorate; one's own faith in all this."[19] Faber tells of a seminary graduate who, in reflecting on a sickbed conversation he himself had had, made the remark "that in this conversation he was reduced to falling back on the faith of his

---

[16]M. L. Peel, "Theological Education in America," in *Vox Theologica* 33 (1962-63): 85ff.

[17]We continue to use the name "practical theology"—the name which has won a fixed place for itself in the Protestant theological world—in spite of the objections which can be raised against it. The adjective is to be understood as describing the object of the study. "Practical theology" is *praxeology*: the systematic study of the vital manifestations and ministries of the church. For the meaning of *praxis* see Romans 12:4 and the Greek name for the Acts of the Apostles.

[18]H. Faber, *Leren voor Dominee*.

[19]Ibid., p. 3; cf. p. 14.

infancy." The chasm between the problems of the pastorate and the theological learning one has acquired, it often turns out, is much too deep. Even young ministers who have learned to theologize with their feet on the ground—with an eye to the problems of the church and the world—frequently have a hard time being pastoral, from their vantage point, in sermons, conversations, and church education. The theologian, the pastor, and the believer—often these are three distinct roles. But for the pastorate it is essential that the three (correct theological attitudes, insight, and knowledge; correct pastoral attitudes, insight, and skills; and "the faith of the person") be integrated. This integration cannot be postponed till theological study has been completed; it cannot be accomplished in a few months by means of special courses; it has to be realized in a process of coincidental convergent growth, a fusion, in the heart of a believing, theological, pastoral person. When the development of the theologian-pastor is not from the start one which tends in the direction of this unity, it necessarily leads to the uncertainty signaled by Faber.

The second objection against the removal of practical theology from the theological curriculum flows directly from the nature of theology. Karl Barth once posited the thesis[20] that instead of speaking of "theology" it would be better to speak of "theo-anthropology." Theology has to do "with God as the God of human beings; for that reason precisely, therefore, with people as the people of God." The term "theology" is not really adequate "because it fails to make visible this decisive dimension of its object." If in theology the object is the knowledge of God, and if theology is a service to the church and to the pulpit, then for that reason alone the human person—i.e., the person who reads the Bible, listens to sermons, and reflects on both Bible and sermons—is relevant. Then, too, the whole communication process between Bible writers and Bible readers, between preachers and congregations—all that happens in the sphere of the knowledge of God: reading, listening, reflection, prayer, and especially interpersonal relations—is theologically relevant. Theology is not only the study of the knowledge of God; it is also the study of the process of getting to know God, of the events which happen between God and human beings, and between persons, with a view to the process of getting to know, and knowing God. In other words, theology's field of study embraces all factors essential to knowing God, functions of his revelation and his companionship with us human beings, including the functioning of the faith-community, pastoral role-fulfilment, and pastoral communication. A theology of which something like pastoral theology was not an essential component could not possibly include these features in its field of inquiry. So if we plead for the retention of practical theology, the motive lies not only in the "wholeness" of the person who studies theology with an eye to the pastoral ministry, but also in the "wholeness" of the theology which aims to be a ministry to the church.

---

[20]K. Barth, *Evangelical Theology: An Introduction,* p. 12.

3. PRACTICAL THEOLOGY — A DISTINCTIVE DISCIPLINE

The preceding section should have made it somewhat clear that the op-posing positions we described at the beginning of this part do not pose a real dilemma for us. This is not to say that we want to reserve any part of what Barth called the "theologically hollow theory of a trade" (*Handwerkslehre*). Once bitten by a practical theology of that caliber, one is bound to be twice shy—theolog-ically. O. Haendler, in his discussion of the methodology of catechesis, remarks: "Mistrust of psychology is based here, as everywhere in the church, on the very real danger that something important, even decisive in human life, will be rel-ativized into a merely psychological process."[21] His formulation of the issue is debatable,[22] but his meaning is clear: every practical theology which borders on psychologism or sociologism is bound to evoke deep distrust. The reason is not only that it relativizes the crucial dimensions of human existence but also that—even apart from the practice of practical theology—it is unscientific and deadly to the pastorate.

We have no desire, therefore, to ignore the warning signs held before us as we begin our journey in the direction of what happens, in the exercise of the pastoral role, in and between persons, and between God and the human person. It is an idle question, says Karl Barth, how those who proclaim the word of God "should approach this or that modern man, or how they should 'bring home' the word of God to him."[23] "The task of the preacher is to speak this outward Word in such a way that it reaches the man who hears it," affirms Gustaf Wingren,[24] but he adds: "It is not possible to say anything further about the entrance of that Word." In any case, preaching must certainly be "God's own speech to men."[25] This address to human beings "does not take place through any sort of psychologically studied approach on the part of the preacher but exclusively as, without artifice, the sermon reproduces the meaning of the pas-sage as a word to the listening people."[26]

But is the issue of what happens interpersonally in pastoral role-fulfilment an idle question? Is it idle because it concerns the word of him who declares that his word will not return empty (Isa. 55:11)? Is it idle because—as Miskotte puts it—"preaching and instruction . . . are a happening on which one does not know how it happens"?[27] But could not the sequel (". . . although on the other hand one knows very well that when certain things are denied or neglected, it

---

[21]O. Haendler, *Grundriss der praktischen Theologie*, p. 281.

[22]At stake is not a "psychological process" but something which happens between God and human beings and which can be made psychologically transparent from top to bottom.

[23]K. Barth, *Evangelical Theology: An Introduction*, p. 182.

[24]G. Wingren, *The Living Word*, p. 209.

[25]Ibid., p. 19.

[26]Ibid., p. 20.

[27]K. H. Miskotte, *When the Gods Are Silent*, p. 103.

is not to be expected that anything of consequence will happen") apply perhaps to that interhuman happening? And would it not be a promising enterprise to ask what these forms of denial and neglect are and see whether as theologians we could not make some progress? There is really no need to proceed in the direction against which Wingren warns, that of a psychological hatching-out process; but it sounds a trifle too naive when he posits that "it is not possible to say anything further" about the entrance of the word in human life. The sciences which deal with interhuman happenings have said enough about the subject that "theo-anthropology," after eavesdropping in the workshops of these sciences, should at least have the courage to formulate a number of questions.

This inquiry and this search for answers is, then, the business of theology. It is the business of theology, not just to avert the dangers of psychologism and sociologism, but because in the problematics of the interaction between humans the issue is "to know God"—a genuinely theological inquiry.

We have quoted Wingren's words to the effect that "it is not possible to say anything further" on the subject of what happens between preacher and listener. An examination of the literature of practical theology would not lead to such a negative conclusion, however; much more striking in this literature is that all sorts of things are being said and all kinds of suggestions are being made, without it being clear on what grounds this is being done. What S. D. Fokkema said of theory formation in pedagogics certainly applies to theory formation in practical theology—namely, that in regard to issues in which it seeks to be empirical and practical, too, its theory shows a distinct tendency toward being untestable. We do not in the least mean that assertions are being launched "in the blue." In the literature on the pastorate and church practice in general, one can discern much practical wisdom and see the evidence of well-worked-through experience. One can learn much from it—in the same way that a young preacher can learn from a seasoned older colleague. But practical wisdom and personal experience cannot adequately serve as bases for a theory which is indispensable in protecting our praxis from a plunge into the arbitrary. "Nothing is so practical as a good theory." For the formation of theory more is needed than practical—i.e., personal—experience, more also than the insight which comes from wisdom or personal gifts. Theory formation must be based on knowledge which has been acquired methodically; on experience which demonstrably rests, not on what is incidental and individual, but on phenomena which regularly recur under certain conditions.

In practical theology we are nowhere near the point where we can even start such theory formation. This is not to say that this is the first time a call for attention to this matter has been issued in practical theology. J. Waterink already did this emphatically in 1923.[28] But thirty-six years later H. O. Wölber was led to state that practical theology had not yet entered this field.[29]

This will never happen, it seems to us, if no effort is made to develop a

---

[28]J. Waterink, *Plaats en Methode van de ambtelijke Vakken.*
[29]H. O. Wölber, *Religion ohne Entscheidung,* pp. 217ff.

clear and unambiguous conceptual apparatus. In our discipline it sometimes seems as if terms are used as the most individual expressions of the most personal insights, or—worse—as if common terms are employed but each uses them to mean something different. To give an example or two. Some use the word "proclamation" as a synonym for preaching; others use it to embrace preaching, pastoral care, catechesis, etc.; for still another group "proclamation" stands for the transmission of the message of God which does not proceed from a text and does not occur in a church service; still others wish to use the word only for bringing the gospel to people who have never heard it; a fifth conception is that proclamation is the central component in all speech from, and about, the word of God; proclamation, it is said, is in any event communication by means of words, a speech-event, although deed proclamation is also mentioned. Another example: pastoral care is a special form of preaching or proclamation, namely, to the individual; pastoral care is a special *application* of the gospel, say others; pastoral care embraces preaching, catechesis, and the spiritual guidance of the individual, say people in Roman Catholic circles; pastoral care is the task of officebearers, say some; pastoral care is typically the task of the laity, say others.

The situation becomes still more confusing if one compares precise definitions. Pastoral care is sometimes described as "the guidance of souls" and at other times as the opposite of the "guidance of souls." At the root of this conceptual confusion is, of course, a difference in insight. The problem of standardization in terminology is more than a linguistic problem. But it is that, too, and before that it is a matter of simply listening to one another.

[When this is not done adequately, one can fall victim to strange convolutions of thought. This is evident from a passage listed from the—in many respects—excellent, one could say "classic," book of Eduard Thurneysen, *A Theology of Pastoral Care*. Thurneysen, posing the question where pastoral care belongs in church and theology, goes on to say: "The theological textbooks unanimously place it within the discipline of *practical theology*. They therefore affirm that pastoral care is concerned with proclamation in the broadest sense of the word. For the act of proclamation or preaching is the proper subject of all practical theology." He forgets that this last assertion is his own and not that of the theological textbooks. They do not confirm his thesis that pastoral care is concerned with proclamation or preaching.]

The challenge to practical theology can perhaps best be defined if we first listen to what the poet Gerrit Kouwenaar says of poetry: "In a poem one is ultimately interested, not in naming things, but in invalidating the names which have taken the place of the things themselves—the abstract clichés which block the perception of the real." A pronouncement like this must not be taken too absolutistically, of course. Alongside Kouwenaar's assertion that in a poem the point is not the naming of things, one should posit that for poetry naming things is also essential. Kouwenaar's intention was expressed much earlier by Rilke in these words:

I am so afraid of man-made words:
They pinpoint it all so clearly.
This they call a dog and that a house,
And this the beginning and the end is there.

I also fear their minds: they toy with tongues in cheek,
They know it all, what was and will be;
No mountain, for them, has any majesty left,
Their own gardens and goods are nearly as tall as God.

I must ever warn and shield: Keep your distance.
I love to hear things sing of themselves.
You touch them: they freeze and fall silent.
You are the destroyer of things for me.

Words, names, and stereotyped expressions can deafen us to the voices of the things themselves, so that for the deaf the things have died—a personal and original relationship with them has become impossible.

Whatever the source of Rilke's fears—an estheticism with mystical overtones, perhaps—from one's own experience one can know how real the threat is which so oppresses Rilke. One can't tell a thing to the person who already knows the words—he is no longer receptive. For the sake of communication we have no choice but to work with descriptive words. We speak of love, hate, avarice—names for extremely complex phenomena. But we had better be aware how relative such designations are and be alert to the fact that two behavior complexes may strongly resemble one another, even be describable in the same terms, yet be very different. There is "hatred" and hatred, "love" and love; even more emphatically: not every "libertine" is a libertine, not every "atheist" an atheist, not every "Christian" a Christian. People in the humanities sometimes speak with a hint of condescension about the "dead formulas" used in the natural sciences; they prefer the living word. They forget that the formula offers a possibility of exact and nuanced designation, in which the essential finds its permanent and indelible expression.

Rilke loves to hear things sing into his ears. Kouwenaar wants to see things as they are, hear what they themselves have to say, not what is said about them in a name. He wants to get behind the report to the reality, back to self-naming and self-reporting reality. The poet would then try to repeat the self-report.

This typically poetic intention is also a typically scientific intention. Perhaps we even have to get behind the names "poetry" and "science." To relate thus—with complete openness—to the phenomena is to be genuinely human and really honest—and the only way to arrive at understanding.

Part of the business of practical theology, one which will require a lot of attention for the time being, is the "invalidation of the nomenclature." It means looking at the phenomena as such: the attempt to ascertain their essential characteristics. In this effort practical theology will have to look in two directions.

Like pedagogics, it is both an empirical and a normative discipline. It must make transparent the praxis of the church; read the phenomena down to their essential characteristics; investigate the needs and possibilities of church practice. Its task is to track down the revelational data which are relevant to churchly praxis; interpret and organize them with an eye to that praxis. Orienting itself to the praxis and to the word of God which applies to it, it must begin to formulate theory on behalf of that praxis. In the nature of the case, it is impossible for the practical theologian to do all this alone. He would have to be at once an exegete, a systematic theologian, a psychologist, and a sociologist—to say nothing of the historical research which needs to be done in practical theology. It even seems impossible for practical theology to undertake these tasks on its own by means of interdisciplinary teamwork. It will repeatedly have to call in the aid of, or make use of the results of, its theological sister-disciplines and other sciences.

In light of all this, practical theology must necessarily have at its disposal a clear and unambiguous conceptual apparatus—one, moreover, which is multidimensional. Not much can be achieved with current labels and terms. Practical theology cannot, for instance, ask the practitioners of biblical theology to provide data about "pastoral care" in the New Testament. The word does not occur in the New Testament, and it is not certain, therefore, that the phenomenon so designated in a certain kind of praxis makes its independent appearance in the New Testament. Should it ask for data on "proclamation"—to use a rather popular word for preaching—it will get to hear about *kēryssein* and *kērygma*; it would then learn a variety of things which are certainly relevant, but perhaps not accept a variety of things equally relevant. If it should ask psychology to say something, say, about the psychological effect of conversion; or social psychology about the experience of the communion of saints; or sociology about the structure of a congregation, then—in the absence of more precise conceptual definition—these sciences could not do a thing with the terms.

Practical theology needs concepts—i.e., definitions which embrace its knowledge of the essential characteristics of phenomena occurring on its terrain—which are directly translatable in terms of the sciences with the help of which it must deepen and enrich its fundamental insights or gain its experience.

Only within a pastoral theology equipped with such an apparatus can the systematic formation of theory take place which would enable it, not just, as now, incidentally, in hit-or-miss fashion, but regularly and systematically, to serve church praxis with expert information.

The purpose of this study is not to present such a conceptual apparatus to practical theology but to make a contribution in that direction.

4. THE TASK OF PRACTICAL THEOLOGY

The preceding section may have created the impression that we lost sight of something stated earlier, namely, that practical theology also has a task with reference to the training and formation of the future pastor. We discussed doing practical theology as a science. This, we said in passing, not for the sake of the science itself, but for the purpose of offering systematic guidance to the church. But equipping people for the work of the pastorate is something else.

We deemed it important to stress that practical theology must function as a "science." It is not the practical end of the curriculum—as has been suggested. It is part of theology with a methodology of its own. But alongside its scholarly task, practical theology—as is true of the entire academic scientific enterprise— has the duty to train. We gladly agree with these recent practitioners of practical theology who say its task is not to teach future pastors a few practical tricks. This, to our mind, is no training. We would dare venture the suggestion that the task of practical theology is to make a contribution to the vocational training or professional equipment of the pastor. But that is not peculiar to practical theology; it is one of the tasks of every theological discipline.

Nor can we describe the special task of practical theology as teaching educands to preach, catechize, and give pastoral care. The theological student who is a pastor-in-training learns this in each of the theological subjects— explicitly even, when these are taught practically and functionally. It is to be feared that with that understanding practical theology then degenerates into a discipline which can no longer be called theological, because in homiletics it tends to give attention only to rhetoric, in catechetics to the principles and practice of teaching, in poimenics to pastoral psychology. In our opinion, it can be more effective and offer its own contributions better—from the perspective both of training students and that of a scientific enterprise—if it is no longer hampered by an exclusive schema of "vertical" subjects (homiletics, catechetics, poimenics) but also cuts through these subjects horizontally with a doctrine of the functioning of the church and a doctrine of pastoral role-fulfilment.

A doctrine of churchly functioning would treat questions like these: How— ideally and in fact—does the church function in preaching, church school, pastoral care, worship, and diaconal ministry; and how should the congregation be structured and organized with a view to these functions?

The doctrine of pastoral role-fulfilment would treat especially the problematics of pastoral communication in preaching, teaching, and pastoral care.

For training purposes the doctrine of pastoral role-fulfilment would have to be given special emphasis. In such a doctrine, however, no detailed prescriptions can be given for a variety of concrete situations. A pastor-in-training would not greatly benefit from such instruction: one of the first discoveries he or she will make in practice is that every situation is unique. What he can be taught, in our opinion—at least when the formation of theory has advanced somewhat— is how he can analyze a situation or at least how he can plan a new situation in order to comprehend or gain insight into the existing one. What he may also learn—provided the condition mentioned in the previous sentence has been met—is what is essential for pastoral communication.

5. THE PLACE OF OUR SUBJECT IN THE FIELD OF PRACTICAL THEOLOGY

It was our belief that the approach to a problem in practical theology followed in this study made these introductory reflections necessary. By way of a selective summary of the preceding we can now offer an introduction to our real subject.

Practical theology occupies itself with the *diaconic* forms of churchly praxis (the division of "vertical" subjects) and more precisely with the church's functioning and pastoral role-fulfilment in those forms (the horizontal cross-section of these subjects). In the doctrine of pastoral role-fulfilment it occupies itself especially with problems of communication in the different forms. Its task in relation to these problems is defined, first, by its scientific responsibility: the formation of theory, particularly with a view to offering expert information on church praxis; and, second, by its responsibility to train: the equipment of the pastor-in-training.

With a view both to the formation of theory and the training of pastors, practical theology needs to develop a conceptual apparatus which can make its questions operational for research purposes. This apparatus must also be able to serve in developing a body of guidelines for equipping pastors.

Within this framework, so understood, the present study intends to offer a contribution toward the development of this conceptual apparatus. The subject lies within the context of the doctrine of pastoral role-fulfilment, and our attention will be limited to three forms of churchly praxis: preaching, catechesis, and pastoral care. Within this area the problems of pastoral communication will be subjected to closer scrutiny, and that only in part, namely, from the perspective of the "agogic" component in pastoral role-fulfilment.

Part II offers a model of pastoral role-fulfilment. Part III attempts to ascertain what the "agogic" is. And Part IV views pastoral role-fulfilment as an "agogic" situation.

II. Pastoral Role-Fulfilment

1. INTRODUCTION

The association of the concepts "pastoral role-fulfilment" and "agogy" may well be expected to evoke spontaneous resistance. Strong emphasis is given nowadays to people "coming-of-age"; in the churches this focus expresses itself in the emphatic attention given to the "laity." The layperson, once viewed as object, is now seen as "subject with a unique calling and responsibility."[1] From the same perspective, in part at least, the pastoral relationship is discussed in terms of "availability," "partnership," or "ministry." "Agogy," with its potential for concretization as pedagogy, psychagogy, and even demagogy, does not seem to fit in this context. The word suggests a people "underage" plus a (probably) authoritarian, in any case a superior, figure, who leads or directs those people and has a private agenda for them.

The premise of this study is, nevertheless, that the connection between pastoral role-fulfilment and "agogy" is possible; more: that the agogic element is inherent in pastoral role-fulfilment. This last statement implies that, in our opinion, the agogic element is not an independent phenomenon alongside pastoral role-fulfilment but a function of it. When the "subject" in pastoral role-fulfilment is correlated with another "subject," then an agogic "flow of power" runs through the correlation in the (interpersonal) field which has come into being. The purpose of this study is to isolate that functional component for the purpose of examining it in its uniqueness.

In order to arrive at this abstraction it is necessary, in the first place, to design a model of pastoral role-fulfilment. To avoid misunderstanding we do wish to point out, incidentally, that the purpose of a model is only to make a complicated phenomenon somewhat manageable and translucent in its fundamental structure—this, with a view to developing a body of theory concerning it. A model, says C. A. van Peursen,[2] is not a photographic reproduction. One

---

[1] H. Kraemer, *A Theology of the Laity*, p. 72.
[2] C. A. van Peursen, *Filosofische Oriëntatie*, p. 155.

cannot say of a model that it reproduces reality; one can only say that it is a way of conceiving it. It is a way of saying: these are the essential characteristics to the extent that we can now ascertain them; this is a way of picturing their interconnection. This, in simplified form, is the framework of the phenomenon. A model is a phase in the formation of theory concerning a given phenomenon. It is less a way of giving answers to questions which can be raised than a means of tracking down issues and a way of formulating a problem.

Our point of departure is that pastoral role-fulfilment mediates the coming of God in his word. So, first, we must determine what the word of God is and does; next, what the structure is of this coming of God in his word and what the dynamics are in which the person, to whom God comes in his word, is involved.

2. THE TERM "PASTORAL ROLE-FULFILMENT"

Our attention in this study is focused on a single component in the complex we have designated "pastoral role-fulfilment" (Dutch *Het pastoraal optreden*). The term "role-fulfilment" (*optreden*) has a variety of nuances, each of which evokes a different image. The Dutch word *optreden* probably comes to us from the vocabulary of the theater. "To tread upon" (*optreden*) is first of all to tread upon the boards, as in the phrase "as good an actor as ever trod the boards," and hence to appear before a public. The appearance of an actor before a public alone, however, does not suffice to call it *optreden*; for that he must act his role before the public.

Another meaning of the word comes into view when mention is made of the *optreden* of the police, or a teacher, or a father who believes that the situation on the street, or in class, or in the home no longer allows him to keep his distance, and says: "I believe I have to make an appearance and act" (*gaan optreden*). *Optreden* then means "to make an appearance for the purpose of intervening (in a situation)."

Both senses of the word have in common a relationship to others—a public before which one acts, other people in relation to whom one acts.

The use of the word *optreden* as a rule entails the idea of a certain role, a function, a capacity in which one acts. One does not simply act; one acts in the capacity of. . . .

So with the term "pastoral role-fulfilment" we mean the official activity of one who is called to be pastor in face-to-face contact with another, or others, for whom he or she is called to be pastor. There are a number of distinguishable forms of pastoral role-fulfilment; in this study we shall limit ourselves, in the main, to those of preaching, catechesis, and pastoral care.

The adjective can simply mean that we are concerned with the role-fulfilment of a pastor. But one can sometimes say of a pastor that he does not act very pastorally. We value the ambiguity which is thus present in the term "pastoral role-fulfilment," but our interest is in the kind of role-fulfilment which is pastoral indeed.

3. THE SPECIFIC CHARACTER OF PASTORAL ROLE-FULFILMENT

In order to construct a model of pastoral role-fulfilment we must distance ourselves from the forms of pastoral role-fulfilment known to us. In a previous chapter we pointed out the importance of what the poet Gerrit Kouwenaar called "the invalidation of the nomenclature." We cannot simply proceed to do this, however, for then the thing we want to study will elude us. One can observe pastoral role-fulfilment only in the forms in which it appears.

The question is, What is the most essential element of pastoral role-fulfilment in preaching, catechesis, and pastoral care? In our view it is this: In addressing a congregation, in instructing the members of a church, in assisting parishioners in their problem situations there is a person who acts, not on his own, not by virtue of his own superiority—in whatever respect that may be— but in the name of the Lord of the church, and with the word of God. In fulfilling the pastoral role in each of these forms a large measure of the typical action of a speaker, a teacher, or a counsellor may be present, but the unique and essential element in pastoral role-fulfilment lies in being sent by specific mandate of the Lord, who wishes to "make an appearance" himself in the role-fulfilment of the pastor, by means of the word of his revelation laid on and entrusted to him. At the heart of pastoral role-fulfilment is not the activity of a human being, but *the action of God who, by way of the official ministry as intermediary, comes to people in his word*. It seems both necessary and possible to take this position as our point of departure for the construction of a model of pastoral role-fulfilment.

4. THE WORD OF GOD IS (a) THE FORM OF THE LORD'S PRESENCE

The core of pastoral role-fulfilment is, then, the action of God who comes to people in his word. We could simply have said "the word," or "the ministry of the word," but the danger of abstractness could not then be avoided.

What is a word? Says Gerhard Ebeling: "Buried as we may be under a mass of written and printed words we dare not overlook the fact that the essence of a word discloses itself only when it is spoken—hence as an oral word-event. The basic model of a word-event is, therefore, not a pronouncement which one can abstract from the speech situation; rather, the speech-event is to be characterized as communication. For the word occurs between two partners, makes participation possible, creates communication."[3]

Hence the word is what is spoken, "the breath of one's mouth" (cf. Ps. 33:6). A word cannot be separated from a person who speaks, a voice in which the word comes alive, or eyes which look at the speech partner. To take a word out of its speech context and to write it down or to print it is to run the risk of incurring an essential loss. The poet Leo Vroman expressed the pain of this loss in a poem called "To the One Who Reads This."

> *Printed letters I am showing you here;*
> *With blood-warmed words I cannot speak,*
> *Nor extend a hot hand from this paper.*
> *What can I do? I cannot reach you.*

All he can do is ask the reader to put his or her hand on the paper or to say aloud the written word that is "petrified in print." Words can be a diversionary maneuver, or a barrier, or a curtain of smoke, but the word which one person speaks to another is the form in which the one goes to the other in order to enter the other's thoughts, feelings, and experience. " 'Word' or 'saying' is the simple but genuine form in which person communicates with person."[4]

The expression "the word of God" may be a reference to Holy Scripture, but it must not be forgotten that even then it means "God has spoken and still speaks."[5] According to Calvin, the highest proof of the truth of Holy Scripture is the fact that God in person speaks in it (*dei loquentis persona*);[6] Scripture derives its authority from him. The only legitimate manner of dealing with Scripture is to listen to God speaking. "The word of God," says H. Bavinck, "is never detached from God, Christ, the Holy Spirit; it has no existence in itself; it cannot be separated deistically from its creator and author." "Where it is, God is present."[7]

Martin Buber tells the story of the Hassidic rabbi Sussja of Hanipol: "At the beginning of the presentation when his Master, the great Maggid, recited the text of Holy Scripture which he wanted to interpret, and began with the words of Scripture 'And God said' or 'And God spoke,' ecstasy seized him and he screamed and moved so wildly that he disturbed the circle around the table and had to be led out. Then he would stand in the hallway or woodshed, beat upon the wall, and cry out: 'And God spoke!' "[8] In its depiction of the ecstatic emotionalism of Hassidism this story is typical. But one cannot leave it at that. Sussja is the person who really experiences what to us has become all too familiar: that there is another who speaks to a person, who makes his word go

---

[3]G. Ebeling, *The Nature of Faith*, pp. 185-86.

[4]K. Barth, *Church Dogmatics*, II/2, p. 97.

[5]R. Schippers, "De Dienst des Woords," in *Van den Dienst des Woords*, p. 12.

[6]J. Calvin, *Institutes of the Christian Religion*, I.vii.4 (McNeill edition, p. 78).

[7]H. Bavinck, *Gereformeerde Dogmatiek*, IV, 439.

[8]M. Buber, *Der Grosse Magid und seine Nachfolge*, p. 138.

forth to people, and who thus lets those people participate in his thoughts, feelings, striving—in short, *his life*; and that other is God.

We can understand even better what that means when we see the negative—the absence of the word of God, his silence. Consider this story: Saul and his army are encamped at Gilboa before the battle with the Philistines (I Sam. 28:4ff.). When he sees the Philistine army, he is afraid and "his heart trembles greatly." He knows how inadequate his possibilities are. In that situation only one thing is important: Is "the Other" present? "And when Saul inquired of the LORD, the LORD did not answer him, either by dreams, or by Urim, or by prophets" (v. 6). The silence is total, and Saul now experiences the reality of what Samuel announced to him long before: "You have rejected the word of the LORD, and the LORD has rejected you . . ." (I Sam. 15:26). The same experience is expressed at the beginning of Psalm 22: "My God, my God, why hast thou forsaken me? . . . O my God, I cry by day, but thou dost not answer; and by night, but find no rest" (vv. 1-3). The person who does not hear the word of the LORD is abandoned and rejected; he has "descended into hell."

J. T. van Veenen has pointed out that, just as in Genesis Yahweh appeared in the angel of the LORD, so in prophecy Yahweh makes himself known in the form of "the word." "The word is the form of his presence, distinct but not separated from him." "When we, by analogy with Genesis, would expect: 'the angel of the LORD came to him' we read instead: 'the word of the LORD came to him.' The word is the form [Dutch *gestalte*] in which Yahweh emerges from his hiddenness and meets the person. This form of presence [Dutch *nabijheids-gestalte*] is so concrete and tangible that it can be said: The word of the LORD came to Hosea, Joel, and the like; indeed, Amos *sees* the word which comes to him (1:1)."[9] In the Old Testament it is not as if one must now think of a person whose name is "the Word." The form of Yahweh's presence is the word which proceeds from his mouth and is heard in one's ears—directly, intelligibly, and in one's own vernacular.

In the New Testament the apostles are called witnesses of this word, "the word of life," which they heard, and saw with their own eyes, and touched with their own hands (I John 1:1-2). In the words of Jesus Christ they heard it; in his entire appearance they saw it; for God who spoke of old by the prophets "has spoken to us in these last days by a Son" who does not simply speak the word which God reveals but "reflects the glory of God and bears the very stamp of his nature" (Heb. 1:1, 3). What God has to say to us, and to share with us, is audible and visible in him—as concretely as a human being who participates in our lives. He is the Word who became flesh, says John in his prologue, a human being environed in our reality. This is the aim of what John says about the Logos who was in the beginning with God and by whom all things were made. Says Adolph Schlatter: "Contemporary teachers of Judaism drew up a variety of

---

[9]J. T. van Veenen, "De profetische Prediking," a chapter in *Wegen der Prediking*, ed. by C. W. Mönnich, pp. 195ff.

doctrinal positions about the divine reason and the divine word, being stimulated by Greek philosophers and their theses about the provenance of things from thought. It's easily possible that John's reference is to them. What he intends in these verses, however, we must take, not from opinions and books foreign to him, but from the gospel itself."[10] Karl Barth remarks that, if one asks why John uses the Logos concept as a question in historical genetics, one faces a host of possibilities. "What is certain is that he had no intention of honoring Jesus by investing him with the title of Logos, but rather that he honored the title itself by applying it a few lines later as a predicate of Jesus." He is "the divine self-communication proceeding from person to person and uniting God and man"[11]—Immanuel.

Ad den Besten summarizes everything we have said so far about the word of God in a song composed for the confirmation of new members:

Before I asked of you a thing,
You gave your word to me;
For the living of my life that is enough,
And for the dying of my death as well.

Your word is deed, Father;
Was manna in the wilderness,
Became human—is nearer to me
Than those who are my neighbors.

5. THE WORD OF GOD IS (b) THE REVELATION OF THE NAME

"The Word became flesh and dwelt among us . . . and we beheld his glory" (John 1:14). This text is the point of convergence for a number of scriptural lines. In what follows we shall point out a few of them.

The presence of the incarnate Word is described in Greek by the word *skēnoun* ("to dwell as in a tent"). According to Michaelis, this "does not refer to the temporary and transitory element in the earthly existence of the Logos but is designed to show that this is the presence of the Eternal in time."[12] In his commentary on John, F. W. Grosheide says: "*Skēnoun* reminds one of the tent of testimony, the dwelling of God among his people, and the *shekinah.*"[13] Karl Barth asserts that the tabernacle, the "'*ōhel mō'ēḏ* (the place of conversation or rendezvous between Yahweh and Moses)," in the Septuagint is called *skēnē*

---

[10]A. Schlatter, *Das Evangelium nach Johannes* (Erläuterungen zum Neuen Testament), I, 63.

[11]K. Barth, *Church Dogmatics*, II/2, pp. 96-97.

[12]*Theological Dictionary of the New Testament*, VII, 386.

[13]F. W. Grosheide, *Johannes*, I, 95; J. H. Bernard, *St. John* (International Critical Commentary), I, 21: "The verb *skēnoun* would always recall this to a Jew."

martyriou: "The place of self-attestation, the revelation of God." He considers it likely that there is a connection between this description of the tabernacle and the fact that the dwelling of the Logos among the people is described as *skēnoun*. The implication is that in Jesus Christ, the incarnate Word of God, we are dealing with him "who attests, reveals, and proclaims Himself."[14] First, Sinai was God's place of revelation and rendezvous; in the wilderness it was the tent of meeting; in the promised land, the temple. In the New Testament Jesus is "greater than the temple" (Matt. 12:6); or rather his dwelling among us, his appearance in word and works, his life, death, and resurrection. The *word* dwelt in the tent of meeting or in the temple. Instead, we hear that the glory of the LORD, the face of the LORD, and especially the name of the LORD indwelt it. W. Eichrodt says that these keywords changed from being "descriptions of the God who appears visibly to becoming theological concept-words for the presence of the transcendent God."[15] It is a question whether this is a felicitous way of saying it; in any case, these words regularly denote God's presence *among*, and especially *for,* his people.

This comes out most vividly in the connection often made between the sanctuary and the name of the LORD. The law for the altar proclaims: ". . . in every place where I cause my name to be remembered I will come to you and bless you" (Exod. 20:24). In Deuteronomy, (I, II) Kings, and (I, II) Chronicles, the temple is recurrently described as "the place which the LORD will choose to cause his name to dwell there," "a house for the name of the LORD," or "the house which I have sanctified for my name." And always connected with this is the idea of the LORD's coming with his blessing. In answer to Solomon's prayer that the LORD may be attentive to the prayers which would be offered in the place of which he said "My name shall be there" (I Kings 8:29), the LORD replies: "I have consecrated this house which you have built, and put my name there for ever; my eyes and my heart will be there for all time" (I Kings 9:3; cf. II Chron. 7:16). The indwelling of the name "in this house" affords Israel the certainty that the LORD will hear and help them when they cry out to him in their distress (II Chron. 20:9).

So what is true of the word of God can also be said of the name of the LORD: the name is "the form of Yahweh's nearness." But more than with the word, there is reason here to suspect a personification: the name has a house; its dwelling is among the people. One must, however, be careful with such an observation. The name, which dwells in the sanctuary, is repeatedly connected with verbs of prayer and confession: *qārā'* and *zākar.* The name of the LORD is invoked, announced, proclaimed, made known, brought into remembrance. When God makes known his name to Moses he adds: "This is my name for ever, the name by which I am to be remembered from generation to generation" (Exod.

---

[14]K. Barth, *CD*, IV/3/2, p. 612.
[15]W. Eichrodt, *Religion in Geschichte und Gegenwart,* IV. col. 1601, s.v. *Offenbarung.*

3:15). The name of the LORD dwells in the midst of the people; i.e., there is a place where the LORD is present to hear when an appeal is made to him on the basis of his self-disclosure; when the people bring to his remembrance what he has revealed of himself in his name. The name is less a personification than a concentration of the LORD's presence in one place.

Our starting point is that at the core of pastoral role-fulfilment is the action of God who comes to people in his word. The word of God, as we have seen, means that he draws near to people, and creates communion, in self-disclosing and self-committing speech. So near does he come that "the Word" came to dwell among us, as "the name" dwelt among people in the house of the LORD. Looking back from the appearance of God in the incarnate Word to what was said about "the name," we shall be able to see still more clearly what "the coming of God in his word" entails.

Numerous efforts have been made to offer a linguistically responsible and etymologically correct derivation of the name Yahweh—none of them completely satisfactory.[16] The problem, as Vriezen comments, belongs to the history of religion, not to theology. "Theologically important is what the Israelite meant by the name, what the name meant *to him*."[17] We would prefer to say: theologically important is how the name functions in God's revelation. Investigation shows that central to the name are notions of coming, appearing, and being present.

When God appears to Moses in the burning bush, Moses asks what he must answer when the Israelites inquire about the name of the God who has sent him. "God said to Moses, 'I AM WHO I AM.' And he said, 'Say this to the people of Israel, "I AM has sent me to you" ' " (Exod. 3:14). "I AM WHO I AM" and "I AM" express the significance of the name Yahweh.

What is striking in this declaration is, first of all, the rejection of the question. J. L. Koole remarks: "The LORD neither can nor will simply make known who he is; it is necessary to maintain some distance—a sense of the wholly otherness of God."[18] We encounter a similar rebuff in Judges 13:18: "Why do you ask my name, seeing it is wonderful?" God cannot be named. He cannot be placed alongside something or someone else under one denominator. He is incomparable: "Who is like thee, O LORD, among the gods? Who is like thee, majestic in holiness, terrible in glorious deeds, doing wonders?" (Exod. 15:11). God is the one who works wonders (Ps. 77:14)—and the person who has caught a glimpse of these wonders must confess: "Such knowledge is too wonderful for me; it is high, I cannot attain it" (Ps. 139:6).

God is who he is—incomparable. In the same breath in which he declares his name he says there is no appropriate name for him. This concealment does

---

[16]Cf. G. Quell, *TDNT*, III, 1065ff., s.v. *kyrios*; T. C. Vriezen, *An Outline of Old Testament Theology*, 2nd ed., p. 342.

[17]T. C. Vriezen, *An Outline of Old Testament Theology*, p. 342.

[18]J. L. Koole, *De tien Geboden*, p. 63.

not diminish God's self-disclosure, however; rather, it *qualifies* his self-disclosure. When Isaiah 45 refers to God's hiding himself, the reason is only to accentuate the confession of his saving nearness. "Truly, thou art a God who hidest thyself" (v. 15). Thus God is God—namely, the "God of Israel, the Savior." God is not the God who is "just" there, nor can he "just" be known. Non-Israelite nations will have to acknowledge to Israel: "God is with you only, and there is no other, no god besides him" (v. 14). In this concealment Jesus discerns the good pleasure of the Father, for which he thanks him who has hidden "these things from the wise and understanding" and "revealed them to babes" (Matt. 11:25). For that reason the self-concealing God can say to Israel, "the children": "I did not speak in secret, in a land of darkness" (Isa. 45:19; cf. 48:16). For "the offspring of Jacob" he is not beyond finding or approaching, but the redeemer who does not put his own to shame, leaving them helpless, with empty hands, and in unrequited expectation (Isa. 45:17). He wants to be their God; his self-concealment is only a way of being ready for those who would witness his wondrous deeds. "I AM WHO I AM"—this word (*dābār*) is a reference first of all to the *dᵉ bîr*, the innermost sanctuary (Ps. 28:2), where dwells the name, in holiness and unapproachable light, in order that those among whom he dwells may call upon him for help. The presence of the name, then, is the presence of One who is incomparably different from the gods.

But the name has a second element which must be understood, namely, that God is present and prepared. H. Renckens, S.J., remarks that from the story in Exodus 3 "it does not necessarily follow that the name Yahweh is in fact connected with the similar-sounding Hebrew verb 'to be'; what does follow is that the real content of the word 'to be' must be ascribed in some fashion to the God of Israel."[19] It is important, then, to determine what the real content of the verb "to be" is. It can certainly not be "the unmoved and unchanging being in which Plato situated the divine."[20] Says N. H. Snaith: "The God of the Hebrews was essentially active in the world which he had made. We regard it to be of the utmost importance that this fact should be recognized throughout the whole of Old Testament theology. He was no static God in the sense of the philosophers." "Jehovah is always active, always dynamically here, in this world. The Hebrew does not say that Jehovah *is*, or that Jehovah *exists*, but that he *does*. Properly speaking, the Hebrew verb *hayah* does not mean 'to be' so much as 'to come to be.' Hebrew has no real verb of 'being' but one of 'becoming.' The verb is active and not static. This attitude is most strongly marked in the Hebrew idea of God. Jehovah is known by what he does in the world. The whole of the religion is therefore concerned with the relationship of God and man."[21]

[Psalm 10 pictures the wicked as persons who consistently think "there is no God" (v. 4). This is "not a denial of the divine existence, but of his presence

---

[19]H. Renckens, S.J., *De Godsdienst van Israël*, p. 90.
[20]H. M. Kuitert, *De Mensvormigheid Gods*, p. 193.
[21]N. H. Snaith, *The Distinctive Ideas of the Old Testament*, pp. 47-48.

and interposition."[22] According to the wicked, God is not actively involved in what happens here and in what people do. "Thou wilt not call to account" (v. 13). To the pious, who is the victim of the hatred of the wicked, it may seem that the wicked are right. ". . . He will never see it" (v. 11). In his distress he calls upon the name of the LORD: "Why dost thou hide thyself in times of trouble?" (v. 1). But in his despair he does not separate himself from the name; and knowledge of the name brings him to the peace of faith: God is involved in my life and destiny. "Thou dost see; yea, thou dost note trouble and vexation, that thou mayest take it into thy hands" (v. 14).]

God's being is being "actively present";[23] "a personal relatedness of his being to the world" (Vriezen); "being present effectively, actively, protectively. The name Yahweh simply means that he is very near, present and shows it."[24]

Third, the name embraces the notion of continuity. 'Ehyeh may also be translated "I shall be." Yahweh is he who will be; he will be who he is. In a few instances in the Old Testament this is expressed in words also used in John's Revelation: the first and the last. God, who is present at the beginning, will also be present at the end: "I am He; I am the first, and I am the last" (Isa. 48:12; cf. 41:4; 44:6). The LORD is not only concerned with people; he is concerned with people in their histories, and with the history of the people. He lives with them through their histories; he has his own active history with them. Continuity does not mean a static fixity, therefore; the contrary is the case. He is not so much the fixed point in the turning of the times; he is in motion—think of hāyâ—and yet in motion and tumult the same. "What God has been in the past he is equally in the present and will certainly be in the future."[25] He is the living God. "He does not remain behind; nor is he tied only to an action of long ago. He does not live only in a memory which in time grows dim. He is also the God of the present."[26] Making his appeal in the name of the LORD a penitent pleads in Isaiah 63:17: "Return. . . ." He cries to God to rend the heavens and to come down (64:1), to accomplish his incomparable deeds (64:3), in order to make his name known to his adversaries (64:2) so that they may see what they had not heard, perceived, or seen from of old: a God who works for those who wait for him (64:4).

The word of God is, then, the revelation of this name. When the LORD proclaimed his name to Moses, Moses heard: "The LORD, the LORD, a God merciful and gracious, slow to anger, and abounding in steadfast love and faithfulness, keeping steadfast love for thousands, forgiving iniquity and transgression and sin, but who will by no means clear the guilty, visiting the iniquity of the

---

[22]C. A. Briggs and E. G. Briggs, *The Book of Psalms* (International Critical Commentary), I, 77.

[23]H. M. Kuitert, *De Mensvormigheid Gods*, p. 193.

[24]J. L. Koole, *De tien Geboden*, p. 63.

[25]J. de Groot and A. R. Hulst, *Macht en Wil*, p. 151.

[26]A. R. Hulst, *Het heilige Volk*, pp. 39ff.

fathers upon the children and the children's children to the third and the fourth generation" (Exod. 34:6-7). One could say that these words, in which God proclaims his name, are the constituents of the name. Whatever is contained in the name is explicated by the word. The "open" name Yahweh sums up everything that is unfolded in the word. The fulness of that name has come to dwell among us in the Word who became flesh. In the concealment of cradle and cross God was with us. Those who recognized in him only the son of the carpenter (Matt. 13:55, 57) took offense at him, but those who believed have seen his glory (John 1:14).

The name thus signifies the presence in concentration of a holy God; it reveals the presence of the God who goes with his people as One who cares; and it sums up the continuities of his dealings with them in history. The Word, spoken and incarnate, is the explication of the name.

6. THE WORD OF GOD IS (c) THE REVELATION OF THE TRUTH

The Significance of "Truth"

When the Word comes to dwell among people and displays his glory, it means that the fulness of "grace and truth" is revealed to them (John 1:14). Before Pilate Jesus declares: "For this I have come into the world, to bear witness to the truth" (John 18:37). The coming of God in his word implies that the truth is made public; and the pastoral role-fulfilment which mediates the coming of God therefore has everything to do with making truth public. In order to understand the phenomenon of pastoral role-fulfilment it is necessary, then, that we get some insight into what is meant here by "truth."

Referring to the concept of truth in philosophy, G. Gawlick remarks: "Philosophy has not been able to provide a definition of truth which precisely fits the contents and is exempt from formal objection. The concept signifies something which eludes definition by its simplicity in origin."[27] But the concept itself is not simple. To describe its complexity Gawlick points toward its numerous opposites, e.g., falsehood, untruth (error or lies), and illusion. The concept becomes still more complex when we note the different ways and connections in which the Bible speaks of truth. For example, Scripture refers repeatedly to "doing the truth" and "walking in the truth," and to combinations like "truth and mercy," "righteousness," "salvation," and "light." From this usage it is evident that the definition of truth employed by Albertus Magnus and Thomas Aquinas (*veritas est adaequatio rei et intellectus*: "truth is the correspondence of thing and understanding") cannot, if ever, be applied to the *biblical* notion of it.

To clarify this issue it may be useful to distinguish between the so-called

---

[27]G. Gawlick, *RGG*, VI, col. 1518ff., s.v. *Wahrheit*.

Greek concept of truth and the manner in which the Bible speaks of it—knowing, meanwhile, that more than this is needed, particularly in reference to the use of the word "truth" in the New Testament.[28] Ĥ. W. Rossouw, in answering the question what the truth content is of the word with which faith knowledge correlates, reduces the difference to a succinct formula when he says that the concern here is not a "metaphysical-idea" truth but a "redemptive-historical and eschatological" one. The truth of the word does not appeal to the *theoria* (contemplation) of noetic thought but makes its claims upon the heart's trust.[29] Because there were as many "truths" as there were facts, the Greeks, according to Rudolf Bultmann, raised the question of *the* truth. "This is the question of true being in the absolute sense, which man must know if he is to find his way in his puzzling existence."[30] To the Greeks *alētheia*, truth, is the ideal support system (Dutch *bestand*) behind the things of sense.[31] This is what human beings want to know in order to have stability in a world in which they must live with, and in the midst of, facts which appear to them as contingent concretions, which as such continue to escape them, but in which they would discern the enduring sense and of which they would know permanent being. The Greek idea of revelation, says A. Oepke in this connection, refers to what is at all times, even though concealed behind empirical being.[32] This way of putting the problem is not found in Scripture. This becomes very clear when we compare the biblical idea of revelation with the Greek notion described above. We shall discuss this issue in the context of Oepke's article.

[In the Old Testament Yahweh reveals himself as the Lord of history. "Because Israel's religion is nourished by history, it is characterized by a historical orientation. The essential thing in the biblical view is not to be found in what always is, but in what happens. History, i.e., that which happens, is the work of Yahweh." Revelation is not "the impartation of supernatural knowledge" but "the action of Yahweh." "It is the removal of his essential concealment, his self-offering for fellowship." The most distinctive feature of Old Testament revelation is most clearly expressed in its reference to the future. In the New Testament, too, "revelation" denotes, not the impartation of knowledge, but the actual unveiling of intrinsically hidden facts or, theologically, "the manifestation of transcendence within immanence." In brief, "revelation in the NT is the self-offering of the Father of Jesus Christ for fellowship."[33]

In his expositions of the concept of truth J. H. Vrielink follows closely what Oepke has written about revelation.[34] "In order to understand the unique

---

[28]Cf. R. Bultmann, *TDNT*, I, 232ff., s.v. *alētheia*; J. H. Vrielink, *Het Waarheidsbegrip*, pp. 70ff.

[29]H. W. Rossouw, *Klaarheid en Interpretasie*, p. 176.

[30]R. Bultmann, *TDNT*, I, 239.

[31]J. H. Vrielink, *Het Waarheidsbegrip*, p. 67.

[32]A. Oepke, *TDNT*, III, 567ff., s.v. *apokalyptō*.

[33]A. Oepke, *TDNT*, III, 591.

[34]J. H. Vrielink, *Het Waarheidsbegrip*, pp. 117ff.

character of the *'emet*-concept, we must bear in mind that it concerns primarily 'a-being-together.' " "*'Emet* primarily signifies the community relationship, immediately and centrally, as it functions in life in its fulness, not the abstract knowing relationship between thought and being in their correspondence. Much more inclusive than the knowing relationship, *'emet* describes the total conduct, and that as one which is reciprocally trustworthy and which one can expect of the other."[35] "Hebrew truth, in contrast with the Greek *alētheia* concept, is not 'profound': it realizes itself in the external reality of history, in concrete, personal covenant relationships in time."[36] "Yahweh's historical truth demonstration par excellence is for Israel the exodus from Egypt. There his *'emet* came to light decisively and with a strong hand."[37] Vrielink discerns the influence of the Greek notion of truth in the New Testament. His conclusion is that in the New Testament "the Old Testament *'emet* and the Greek *alētheia* meet, in order to unite in a peculiar fashion and a religiously relevant idiom, so that the cognitive significance of *alētheia* is taken up in the inclusive *'emet*"; which is to say that "the Greek noetic is taken up into the personal community relationship."[38]]

For us it is important now to ascertain that in Scripture "truth" cannot be abstracted from the concrete events which happen to us in history. *'Emet,* says Barth, "indicates first the specificity of a process or state of affairs, and so its solidity, force, and permanence, and therefore its authenticity, validity, necessity, and unassailability." ". . . Properly and decisively and therefore in truth, the truth is seen throughout as a predicate of a prerogative of God as the LORD who speaks and acts in Israel. As numerous places in the Psalms have it, it is *thy* truth." "How God speaks and acts and at the same time *what* he wills and seeks and creates with his speaking and acting: this is true as such."[39] The name Yahweh can be biblically paraphrased as "I shall show myself to be who I am." "In his historic actions and words Yahweh is the real God. We must not look for his *'emet* (his authentic Godness) behind these actions and words."[40] The name Yahweh is a reference to history, to his acts of covenant faithfulness, in which God reveals his truth, not "something about" the truth which can be deduced from those deeds. God's actions are works of truth; in all his deeds the truth shines. This makes the Psalmist sing: "This is God, our God for ever and ever" (Ps. 48:14). In Psalm 77 one hears the voice of a person who has lost his footing and doubts the *'emet* of the LORD promised in the name (vv. 8-10). What is the solution? It comes in verse 11: "I shall call to mind the deeds of the LORD." In the concreteness of the covenant deeds of the LORD he finds the LORD: "Thou art the God who workest wonders" (v. 14). In an article about the Old

---

[35]Ibid., p. 60.
[36]Ibid., p. 67.
[37]Ibid., p. 68.
[38]Ibid., pp. 104, 110.
[39]K. Barth, *CD*, II/1, p. 207.
[40]H. M. Kuitert, *De Mensvormigheid Gods*, p. 244.

Testament prophets A. Jepsen writes: "The prophets do not announce general truths about God but speak in the name of God who was there, has spoken and acted, and who is coming." "The presupposition of every prophetic message . . . is the remembrance of the deeds of the God of Israel who has made his history with them from the start."[41]

Jesus Christ, in being witness to the truth, still transcends this level. He does not just *bring* the word, he *is* the Word (John 1:1ff.). He does not just *proclaim* the truth, he *is* the truth (John 14:6). "He brings the *alētheia*, not simply as an impartation mediated by His Word, but as He sanctifies Himself for them (Jn. 17:19)."[42] His historic appearance, his words and works, in short, the whole of his history, not only makes the truth visible but realizes it. "The issue in the truth of his word concerns not what God is in himself but what kind of God he is in his address to the sinner. The truth of that word is Jesus Christ, the crucified one, the risen and therefore the living Lord. . . ." "Jesus Christ is himself the original expression of the canonical truth of salvation—not as a metaphysical principle but as the living Lord who has come to the sinner in his living Word. . . ."[43]

How Are Truth and Reality Related?

One of the theological presuppositions of preaching, says A. D. Müller, is that God speaks with us here and now—and we gladly agree. But it seems dangerous when he speaks here, as he does, of the need to dehistoricize revelation.[44] H. Schreiner speaks in a similar vein when he says that in giving instruction in the Christian message one must "point past the historicity of revelation to the way toward God."[45] According to him, it is of great importance that the catechism instructor familiarize himself thoroughly with the historical situation of revelation, because "the *sensus historicus* (the historical 'wrapping' and meaning) is the cradle in which the *sensus pneumaticus* (the spiritual address and unconditioned sense) is laid."[46] The above-mentioned practitioners of practical theology—and many others who speak and think in the same way—certainly do not take the story of the acts of the Lord as the mythological guise for a spiritual truth, but they are not sufficiently alive to the peculiar character of the truth of God and its revelation. The peculiar nature of the truth of God lies, in our opinion, in this, that its "genuineness"—perhaps the most adequate translation of *'emet*—its "true reality" appears in what he does in his *act*-ive address to people.

---

[41]A. Jepsen, *RGG*, V, col. 628, s.v. *Propheten*.
[42]R. Bultmann, *TDNT*, I, 246.
[43]H. W. Rossouw, *Klaarheid en Interpretasie*, p. 176.
[44]A. D. Müller, *Grundriss der praktischen Theologie*, p. 160.
[45]H. Schreiner, *Evangelische Pädagogik und Katechetik*, p. 183.
[46]Ibid., pp. 162ff.

[Dietrich Bonhoeffer puts the matter at issue here with special clarity in one of the letters in which he discusses Bultmann. Bonhoeffer believes (rightly or wrongly; it need not be settled here) that Bultmann has gone off "into the typical liberal process of reduction." "My view," says Bonhoeffer, "is that the full content, including the mythological concepts, must be kept—the New Testament is not a mythological clothing of a universal truth; *this mythology* (resurrection, etc.) *is the thing itself.*"[47] R. Schippers expresses the same thing with pungency when he says that "scientifically it must be known that in fact the gospel cannot remain gospel without the four Gospels."[48] H. N. Ridderbos clearly demonstrates the error of "the opinion that Paul considered the knowledge of the historical Jesus . . . to be of little or no significance, and that for his own preaching and views of Christ he trusted exclusively to that which he was given by the *pneuma.*" It is not in keeping with the specific character of Paul's preaching to construe a contrast between the pneumatic and the historical knowledge of Jesus Christ. Paul's Christology is "not timeless and inward"; "the historical and objective aspects of Christ's coming into the world, his suffering, death, and resurrection, constitute" its backbone. When Paul mentions the hidden wisdom of God which God reveals by the Spirit to "them that are perfect" (I Cor. 2:6ff.), the expression "refers to the knowledge of that which occurred in and with the 'historical' Christ."[49]]

Witnessing to the Truth

It is decidedly significant that the word group surrounding the phrase "to witness" forms a central category of revelation in the New Testament.

To reproduce the literature on this word group would take us too far afield; a modest summary must suffice.

[The witness has a very specific function in a process. By reporting his observations he provides the judge with knowledge of the actual events on which the trial turns. It is the witnesses, both in the Old Testament and in rabbinic Judaism, who provide legally admissible evidence.[50] In rabbinic Judaism only the evidence of the eyewitness was admissible; even the most obvious inference was not. In New Testament usage, where *martyrein*, etc., is used to characterize the apostolic preaching, the main feature is the eyewitness motif.[51] Especially in Luke the concept of witness plays an important role. ". . . The fact that Luke applies the concept of the witness to the content of the Gospel is grounded in

---

[47]D. Bonhoeffer, *Letters and Papers from Prison,* the enlarged edition by Macmillan, p. 329.

[48]R. Schippers, *De Geschiedenis van Jezus en de Apokalyptiek,* p. 22.

[49]H. N. Ridderbos, *Paul and Jesus,* pp. 57-58.

[50]R. Schippers, *Getuigen van Jezus Christus in het Nieuwe Testament,* pp. 8ff., 19ff.

[51]Ibid., pp. 100ff. At the least the statement applies to Luke as author. In the Johannine writings the emphasis is on the authority of the witness.

his marked concern to expound clearly the historical foundations of the evangelical message. At issue are, not doctrines, myths, or speculations, but facts which took place in the clear light of history at a specific time and place, facts which can be established and on which one can rely."[52] Gerhard Kittel points out that from a comparison between Acts 6:1ff. and 1:20ff. it can be established that the *diakonia, tou logou,* "the essential content of the office of the Twelve which they cannot surrender," consists of the witness about Jesus.[53] This is evident also from Luke 1:2: The *ap' archēs autoptai* have become *hyperetai tou logou* (1:2); "because these men were eye-witnesses, they had an essential qualification for the ministry of the Word, namely, acquaintance with the *pragmata,* with the facts concerning Jesus Christ, about whom the Word is the witness and message."[54]]

Use of the word "witness" as a category of revelation demonstrates that the coming of God in his word is directly related to his appearances: his self-attestation in his deeds. *There* and *such* is our God; he wants to be known and believed through his self-communication by action.

There is no truth of God other than the truth which has become visible, audible, and tangible. God's truth is God's "real-ity" (Dutch *werk-elijkheid*). This means that the scriptural story is not "just" a story. The narrative, says K. H. Miskotte, is teaching, and the teaching comes from above, from the order of divine truth. "We are thrown off the track when we interpret the narrative as a myth which has formed around a 'historical' kernel, the livery of a universal truth, an illustration of an admonition. The event, the truth, the Commandment are not to be enucleated from the time process in such a way that we recover rational or superrational data while the narratives remain as empty shells." "We all have in our blood the religious notion of an eternal content in an accidental form; and it also seems to relieve us of many intellectual difficulties and emotional. impediments. Nevertheless, such a reduction from the concrete to the abstract, from the accidental to the general, dare not be applied here."[55]

For pastoral role-fulfilment in the ministry of the word this means that it cannot be part of its agenda to "dehistoricize" (Müller): to push oneself through the historicity of the narrative toward the way to God himself. The historical "wrapping" is not the cradle in which the "spiritual address" is laid (Schreiner). To offer a biblical analogy one could say with a variant rendering of the centurion's exclamation: "Truly this reality is the truth of God!" (cf. Mark 15:39). The word of God, and the narrative of its happening, discloses the truth; it does not provide the material from which the truth could be deduced. The knowledge of God's truth does not have to be enucleated from his word; this truth must be

---

[52]H. Strathmann, *TDNT,* IV, 492, s.v. *martyreō.*
[53]G. Kittel, *TDNT,* IV, 115, s.v. *legō.*
[54]Ibid.
[55]K. H. Miskotte, "The Narrative," in *When the Gods Are Silent,* pp. 199ff.

heard in the word in the same way that the witnesses *saw* it in "the acts of the Lord."

7. THE WORD OF GOD (d) ACTUALIZES SALVATION

The word of God reveals the truth of God: his faithfulness, the genuineness and reality of his presence for people. We can also say all this in the words of the heading of this section: The word of God actualizes salvation. When God comes in his word, then by that token he has turned in love toward people; then he has acted on behalf of people; then he has communicated with people. When God comes in his word, then by that token salvation is there; then people are being healed and situated in the peace, the righteousness, and the life of the Kingdom.

Now pastoral role-fulfilment mediates the coming of God in his word: i.e., pastoral role-fulfilment leads to healing and communication of salvation. It is a ministry of mediation which serves the realization of salvation. For that reason it makes sense to take this dynamic, already present in the preceding, and make it explicit.

Should someone say: "Show me a person who participates in salvation," we could not do better than point to the person who constitutes the "I" of the Apostles' Creed. Nowhere is it clearer what it is "to participate in salvation" than in these unembellished sentences, in which a person links his or her name with *the* name: "I believe. . . ." A peculiarity of this Creed is that it consists of a summary of a series of facts. The speaker in the Creed does not speak of truths to which he adheres or of convictions which he has adopted but of facts and of future events of which he knows that they will be facts because they have been promised and are, in principle, already in process. In the preceding section we referred to the significance of *martyria* as a category of revelation. In view of its fact consciousness we could characterize the Apostles' Creed as a response to the *martyria*. We have already seen that, according to R. Schippers, the main motif in the word group "to witness" is the eyewitness motif; and witness is a report of what has happened. But that report is a testimony: it is not given to satisfy anyone's curiosity. When Luke says that in writing his story he went to work with accuracy (*akribōs*), he also makes plain the reason for this precision— namely, that his readers might know the truth concerning the things of which they had been informed (Luke 1:1-4). According to Schippers, a second motif is directly connected with the primary one: the *martyria* concept has a legal color. "The witness plays his role in the adversary situation of the legal process." The facts must be imparted in order that people may make up their minds about God and his saving actions on the basis of known facts. In conclusion Schippers says: "In essence, to witness concerning Jesus Christ, in the New Testament, is to speak about him—whether in self-attestation by Jesus, or by the Father, or by the Spirit, or by the eye- and earwitnesses of his teaching and action—in order by this witness to persuade people to make the big decision. It aims to move people to the positive pronouncement of a faith which breaks at the root with the unbelieving rejection of the Word which became flesh and dwelt among us and revealed his glory, not least in the resurrection from the dead. Thus this witness, with its knowledge and report of the facts, serves the justice of God."[56]

To say the words of the Creed "I believe . . ." is by that action to make "the big decision." Still, more takes place than that the one who recites the Creed acknowledges the factuality of the facts to which witness is given. This is also evident from the structure of the Apostles' Creed. It is more than a summary of facts; it is a story told in a few pivotal words. Very succinctly but without omitting anything, the Creed tells the story of the salvation that has come. At this point we need to focus attention on the role which the story plays in the disclosure of salvation.

[W. H. Gispen, in his book on Israel's "compulsion" to tell stories, points out the phenomenon that "Semites in their literature showed a great preference for the tale, the story—a tendency which arises from their love for the concrete and their distaste for the abstract." He believes that this preference is so strong that we can speak of the storytelling compulsion, by which he understands "the tendency to form larger units, or books." This preference for narrative may even be detected in books which are not directly narrative. "The Pentateuch is one unit—one grand narrative history." "Even in Leviticus, which is composed almost completely of laws, there is inner and outer unity. This shows that unity was there by design."[57] The same tendency may be detected in the New Testament. One of the characteristic features of the Gospels, according to R. Schippers, is that "they tell the story of Jesus as it unfolds within the horizon of the 'holy history' as told prophetically in the Old Testament."[58] With reference to the Gospel of Matthew H. N. Ridderbos says: "The remarkable arrangement and the alternation of the words and works of the Lord is proof that a basic plan and design underlies the narrative of this book."[59] It is not hard to discover that this plan conforms to the schema of the Old Testament story of the history of the LORD with his people.]

One would think that something more is afoot than a particular specimen of a general phenomenon in Semitic literature—the tendency to form progressively larger units. The movement is not so much *toward* the unity of the story; it proceeds *from* a unity. Yahweh makes his history with people from creation to consummation. He realizes the promise "And I will walk among you, and will be your God, and you shall be my people" (Lev. 26:12). He travels with his people through the times as a shepherd with his flock. Thus, in the continuity

---

[56]R. Schippers, *Getuigen van Jezus Christus in het Nieuwe Testament,* p. 199.
[57]W. H. Gispen, *Israëls "Verhaaldwang,"* p. 22.
[58]R. Schippers *De Geschiedenis van Jezus en de Apocalyptiek,* p. 6.
[59]H. N. Ridderbos, *Mattheüs,* I, 19.

of his covenant, in constant interaction with his people, he is God. Thus he reveals himself and is known. It is not the case that one takes the incidental deeds and words of the LORD and afterward makes a single story out of them. All the action took place and all the words were spoken in the history of God's association and self-communication with his people. The deeds of the LORD together form the work of the LORD, and his words are the *word* of God. His acts can be known only from the perspective of the whole of his work; the words can be understood only from the perspective of the word. Every part derives its meaning from the totality of the one story which has its center in the gospel of the Word which became flesh and dwelt among us.

This story is not just the story of God in his association with people; it is also the real story of human beings. Just as nothing of value can be said about, or understood of, God outside the story, so nothing of saving significance can be said or understood of people outside the story. The "I believe" of the Apostles' Creed is therefore not just an acknowledgment of the factuality of certain facts: it is the adoption of the story and therein the adoption of the history of God's works and words as the history of the salvation of this person who says: "I believe."

[The Apostles' Creed is akin to confessions such as those of Deuteronomy 26:5ff. and 6:21ff. In Deuteronomy 6, fathers are instructed to tell their sons: "*We* were Pharaoh's slaves in Egypt; and the LORD brought *us* out of Egypt with a mighty hand." Martin Noth points out that such a statement cannot simply be explained in terms of the solidarity of the people through the ages. "The issue is much more a matter of the constantly renewed re-presentation of past events."[60] With the first we can agree: it is not so much a sense of historic solidarity with his people which causes the believer to apply the history of salvation to himself, as the conviction, in the context of the covenant and in fellowship with the people of the LORD, that one is bound up with him who works salvation, who is the first but also identifies with those who are last (Isa. 41:4). It does not seem quite correct to speak of "a constantly renewed re-presentation." One thinks almost involuntarily, in this context, of the well-known quote from the *Pesahim* tractate in the *Mishnah*: "In every age man is under obligation to regard himself as if he had been delivered out of Egypt."[61] The Jew celebrating the Exodus knows: this has happened to *me*, for not only is this people my people, but what is more: this God is my God. I belong to the covenant in which the LORD has accomplished this act of redemption.]

"Consequently," says Wingren, "the distinction between subjective and objective loses its meaning, for the *kerygma* implies that when we speak of Christ's death and resurrection—that unique, objective event, far back in time and distant in space—we speak of an event in the life of man, an event that

---

[60]M. Noth, "Die Vergegenwärtigung des Alten Testaments in der Verkündigung," in *Evangelische Theologie* 12 (1952-53): 12.
[61]Quoted by J. Behm, *TDNT*, III, 733, s.v. *klaō*.

happened to the man sitting listening in the pew. We are talking about him when
we are talking about *Christ*. We do not first speak of the objective event and
then try to find a way of applying it to men, for the *kerygma* concerning Christ's
death and resurrection man is already present; the hearer is there in the passage
when the minister opens the New Testament."[62] We could also say: he was
already in the story, for it is the story of a history which embraces him from the
very beginning; it is the story of "the works" of which man and "his" salvation
are the focus.

[It is said that H. F. Kohlbrügge once answered the question "When were
you converted?" with the laconic reply "On Golgotha." "This answer," says
Barth, "with all its fundamental implications, was not the witty retort of an
embarrassed and unconverted man, but the only possible and straightforward
answer of a truly converted Christian. The events of faith in our own life can,
in fact, be none other than the birth, passion, death, ascension, and resurrection
of Jesus Christ, the faith of Abraham, Isaac, and Jacob, the exodus of Israel
from Egypt, its journey through the desert, its entrance into the land of Canaan,
the outpouring of the Holy Ghost at Pentecost and the mission of the apostles
to the heathen." "Have I experienced anything more important, incisive, serious,
contemporary than this, that I have been personally present and have shared in
the crossing of Israel through the Red Sea but also in the adoration of the golden
calf, in the baptism of Jesus but also in the denial of Peter and the treachery of
Judas, that all this has happened to me here and now?"[63] *Re*-presentation is
superfluous. Nor do I—as S. Kierkegaard thought—need to become contem-
poraneous with the moment in which salvation was effected. The saving action
implicated me; I was involved when it happened. "I have been crucified with
Christ," declared Paul (Gal. 2:20). He reminds the church: ". . . and you were
buried with him in baptism, in which you were also raised with him" (Col. 2:12;
3:3). "God made us alive together with Christ . . . and made us sit with him
in the heavenly places in Christ Jesus" (Eph. 2:5-6). The story of the LORD—of
the covenant, of reconciliation, of salvation—is *our* story.]

But are these not grand and empty words? In the experience of a pastor
that can be a problem as big as life. There one is bound to encounter a man like
Gideon. "The angel of the LORD appeared to him and said to him, 'The LORD
is with you, you mighty man of valor.' And Gideon said to him, 'Pray, sir, if the
LORD is with us, why then has all this befallen us? And where are all his
wonderful deeds which our fathers recounted to us, saying, "Did not the LORD
bring us up from Egypt?" ' " (Judg. 6:12-13). For this young man *the* story has
become just another story; rather, he has lost his connections with it. The situation of the moment does not hang together with what the story has led him to
expect. It is his grief that the right hand of the Most High has changed (cf. Ps.
77:11). The reality of experience is diametrically opposed to reality as told. His
experience in no respect resembles what he ought to believe. In this Gideon is

---

[62]G. Wingren, *The Living Word*, p. 28.
[63]K. Barth, *CD*, I/2, p. 709.

not alone; his experience is that of practically everyone who grew up with the stories told by the fathers. But weren't those stories the word of God? In the heading above this section we wrote: "The Word of God Actualizes Salvation." Wouldn't it be better, in light of our actual experience, to put that short sentence in the interrogative?

Before we proceed to do that, we must make an effort to understand better what we mean by the phrases "the word of God" and "the coming of God in his word." In view of the biblical idiom concerning "the word of God" it is not strange that the word of God actualizes, or effectuates, something.

[Take, for instance, Psalm 33. "The word of the LORD" (v. 4) parallels "all his work." "By the word of the Lord the heavens were made, and all their host by the breath of his mouth" (v. 6). "For he spoke, and it came to be; he commanded, and it stood forth" (v. 9). An account of events in the Old Testament often begins with the phrase "And it came to pass" (wayy^{e}hî). The same verb is occasionally used to denote the coming of the word of the LORD to someone: e.g., the word of the LORD came (hāyâ) to Jeremiah (Jer. 1:2). The same word serves to explain the name Yahweh and characterizes this God as the God who is present, attentive, and effective. The word of God is not just a vibration in the air: it breaks into a situation and creates a new one. It is a dynamic presence: "Is not my word like fire, says the LORD, and like a hammer which breaks the rock in pieces?" (Jer. 23:29). When that word comes, something must happen: "The LORD has sent a word against Jacob, and it will light upon Israel; and all the people will know . . ." (Isa. 9:8-9). The word is like a messenger whom the LORD sends out and who does not return without effecting his purpose: "it shall accomplish that which I purpose, and prosper in the thing for which I sent it" (Isa. 55:11). The word of God is living and active (Heb. 4:12); it is at work in believers (I Thess. 2:13); it is the power of God (I Cor. 1:18; cf. Roman. 1:16); it is able to save souls (James 1:21).]

The preceding, and especially the words of Scripture quoted out of context, may create the impression that the word of God is a mysterious power which actualizes salvation (or judgment) in a somewhat magical manner. To remove that misunderstanding—and at the same time to discover points of view which will prove significant for pastoral role-fulfilment and some dynamic components in it—we wish to make three observations.

We have already seen that the word of God may never be abstracted from the speaker. The word of God is his speech: he is always present when he speaks; it is always the word which proceeds from his mouth. The word of God is the *dynamis theou* (power of God) because God is the subject of that word. Says G. Kittel: "Not in itself as a magical entity, but as the Word of God, i.e., the Word spoken and used by God, the Word is efficacious." The image of the weapon is sometimes used with reference to the word of God; the image focuses our attention primarily on him who uses it: only in his hand is it effective.[64]

Second, a word of power, in the nature of the case, is the verbalization

---

[64]G. Kittel, *TDNT*, IV, 118, s.v. *legō*.

of a thought or desire, or knowledge of an event, or the like. The creation-word of God is a command, i.e., an authoritative expression in the words of his will. The benediction of God is a promise, i.e., the expression of his readiness and intent to bless. The gospel is a message of salvation: a communication of what God has done to, and on behalf of, people. "Evangel" characterizes the word of God as "the message of the great transformation, of the redemptive intrusion of God."[65] Paul says that the gospel is the power of God for salvation (Rom. 1:16). But the gospel is not a power simply as "words"; it is that as "word of the cross" (I Cor. 1:18), as "the gospel of God which he promised beforehand through his prophets in the holy scriptures, the gospel concerning his Son, who was descended from David according to the flesh and designated Son of God in power according to the Spirit of holiness by his resurrection from the dead, Jesus Christ our Lord . . ." (Rom. 1:1-4).

[Rudolf Bultmann is right when he says: "In the 'word,' then, the salvation-occurrence is present. For the proclaimed word is neither an enlightening *Weltanschauung* flowing out in general truths, nor a merely historical account which, like a reporter's story, reminds a public of important but bygone facts."[66] But this does not necessitate a split between kerygma and history. For, as H. Diem remarks against Bultmann *cum suis*, "The whole content of the Gospel message and proclamation flows from the real history of Jesus Christ."[67] It is this content which constitutes the power of the word of God proclaimed as gospel; the power of the word of God is a power "which, rooted in a historical act, brings deliverance. . . . It has its origin in a decisive divine act."[68] This gospel, the message of what has happened, is the gospel of salvation (Eph. 1:13), of peace (6:15). The content of the message is decisive: Christ and his work. The word of the cross (I Cor. 1:18) is the word of reconciliation (II Cor. 5:19), of grace (Acts 14:3; 20:32), and of life (Phil. 2:16). It is the word that is "able to save your souls" (James 1:21).]

The word, as we saw, implies a speaker. Further, it has content. A third characteristic, as Luther points out, is that it calls for the hearing ear: *natura verbi est audiri* ("It is the nature of the word that it be heard").[69] Failing to reach the ear of the one for whom it is intended, the word falls short of becoming a "word-event." It is then no more than a blowing out of air (*flatus vocis*). Where there are no ears, there is no sound; where there is no understanding, there is no word. A reality I have not observed does not "really" exist for me. A word I have not heard or understood is not for me a really existing word; it communicates nothing; it is not significant for me.

One could ask whether the same is true for the reality of the word, i.e.,

---

[65]H. N. Ridderbos, *The Authority of the New Testament Scriptures*, p. 54.

[66]R. Bultmann, *Theology of the New Testament*, I, 307.

[67]H. Diem, *Dogmatics*, p. 132.

[68]W. Grundmann, *TDNT*, II, 309, s.v. *dynamis*.

[69]M. Luther, *Werke* (Weimarer Ausgabe), Vol. IV, p. 9, l. 18.

the speech of God. Dogmatics refers to *creatio ex nihilo* by the word. Abraham believed in God, "who calls into existence the things that do not exist" (Rom. 4:17). Ezekiel is told, be it in an allegorical vision, to prophesy to dry bones, "and lo, they were very dry" (Ezek. 37:1-10). Both in creation and in redemption the word of God goes forth to what is not as well as to the dead. When he commands, it is there (Ps. 33:9). "At the beginning of every relation of man to the Word stands the passive 'expressed . . . in the image of birth' (cf. I Peter 1:23; James 1:18)."[70] The word of God "works," it seems, even when there is no ear to hear.

Trying to understand the preceding—the urge to do this could be an indication that what Luther said about the *natura verbi* also applies to the word of God—we become strongly aware of the limits of our imagination. Calling the nonexistent into being—the idea refuses to be visualized. Perhaps it is not necessary. The references to God's creative speech are given, not to indicate the relationship between God and the nonexistent but between God and the existent. What is, exists only because God called it into being; when it was not, God called it that it might be. The meaning of *creatio ex nihilo* is that what is exists solely by the grace of God, is absolutely dependent on him and subject to him. It would not be there if he had not called it into being. In this perspective Ezekiel's vision becomes meaningful. The dry bones represent Israel: "Behold, they say, 'Our bones are dried up, and our hope is lost; we are clean cut off' " (37:11). Israel has sunk into the impotence of nonbeing. But then comes the LORD: "Behold, I will open your graves and raise you from your graves, O my people. . . . and you shall know that I am the LORD" (37:12-13). These last words express the motive for the passive of which Kittel says that it stands at the beginning of every relation of man to the word. The word "passive" does not quite seem to fit; the relation between a person and the word of God starts with the sovereign speech of him who, in creation and redemption, is the first, and who shows himself to be who he is, Yahweh, the One who is caringly present. And the person to whom the word of that God comes will know him as Yahweh, the God of the covenant, the God of the eternal *'ᵉmûnâ* (faithfulness).[71] That God is the God in whom Abraham believed (Rom. 4:17). Justice is done to this aspect of the word of God when it is called a decree or proclamation. It is never the kind of communication which can simply be received as information; nor does he offer an opinion which a person may or may not share. On the contrary, the LORD comes and stands forth, calling, and then the incident occurs "at which the two ears of every one that hears it will tingle" (I Sam. 3:11), namely, God's very own speech.

It now seems evident that Luther's remark about the nature of speech in general is true, in the most absolute sense, of the speech of God: it *demands* that it be heard. In numerous places the Bible requires of a person that he must

---

[70]G. Kittel, *TDNT*, IV, 118-19, s.v. *legō*.
[71]Cf. Hosea 2:20.

hear and heed a given word, listen to it, obey it, or believe it. When the LORD "comes and stands forth" Samuel must answer: "Speak, for thy servant hears." It is as if Samuel is saying "I do not yet know you, but I want to be your servant and serve in knowing you. How? By listening!" God's servants are people who listen; God's people are a listening people. Our Christian religion is a religion of faith by hearing, the hearing of the word.

Natura verbi est audiri. The connection between the word and hearing it is so close that in Hebrew a form of the verb "to hear" is sometimes used to denote the act of proclamation.

[An example occurs in Isaiah 52:7, where the messenger of good tidings is pictured as *mašmî(a)' šālôm* and *mašmî(a)' yᵉšûʻâ* (lit. "one who causes peace to be heard" and "one who causes salvation to be heard"). The noun *šᵉmûʻâ*, derived from the verb *šamaʻ*, can mean "message," "tidings,"[72] "revelation," or "oracle."[73] The word also occurs in Isaiah 53:1 where the KJV has "Who hath believed our report?" From the passage a line can be drawn to the New Testament where it is quoted in John 12:38 ("Lord, who has believed our report?") and Romans 10:16 ("Lord, who has believed what he has heard from us?").

In their commentary on Romans, W. Sanday and A. C. Headlam offer two meanings of *akoē*: "The faculty by which a thing is heard" and "the substance of what is heard." The second meaning is the one, in their opinion, which is intended in Romans 10:16 ("Who has believed what he has heard?"). Commenting on verse 17 they say, "It shades off into the first, 'faith comes by hearing.' "[74] It seems somewhat risky to speak of one meaning "shading off" into another, but it seems justified here. Translating a word from one language to another is always an attempt at approximating the meaning of the original as closely as possible. *Šᵉmûʻâ–akoē*, in the passive, signify "that which is heard." Now what is heard is not always identical with what was said (and therefore what should have been heard), but the intent of the speaker is that the two be identical. When the purpose of an author is to stress the importance and necessity of hearing what is said attentively, obediently, and believingly—as in the context of the two passages, Isaiah 53:1 and Romans 10:16—it is not strange to name that "which is proclaimed" with the word for that "which is heard." There *was* something to be heard, for something was said; but was it heard in reality—in faith? In this way Paul comes to use *akoē* as a parallel to *euangelion*: not all have heeded the *euangelion*, for it is, as Isaiah said earlier, 'Who has heard our *akoē*?

Gerhard Kittel seems to go too far when he says that *akoē* became a technical term for "proclamation" or "preaching."[75] At least it is doubtful that

---

[72]Cf. I Samuel 4:19; Proverbs 15:30; 25:25; Jeremiah 49:14.

[73]Cf. Isaiah 28:9.

[74]W. Sanday and A. C. Headlam, *The Epistle to the Romans* (International Critical Commentary), p. 297.

[75]G. Kittel, *TDNT*, I, 221, s.v. *akouō*.

akoē means preaching in Galatians 3:2 and 5. The term *logos akoēs* occurs in two other places—too few to infer that it is a technical term. We do believe that precisely the combination *logos akoēs* says something important about the word of God which comes to us as preaching. In Hebrews 4:2 the expression stands for "the message that was preached." The gospel is proclaimed to us as it was to Israel. The *Logos akoēs* did not profit them; they heard it but did not believe it; they did not hear it as they should have, as the word intends itself to be heard. The same expression occurs in I Thessalonians 2:13 in a rather complicated construction: ". . . when you received the word of God which you heard from us . . . the word of God." What Paul preached was to them God's word—as indeed it is, says Paul. Our paraphrase "what Paul preached" occurs in his words as *logos akoēs (par' hemōn) tou theou*. Two things strike us in this description. First, it is striking that Paul speaks already here of *logos tou theou*. He does not for a moment suppose that the Thessalonians have accepted *his* word as though it were God's. Second, it is noteworthy that he does not simply speak of *ho logos tou theou*. Something must be added—something which indicates the specific character of the situation in which the word appeared. This indication is given by the use of *akoēs*. Says Hermann Diem: "The specific character of the truth of this *logos akoēs* lies in the fact that it [the truth] cannot be lifted out of the concrete event-sequence of obedient preaching, hearing, and believing."[76] *Akoē* says that the word "came to pass" in a situation of human speech-and-hearing; it proceeded with great personal directness—from "mouth" to "ear."]

When the word of God comes, the human ear must be ready to hear. Then the word "works" (*energeitai*, I Thess. 2:13), and is a power of God. Our Lord makes this very plain in the parable of the sower. "As for what was sown on good soil, this is he who hears the word and understands it; he indeed bears fruit" (Matt. 13:23). "There is," says R. Schippers in reflecting on this parable, "a mysterious correlation between seed and soil. . . ." "The word of God is not powerful apart from the human heart which hears and keeps it."[77] The context of Matthew 13:14-15 shows that the expression "to hear and understand" is an allusion to Isaiah 6:9-10. Understanding there is a function of the *heart,* a word which in the Old Testament consistently refers to human beings in their totality and unity. It is, says Behm, "first the principle and organ of man's personal life. It is the focus of his being and activity as a spiritual personality."[78] The issue in hearing and understanding the word, without which the word is powerless, is an intensely yielded and dedicated listening such that a person achieves rapport with the word from within the core of her existence. This comes out clearly in Mark's reading of the interpretation of the parable of the sower: "But those that were sown upon the good soil are the ones who hear the word and accept it

---

[76]H. Diem, *Die Kirche und ihre Praxis*, p. 172.
[77]R. Schippers, *Gelijkenissen van Jezus*, p. 29.
[78]J. Behm, *TDNT*, III, 609, s.v. *kardia*.

(*paradechontai*)" (Mark 4:20). The verb *dechesthai* is used in the New Testament, particularly in the book of Acts, for the acceptance of the gospel. "The use of *dechomai* in this connection—it is an equivalent of faith—shows us that in the total NT view man's existence over against God is limited to the reception of His gift. It has no immanent possibilities. In hearing the message, however, man is liberated for decision in relation to it."[79] The issue at stake here has been stated most clearly by Karl Barth: "The Word of God is not spoken merely to a psycho-physical individual in time which is simply the functioning organ of another author . . . , but to a subject who is himself at all points the author, accomplishing this movement freely, independently and spontaneously. The Word of God, demanding hearing and obedience, presupposes a *productive* subject. . . . Otherwise what would be the sense of God speaking to him and not simply disposing of him."[80]

"The word of God actualizes salvation." We have wondered whether this pronouncement should not be turned into a question. Being in Christ, taking part in his death and resurrection and ascension—all this is often beyond our capacity to experience it. We hear the word of which the Bible says that it is powerful, but it sounds like an old story in which we have no role: ". . . where are all his wonderful deeds which our fathers recounted to us?" (Judg. 6:13). "We have heard with our ears, O God, our fathers have told us, what deeds thou didst perform in their days, in the days of old. . . . Yet thou hast cast us off and abased us" (Ps. 44:1, 9). "Are his promises at an end for all time?" (Ps. 77:8). Are people like ourselves the lost generation? These are the questions pastors face over and over on their rounds. Sometimes the feeling creeps up on us that *ho logos akoēs tou theou* is a powerless and pathetically human word.

How do we escape this pitiful plight? H. W. Rossouw makes the statement—thereby pointing the way out—that "salvation is a living word-relationship of personal communion."[81] After Gideon has poured out his scepticism regarding the story, i.e., the word of God, the next thing is an event: "The LORD turned to him and said, 'Go in this might of yours and deliver Israel . . . do not I send you?' " (Judg. 6:14). Salvation from God comes to a person in an "address" which tells of salvation; the word comes in the event of one person being spoken to by Another who in Bethlehem has become the Other and participates in our lives. "The gospel does not come," says G. C. Berkouwer, "coolly to inform man of a new objective state of affairs. It invades man's life as a call to belief and conversion, to love and obedience. It is so pointedly directed to the concrete existence of man that we may speak of an essential correlation between faith and salvation. The salvation of the Lord does not fall on the world as rain upon an arid countryside. It creates a personal relation in

---

[79]W. Grundmann, *TDNT,* II, 54, s.v. *dechomai.*
[80]K. Barth, *CD,* III/4, pp. 329-30.
[81]H. W. Rossouw, *Klaarheid en Interpretasie,* p. 248.

which this salvation is experienced and known in love and thankfulness."[82] When Berkouwer refers here to an "essential correlation between faith and salvation," the thought of a possibly meritorious or cooperative kind of faith must be radically excluded.[83] Faith is but "an instrument with which we embrace Christ our righteousness . . . an instrument that keeps us in communion with him in all his benefits."[84] All this, however, does not substract one iota from the significance of "believing," "hearing and understanding," "accepting," "ingesting"—i.e., the profound orientation of the human heart, hence of the whole of one's existence, to the speech of God. Thus God seeks to be our daily companion and ally. He does not simply "utilize" a human being. He chooses the human person—in herself the actualization of salvation—as a partner-in-dialogue who is called to respond in freedom to God's action.[85] "Speak, for thy servant hears" (I Sam. 3:10). To answer thus is to know Yahweh, and to know Yahweh is to know oneself as implicated in the history of salvation.[86] I believe in the LORD who is "the first, and with the last" (Isa. 41:4).

8. MODES OF PASTORAL ROLE-FULFILMENT

In the preceding we have made continual reference to "the word of God." It became plain that this phrase did not serve simply as the equivalent of "Holy Scripture." We confess that Holy Scripture is "the word of God," but that thesis is not reversible. With the phrase "the word of God" we meant "What God says to us human beings and we hear from him." In our situation, we may add, this cannot be something which has not been imparted through Holy Scripture. Our interest, however, lies in another point, namely, in the word of God "coming to pass" or in what we meant by "the coming of God in his word." Of that coming of God in his word we have offered a few characterizations and seen something significant.

If now we are to construct a model for the pastoral role we must analyze

---

[82]G. C. Berkouwer, *Faith and Justification,* pp. 33-34.

[83]Cf. ibid., pp. 36, 42, 80, 188ff., 195; G. C. Berkouwer, *Faith and Sanctification,* pp. 27, 96; *Faith and Perseverance,* pp. 97ff.; *The Work of Christ,* p. 292; *The Sacraments,* pp. 72ff.; *Holy Scripture,* p. 120.

[84]The Belgic Confession, Art. 22; cf. G. C. Berkouwer, *Faith and Justification,* p. 176.

[85]This is indicated especially in the use of *dechomai* (cf. W. Grundmann, *TDNT,* II, 50), which expresses "the reaction to action on the other side." Berkouwer, in *Faith and Justification,* p. 179, warns that grace "does not mean an ontological cutting-off of a part of human life." "The correlation . . . must not become a divine monologue in which man is a mere telephone through which God addresses himself" (pp. 178-79). "Mindlessly to repeat what God says first," according to Van Ruler, "would be pagan" (*Reformatorische Opmerkingen,* pp. 178ff.). "The Word of God must pass through the judicial capacity of the human person."

[86]Cf. K. Barth on this "knowing" (*CD,* IV/3, pp. 184-85).

this complex "coming of God in his word"; in other words, we must offer as it were a "spectral analysis" of this one light. This is necessary because of our assertion that the pastoral role mediates the coming of God in his word. This is not to say that God's coming in his word always requires this intermediary but only that pastoral role-fulfilment finds its meaning in it.

In analyzing the complex phenomenon of God's coming in his word we must first of all distinguish between the *structures* of this coming—the lines along which it takes place—and the *dynamics*. An attempt must be made to abstract from this phenomenon the structural modes as well as the dynamic moments. It must be remembered that these abstractions do not occur as such. The reality of God's coming in his word is dynamic; dynamic moments do not exist by themselves. They are "the power" of the modes without which the modes could not be.

When we trace the structural modes our intention and focus must be clear. We have already declared our intention: we consider "the coming of God in his word" in order to clarify for ourselves the structure of the pastor's role as intermediary of that coming. Our question then is: In what manner does the word of God come to people when it is spoken by persons?

Obviously we cannot simply answer this question by referring to the three forms of pastoral role-fulfilment which constitute our concern in this study: preaching, catechesis, and pastoral care. We have already discovered that these terms are not clear enough and are used in too many different ways. We saw the necessity of "invalidating the nomenclature" (Kouwenaar). But we remain concerned with pastoral role-fulfilment as it takes place in these forms. Hence we must try to track down the "existentials," or basic structures, which determine the shape of these forms.

The New Testament offers a plethora of terms denoting God's coming by a human intermediary. It would take us too far afield, and not serve our purpose, to discuss them all. Our selection is more or less arbitrary, but we believe that with it nothing essential will be left out. The concepts we have chosen—kerygma, didache, and paraklesis—serve individually as the core of a cluster of terms which belong conceptually together.

Before proceeding to a discussion of the structural modes we must say a word about our nontreatment as such of two concepts which in Scripture are nevertheless very important, namely, the concepts of martyria (witness) and prophecy.

With reference to martyria we have already pointed out that the entire word group *martyrein* in the New Testament serves in the first place to indicate that the matter at stake in the gospel is "what has taken place."[87]

---

[87]H. N. Ridderbos, *The Authority of the New Testament Scriptures*, p. 53, points out a number of redemptive historical categories ". . . by means of which we can clearly understand the nature, the content and the form of the New Testament Scripture, and the nature of its authority," namely, kerygma, martyria, and didache. It must be borne in mind that Ridderbos's intention and focus differ from ours.

The gist of the usage of this word group could perhaps best be characterized with the words of 2 Peter 1:16: "For we did not follow cleverly devised myths when we made known to you the power and coming of our Lord Jesus Christ, but we were eyewitnesses of his majesty." In this primary sense the martyria concept applies only to the situation of the small circle of "witness-apostles." According to H. N. Ridderbos, this "testimony can be said to occupy an entirely unique place in the history of redemption. Not everyone can set himself up as a witness, not even one who was, in the receptive sense, a witness of the revelation of God in Christ. The testimony of Christ is the redemptive word, prepared for the world by God once, and for all time. Only those expressly called and entrusted with the task of being witnesses . . . can appear before the forum of history as the witnesses of Jesus Christ."[88] Their testimony, made possible by what they have heard and seen and their hands have handled (cf. I John 1:1-2), is the ground for their own preaching and that of all others.[89] By their witness—this, in the second place—a testimony comes into being which is as it were the possession of the church, kept and preached by it as "the testimony of Jesus."[90] Sometimes the New Testament calls preachers who themselves were not eyewitnesses *martyres* (e.g., Rev. 2:13), but they are so called as *traditores* of the apostolic witness which constitutes the link forged by the Holy Spirit "between the mighty redemptive events wrought in the fulness of time, and the coming church."[91]

Something needs to be added immediately at this point. Speaking of the Johannine writing, N. Brox points out that there "historical events have testimonial value only insofar as the viewers in faith see in them the *doxa tou theou* (the glory of God). Over and over the manner of speaking and arguing creates the impression that the matter at stake is a testimony of the usual sort. Then, however, it appears that the testimony is unacceptable because it is paradoxical in its structure." What kind of paradox? Brox proceeds with this formulation: "A faltering faith is to be supported by witnesses; however, their testimony itself presupposes faith."[92] If this is true for the one who hears it, it is also true for the speaker, who was the first to hear the word. When someone acts as witness of Jesus Christ, then "his rendering witness is simultaneously an act of confession to the contents of his testimony—to the person of Jesus Christ. The object of witness is such that it cannot be witnessed to without the personal participation of the witness."[93] His witness has ceased to be neutral.

It is eminently biblical to say that pastoral role-fulfilment is a ministry in the martyria of Jesus. This means, first of all, that pastoral role-fulfilment is nurtured and determined by the apostolic witness. Whoever speaks in his role

---

[88]Ibid., p. 63.
[89]R. Schippers, *Getuigen van Jezus Christus in het Nieuwe Testament*, p. 145.
[90]Ibid., pp. 192ff.
[91]H. N. Ridderbos, *The Authority of the New Testament Scriptures*, p. 64.
[92]N. Brox, *Zeuge und Märtyrer*, p. 92.
[93]Ibid., p. 108.

as pastor speaks not to make known his opinions, insights, or experiences but to pass on what has been handed down of the things which have happened according to the reliable testimony of dominically designated witnesses. Pastoral role-fulfilment as a ministry in the martyria means, in the second place, that whoever speaks pastorally cannot speak as though he were noncommitted. "The special knowledge presupposed in the witnesses is identical with the conviction of faith which gives them certainty," says Brox. To act pastorally is to act in faith.

Thus the concept of martyria is of great importance for the pastoral role. The core of the pastoral role is that it is martyria—rather, a ministry in the martyria of Jesus. We have said the same thing from another point of view in the description of our starting point—namely, that pastoral role-fulfilment is the intermediary for the coming of God in his word. Now, however, it is our purpose to track down the structural modes of the pastor's role, and a concept which embraces the essence of the entire range of that role clearly cannot be called "a mode" of its fulfilment.

Much could be said for calling prophecy one of the "existentials" of "God's coming in his word." In the Old Testament the prophet is "a man of the word"— an instrument of the instantaneous revelation of God. He is the mouth of the LORD (Jer. 15:19). "I will put my words in his mouth" (Deut. 18:18). He is— this is probably the meaning of nābî' —the man who has been called to speak in the name of God.[94] What especially makes a person a prophet is immediate dealings with God; this appears also from the older word for prophet—rō'-eh, "seer" (cf. I Sam. 9:9).

The role of the prophet in the New Testament church is not entirely clear. In Acts, one sometimes sees prophetic acts as predictors of future events (e.g., Acts 11:27ff.; 21:10ff.). Much more often prophets are mentioned as carriers of the charisma of prophecy who, especially in the church assemblies, exhorted and comforted people by giving a charismatic here-and-now application of the word just heard. Friedrich seems to hit the bull's-eye when he says concerning the New Testament prophet: "The prophet is the Spirit-endowed counsellor of the community who tells it what to do in specific situations, who blames and praises, whose preaching contains admonition and comfort, the call for repentance and promise."[95] He who prophesies, says Paul, "speaks to men for their upbuilding and encouragement and consolation" (I Cor. 14:3). The Old Testament prophets are said to be bearers of comfort: "To give comfort is their finest calling."[96] The New Testament prophets are no different in this respect. The prophet is the man of paraklēsis. The ancient Christian church translated the name "Barnabas"—in which it detected the root nābî' —as huios paraklēseōs (Acts 4:36).

---

[94]T. C. Vriezen, *The Religion of Ancient Israel*, p. 206.
[95]G. Friedrich, *TDNT*, VI, 855, s.v. *prophētēs*.
[96]O. Schmitz and G. Stählin, *TDNT*, V, 790, s.v. *parakaleō*.

"God's coming in his word" certainly occurs in prophecy, too: the true prophet is the mouthpiece of the LORD. Nevertheless, we believe it is less correct to call prophecy a *mode* of pastoral role-fulfilment. First of all, prophecy is more than a line in the fundamental structure of pastoral role-fulfilment. What is true in the New Testament of martyria is true of prophecy, in the Old Testament especially: it is one of the constituents of inscripturated revelation. Pastoral role-fulfilment proceeds from and leans on prophecy in this sense.

Second, one gets the impression from the New Testament that prophecy is in part a very special charisma which showed up incidentally (think of the direct predictions of Agabus), and in part a gift which can be understood functionally as paraklesis. The very special and incidental gift can hardly be viewed as an "existential"; what occurs regularly can better be called simply paraklesis rather than prophecy—a word which evokes so many—to us irrelevant—associations and is therefore not very useful. In addition the word "paraklesis" embraces nonprophetic paraklesis which certainly belongs to the fundamental structure of pastoral role-fulfilment.

Third, though the central function of prophecy may be paraklesis, its operation is not restricted to it. Especially the Old Testament prophets often acted as carriers of the kerygma; and, according to Eduard Schweizer, for Luke the New Testament prophets were the teachers of the church (cf. Acts 13:1; for Paul this is not so). In the model of pastoral role-fulfilment we wish to design, the different modes need to be distinct in their uniqueness; the concept of "prophecy" would only blur the picture.

And so we shall restrict ourselves to the modes of kerygma, didache, and paraklesis.

[In selecting these three fundamental concepts we display a certain similarity to K. Barth. Barth describes the ministry of the church—and this includes the calling of every Christian—with the word "witness." In that witness he distinguishes three components: "declaration, exposition, and address, or the proclamation, explication, and application of the Gospel as the Word of God entrusted to it."[97] A. A. van Ruler makes the same distinctions when he speaks of the churchly character of preaching: "The apostolic kerygma, in its churchliness, acquires the form of didache (instruction) and the form of paraklesis (admonition)." In the application "kerygma automatically turns into paraklesis."[98] The difference between these schematisms and ours will become plain in the following.]

9. THE MODE OF KERYGMA
The Kerygma Is the Proclamation of a New State of Affairs

Our selection of the words by which we describe "God's coming in his word by the intermediary of pastoral role-fulfilment"—we have said it before—

---

[97]K. Barth, *CD*, IV/3/2, p. 843.
[98]A. A. van Ruler, *Reformatorische Opmerkingen*. p. 181.

is somewhat arbitrary. This is also true of the word "kerygma." In addition to *kēryssein* the New Testament uses several words which differ little or nothing from this word.[99]

[Among the synonyms a large place must be given to words which share the stem *angel-*, words which always carry the thought of announcement or proclamation. It is especially *euangelizesthai* (with the substantive *euangelion*) which indicates the uniqueness of *this* announcement. This word combination is bound to capture our attention as we reflect on kerygma.[100]]

Compared with the verb *kēryssein* (61 times in the New Testament) the noun *kērygma* is relatively rare (8 times). Friedrich notes here that the accent lies not on the *kērygma* as such but on the action of proclaiming.[101] This proclamation, however, is always proclamation of Jesus, the Kingdom of God, the gospel, the word. The biblical use of *kēryssein* implies the *kērygma* as content of proclamation. For us, of course, the action is the most important—we're talking about the pastor-in-action in his role. Still, we do not speak of *kēryssein* as a mode of pastoral role-fulfilment but of *kērygma*. Because this word has a double meaning embracing the action of proclaiming as well as its content it is all the more useful for our purpose. The kerygma is not exhausted by the action of a human being; by the role-fulfilment of a human being in the kerygma the word of God "comes to pass": God draws near, he reveals his name, he makes the truth public, and so actualizes salvation.

Since Martin Kähler has pointed out the enormous significance of kerygma as a key to understanding the New Testament, this concept has been at the center of theological interest.[102] For our purpose it is enough—rather than joining in the discussion—to ask: What does it mean that the complex phenomenon of "God's coming in his word by the intermediary of pastoral role-fulfilment" is described, among others, with the word *kērygma* (and related terms)?

It can be said, first, that kerygma is proclamation. Although the word *kēryx* is used only three times in the New Testament,[103] the kerygma is inconceivable without someone to bring it. The one who brings it is then the messenger, i.e., someone who has been sent for the purpose of making known precisely *this* news at *this* moment to *these* people. It is not his calling to share his insights or to offer material for discussion. *Kēryx/kēryssein* always imply the concept of "an authoritative, festive, and public proclamation which calls for observance."[104]

---

[99]G. Friedrich, *TDNT,* III, 683ff., s.v. *kēryx.*

[100]G. Friedrich, *TDNT,* III, 711-12; cf. also C. H. Dodd, *The Apostolic Preaching,* p. 8.

[101]G. Friedrich, *TDNT,* III, 704, where other combinations are mentioned as well.

[102]Cf. H. N. Ridderbos, *The Authority of the New Testament Scriptures,* pp. 56ff.

[103]In I Timothy 2:7 and II Timothy 1:11 Paul so describes himself; in II Peter 2:5 Noah is so designated.

[104]H. Cremer and J. Kögel, *Biblische-Theologische Wörterbuch,* s.v. *kēryssō,* p. 599; G. Friedrich, *TDNT,* III, 712-13, s.v. *kēryx,* points out the connection between *apostellein* and *kēryssein.* "A preacher is not a reporter who recounts his own experiences, but the authorized agent of someone higher."

What he does is more than, and different from, providing items of information. The herald proclaims a new state of affairs. Friedrich expresses it clearly with reference to Jesus' public action in the synagogue of Nazareth, where Isaiah's prophecy (61:1-2) became kerygma: "When heralds proclaimed the year of jubilee throughout the land with the sound of the trumpet, the year began, the prison doors were opened, and debts were remitted. The preaching of Jesus is such a blast of the trumpet."[105] Referring to the messenger of Isaiah 52:7—the herald, the real subject of all *kēryssein* and *euangelizesthai*—Friedrich declares: "The messenger publishes it, and the new age begins. He does not declare that the rule of God will soon commence; he proclaims it, he publishes it, and it comes into effect." And speaking of Matthew 11:5 ("the poor have good news preached to them") he says: "The message actualizes the new age."[106]

The Kerygma Implicates People in the Story

The kerygma, then, is in the first place an authoritative proclamation which puts into effect a new state of affairs: that's when it begins. This is not something, however, which the proclamation brings about as such; this happens by way of the kerygma of the *m^ebaśśēr,* the messenger, who is the real subject, and by way of the proclamation of the gospel which is the content of it. About the "evangel" we wrote before: it is the story of the mighty works of God in Jesus Christ. By the kerygma—and that's the second point we need to notice—the redemptive events contained in the gospel come to stand, as it were, perpendicularly upon the situation here and now.

Children, when they play, often speak conditionally: "This could be our house and you would be dad." They are apparently aware that there's a break between the reality of the game and the "real" reality. We also often encounter that conditional element in our lives. In our thoughts and speech about the "real" life we have to use formulas like "if . . . , then. . . ." There are conditions to be fulfilled beyond our power to fulfil them. The kerygma, however, speaks unconditionally about our hopes and longings, even about things that are infinitely beyond them. It says: ". . . the old has passed away, behold, the new has come" (II Cor. 5:17); "Behold, now is the acceptable time; behold, now is the day of salvation" (II Cor. 6:2); "once you were darkness, but now you are light in the Lord" (Eph. 5:8); "man, your sins are forgiven you" (Luke 5:20). *The kerygma proceeds from conditions fulfilled in Jesus Christ.* It does not offer an exposition and application of the story of Christ's redemptive work; it implicates the hearer in that story. It tells him he was there: at the crucifixion and in Joseph's garden. It reveals the name: "I am here"; it causes the actual reality of the truth to appear; it actualizes salvation. It relates our lives here and now to him "who is the same yesterday, today, and for ever" (Heb. 13:8), who is "the first and the last" (Rev. 1:18). It links our present with the redemptive historical

---

[105]G. Friedrich, *TDNT,* III, 706-07.
[106]G. Friedrich, *TDNT,* II, 708, 718, s.v. *euangelizomai.*

past so that it becomes present to us; it makes the future relevant to us; it confronts us today with a choice for life or death (Deut. 30:15); "behold, now is the day of salvation" (II Cor. 6:2); "Today, when you hear his voice, do not harden your hearts" (Heb. 3:7).

The kerygma concretizes that which Stählin calls the consistent tendency of the New Testament, namely, that the entire emphasis falls on the present, "for all the essentials which the NT has to proclaim are basically brought together in the present." "In this *nyn* the past of Christ and the future of Christ are both comprehended as the present of Christ."[107] This does not constitute a denial of time and history, but rather an act of implicating persons in history in "him who is," and in the *m^eḇaśśēr* who says: "Today this scripture has been fulfilled in your ears" (Luke 4:21). He could say that because in him the Kingdom came and all God's promises "find their Yes in him" and "we utter the Amen through him" (II Cor. 1:20).

The Kerygma Brings about the Healing of Life

The kerygma, we have observed, is the authoritative proclamation which draws the immediate situation of the listener directly into what has "once-for-all" taken place,[108] as well as into what, in Christ, we eagerly expect (cf. Heb. 9:28). And then it begins. "Today . . . if you hear his voice."

What begins? The Bible offers a number of words for it: the year of jubilee, the day of salvation, the Kingdom of God, the new life. We can also describe it differently, as, e.g., in the words of Friedrich: "The proclamation of the age of grace, of the rule of God, creates a healthy state in every respect."[109] Or in those of Hermann Diem: "The event of proclamation consists in this, that a person, receiving the offer of forgiveness, experiences her 'dubiousness' [German *Fragwürdigkeit*] as having been overcome by God in grace and judgment and so acquires the freedom, in faith, to overcome it herself."[110] The life of a human being who welcomes the kerygma becomes healthy, new, meaningful. On the basis of the proclamation of a new state of affairs, which among other benefits includes justification, life begins anew in freedom. Not that the person begins her life anew; God begins with her anew; and this means that she can walk "in newness of life" (Rom. 6:4).

The impact of the kerygma on human existence has been inimitably expressed in Martinus Nijhoff's grand poem *Zero Hour*.[111]

[Prose summaries and poetic quotations of this 13-page poem follow.— *Tr.*]

---

[107]R. Stählin, *TDNT*, IV, 1122, s.v. *nyn*.

[108]Cf. Romans 6:10; Hebrews 7:27; 9:12; 9:28; 10:10; I Peter 3:18.

[109]G. Friedrich, *TDNT*, II, 720, s.v. *euangelizomai*. He makes this point in the same context as the statement: "Signs and wonders accompany the evangelical message."

[110]H. Diem, *Die Kirche und ihre Praxis*, p. 168.

[111]M. Nijhoff, "Het Uur U," in *Verzameld Werk*, I, 225ff.

On a hot summer day a man passes through the street (street: symbol of a self-satisfied, well-to-do society).

> *He wore not a thread*
> *Which could help you to tell*
> *A man from a man.*

Everyone who would normally walk the street that hour has broken the pattern; only a group of children play in it. At the appearance of the man, "zero-hour" (a military expression) breaks and everyone knows:

> *Now it begins; now*
> *Ends the uncertainty*
> *Of my allowance of time.*

There arises

> *. . . a stillness of the sort*
> *In which things are heard*
> *Which no ear ever caught before.*

The stillness turns into the sound of music and a quiet nervous tension comes over the street.

> *Desire, strangled,*
> *A child murdered in a well,*
> *Calls, suddenly awakened,*
> *For playthings and playmates.*

The doctor, who has recently moved into the street because it seemed to him that an established practice offered greater material reward than the medical research work he had done before as an assistant, sees himself once again at the quiet clinic.

> *The judge saw himself stand*
> *Without robes, without cap, without frills:*
> *Clothed only in justice*
> *And with upraised hand*
> *He stands by his oath:*
> *In the name of righteousness*
> *He pardoned crime*
> *And confessed his own guilt.*

"The woman nobody knows"—virginal prude or loveless prostitute—sees herself naked as Diana in the woods. Everyone feels a pang of paradisal euphoria.

> *One moment the spirit (of the street)*
> *Lost in distant visions*
> *Had entered, like the camel,*
> *Through the eye of the needle,*
> *But in what land did it come?*
> *It was earth. The land was its own.*

The dream slowly disappears.

People breathed out, as if relieved,
Their Amens of good riddance.

The man walks on, and when it is clear he will never come back:

The whole street, in short,
Each and everyone—
With the exception of one,
And the attentive reader will know
It was the judge—
Waved, except for the judge,
Waved on the man
—the expression be pardoned—
With the sign of a holy kiss-off.

[The poem continues, but enough has been quoted to make our point: the life-changing element of kerygma. Through the eye of the needle, in the moment when the word comes to pass, a person arrives in her own land and becomes the person she really is or is meant to be. It is not automatic; it requires a decision, the word of the LORD which is both acquittal and invitation must be accepted "this day" (Deut. 26:17-18)—an act illustrated in the poem by the judge who confesses his own sin. But then it really begins—this new life—in one's own land. Through the kerygma—and that is the third aspect which struck us in this concept—a person comes alive, becomes aware of self; one's dream, the real truth about oneself, becomes actuality.]

The person who hears and heeds the kerygma does not become other than she is; she becomes the one she really is. She can then be the one she was meant to be and overcome her own "dubiousness." God has spoken his Yes to her; now she can say Yes to herself.

The Kerygma Relates to the Church Situation

One more question: Is not kerygma a mode of the "apostolate" more than of the pastorate?—to use this rather dubious distinction for a moment.[112] The act of *kēryssein*, taken literally, takes place under an open sky. "*Kērygma* is the herald's cry ringing out in the streets and villages and in houses."[113] An illustration in Bouyer, quoted by Weterman, helps to clear up the ambience of *kē-rygma*:[114] Some weeks before the coronation of a new king a man in a strange costume, whose name nobody knows, makes his appearance somewhere in Lon-

---

[112]Terminologically dubious; cf. John 10:16: "And I have other sheep, that are not of this fold; I must bring them also. . . ."

[113]G. Friedrich, *TDNT*, III, 713, s.v. *kēryx.*

[114]J. A. M. Weterman, "De Verkondiging van het Woord Gods," in H. Boelaars, *Levende Zielzorg*, p. 186.

don. From a little attaché case, which bears the seal of the royal monogram, he takes a document and reads the message of the sovereign, couched in old Norman French. This, says Weterman, is an excellent picture of the preacher acting in the mode of kerygma. To a certain extent this can be granted. Of the preacher Weterman says further: "He is no professor giving a lecture. He is not the propagandist for the party line. He does not depend on approval. He does not ask for attention to himself." As for what he communicates, "it is not theory, not a worldview, it is not 'views' of any kind; it is a message, news, facts."

In some ways this picture is accurate; still, it raises questions. The cry of the herald which, in the days when *kēryssein* was common, rang out in the streets did not offer, in official, solemn tones, what the people who heard it already knew: it was *news*; they heard what they could not have heard before. K. H. Miskotte, in his impassioned plea for vital proclamation, cites an example which reminds us of Bouyer's, but intends to illustrate what preaching is not. At a convention of the Republican Party in the United States someone is informed that the party has chosen him as candidate for the presidency. But he, as well as everyone else, had known of it for weeks. This action, says Miskotte, so far from being meaningless, is "beautiful." But it is "ceremony for the sake of ceremony."[115]

Can kerygma ever be more than an appealing ceremony when brought to people who are already informed, have been initiated, and are fully in the fellowship of the church? Can the kerygma be kerygma, i.e., *news* in the full sense of the word? Must not this mode be reserved for the action of the church outward; while within the church restricts itself to didache and paraklesis, the exposition and the appeal? Abraham Kuyper took this position,[116] and Sillevis Smitt declares outright: "The ministry of the word in the gathering of believers has the character neither of kerygma nor of martyria, nor of propheteia, but that of homilia."[117] Remembering the picture of the party convention, one has to agree that there is much to be said for this position.

But more important than this is the material which argues against it. J. T. Bakker points out that there is no watertight division between the missionary situation on the one hand and that of preaching in the Christian community on the other. Should *kērygma* and *homilia* become parallel but isolated entities, that could lead to a church which meets behind closed doors. "The upbuilding of the church and its evangelizing activity belong together and one of the roots of

---

[115]K. H. Miskotte, *Om het levende Woord*, p. 265.

[116]A. Kuyper, *Encyclopaedie*, III, 488, 518. Cf. C. H. Dodd, *The Apostolic Preaching*, pp. 7ff., who defines *kēryssein* as "the public proclamation of Christianity to the non-Christian world." In view of Acts 15:21; 20:25, this definition can hardly be taken as exclusive.

[117]P. A. E. Sillevis Smitt, Thesis 19, accompanying his dissertation, *De Organisatie van de Christelijke Kerk in den apostolischen Tijd*.

this unity is preaching as kerygma." Paul speaks unblinkingly of his church-building activity as the proclamation of the gospel.[118]

Of even greater significance is the following consideration. In the post-apostolic era the work of Christ was viewed especially under the rubric of the doctrine he came to teach, a consequence of which was a trend toward moralism and nomism. In that framework preaching became one-sided, turned into admonition and instruction. The Reformation, stressing the justification of the ungodly, returned to the kerygmatic character of preaching which includes the act of "proclaiming and publicly declaring to each and every believer that . . . God . . . truly forgives all his sins" (Heidelberg Catechism, Q. 84). According to Bakker, "there can be no Sunday in our lives on which we would no longer need the parable of the prodigal son, rather, of the waiting and forgiving Father, as the final and decisive Word of God—also for our Christian life."[119] Says Wingren: "It is false intellectualism to separate those who belong to the church from the missionary *kerygma*." "The idea in the background" appears to be "that once anyone has heard the Gospel he ought to go on. . . ."[120]

The kerygma in the church, as a mode of pastoral role-fulfilment, accentuates the importance of the present. One could say that the kerygma belongs especially in the church because never before has it been "now," because the person who hears it has never been this person before and her situation has never been the situation of this moment. The entire word of God gathers itself together in the kerygma and focuses on the unique present. However it was yesterday, however it will be tomorrow—"this is the day of salvation." "Today, if you hear his voice, harden not your hearts." "See, I have set before you this day life and good, death and evil" (Deut. 30:15). Here salvation stands perpendicularly upon the situation of this person and the *meḇaśśēr* cries out: "Behold your God!" (cf. Isa. 40:9).

10. THE MODE OF DIDACHE

Didache or "Catechesis"?

The Acts of the Apostles ends with the information that Paul, staying at home, welcomed all who came to him, "preaching (*kēryssein*) the kingdom of God and teaching (*didaskōn*) about the Lord Jesus Christ . . ." (28:31). In addition to kerygma there is, in the complex phenomenon of "God's coming in his word by the intermediary of pastoral role-fulfilment," also the component of didache. Before investigating the nature of the mode, we must first try to justify the choice of the word "didache."

---

[118]J. T. Bakker, *Kerygma en Prediking*, Inaugural, p. 25.
[119]Ibid., pp. 26ff.
[120]G. Wingren, *The Living Word*, p. 18.

In the first place, one could ask why, for our purpose of designating instruction, the typically ecclesiastical term "catechesis" was not chosen. According to Beyer, the apostle Paul used *katēchein*, a rare word in classical Greek and not found at all in the Septuagint, as "a technical term for Christian instruction . . . to emphasize the particular nature of instruction on the basis of the Gospel."[121] According to Bijlsma it is "a typical New Testament word for reliable instruction."[122] It cannot be denied that in time "catechesis" became a technical term for church instruction. In the postapostolic period the word was used to describe baptismal instruction; still later, candidates for baptism were called *catechumeni*; and Augustine, in *De Catechizandis Rudibus*, uses the verb for the first time in Latin in the sense of giving instruction in the Christian faith to those who are ignorant of it.[123] It is possible that the usage of this word group for church instruction goes back to Paul's use of *katēchein*. It is difficult, however, to conclude from the three instances where it occurs in Paul that he intended to create a technical term.

Romans 2:18. The point here is that the Jew boasts of knowing what is excellent because he is "instructed in the law" (*katēchoumenos ek tou nomou*).

I Corinthians 14:19. Paul asserts that in the worship assembly he would much rather speak "with my mind" than in glossalalia "in order to instruct others" (*hina kai allous katēchēsō*).

Galatians 6:6. Here Paul probably refers to the responsibility of the educand toward the teacher in the matter of material support when he says that the person who is taught (*ho katēchoumenos*) should share all good things with him who teaches (*tō katēchounti*). Here alone one gets the impression that Paul expresses himself in terms which are current for a well-known process.

It needs to be remembered, however, that the rest of the New Testament gives no evidence that these terms were the usual ones. Checking out the other instances where *katēchein* is used—Luke 1:4; Acts 18:25; 21:21, 24—one gets the impression that to Luke the word connoted a provisional, incomplete, sometimes even an ill-founded, knowledge. Luke undertook to investigate the beginnings of the Christian story and to render an account of them in order that Theophilus might know the truth concerning the things of which he had been informed (*peri ōn katēchēthēs logōn*). Apollos "had been instructed" (*ēn katēchēmenos*) in the way of the Lord, but there were such gaps in his understanding that Priscilla and Aquila found it necessary to expound to him the way of God more accurately (Acts 18:25-26). In Acts 21:21, 24, *katēcheisthai* is used to indicate that a story is going around which is no more than idle gossip and which Paul can invalidate by acting in a certain way.

So it seems to us that, in view of Luke's use of the word, it is hard to maintain that *katēchein* is a "typical New Testament word for reliable instruc-

---

[121]H. W. Beyer, *TDNT*, III, 638-39, s.v. *katēcheō*.
[122]R. Bijlsma, *Kleine Catechetiek*, p. 38.
[123]Cf. Surkau, *RGG*, III, col. 649, s.v. *Katechetik*.

tion." There is more to be said for the opinion of Abraham Kuyper that "*ka-tēchein* in the New Testament refers to instruction which rests entirely on authority and thus to instruction in the interest of those who are not in a position to investigate things for themselves but acquire their knowledge *per traditionem.*"[124]

Apparently, then, no objection needs to be made against using "catechesis" as a name for one of the modes of pastoral role-fulfilment. The word has been around for a long time as a typical churchly expression for which there is no easy substitute. But it seems unprofitable for the purpose of saying anything characteristic or specific about that instruction even when it takes place in the form of catechesis.

Didache or "Didaskalia"?

We need to choose a substantive, then, that is derived from the verb *didaskein*. Two possibilities present themselves: *didachē* and *didaskalia*. Both words are used in the New Testament to describe the action as well as the content of instruction. According to Berkelbach vander Sprenkel, "it is not easy to draw a line of distinction between 'didachē' and 'didaskalia'; it is true that the first refers more to a doctrinal complex . . . ; and the second to the action but equally to the content of the instruction."[125] If this opinion were correct we would prefer "didaskalia" as a keyword for the second mode of pastoral role-fulfilment. A comparison of the ways in which the two words are used in the New Testament, however, shows nothing of the tendency just indicated. One would rather say that the precise opposite is the case, i.e., that *didachē* is more oriented to the act of teaching.[126] *Didaskalia* occurs twice in the Gospels,[127] and there in a quotation from the Old Testament where it clearly has the significance of "the substance of a teaching." The overwhelming majority of instances where *didaskalia* occurs is in the Pastorals. *Didaskalia* then has the definite article and signifies the well-known doctrine accepted in the churches. *Didachē* can have a similar meaning, but that, though standard in the postapostolic age, is an exception in the New Testament.

We would certainly not want to say that pastoral role-fulfilment has nothing to do with "the well-known doctrine," especially not if doctrine is understood as "the severely disciplined—because utterly bound to its object—pointer to the Lord of human beings, to his word, will, and action."[128] Pastoral role-fulfilment must be subject to this discipline of doctrine if it is to be truly intermediary of

---

[124]A. Kuyper, *Encyclopaedie*, III, 504.

[125]S. F. H. J. Berkelbach vander Sprenkel, *Catechetiek*, p. 135.

[126]According to M. Scott Fletcher, *Dictionary of the Apostolic Church*, p. 550, s.v. teaching, *didachē* in general signifies "the act" and *didaskalia* "the substance" of teaching. Cf. K. H. Rengstorf, *TDNT*, II, 161, s.v. *didaskō*.

[127]Matthew 15:9 and the parallel Mark 7:7 where Isaiah 29:13 is quoted: "teaching as doctrines the precepts of men"; cf. Galatians 2:22.

[128]K. Barth, *Der Dienst am Wort Gottes*, pp. 14ff.

the coming of God in his word. But God's coming itself cannot be determined in its structure by that doctrine; for the doctrine is secondary to the word through which God's coming takes place.

So for us the second mode of pastoral role-fulfilment is that of didache. In this word, more than in *didaskalia*, at least within the linguistic circle of the New Testament, the dynamics and freshness of the word-event come through strongly.

Old Testament Didache: Initiation

We shall now try to ascertain how didache affects the image of pastoral role-fulfilment. To that end we must first savor the spirit of didache in the world of the Old Testament. A remark by N. Drazin can help us find our way: "Jewish education was rather synonymous with life. It unfolded life, giving it direction and meaning. In fact a modern Hebrew term for education, *Ḥinuk*, from a root found twice in the Bible in the sense of to 'train,' etymologically means dedication or initiation. . . ."[129] One of Drazin's references is Proverbs 22:6: "Train up (*ḥanook*) a child in the way he should go, and when he is old he will not depart from it." *Ḥānak* and *hᵃnukkâ* as a rule refer to the dedication of a house or temple.[130] *Hᵃnukkâ* is something like the transfer to an object of the dedication which makes it fit for use in worship. It may be taken more broadly: to consecrate a thing—temple or house—to its purpose. This idea fits well with the picture of a road, as used, e.g., in Proverbs 22:6. The "way" is the life of a person seen from the perspective of its destination. Lives do not just "run out": as a rule, they go somewhere. Every life has its own purpose; to direct oneself to that end is mandatory; in order to be able to direct oneself to it a *hᵃnukkâ* is needed—a "transfer of dedication."

However rarely the word is used in the Old Testament for this purpose, there is probably not another which so well reproduces the atmosphere of Jewish upbringing and therefore of Jewish didache, which is the core of that upbringing. This appears most clearly in the family where the upbringing, and hence the didache, begins and belongs. The duty of the parents included more than just warning the children against wrongdoing and telling them to be good. "And these words which I command you this day shall be upon your heart; and you shall teach them diligently to your children, and shall talk of them when you sit in your house, and when you walk by the way, and when you lie down, and when you rise" (Deut. 6:6-7). The father makes God's faithfulness known to the children (Isa. 38:19): "the glorious deeds of the LORD, and his might, and the wonders which he has wrought" (Ps. 78:4).

The "transfer of dedication" consists especially in the initiation of the

---

[129]N. Drazin, *History of Jewish Education*, p. 12.

[130]The verb occurs in Deuteronomy 20:5, I Kings 8:63, and II Chronicles 7:5; the noun in Numbers 7:10-11, II Chronicles 7:9, Nehemiah 12:27, and Psalm 30:1.

child into the story of Yahweh and his people: it implicates him personally so
that it becomes his story. The child is initiated into the story with a view to the
way he has to go. The "way" did not begin when he was born: it started with
the exodus. He was there when it happened: his way cannot be other than the
way of his people; it is the way on which Yahweh brought him with his people
out of Egypt, out of the house of slavery. This didache is not primarily an
explication of history, or of the words and works of Yahweh. It is first of all the
act of implicating the young Israelite in the story of salvation. He learns to say
and to experience "we"—the "we" of the covenant.[131]

Old Testament Didache: Guidance on the Way

A person—and a road: not hard to picture. A person and a road: that's the
image which forms the background of what we—with an anachronistic expression—have called Old Testament didache. The Old Testament contains numerous
references to the way of God, of the LORD, of the good and right way, the way
of the statutes, the testimonies, and the commandments of the LORD.[132] The way
which leads to the true destination, both for the person and the people, is a
definite way. But that "way" must be learned. In order to find it, and to walk
in it, one needs *tôrâ*. T. C. Vriezen has written that *tôrâ* "is proof of God's
continuing care for his people, especially what is constant in the guidance he
gave to the people with whom he entered a covenant. . . . Not only does God
warn, predict, or aid in a particular situation, but he also teaches, instructs, and
educates. All this comes to expression in the *tôrâ* of God by which he instructs
his people."[133]

When one encounters *tôrâ*, it is a mistake immediately to think of the
usual rendering "law." Referring to the Old Testament, Martin Buber writes:
"The Torah of God is understood as God's instruction in His way, and therefore
not as a separate *objectivum*. It includes laws, and laws are indeed its most
vigorous objectivizations, but the Torah itself is essentially not law. A vestige of
the actual speaking always adheres to the commanding word; the directing voice
is always present, or at least its sound is heard fading away. To render Torah by
'law' is to take away from its idea this inner dynamic and vital character."[134]

---

[131]The mandate to tell the children occurs, among other places, in Exodus 10:1ff.;
12:24ff.; 13:8ff.; 13:14ff.; Deuteronomy 4:9; 6:20ff.
[132]For example, in Psalm 25:4, 5, 8, 9, 10, 12; Psalm 119:1, 3, 5, 9, 10, 14, 21,
27, etc. N. H. Ridderbos, *Psalmen*, I, 262, remarks on Psalm 25:4 that "way" is the
keyword of this psalm: "They are the ways on which the LORD walks and causes the
righteous to walk. . . ."
[133]T. C. Vriezen, *Hoofdlijnen der Theologie van het Oude Testament*, p. 196. An
English translation of this book, *An Outline of Old Testament Theology*, is based on a
second enlarged edition of the Dutch work (1955). The above quotation is from the
original Dutch edition of 1949. Cf. the English translation, pp. 253ff., 263ff.
[134]M. Buber, *Two Types of Faith*, p. 57.

Torah is "direction, instruction, information." It points out the way, offers guidance on the road. It is the word of revelation in which God comes to a person.

Especially the priests serve God by giving *tôrôt*: life-shaping pointers for concrete situations. And writings which embody commandments, but also stories, poems, genealogies, and proverbs, called the Torah in their totality, are the means by which God's coming to direct and redirect his people continually takes place. Hence the Torah is not a codebook of commandments and precepts which restrict human beings in their movements. It is a hand pointing out the way— *the* way. "It shall come to pass in the latter days that the mountain of the house of the LORD shall be established as the highest of the mountains, and shall be raised above the hills; and all the nations shall flow to it, and many peoples shall come, and say: 'Come, let us go up to the mountain of the LORD, to the house of the God of Jacob; that he may teach us his ways and that he may walk in his paths.' For out of Zion shall go forth the law . . ." (Isa. 2:2-3; Mic. 4:1-2). To direct a person to her destination, to initiate her into the story, to take and lead her on the way—that is the Jewish didache.

To get the total picture even more sharply into focus we shall now direct our attention to *ḥokmâ*.

Old Testament Didache: Instruction in the Way of Wisdom

According to Vriezen, "wisdom is a more pedagogical expression of the moral element in religion, different from that given by the laws; fundamentally the laws are looked upon as received directly from God, while wisdom is, as it were, the human reflection of this."[135] There is certainly more to be said about *ḥokmâ*, as there is about the similarity and difference between *tôrâ* and *ḥokmâ*, but it does give us the clue that *ḥokmâ* has its own function in the realm of Jewish didache. Vriezen, whom we just quoted, speaks of the "more pedagogical expression of the moral element in religion" and "the human reflection" of God's revelation in the Torah. Abramowsky says almost the same thing with more wit and less precision: "Here the high order of law has been converted into the small coin of practical shrewdness."[136]

With *ḥokmâ* we have arrived at the concerns of every day in which a person is not continually pondering heavy problems or confronting "the ultimate questions," but does have to face with insistent regularity the question "Now what do I do?" There are a thousand and one situations at work, in the family, and in dealing with people, with oneself, or things in which one cannot ask a priest for *tôrâ*, in which there is no precept in law, and in which God has given no revelation by a prophet—situations in which one must come up with one's own answer. Knowledge of "the way" is not enough: one also needs knowledge of affairs, a perspective on specific situations, insight into problems. "He has

---

[135]T. C. Vriezen, *An Outline of Old Testament Theology*, p. 315.
[136]R. Abramowsky, *Das Buch des betenden Gottesvolkes*, II, 220.

showed you, O man, what is good; and what does the LORD require of you but to do justice, and to love kindness, and to walk humbly with your God?" (Mic. 6:8). But the person who knows this does not, by that token, "have all the answers"; she still has to manage in the midst of the complexities of daily life.

It is to this pressure that *ḥokmâ* addresses itself. The reference, says Fohrer, "is to prudent, considered, experienced and competent action to subjugate the world and to master the various problems of life and life itself."[137] The person who is wise is equal to the demands of life, not because she is a superior person; wisdom begins—and this is the essential and unique feature of the Israelite concept of *ḥokmâ*—in "the fear of the LORD" (Prov. 1:7; 9:10; Ps. 111:10). That "beginning" must be understood in a twofold sense, namely, as the main part and as the source and starting point of wisdom. Wisdom consists in the first place in, and proceeds from, the fact that a person has turned in awe and trust to the LORD, goes and seeks his way, and departs from evil (cf. Job 28:28; Prov. 8:13).

The acquisition and possession of wisdom in this sense is not the privilege of individuals or of a special class of people. Nor is this wisdom viewed as valuable only at a certain time or within a certain culture. It is universal. One can, however, speak of *ḥokmâ* in a more particular and concentrated sense. Then the reference is to a general ancient eastern phenomenon which in Israel acquired its own form and was represented by certain persons, the *ḥᵃkāmîm*, as well as by certain writings, the wisdom literature.

It is no small job to determine what kind of people the *ḥᵃkāmîm* were.

[According to W. H. Gispen, "Israel, with its wise men and women, and its practice of wisdom, was a part of the people of the Near East. The *ḥokmâ* literature is international. The wise person in Israel, who knew and used much of the literature and who even gave space to non-Israelite practitioners of wisdom in the wisdom literature of the Old Testament, was a person of broad perspective and universally human ideals, a person who understood well the art of living."[138] "The wise man was most likely to be found among the élite, i.e., among people of much leisure and a good education. Numerous indications point to the theory that the wise were to be found especially at the royal court."[139]]

Whether or not they formed a separate class, in Israel, too, some people stood out because they had a better-than-average grip on life, a clearer insight into it, and a more extended and nuanced experience of it—people who were therefore called "wise."[140] These wise ones fulfilled a special twofold function. Jeremiah (18:18) places in sequence (1) the priest as a man of *tôrâ*, instruction

---

[137]G. Fohrer, *TDNT*, VII, 476, s.v. *sophia*.

[138]W. H. Gispen, *De Wijze in Israël*, p. 15.

[139]M. A. Beek, "De Prediking der bijbelse Wijsheid," in C. W. Mönnich and F. J. Pop, *Wegen der Prediking*, p. 352.

[140]G. Fohrer, *TDNT*, VII, 476, observes that the translations "wise" and "wisdom" are unfortunate and to a degree inexact. It will prove hard, however, to find a substitute expression spacious enough to accommodate this hard-to-define phenomenon.

in cultic matters; (2) the prophet as the man of *dābār*, the word of revelation from God; and (3) the wise one as the man of *'ēṣâ*, or counsel. It is possible that the wise man is the political leader, as Gispen supposes on the basis of a comparison of this text with Ezekiel 7:26.[141] In any case, he is called *ḥākam* and proves to be the person who, when others are desperate, provides counsel; he is a *yō'ēṣ* who is so urgently needed in critical circumstances.[142]

But the wise man functions in still another manner, namely, in the didache, in teaching the people and especially the youth. In this capacity he turns up in Ecclesiastes 12:9 where it is said of Qoheleth that he "taught the people knowledge, weighing and studying and arranging proverbs with great care."

Something needs to be said about the nature of this instruction. An important part of it was probably the act of inculcating bits of wisdom, of which we know a few from collections like the book of Proverbs. Still, this instruction in wisdom was not exhausted by the transmission of proverbs. One wisdom teacher defines the intent of his activity like this: "I have taught you the way of wisdom; I have led you in the paths of uprightness" (Prov. 4:11). The wisdom teacher, too, knows of a way which his pupil must go. His instruction also has the character of *ḥanukkâ*, of initiation, of directing a person to his destination. When wisdom calls—by way of a teacher—the heart must pay attention (Prov. 8:5). It is not enough simply to take over established wisdom, precodified answers, prefabricated solutions. The aim of the teacher is to give "prudence to the simple, knowledge and discretion to youth" (Prov. 1:4). The pupil must himself try to become wise (Prov. 8:33), for then he finds life (8:35).

[The words used in close association with *ḥokmâ* indicate again and again that the acquisition of wisdom does not consist in learning prevailing profundities. The person who gains wisdom gains *'ēṣâ* (counsel), *tebûnâ* (understanding), and *bînâ* (insight), and thus *geburâ* (power). Only God has this wisdom in perfection. "With God are wisdom and might; he has counsel and understanding" (Job 12:13); ". . . his understanding is beyond measure" (Ps. 147:5; cf. Isa. 40:14). God can fill a person with his Spirit, with ability and intelligence, with knowledge and all craftsmanship (Exod. 31:3). Solomon asks the LORD for an understanding mind (lit. "a hearing heart") to "discern between good and evil" (I Kings 3:9). The wise person has an attentive, listening heart: "True reason is the act of perceiving, hence not the knowledge which is self-created and self-contained, but communication received from God by attentive listening."[143]]

The wise person is one who lives in the fear of the LORD, and in whom something appears of the profile of the coming Messiah: "And the Spirit of the LORD shall rest upon him, the spirit of wisdom and understanding, the spirit of

---

[141]W. H. Gispen, *De Wijze in Israël*, pp. 16ff.

[142]Cf. Proverbs 11:14; 15:22; 24:6.

[143]W. Vischer, "Alttestamentliche Vorbilder unseres Pfarramts," in *Gottesdienst-Menschendienst: Eduard Thurneysen zum 70. Geburtstag*, p. 269.

counsel and might, the spirit of knowledge and the fear of the LORD. And his delight shall be in the fear of the LORD" (Isa. 11:2-3).

To sum up: To be truly human, according to the Old Testament, is to be implicated in the story of the covenant, to live in the fear of the LORD, to walk in the way of the LORD amid the complexities of the life of every day, at work and in social activities. It is to be directed in all this toward the destination which assumes the shape of the One who is to come, who will fill the heart with the knowledge of the LORD (Isa. 11:9). To help human beings gain and experience this humanity is the purpose of didache in its various forms. These forms change, and sometimes disappear, in the New Testament era and in the Christian church. But the mode of didache, which codetermines the structure of pastoral role-fulfilment, remains. The coming of God in his word, in the differing dispensations, forms a unity. That divine "coming" and its human intermediary can be understood only in terms of that unity.

"The Teacher Is Here . . ." (John 11:28)

The first thing that strikes us as we consider didache in the New Testament is that the verb *didaskein* occurs most frequently in the Gospels and the first part of Acts. It is used mainly in the atmosphere around Jesus and in the mother church at Jerusalem. Jesus himself is pictured again and again as the teacher. Mark informs us that Jesus taught, "as his custom was" (10:1), and that the chief priests and the scribes feared him precisely "because all the multitude was astonished at his teaching (*didachē*)" (11:18). Repeatedly Jesus was teaching (*ēn didaskein*), especially on the sabbath, in the synagogues and in the temple.[144] That's how people knew him; they addressed him therefore as *rhabbi, didaskale,* and *epistata*.[145] Both in the manner of his public performances and in the subjects he discussed, Jesus clearly resembled the teachers of Israel.[146] One could ask at this point whether, for the purpose of determining the nature of didache as a mode of pastoral role-fulfilment, it is not enough to attempt to get a clear picture of Jesus as Teacher and of his didactic activity.

[This is obviously the opinion of J. M. Price. Jesus Christ, he observes, has long been known to us "as a revealer of God, a healer of human ills, and a redeemer from sin. Only in recent years has much thought been given to him as teacher." It has become increasingly clear that the Lord placed a heavy emphasis on teaching, i.e., on "educational activity."[147] Here Price adds: "Chris-

---

[144]E.g., Matthew 13:54; 26:55; Mark 1:21; 6:2; 12:35; Luke 4:15, 31; 6:6; 13:10; 19:47.

[145]R. Bultmann, *Jesus,* p. 43, points out that the title "Rabbi" would designate Jesus as a member of the profession of scribes. When they used this title, it was as if people addressed him as "Herr Doktor."

[146]E. Lohse, *TDNT,* VI, 964, s.v. *rhabbi*.

[147]J. M. Price et al., *A Survey of Religious Education,* p. 37.

tianity is looked upon as a school with Christ the founder and Master Teacher, the leaders as assistant teachers, the enlisted nations as pupils, and the Bible as the textbook. Thus the educational idea is prominent." Simple as this model of Christianity is, the model of pastoral role-fulfilment which could be derived from it would be equally simple: a Sunday School with teachers who in the manner of Jesus engaged in "educational activity."

We reject this model, however, not because of its simplicity but because of its blatant inaccuracy. True, Jesus does appear in the Gospels especially as teacher. But Price neglects two cardinal facts: he ignores the astonishment Jesus' teaching aroused; and he fails to notice that the writings which picture Jesus as teacher are *Gospels.*]

Jesus was a teacher. He was acknowledged as such; the multitudes had no difficulty regarding him as at least the equal of the scribes—the similarity was obvious. It was also clear to them that there was a difference—a difference indicated in the Gospels by the word *exousia*: the multitudes were astonished at his doctrine, "for he taught them as one who had authority, and not as their scribes" (Matt. 7:28-29; cf. Mark 1:22, Luke 4:32). According to Price, we have learned that Jesus, whom we already knew as revealer, healer, and redeemer, is also and especially a teacher. But "the multitudes" had a very different experience. "And they were all amazed, so that they questioned among themselves, saying, 'What is this? A new teaching! With authority he commands even the unclean spirits' " (Mark 1:27). They discovered the astonishing uniqueness of a teacher who did not, like the rabbis, limit himself to the law and the tradition, but acted with immediate authority. Here is One who not only unfolds old truths but opens new perspectives, revealing God and authenticating his doctrine by healing the sick and saving sinners. "A new doctrine with authority!"

This difference between Jesus and the scribes came out in his manner of speaking. Says Gould: "They had, and constantly cited, external authority for their teaching. They said, *Rabbi* says *this.*"[148] When Jesus quotes the authorities of old, he does it only to place over against them his "but I say to you" (Matt. 5:21ff.). The difference between Jesus and the scribes, according to Gould, consisted in the fact that they appealed to "external authority" while his authority was internal, "proceeding from vision." The next sentence shows what he means by this: "The difficulty with the scribes . . . is that they carry external authority into the realm of intuitive truth."

If this were true, then Jesus would be no more than a reformer of the didache. It is not likely that the multitudes were beside themselves with astonishment over this alone. The Gospel of Mark presents a different picture. First it reports that people were astonished by Jesus' doctrine (1:22). Then Mark tells the story of the healing of a man with an unclean spirit (1:23). Then follows: "And they were all amazed, so that they questioned among themselves, saying,

---

[148]E. P. Gould, *A Critical and Exegetical Commentary on the Gospel according to St. Mark* (International Critical Commentary), p. 22.

'What is this? A new teaching! With authority he commands even the unclean spirits, and they obey him' " (1:27). What happens here is something other than that a teacher has appeared who speaks from an intuitive knowledge of the truth and so arouses astonishment. The authority present here is not inner, but *messianic*. Here is a teacher who speaks with *exousia*; who has *exousia* to forgive sins on earth (Mark 2:10); who commands the wind and the sea (Mark 4:41); who rebukes evil spirits and a fever (Luke 4:35, 39). From his works and words it is apparent that he is the One who was to come (Matt. 11:2ff.). Unlike the scribes, Jesus does not appeal to authorities. He himself exercises an authority which is absolute; but in a sense it, too, is "external authority." Before his resurrection, as well as after, Jesus acts only in the power of the *exousia* granted him.[149] He knows that he has been sent by the Father as the Son of man on whom the Father has set his seal (John 6:27), who has come to do the will of him who sent him (6:38), to accomplish his work (4:34). This is how he wants to be known and believed.

[The uniqueness of Jesus' didache, by comparison with the rabbinical, comes out clearly, notwithstanding the similarity, in Jesus' *parables*. At first sight this uniqueness does not appear very noticeable. Scribes, too, used parables in their discussions, both to illumine and to establish an argument.[150] People were not surprised to hear Jesus tell a story. They were familiar with the practice and often knew the metaphors he used; several of them were taken from traditional Jewish religious imagery.[151] When Jesus began to tell a parable, people must have felt that they were on familiar ground. But when he continued, they discovered that his parables, too, were absolutely astonishing. In form they were like, but actually they were very different from, those of the scribes. They used parables to make difficult matters simple; Jesus confronted them with the mystery of the Kingdom by means of parables. If they had ears to hear, the story inevitably brought them to the questions "Who is he?" and "Who am I?" By their stories the scribes brought the minds of their listeners to a restful conclusion; but with Jesus the high-powered tension of the gospel was present from the beginning. The whole parable is aflame and every word glows with the fire of the last things. Jesus does not use parables to clarify his argument, as the rabbis do; he does not try to prove anything: he speaks with authority and does it with images.[152]

When Jesus tells a parable, the word comes to pass: God draws near to

---

[149]Matthew 28:18. References to the authority given him occur frequently in John: 5:19, 27; 7:16, 18; 8:26, 27; 15:15; 17:2, 8, 14. Inherent in the concept of *exousia* is "full power" (cf. W. Foerster, *TDNT*, II, 560ff., s.v. *exestin*).

[150]A. Oepke, *TDNT*, V, 750, s.v. *parabolē*.

[151]Dahl, *RGG³*, II, col. 1618, s.v. *Gleichnis und Parabel*, mentions the metaphors of father and child, master and slave, the banquet in the Kingdom, and the harvest at the end of the world.

[152]Cf. O. Noordmans, *Dingen, die verborgen waren*, pp. 14ff., and A. M. Brouwer, *De Gelijkenissen*, p. 57.

people; he reveals his name; he reveals his truth as relevant and present reality; he actualizes salvation. The Kingdom of heaven comes near in the parables; the mystery of the Kingdom becomes manifest in Jesus: a mustard seed, small and of no account; a treasure in a field. Jesus is more than the mouth which tells the stories; in the stories he reveals himself in his hidden—but apprehensible-by-faith—glory. "The parables are, no different from his miracles, self-attestations of Jesus."[153] "I who speak to you am he" (John 4:26). Nonintimates are challenged to think by the parables; each calls for a response, a decision of faith.]

We noted above that Price—who pictured Jesus as the teacher who constitutes a model for the church—neglected to pay attention to people's astonishment over the *exousia* of this teacher of whom the Gospels speak. But neither does he notice that the writings which present Jesus as teacher are *Gospels*. So much attention has been given in recent years to the unique kerygmatic character of the Gospels that we need to add very little now.[154] The Gospels intend to be only gospel: they announce that the Kingdom of heaven has come. The key to the understanding of the unique nature of the Gospels is given by John in a statement which applies to all the Gospels, not just to his own: "These [the signs described in this Gospel] are written that you may believe that Jesus is the Christ, the Son of God, and that believing you may have life in his name" (John 20:31). When the Gospels report that Jesus was a teacher and how he taught, then that, too, is kerygma: these statements, too, intend to bring the reader to an astonished "Who is this?" and "What is this?" They intend to bring the reader to the astonishment and consternation of the multitudes, to the recognition of his *exousia*, and to the confession: "You are the Christ, the Son of the living God!" (Matt. 16:16). The "assistant teachers" cannot take a peek into the Gospels to see how the Master did it and what they can learn from him in their ministry of didache. The nature of didache, as a mode of pastoral role-fulfilment, cannot be determined from what the Gospels say about Jesus as teacher. *The didache of the church certainly has everything to do with the didache of the Lord, but it cannot be a continuation, still less an imitation, of it.*

The Didache of the Church

We shall now try to determine how the didache of the church relates to the didache of Jesus Christ. For our point of departure we have chosen the conclusion of Matthew's Gospel (28:18-20). Our attention will be focused in particular on verse 19, the so-called Great Commission. As is well known, the authenticity of these words as words from our Lord has been challenged on a

---

[153]K. Frör, *Biblische Hermeneutik*, p. 295. In a note Frör remarks: "There is a considerable consensus today on this point."

[154]For a summary of this discussion see Bornkamm, *RGG*, II, col. 749ff., s.v. *Evangelien*.

number of grounds. We can bypass this issue. The conclusion of Matthew's Gospel is clearly not an appendix to the Gospel, but its culmination: the *proclamation* of his *exousia* (v. 18) and the *promise* of his continuing fellowship with the church which allows itself to be integrated into his messianic work (v. 20b). The church derives its *raison d'être* from the imperative (vv. 19-20a), which rests in "the indicatives of messianic fulfilment and the promise of the Spirit."[155] In the absence of this imperative there could be no redemptive-historical necessity for the church. The New Testament and the history of the church would have lost their meaning.

The question whether the missionary command was given only to the apostles or to the whole church is of little significance for our study.[156] The truth is: In the mandate to the apostles a model is given, as it were, for the functioning of the church, viewed from a specific perspective: Make disciples (*mathēteusate*) . . . baptizing (*baptizontes*) . . . teaching (*didaskontes*). Even if the command to bring the gospel *to all the nations* had been given only to the apostles and fulfilled by them, this still would not diminish in the least the significance of this passage for the determination of the church's didache. The linkage *mathēteusate–didaskontes*, which occurs only here, discloses the true nature of this didache in its connection with and distinction from the teaching of Jesus Christ.

O. Michel[157] has provided clear insight into the structure of Matthew 28:19-20. "It consists of very diverse materials which, however, have now been drawn into a certain theological whole. The opening words are formed by the word of revelation and authority, verse 18b (*edothē moi pasa exousia*), which forms the foundation of the entire composition. Then follows, as a consequence, the real missionary command, verse 19 (an imperative *mathēteusate* with two connected participles: *baptizontes* and *didaskontes*). The real missionary command, the middle member of the composition, carries the mandate of the Risen One; . . . the promise of verse 20: *egō meth' hymōn eimi* constitutes the conclusion of the composition." In the period of Jesus' walk on earth the multitudes spied or suspected with astonishment something of messianic *exousia* in his public actions. They were not mistaken. "All things have been delivered to me by my Father" (Matt. 11:27), said Jesus. But his messianic glory was concealed and basically knowable only by the person to whom the Father, who is in heaven, revealed it (Matt. 16:17). Only after the completion of the messianic work of redemption—suffering and resurrection—is the messianic *exousia* proclaimed openly. The prophecy of Daniel 7:13-14 is now fulfilled: The Son of man presents

---

[155]J. C. Hoekendijk, *Kerk en Volk in de Duitse Zendingswetenschap*, p. 224.

[156]Cf. H. N. Ridderbos, "De Apostoliciteit van de Kerk," in J. Ridderbos, *De apostolische Kerk*, p. 71; *The Coming of the Kingdom*, p. 373.

[157]O. Michel, "Der Abschluss des Matthäusevangeliums," in *Evangelische Theologie* 10 (1950-51): 19.

himself in his royal dignity, and in the consciousness of that dignity he sends his apostles to all the nations.[158]

In the light of his royal dignity one would expect another mandate: Make all the nations into my subjects. But the Messiah-king remains the "teacher"— *mathēteusate*, his order runs, "make them my disciples." From this mandate *mathēteusate . . . didaskontes*, it is clear that the didache of the church does not replace the didache of Jesus. Jesus Christ remains the teacher: the apostles and the church, by their didache, can only lead people into the discipleship of this teacher.

[Here we must point out a remarkable phenomenon. The Gospels, we have noted, refer frequently to Jesus' activity of *didaskein*. One would expect that the verb *manthanein* (to learn), which corresponds with *didaskein* as a description of the activity of the pupil, would also occur frequently. This is not the case, however; in the entire New Testament *manthanein* occurs only 25 times, of which only a few instances are found in the Gospels. On the other hand, the noun *mathētēs* occurs frequently—in the Gospels and Acts alone more than 250 times. The conclusion to be drawn from this is that Jesus' *didaskein* corresponds not so much to *manthanein* as to being *mathētēs*. One comes to this teacher not first of all to be instructed by him, but to be his disciple.[159]]

To observe clearly the utter uniqueness of the didache of Jesus Christ, we must consider the significance of discipleship somewhat more closely. Like Jesus, the scribes, too, had a circle of students around them. The relationship in which the disciples stood to Jesus was of quite a different nature, however, from the one in which rabbinical students stood to their Rabbi. For while they had to apply to their teachers to be admitted into their schools, Jesus *called* his followers into discipleship. He does not instruct them for the purpose of making teachers out of pupils, who can then take the place of the master, but lays it down once for all that he is Lord, and the disciples his servants (Matt. 10:24b).[160] In the fulness of his messianic *exousia* Jesus says: "Follow me!" (Mark 2:14). He builds, not an audience but a body of people bound to him personally. They are a band of disciples who have "died out" to other claims and as a "posthumous community" have a character far different from other communities.[161] They must not look to what is behind them (Luke 9:62); they must leave everything (Mark

---

[158]H. R. Boer, *Pentecost and Missions*, p. 145: "When Jesus said . . . 'Go ye *therefore*' . . . he spoke consciously as Lord of lords and King of kings under whose aegis his subjects would herald the new reign that had been inaugurated."

[159]K. H. Rengstorf, *TDNT*, IV, 390, s.v. *manthanō*. "A fundamental mark of Jesus in the tradition is that they are called by Him to discipleship" (p. 444).

[160]The preceding nine lines are a free translation of a quotation from E. Lohse, *RGG³*, IV, col. 1286, s.v. *Nachfolge Christi*. Cf. also E. Lohse, *TDNT*, VI, 964, s.v. *rhabbi*.

[161]P. S. Minear, *Images of the Church in the New Testament*, p. 147.

10:28); they must "hate" those to whom they are bound with ties of love[162] even their own lives (Luke 14:26); they must deny themselves and take up their cross (Mark 10:34); there must be no other relationship of trust and obedience than to him.[163]

At the moment the risen Lord can openly proclaim his messianic *exousia*, which has now been fully given to him, he gives to the Twelve—who are the foundation and representation of the people of God who have been called out of every generation, tongue, and nation, the messianic community of the new age[164]—the mandate: *Mathēteusate*— "Make them into what you yourselves are! Call them into the duodecimal whole of end-time Israel!"[165] They have reached "the highest rank among Christians," but on the narrow road of discipleship it must become a multitude which no one can number (Rev. 7:9). "The Twelve can and will be innumerable."[166]

During Jesus' sojourn on earth people become disciples because he *calls* them. In the call from the Lord the kerygma comes to pass; in the claim which the Messiah makes on a person, the messianic kingdom directly confronts the person. A new state of affairs is proclaimed to her: today, in the hour of her call, it goes into effect. Zero hour has dawned. When Christ commands the apostles to disciple all nations, he does not mention the kerygma. They must do this, "baptizing them in the name of the Father, and of the Son, and of the Holy Spirit."

Just as previously the Lord came to a person and said: "Follow me!" so now the Lord comes to a person in baptism to fit him or her into the messianic community. When Christ commissions the apostles: "Make disciples . . . baptizing," he commands them to go into the world with the kerygma of the name and the baptism in the name which is bound up with it.[167] Mention of baptism here does not mean that baptism replaces the kerygma: baptism is kerygma in concentrated form, focused directly on the recipient.[168] The identical thing which

---

[162]O. Michel, *TDNT,* IV, 690-91, s.v. *miseō*: "The reference is not to hate in the psychological sense, but to disowning, renunciation, rejection. . . . This abnegation is to be taken, not psychologically or fanatically, but pneumatically and christocentrically."

[163]K. Barth, *CD,* IV/2, p. 536. Cf. p. 537: the Son of man who as the Son of God speaks in the name and with the full authority of God, demands trust and faith in the form of obedience to himself. "This is the commitment to Him which constitutes the content of the call to discipleship."

[164]K. H. Rengstorf, *TDNT* II, 326ff., s.v. *dōdeka*.

[165]K. Barth, *Auslegung von Matthäus 28,16-20,* p. 13.

[166]Ibid., p. 14.

[167]For the meaning of *eis to onoma,* see A. Oepke, *TDNT,* I, 539, s.v. *baptō.*

[168]E. Dinkler, *RGG,* VI, col. 630, s.v. *Taufe,* comments that Paul felt no tension between word and sacrament. "The issue both in the word of proclamation and in baptism is the presence of God and Christ (II Cor. 5:20; 1:21ff.) and thus the presence of the redemptive event in the here-and-now (II Cor. 6:2)." This is the light in which one must view the use of *baptizein* in place of *kēryssein* in Matthew 28:19.

the Word proclaims to us and thus promises with legal validity, the sign of baptism tells us *in a different manner.*[169]

It is by baptizing that the apostles will make the nations disciples of Christ. In kerygma and baptism a new dimension comes to light: the Kingdom has come and people may live in it as disciples of the Lord.

The fact that discipleship truly is the following of a way, a continuous life with Christ, comes to expression in the second term which qualifies more precisely the activity of discipling: *didaskontes autous tērein panta hosa eneteilamēn hymin.*

We must note first of all that Jesus speaks of "all the things which I have commanded you." His reference is to what he himself has taught his disciples— *his* didache. But now that he has openly declared that all *exousia* has been given to him, that he is the Son of man to whom was given dominion and glory and royal power (Dan. 7:14), he can sharply define the true nature of his didache. His didache was truly a new teaching *kat' exousia* (Mark 1:27); what he taught his disciples was more than the knowledge imparted to them; it consisted of commandments (*entolai*) by which to govern their lives. Now that the didache has been given by the messianic teacher, the time of teaching in an absolute sense has been brought to a close.[170] The apostles, and the apostolic church in general, do not "teach" as Jesus "taught." After the messianic teacher there is really no room any more for a "teacher": there is but one teacher and master, the Christ (Matt. 23:8, 11). It is their task to pass on his didache, which completely controls their lives, as they received it from *the teacher.*[171]

With reference to the discipling-by-teaching mandate we must—in the second place—take note of what J. H. Bavinck has written: "It is deserving of our attention that we are not told: 'teach them all that I have commanded you.' That would have been a relatively simple matter of regular catechizing and continuing education. The words 'teach them to observe' include much more than that. They include the necessity of pedagogical skill and tact, pastoral wisdom and caution. The challenge is gradually to accustom the feet of inexperienced believers to the way of peace."[172] By characterizing his didache as "all that I have commanded you" Christ indicates that what he has taught cannot be received as information in the manner of students in a lecture hall but is determinative for the way his followers have to go. Discipleship is "followership"; it is a matter of living a certain way; it is a continuous being with Christ, as abiding in his word (John 8:31). If now the apostles, and through them the apostolic church, receive the mandate to disciple the nations also by means of

---

[169]H. Diem, *Die Kirche und ihre Praxis,* p. 136.

[170]In regard to the absolute use of *didaskein* in the Gospels, see K. H. Rengstorf, *TDNT,* II, 144ff., s.v. *didaskō.*

[171]Cf. G. Schrenk, *TDNT,* II, 544, s.v. *entellomai,* and H. Riesenfeld, *TDNT,* VIII, 141, s.v. *tēreō.*

[172]J. H. Bavinck, *Alzo wies het Woord,* p. 143.

didache, this implies that the didache is focused on that continuity. Didache is guidance on the way, the way of following Christ, the way that is Christ. Earlier we saw that the term h^anukkâ is the clearest characterization of Jewish upbringing and the education which constitutes the core of that upbringing. What is true of Jewish upbringing is true of the mode of didache: it is "a transfer of dedication" with an eye to a person's destiny and the way he or she has to go. The baptism bound up with the kerygma is the incorporation of a person in a disciple-community in fellowship with the Lord (Mark 3:14); didache is initiation in the life of discipleship, the "imitation" of Christ.

In saying this we do not mean to imply that the didache is first of all *ethical* instruction. In the first place, the use of *didaskein* in the New Testament does not permit this. A few scholars think that didache has particular reference to the ethical,[173] but H. N. Ridderbos has demonstrated—especially contra K. H. Rengstorf—that "teaching" and "to teach" in the New Testament have a very comprehensive significance. It consists, among other things, in the "further unfolding of the implications of the redemptive events and their further progress."[174] Didache unfolds the meaning and implications of what was revealed in the kerygma; it points out the implications of the great events of redemption. Didache includes the exposition of Scripture and demonstration from the Scriptures that Jesus is the Messiah.[175]

In the second place, the phrase "living in discipleship" cannot be taken in a strictly ethical sense. Our discussion of the concept of discipleship in the Gospels has already brought this out. It would become even plainer if we should trace the concept of discipleship in the Epistles. This, however, would take us too far afield. We simply wish to point out that, particularly in Paul, the life of discipleship is viewed in the closest relationship to Christ himself and to his history, which is the history of salvation.[176] The person who is "in Christ" belongs to "the body of Christ," has been transferred from the sin-and-death sphere of the first Adam into the righteousness-and-life sphere of the second.[177] She is justified by faith in him, and she died and is risen in him. But Jentsch is correct when he remarks: "Without actualization in discipleship faith remains

---

[173]C. H. Dodd, *The Apostolic Preaching*, p. 7, asserts that "teaching (*didaskein*) is in a large majority of cases ethical instruction." But in addition it can be what we call "apologetics" or, especially in John, exposition of a doctrinal point.

[174]H. N. Ridderbos, *The Authority of the New Testament Scriptures*, p. 74.

[175]K. H. Rengstorf, *TDNT*, II, 144, s.v. *didaskein*.

[176]Consider the use Paul makes of the expression "in Christ" and the "body of Christ." Cf. K. Barth, *CD*, IV/1, p. 622: "It will be well to try to survey together the different meanings within which the word *sōma* oscillates. . . ." P. S. Minear, *Images of the Church*, pp. 173ff., points out the various meanings of the word: "This variety of meanings should warn us against . . . importing into each occurrence of the analogy the range of meanings which it bears in other passages" (p. 174). For an extensive treatment of the term "body of Christ" and its connection with discipleship, see D. Bonhoeffer, *The Cost of Discipleship*, pp. 180ff., and *The Communion of the Saints*, pp. 97ff.

[177]A. Oepke, *TDNT*, II, 542, s.v. *en*.

a pious emotion. Hence one can speak of being-in-Christ only when the fiduciary series 'knowing, acknowledging, and confessing' corresponds to the obedience series: 'to hear, to heed, to obey.' I am in Christ, then, when I am prepared for *obedience in affliction* and the *new obedience*."[178] Life in discipleship—in other words, life in Christ, as a member of the body of Christ—is life in the faith which works through love (Gal. 5:6). Didache is directed toward the totality of that life and all its aspects. It cannot be merely "ethical" instruction; it cannot be merely "doctrinal" instruction either. Distinctions of this sort fall short and do less than justice to the New Testament *martyria*, in which "the ethical" is not separate from "the doctrinal." Didache is "an aid to faith" as "an aid to living," but in the same breath one has to say, "an aid to living" as "an aid to faith."

"You Then Who Teach Others . . ." (Rom. 2:21)

Didache, so conceived, makes certain demands on the pastoral role. In the Western Church, according to F. Melzer, writing on the teaching process, the academic professor, representative of rationality, is the master model. Over against this model he places the guru, the Hindu master who does not lecture but "is."[179] It is not Melzer's view that we must have the guru in the place of the professor. "We need both . . . more correctly: we need the holistic model which stands behind or above both." Of this holistic model Jesus is the "original type." That type is also present in the apostles. They did not just propagate a doctrine, "they themselves went the way of this doctrine and drew many with them on this way into eternity."[180]

One could raise the question whether one can really speak of a "higher model" which embraces the essential elements both of the academic professor and the guru; perhaps both the professor and the guru are alien, at bottom, to "the religion of the New Testament."

In any case the mode of didache calls for a style of pastoral role-fulfilment which differs from the style of the professor. The didache as initiation into discipleship calls for a person who himself lives "the way" and is exemplary in his entire life, not just in what he says as a teacher.

Against this background the warning of James is very much in place: "Let not many of you become teachers, my brethren, for you know that we who teach shall be judged with greater strictness. For we all make many mistakes . . ." (James 3:1-2a). This warning is all the more dramatic when it is put alongside of what Paul writes to one who calls himself a Jew in Romans 2:17-24. This person is sure that he is "a guide to the blind, a light to those who are in darkness, a corrector of the foolish, a teacher of children" (2:19-20). The question which confronts everyone who wishes to be a teacher in the didache is this:

---

[178]W. Jentsch, *Handbuch der Jugendseelsorge*, II, 41.
[179]F. Melzer, *Der Guru als Seelenführer*, p. 9.
[180]Ibid., p. 39.

". . . you then who teach others, will you not teach yourself?" (v. 21). Hitherto, says H. Thielicke, Protestantism has given "far too much thought to faith and far too little to the problem of credibility."[181] Credibility will be there only when the person who teaches makes serious work of his faith. This does not mean that he must be morally perfect. But "we do have to know whether he lives, whether he exists, in the house of the dogmas he proclaims. . . . Does he really live in his doctrinal house? . . . Does he do his thinking, feeling, and willing in it? Or are the pulpit and his study places outside of this world, separated from the pleasant normalities of his existence?"[182]

In concluding our reflections on didache, we must take a look backward. In the Old Testament the heart of the didache is h^a nukkâ: the father inducts his child into the way he or she must go—into the story and the way of his or her people. Didache is also tôrâ—the voice which instructs—and hokmâ, instruction in the paths of uprightness (Prov. 4:11) in order that one may really live (Eccl. 7:12). In the New Testament this is all taken up in the instruction which guides a person in the way of discipleship and life in the messianic community.

It is characteristic of the mode of kerygma, we observed, that it relates the word proclaimed directly to the present; in the kerygma the salvation preached stands squarely over against the situation of the person in the "now" who hears it. In thinking of the mode of didache one pictures a horizontal line: salvation appears on the road we have to travel day by day, step by step, through the complexities of life. God comes to us in his word through the intermediary of pastoral role-fulfilment also in the mode of didache. The Lord calls: Follow me!

11. THE MODE OF PARAKLESIS

A Third Mode

In the dynamic structure of God's coming in his word through pastoral role-fulfilment, the modes of kerygma and didache are fairly easy to distinguish. In the kerygma God enters human life with his salvation; in the didache God points out a new way of life.

Now if we read the New Testament carefully we encounter, as it turns out, something still different—something which is not separate from kerygma and didache but which lies in a different sphere from that of the authoritative proc-lamation of salvation and the didactic unfolding of it. Activities like the following are mentioned: to appeal, to beg, to beseech, to invite, to entreat, to ask, to urge, to conciliate, to exhort, to give or receive encouragement, to console, to comfort. Checking them out, one discovers they are all translations of *parakalein*.

The New Testament clearly teaches that *paraklēsis* is a necessary element in the life and activity of the church.

---

[181]H. Thielicke, *The Trouble with the Church*, p. 15.
[182]Ibid., pp. 5-6.

[Paul mentions *paraklēsis* among the charismata given to believers with a view to the activities to be accomplished in the church (Rom. 12:8). Timothy is mandated to give special attention to the public reading of Scripture, to *paraklēsis*, and to teaching (I Tim. 4:13; 6:2). Titus must appoint elders in the church of Crete who are able *parakalein* on the basis of sound doctrine (Tit. 1:9).]

Thus, next to kerygma and didache the New Testament offers still another pastoral activity with a quality of its own. This activity can be singled out in the word "paraklesis," provided one remembers that a variety of other words help to define its nature more precisely.[183]

[Indeed, the question can be raised why we do not designate this third mode of pastoral role-fulfilment as *parenesis*, a term that is especially current in the field of homiletics. The argument against its use is, in the first place, that the noun does not occur in the New Testament and the verb only twice (Acts 27:9, 22), and that in a context which is hard to associate with pastoral role-fulfilment in the church. In the second place, *parenesis* is a technical term in rhetoric: it is, according to Huyser, "practical in nature and consists in a series of concrete prescriptions for living which are barely related to each other." As a homiletic concept, says Huyser, *parenesis* "stands for the official admonition which a preacher directs to a congregation."[184]

This selection is possibly defensible when it is a matter of isolating a certain element in preaching from a strictly formal, rhetorical viewpoint. Our purpose is rather to construct a model of the complex phenomenon of "God's coming in his word through the intermediary of pastoral role-fulfilment." In such a model the fundamental structure of a phenomenon must be laid out. For that purpose we have to go back to its original appearance, i.e., in the New Testament. There we possibly find what in rhetoric is called *parenesis*, but then it certainly is not by itself codeterminative of the structure of the phenomenon under discussion but only in a wider context—a context which the New Testament itself calls *paraklēsis*.]

In order to define the nature of the third mode of pastoral role-fulfilment we must first trace the meaning and usage of *parakalein* and *paraklēsis*, and then the elements added to the picture by words used in close association with *paraklēsis*.

To Ask, to Exhort, to Comfort

According to Schmitz, *parakalein* has a threefold meaning in the New Testament: (1) asking for help (especially in the Synoptics), (2) exhortation, and (3) consoling.[185]

[It must be borne in mind here that what occurs in a lexicon for the word X

---

[183]See O. Schmitz, *TDNT*, V, 796, s.v. *parakaleō*.
[184]P. J. Huyser, *De Paraenese in de Prediking*, p. 4.
[185]O. Schmitz, *TDNT*, V, 794ff., s.v. *parakaleō, paraklēsis*.

as meanings (1) . . . , (2) . . . , and (3) . . . in reality may concern a semantic field of reference with a central core, while for every use of the word one has to ask what is the scope and what are the nuances in this instance. According to A. Robertson and A. Plummer, *parakalein* in the New Testament has "many shades of meaning, radiating from the idea of 'calling to one's side' in order to speak privately, to gain support."[186] Schmitz, too, regards this as the original meaning of the word,[187] but in the New Testament the original sense is far less prominent than the idea of turning to another in speech. The various meanings of *parakalein* may all be brought together under the common sense of "address."[188]]

In any case, one can say that *parakalein* embraces the idea of a calling out—*kalein*: one speaks and another is spoken to; one turns to another in the form of an address—*para*.[189] In other words, *parakalein* contains *the idea of an address to a contingent situation of a person or a group of persons*.

It would certainly not be correct to conclude from this analysis that there is an absolute distinction between paraklesis on the one hand and kerygma and didache on the other. But for paraklesis this specifically focused address to the situation is typical. The fact, then, that the coming of God in his word also takes place in the manner of paraklesis means that God is present, reveals his name and truth, actualizes salvation, not in abstraction from the situatedness of human beings, but in direct connection with it and with a view to it. Were God to come to me only in the mode of kerygma, that could mean: God has come; be silent before him—my realities and interests do not matter. The reality of the Kingdom takes precedence over them. Were God to come to me only in the mode of didache, that could mean: God has come; the road on which life has brought me is no longer important, he has another way for me. When God comes to me in the mode of paraklesis, it dawns on me: God has come and he wants to live in my house and my situation—my situation is important to him. God enters my situation in its concrete "thus-and-nowness," and he appears in it for that very purpose.

Paraklesis, then, can be—depending in part on the situation—a request, an exhortation, or an expression of comfort. But it must be remembered that each of these separate meanings lies in one field of meaning.

[Sometimes the translation of *parakalein–paraklēsis* into the English equivalent is not difficult. When Paul writes to Philemon that he is bold enough to command him to do what is required, but for love's sake prefers *parakalein* (vv. 8-9), the choice of *appeal* is obvious. It is also clear that in the case of Euodia and Syntyche, who live in disagreement, Paul exhorts or *entreats* them to agree

---

[186]A. Robertson and A. Plummer, *First Corinthians* (International Critical Commentary), p. 87.

[187]O. Schmitz, *TDNT*, V, 774.

[188]Ibid., p. 794.

[189]Cf. E. Robinson, *Greek and English Lexicon of the New Testament*, s.v. *para*: "a prep. governing the genitive, dative, and accusative, with the primary signif. *beside, nearby*; expressing thus the relation of immediate *vicinity* or *proximity*."

(Phil. 4:2). In II Corinthians 1:3ff. the subject is doubtless that of *comfort*. But there are also instances where the choice between "exhort" and "comfort" is difficult if not impossible. Stählin points out that in extrabiblical antiquity "the imperative element in *parakaleō* ('to admonish') is always more or less plainly accompanied by the indicative ('to console') and vice versa."[190]

Schlier offers this fine summary: "Apostolic exhortation is a concerned and urgent address to the brethren which combines supplication, comfort, and admonition."[191] This does not mean that Paul, when he admonishes, only wants to comfort. It does mean that admonition is always directly connected with the only comfort of Lord's Day I of the Heidelberg Catechism: "that I with body and soul, both in life and in death, am not my own, but belong to my faithful Savior, Jesus Christ."

"The Parakletic Formula"

At this point we must pay some attention to the use Paul makes of what may be termed "the parakletic formula." He exhorts the believers at Rome "by the mercies of God" (Rom. 12:1); "by our Lord Jesus Christ and by the love of the Spirit" (Rom. 15:30); "by the name of our Lord Jesus Christ" (1 Cor. 1:10); "by the meekness and gentleness of Christ" (II Cor. 10:1). In each instance he uses *dia* with the genitive. "This usage corresponds to that of the causal *per* in requests or oaths," according to Oepke.[192] Paraklesis comes to people who have already received the kerygma. A new state of affairs has been announced for their benefit, the Kingdom has come, the new life has begun. Their life is life in Christ; it is no longer determined by self but controlled by Christ who lives in the person who is called to a new life (Gal. 2:20). They are now baptized; their life is taken up into the story of the mercies of God, of the meekness and gentleness of Christ, of the love of the Spirit.

It has begun—God has begun. Believers can now be addressed in their situations with an appeal to the fact that they are in the story, in God's new beginning, in Christ. The paraklesis constitutes an appeal to the kerygma and to the baptism which was the personal seal of the kerygma; it is a *paraklēsis en Christō* (Phil. 2:1; cf. II Thess. 3:12).

What paraklesis calls for exceeds human possibilities; it is not a moral appeal, but a reminder of what God has done,[193] an exposition of the saving deed already accomplished. It does not call for brand new initiatives and achievements; it calls for fruit-bearing and an answer.

God has begun, says the paraklesis; now it has really begun for you!

---

[190]G. Stählin, *TDNT*, V, 779, s.v. *parakaleō*.

[191]Quoted in O. Schmitz, *TDNT*, V, 796.

[192]A. Oepke, *TDNT*, II, 68, s.v. *dia*.

[193]O. Schmitz, *TDNT*, V, 795: "The exhortation is distinguished from a mere moral appeal by this reference back to the work of salvation as its presupposition and basis."

Just as the Old Testament prophets, in the call to repentance, called people back to the LORD who had at one time called them into his possession, so paraklesis, even when as exhortation it cuts deeply into the situation of "now-and-such," is the appeal to return to the love of God in order to live in it.

The Consolation of Israel

This liberating and redeeming element of New Testament paraklesis—and therefore the big difference between paraklesis and parenesis in rhetoric—stands out more clearly when we trace the background connotations of the concept in the Old Testament and in Judaism. *Parakalein* often occurs in the Septuagint, usually as equivalent of *niham*; it can nearly always, even when it serves as equivalent for another word, be translated by "to comfort."[194] *Niham* means literally: to cause to breathe again, to relieve. The word presupposes a state of pressure and anxiety. But when comfort comes, people can breathe again. From the same stem comes *m^{e}nûhâ*. Naomi wishes that her daughter-in-law may find *m^{e}nûhâ*, "each . . . in the house of her husband" (Ruth 1:9), and that "it may be well" with them (Ruth 3:1). The land Yahweh gives to Israel to possess is called "the rest and the inheritance which the LORD your God gives you" (Deut. 12:9; cf. Ps. 95:11). *M^{e}nûhâ* can be translated "rest" or "resting place": it is the space in which a person is placed and in which life can blossom.

The same idea resides in the Old Testament concept of "comfort." When Yahweh comforts Zion, he "makes her wilderness like Eden" and "her desert like the garden of the LORD" (Isa. 51:3). When Yahweh returns to Zion, that constitutes comfort and—for that is comfort par excellence—redemption (Isa. 52:9). *Niham* frequently occurs with the prefix *min*, meaning "out of." Comfort is a power which draws people *out of* situations of distress. The name Noah, which was mistakenly linked with *niham*, was understood to carry comfort or relief: "Out of the ground which the LORD has cursed this one shall bring us relief from (*min*) our work and from the toil of our hands" (Gen. 5:29). Noah will bring relief from the curse. The words of a psalmist are characteristic for true comfort: "This is my comfort in my affliction that thy promise gives me life" (Ps. 119:50). Comfort is redemption and help (cf. Ps. 86:16-17).

[Commenting on Isaiah 40:1: "Comfort, comfort my people, says your God," Norman H. Snaith remarks: "The command 'Comfort ye' does not mean that consoling words are to be spoken to one in the midst of sorrow in order that the sorrowful one may continue bravely in tribulation. It means that words are to be spoken which will make an end of sorrow, and so will comfort *out of* sorrow, not *in* sorrow."[195] This is true of all real comfort. When comfort comes, the situation changes; when it does not, one can only speak of worthless, empty

---

[194]Ibid., p. 777.
[195]N. H. Snaith, *The Distinctive Ideas of the Old Testament*, p. 181: "It involves the cessation of sorrow."

consolation (Zech. 10:2; cf. Job 21:34). It is about such comfort that Job raises his complaint (Job 16:1ff.). His friends had come to him with good intentions. Their words are more than worth considering. Their arguments are very edifying and they surprise one with the large truths they bring up. But Job, who himself had a solid reputation as a wise man and as one who "comforts mourners" (29:25), has heard it all before (16:2). Were his friends in his place he could do as much: "I could join words together against you and shake my head to you" (16:4). But such words, however full of wisdom, are powerless (16:3). They cannot "comfort out of sorrow"—nothing changes. They do not put a person into "space"; they don't enable him or her to breathe again; they offer no fresh horizons. For that reason Job calls his friends "miserable comforters." Their comfort is not *paraklēsis alēthinē*, (Isa. 57:18, LXX), which offers healing and guidance and brings a person *šālôm* (Isa. 57:18-19).]

It is no wonder that in later Judaism *neḥāmâ* became a term for the messianic salvation in its fulness. Simeon, who expected the *paraklēsis* of Israel, the messianic *neḥāmâ* (Luke 2:25), sang of its fulness with the child Jesus in his arms: ". . . salvation which thou hast prepared in the presence of all peoples, a light for revelation to the Gentiles and for glory to thy people Israel" (Luke 2:30-32). Jesus Christ himself is the *paraklēsis*, the comfort out of sorrow: to captives he proclaims release, to the blind sight, to the oppressed liberty (Luke 4:18); he took our infirmities upon himself and bore our diseases (Matt. 8:17). He is the resurrection and the life (John 11:25). He abolished death and brought life and immortality to light through the gospel (II Tim. 1:10). He delivers all those who through fear of death are subject to lifelong bondage (Heb. 2:15). He is the consolation, for in his death and resurrection the new age begins in which God will dwell with people and "he will wipe away every tear from their eyes, and death shall be no more, neither shall there be mourning nor crying nor pain any more, for the former things have passed away" (Rev. 21:3-4).

Paraklesis is a mode of God's coming in his word through the intermediary of pastoral role-fulfilment. The danger is not imaginary that in this mode in particular the pastor's work will degenerate into joining together pretty words— empty words of consolation or empty words of admonition. They may perhaps be words which, like the words of Job's friends, are wise and valuable in themselves, but they do not break through sin and suffering; they have nothing to do with Easter or the coming Kingdom.

Eduard Thurneysen points out that the pastoral care of Christ himself was pastoral care "within the perspective of a grand hope." His next words are to the point: "For that reason our pastoral care as his disciples cannot be other than the pastoral care of hope. All real pastoral care is as such the pastoral care of hope; it has eschatological character, or it is not real."[196]

In other words, real exhortation is only that which is addressed to people

---

[196]E. Thurneysen, *Der Mensch von heute und das Evangelium*, p. 13.

with the parakletic formula: paraklesis which takes place with an appeal to *the* paraklesis which took place in the appearance and work of Christ: I comfort you, I exhort you—for salvation has appeared. Or, as Paul says it in his paraklesis to the Romans: "Besides this you know what hour it is, how it is full time now for you to wake from sleep" (Rom. 13:11). With reference to *nhm* Snaith remarks: "The root is associated again and again in the Old Testament with the idea of change of mind, hearts, intention." "The Hebrew word *nacham* is . . . a conversion word, and the same applies to *parakaleō*. . . ."[197] Paraklesis, we may say, is an appeal to change, but the appeal takes place within the context of the gospel, the evangel of the new age which has dawned with the coming of Christ: "Arise, shine; for your light has come, and the glory of the LORD has risen upon you" (Isa. 60:1). "The light shines in the darkness"—and we have beheld his glory (John 1:5, 14).

Mutua consolatio fratrum

Because our topic is paraklesis as a mode of pastoral role-fulfilment, we need to raise the question who is responsible for this ministry. Schmitz and Stählin point out that in the Old Testament comforting is God's own proper work: "I, I am he that comforts you" (Isa. 51:12). "As one whom his mother comforts, so I will comfort you" (Isa. 66:13).

But God's comfort does not come only directly and immediately; it also comes through many mediators and channels, especially through prophets.[198] The New Testament offers the same picture. "Blessed be the God and Father of our Lord Jesus Christ, the Father of mercies and God of all comfort" (II Cor. 1:3; cf. Rom. 15:5; II Thess. 2:16). God's *paraklēsis* comes to us through the Scriptures (Rom. 15:4) and through people whom he has called to ministry. When they fulfil their role, God's paraklesis takes place: ". . . we are ambassadors for Christ, God making his appeal through us" (II Cor. 5:20).

Paul makes this statement, thinking of the apostolate. His letters make clear that he often viewed his ministry as a ministry of paraklesis. But the New Testament also shows that this ministry is not limited to apostles.

[In Romans 12:8 Paul mentions *paraklēsis* as one of the gifts given to believers. Timothy and Titus are told that it is part of their task and they are given instruction in the way it is to be done (I Tim. 4:13; II Tim. 4:2; Tit. 2:15; I Tim. 5:1; 6:2; Tit. 2:6). Titus is told to appoint elders able *parakalein* (Tit. 1:9). In addition, believers are summoned to admonish and to comfort one another: ". . . encourage one another and build one another up" (I Thess. 5:11; cf. 4:18). "Take care, brethren, lest there be in any of you an evil, unbelieving heart, leading you to fall away from the living God. But exhort one another every day . . ." (Heb. 3:12-13; cf. 10:25).]

---

[197]N. H. Snaith, *Distinctive Ideas of the Old Testament*, p. 181.
[198]O. Schmitz and G. Stählin, *TDNT*, V, 790, s.v. *parakaleō, paraklēsis*.

It is well for us to bear in mind that whenever the word *parakalein* occurs in the New Testament, we must not suppose that it carries the full weight of the paraklesis concept that we have developed from the material available.

Parakalein is an ordinary word, and when the New Testament, which was written in ordinary language, uses it, it does not necessarily mean, in each instance, to suggest notions of "liberation and redemption," "reminders of salvation in Christ," "the complete renewal of life," etc. When a given letter instructs "admonish one another," the author speaks of *paraklēsis* but he does not necessarily think of "the mode of God's coming in his word." He does not use our concept. He only wants to say: "You are responsible for one another; remember this and exercise that responsibility by being aware of each other and if necessary by talking to each other."

This does not deprive us of the right to make connections and associations. For then our point of departure is not the word which is used as such. It lies elsewhere, but where? Whence is it that members of the church are told they have the calling *parakalein* each other, and that with an eye to salvation? The source of this is the reality that salvation and involvement in it is not a private matter. Together they are in Christ: ". . . one body, and one Spirit, just as you were called to the one hope that belongs to your call, one Lord, one faith, one baptism, one God and Father of us all, who is above all and through all and in all" (Eph. 4:4-6), and they all partake of the one bread (I Cor. 10:17). If one member of the church suffers, all suffer together (I Cor. 12:26). If one member deviates or falls away, then there is a breach in the unity of the church, a break in the fellowship, a fellowship which is with the Lord and in salvation. The matter at stake in mutual paraklesis, the *mutua consolatio fratrum*,[199] is more than the practice of group loyalty. The unity of the church is essential for participation in salvation, for life in "the consolation of Christ." To preserve and to experience that unity—that is the issue in mutual paraklesis. God has come and now we live—communally—with God; therefore, exhort one another. Our joint salvation, our unity, is at stake. To live in the sphere of salvation is to live together, and hence to live in responsibility for each other.

Paul writes to the church at Rome: ". . . I long to see you, that I may impart to you some spiritual gift to strengthen you" (Rom. 1:11). It is as apostle that he writes this; as such he has a special commission and special resources with which to enrich the life of the church. But immediately afterward Paul interrupts himself: ". . . that is, that we may be mutually encouraged by each other's faith (*symparaklēthēnai*), both yours and mine" (1:12). This passage, says Schlier, "must certainly not only be judged as a conventional ploy to win their goodwill."[200] The apostle is also a brother; he is not above the church, he is in the thick of it. The prefix *syn*, says Grundmann, "denotes the totality of persons who are together, or who come together, or who accompany one another, or who

---

[199] An expression from the Articles of Schmalkald, III, 4.
[200] H. Schlier, *Het Woord Gods*, p. 96.

work together, sharing a common task or a common destiny, aiding and supporting one another."[201] Paul expresses this idea in the word *symparaklēthēnai*: he lives in the fellowship of totality and reciprocity and interdependence which is the church; offering comfort, he himself seeks comfort; offering admonition, he opens himself up to admonition. In no other way does he participate in salvation or could he live in it.

The mandate to exercise mutual paraklesis presupposes what it simultaneously serves: "the unity of the Spirit" (Eph. 4:3), "participation in the Spirit" (Phil. 2:1). It is therefore more than the simple prompting: "Do keep an eye on each other." For in this paraklesis it is God, dwelling through the Spirit in the church, who comes to the oppressed, suffering, and erring person. When people address each other through the Spirit—who is the Spirit of life in the body of Christ—God, the God of all comfort (II Cor. 1:3), is the subject of that address.[202]

Now to summarize what we have discovered about paraklesis: *In the paraklesis God comes; it is directed toward the contingent situation of a person; it makes an appeal to the salvation already received; it includes the call to return to the love of God; it calls a person out of his or her sorrow or sin to live in peace; it directs the person to the great eschatological consolation; it is a life-function of the body of Christ which lives in the fellowship of the Spirit.*

Related Words

To sharpen the picture of the mode of paraklesis, we now wish to pay attention to a number of words used repeatedly in close connection with *parakalein/paraklēsis*. These words do not, like *parakalein*, directly denote the activity of speech, even though as a rule encouragement or correction will take place by way of speech. More than *parakalein*, which can be used in a rather formal way, they indicate the nature of the activity and the intention underlying it. Therefore they make more explicit certain aspects of paraklesis.

The verb *paramytheisthai* occurs a few times in the Epistles, as do the nouns *paramythia* and *paramythion*. The meaning of these words is almost identical with *parakalein/paraklēsis*, with this difference that *paramytheisthai*, as Jentsch remarks, more literally means " 'to address as a brother' because something has happened (in the sense of comfort and promise) or because something must happen (in the sense of exhortation)."[203] *Paramytheisthai* means "to encourage,"

---

[201]W. Grundmann, *TDNT*, VII, 766, s.v. *syn–meta.*

[202]It is probably not correct, when thinking of paraklesis, which is certainly a work of the Holy Spirit, to associate it with the name given in the Gospel of John to the Holy Spirit: *Paraklētos*. Jentsch, *Handbuch*, I, 50, remarks: "*Paraklētos* cannot simply be derived from *parakalein*, but has its own conceptual history." Cf. J. Behm, *TDNT*, V, 803ff., s.v. *paraklētos*; D. E. Holwerda, *The Holy Spirit and Eschatology in the Gospel of John*, pp. 26ff.

[203]W. Jentsch, *Handbuch*, I, 51.

"to cheer up": this encouragement proceeds from mutual love and promotes the well-being of the "fainthearted" (I Thess. 5:14).

The verb *nouthetein* (to put in mind, warn, admonish), as well as the noun *nouthesia*, has a more severe sound. The characteristic meaning of *nouthetein* comes out in I Thessalonians 5:14, where believers are told to encourage the fainthearted and to *admonish* the irregular or idle (*tous ataktous*).[204] The correction is directed to people who "have given up," who are not continuing on the road of discipleship. According to I Corinthians 4:14 this correction is for people who have become puffed up "in favor of one against the other" (I Cor. 4:6) and who conduct themselves as though they were kings (I Cor. 4:8). It comes to persons who are "factious" and cause splits (Tit. 3:10), or to those who fall into the sins into which Israel fell on its wilderness journey: idolatry, immorality, putting the Lord to the test, grumbling (I Cor. 10:6-10). These sins and the punishments which followed "are written down for our instruction (*pros nouthesian hēmōn*), upon whom the end of the ages has come" (I Cor. 10:11).

Nouthesia is the task of an apostle (Acts 20:31; I Cor. 4:14; Col. 1:28) or other officebearers (I Thess. 5:12; Tit. 3:10). Like *paraklēsis,* it is the task of every believer (Rom. 15:14; Col. 3:16; I Thess. 5:14; II Thess. 3:15).[205] According to H. N. Ridderbos, *nouthetein* is used to refer to "directive pastoral activity."[206] It seems to us that a heavy emphasis must then be put on the "pastoral" which qualifies the "directing." Paul characterizes his activity in the church at Ephesus with these words: ". . . for three years I did not cease night or day to admonish every one with tears" (Acts 20:31). When he acts "nouthetically" he does it because he experiences his relationship to the church as that of a father to his beloved children (I Cor. 4:14-16). Admonition in mutual paraklesis must take place in the same (family) atmosphere. This is clear from II Thessalonians 3:15: "Do not look on him"—namely, the one who refuses to pay attention to the admonition in the letter—"as an enemy, but warn him as a brother," i.e., he remains a brother and must be treated as such; in this case that means he must be warned.

Nouthesia presupposes the specific solidarity of the family; it is a function of this solidarity. If people are truly bound up with each other, indissolubly, as parents and children, and as children reciprocally in the family, one must help the other to remain "in place," in the fellowship, "on the way," in discipleship to the Lord.

This *nouthesia*—like parental discipline in the home—is *nouthesia kyriou.*

---

[204]W. K. M. Grossouw, *Sint Paulus en de Beschaving van zijn Tijd,* p. 8, says that the word *ataktein,* in Paul's time, "had acquired the almost technical sense of 'playing hooky,' 'goofing off,' going on strike—a meaning which the term undoubtedly has here."

[205][American readers in particular will recognize these texts as the basis for a theory of "nouthetic" counselling advanced and popularized by Jay E. Adams in his books *Competent to Counsel, The Christian Counselor's Manual, More than Redemption: A Theology of Christian Counselling,* and other works. *Tr.*]

[206]H. N. Ridderbos, *Aan de Kolossenzen,* p. 163.

Paul uses this expression in Ephesians 6:4: "Fathers, do not provoke your children to anger, but bring them up in the discipline and instruction of the Lord."

[It is hard to determine precisely the nature of the genitive in *nouthesia kyriou*.[207] Most likely it has in it something both of the subjective and the qualitative. Parents bring up their children; that means concretely that they address themselves to them with *paideia* and *nouthesia*. But they do not do this on the basis of the fact that they know or have the right to determine the place and the "way" of the child: the Lord knows it and determines it. And through the parents, by whose hand God governs children, he puts that child "in place," guides her on her way, and if necessary brings her back. When parents direct and correct children, they are to do this, knowing the Lord and his will in relation to this child, and in his service. That would seem to be the meaning of bringing up children "in the discipline and instruction of the Lord."]

In the church community all admonition is *nouthesia kyriou*. Paul writes to the Christians at Rome: "I am satisfied . . . that you yourselves are full of goodness, filled with all knowledge, and able to instruct one another." (Rom. 15:14). According to H. N. Ridderbos, Paul is speaking here of "goodwill, the desire to be accommodating in social relations with one another" and "the knowledge of God in the practice of life,"[208] both of which are needed for mutual admonition. The "charge" carried by *agathōsynē* and *gnōsis* appears to be somewhat heavier.

The commentaries as a rule remark that Romans 15:13 is the conclusion of the parenesis begun in 12:1 and forms the provisional ending of the letter. Very true, but that is not to say that verse 14 must not be read in one breath with the preceding verse. Verses 13 and 14 are joined by the conjunction *de*, just as they are connected by a form of the verb "to fill": "May the God of hope *fill* you with all joy and peace. . . . I am satisfied that you yourselves are *full* of goodness, *filled* with all knowledge. . . ." Paul is convinced that the Christians in Rome already partake of what he desires for them: "joy and peace" and to "abound in hope" (v. 13); they are "full of goodness" and "filled with all knowledge" (v. 14); thus something of the perfect eschaton they expect is manifest. But then they are also able to instruct and admonish one another: they live together—witness their goodness and knowledge—within "the horizon of hope" (Thurneysen). What is expressed in the parakletic formula applies also to *nouthesia* in the church: it "leans on" the salvation of him in whom the Gentiles hope (Rom. 15:12); it intends to bring back those who have departed from the way of salvation, and so to preserve them in the fellowship of the family and "house of the Lord."

A third word associated with *parakalein*, which also adds to the content of the concept of paraklesis, is *stērizein*, supported twice, with the same mean-

---

[207]Cf. G. Bertram, *TDNT*, V, 624, s.v. *paideia*: "This is the education which the Lord gives through the father."

[208]H. N. Ridderbos, *Aan de Romeinen*, pp. 328-29.

ing, by *epistērizein*. The main sense of this word is "to support," "to fix something so that it stands upright and immovable."[209]

The presupposition of stērizein is the state of being under assault;[210] *the action of stērizein intends to bring the assaulted person to stability and concentration.*[211] That concentration is the orientation of a person toward the salvation that is coming. In their suffering believers must wait patiently, like the farmer who waits for the precious fruit of the earth. "You also be patient. Establish your hearts, for the coming of the Lord is at hand" (James 5:7-8). This concentration does not mean immobility, a posture of simply "sit-and-wait." What is at the point of death needs to be strengthened (Rev. 3:2). The Lord will establish their hearts so that they may be "unblamable in holiness . . . at the coming of our Lord Jesus" (I Thess. 3:13). "Now may our Lord Jesus Christ himself, and God our Father, who loved us and gave us eternal comfort and good hope through grace, comfort your hearts and *establish* them in every good work and word" (II Thess. 2:16-17).

The subject of the strengthening is in the first place God and the Lord Jesus Christ;[212] then the apostles or their helpers;[213] finally the believers themselves are responsible for their own strengthening and that of their brothers and sisters.[214] In Romans 1:11-12 Paul links "strengthening" with "mutual encouragement"; what gives stability, in the sense of a continuing focus on salvation, is that people receive consolation from one another's faith, in the community of commonality and mutuality which is the church. This is true not because faith is so well established and sure but because it is the Lord in whom one believes.

Another word deserving of our attention is *katartizein*. This means to make someone or something *artios*, i.e., such that he or she or it fully meets the demands one must pose to the subject.[215]

[Jesus saw James and John "mending their nets (*katartizontas ta diktua*)" (Matt. 4:21). In extrabiblical Greek *katartizein* is used, inter alia, in medicine for setting a leg and in politics for bringing parties together.[216] In I Peter 5:10 the word occurs—along with the word *stērizein* discussed earlier—in a series of verbs all of which express the idea of stability: "The God of all grace . . . will himself restore (*katartisei*), establish (*stērizei*), and strengthen you."]

---

[209]G. Harder, *TDNT,* VII, 653, s.v. *stērizō*.

[210]Ibid., p. 656: "It presupposes that the Christians who are to be strengthened are under assault and in danger of becoming uncertain or slothful in their faith or walk."

[211]For the idea of concentration and purposeful self-direction, see the use Luke makes of *stērizein* (9:51): "he set his face (*to prosōpon estērisen*) to go to Jerusalem."

[212]Romans 16:25; I Thessalonians 3:13; II Thessalonians 2:17; 3:3; I Peter 5:10.

[213]Luke 22:32; Acts 14:22; 15:32; 18:23; Romans 1:11; I Thessalonians 3:2.

[214]James 5:8; Revelation 3:2.

[215]Cf. G. Delling, *TDNT,* I, 475, s.v. *artios*.

[216]Cf. A. Robertson and A. Plummer, *First Corinthians,* p. 10: "The word is suggestive of fitting together what is broken or rent. It is used in surgery for setting a joint (Galen) and in Greek politics for composing factions."

Whereas *stērizein* means especially to direct to a goal, hence concentration, *katartizein* means to make fit for a purpose, hence to enable someone to fulfil a function. The words of Scripture can make the man of God *artios*, equipped (*exērtismenos*) for every good work (II Tim. 3:17). The idea is not an abstract perfection—an ideal which is foreign to the Bible[217]—but a functional fitness as *"ho tou theou anthrōpos"* to do what he or she has to do as such (*pros pan ergon agathon*). To help him or her get to that point the Scriptures, inter alia, were given.

[In Ephesians 4:11-12 Paul speaks of the officebearers whom Christ has given "for the equipment of the saints, for the work of ministry (*pros ton katartismon tōn hagiōn eis ergon diakonias*)." These words have frequently been used in recent years to indicate the task of training members of the church for the work which the Christian, the ordinary layperson in the church, has to do in the world. For us it is not a question whether Christians are called to such a ministry or whether the church by its agencies must equip them for this ministry; the question is whether these words can be used to support this type of activity.

In the first place, it is somewhat arbitrary to pluck these words from their context. Following *eis ergon diakonias* are the words *eis oikodomēn tou sōmatos tou Christou*. These phrases are in any case parallel. It is not even impossible that all three members (*pros . . . eis . . . eis*) are parallel. If one does not accept this latter position, it is still a question what the relationship between the parts is. Is the work of the officebearer the equipping of the saints, so that they are made fit for the work of ministry and building up the body of Christ? Or are we told that the Lord gave officebearers for the work of ministry and the building up of the body with a view to equipping saints? The latter seems to us the more probable. Abbott, who understands the passage in this way, remarks: "In a connection like this, where offices in the church are in question, *diakonia* can only mean official service." And he says the term *oikodomē tou sōmatos* "describes the function of teachers rather than of hearers."[218] It is probably also meaningful that the reference is, not to *katartizein* or *katartisis*, but to *katartismos*. "*Katartismos*," says Abbott, "is the complete result of *katartisis*." The passage does not describe the process as such but that in which the process of making and becoming *artios* results. The course of the argument in Ephesians

---

[217]E. Brunner, *Das Gebot und die Ordnungen*, p. 616, points out that deliberate preoccupation with the self is totally foreign to the Bible. It arises under the influence of the Aristotelian-Stoic concept of virtue, which aims at the perfection of personality as such. See the English translation *The Divine Imperative*, pp. 167ff.

[218]T. K. Abbott, *Ephesians* (International Critical Commentary), p. 119. He translates: (He gave officebearers) "with a view to the perfecting of the saints unto the work of ministering, unto the building up of the body of Christ." "The most obvious way to interpret this," says Grosheide in his commentary (p. 67), is "to read in the two expressions at the close of v. 12 an explanation of the equipping. But then thus, that *diakonia* effects *katartismos* and *oikodomē* is the content of the *diakonia*."

4:11-13 seems to run like this: The Lord has given a variety of ministers whose task is *diakonia,* the goal of which is the building up of the body of Christ. They are charged with this activity to the end that the saints may attain the state of being *artios,* which consists in being spiritually mature.[219] All official ministry exists for this *katartismos.*]

Katartizein thus means *the activity which aims to mold the members of Christ into real members of that body.* The content of this word could also be subsumed under the didache concept. The reason why we have not done this is that the main idea in *katartizein* is to repair, remaking something in order that it be functionally fit.[220] One could say that *katartizein* presupposes—to use the athlete's idiom—a state of being out-of-condition, resulting in a person's inability to function adequately at her post in the body of Christ.[221]

We will now conclude our consideration of the mode of paraklesis with a few remarks about *oikodomein*—to edify, to build up. This word, too, is used in relation to *parakalein:* "Therefore encourage one another and build one another up . . ." (I Thess. 5:11).[222] When thinking of the biblical use of this word, one must not, as has often been pointed out, confuse it with "edification" in the sense of nurturing a strictly individual religious life. *Oikodomein* may be directed to the individual (cf. Rom. 15:2; I Cor. 14:17; I Thess. 5:11), but *it has the intent of drawing the individual out of her isolation and leading her to her place in the fellowship of the church.*

We noticed earlier that Paul speaks of the officebearer's task in relation to the "building up of the body of Christ" (Eph. 4:12). Two images overlap here: The church is a body, but also a building, "the household of God" (I Tim. 3:15; I Pet. 4:17), "built upon the foundation of the apostles and prophets, Christ Jesus himself being the cornerstone" (Eph. 2:20-22; cf. I Pet. 2:4-6). Christians are fitted into the structure as "living stones" (I Pet. 2:5). It is against this background that the use of *oikodomein* must be seen. Minear is right: "Whatever edifies the brother does far more than improve his moral behavior; it strengthens him in his position in this structured society."[223] The entire complex which is the church, in its differentiation and its unity, is made to build itself up in love (Eph. 4:29). *Oikodomē,* building up the other in the church and building up the church as a whole, is the criterion for a person's behavior in various situations:

---

[219]Verse 13: *ei andra teleion.* The situation is characterized as "the measure of the stature of the fulness of Christ" and comes out in "the unity of the faith and of the knowledge of the Son of God."

[220]Cf. A. Plummer, *Second Corinthians,* p. 378: "In the NT the verb is often used of setting right what has previously gone wrong, rectifying and restoring rather than merely bringing onwards to perfection."

[221]Galatians 6:1, in saying that the church has a duty *katarizein* a member who is overtaken in a "misstep" *(paraptōma),* offers a good illustration of its meaning.

[222]Cf. I Corinthians 14:3 where this set of related words appears: *oikodomē, paraklēsis, paramythia.*

[223]P. S. Minear, *Images of the Church,* p. 164.

one has a duty to ask, not only whether a given behavior is permissible but whether it edifies (I Cor. 10:23; cf. 8:1). All things, especially in the assembly, must be done for edification (I Cor. 14:26); in seeking spiritual gifts and using them one must seek above all the building up of the church (I Cor. 14:12; cf. vv. 4, 17).

To sum up: paraklesis is the mode in which God comes to people in their situations of dread, suffering, sin, despair, error, and insufficiency. God comes to persons to rescue them out of the distress of their situation in order to bring them into life with the church in the enjoyment of the salvation which is in Christ, comforted and courageous in the joy of new obedience. God leads them through this process to their own places and makes them fit to fulfil special tasks within the body of Christ.

12. THE FORMS OF PASTORAL ROLE-FULFILMENT

The Basic Form: The Gathered Community

Pastoral role-fulfilment—to repeat our theme—is the intermediary of God's coming in his word. God draws near to us as the God who speaks to us. He reveals his name and in his name he discloses the marvel of his presence and availability. He makes public his truth as present reality. In all this he actualizes his salvation.

This one process takes place in three modes; in other words, three "measures"[224] define the field of pastoral role-fulfilment: kerygma, didache, and paraklesis. In the kerygma the word occurs as proclamation of the Kingdom of God: salvation is presented in the here-and-now, the "dubiousness" (German *Fragwürdigkeit*) of the person to whom the proclamation comes is overcome, he becomes the person he is intended to be, and he receives new life. In the didache the word occurs as the voice which points out the way, and the person called to the Kingdom is guided on the way of the new life and initiated into discipleship. In the paraklesis the word occurs as personal address with a view to the contingent situation—the "now-and-thus-ness" of a person—to lead him out of sin and suffering, to orient his life to salvation, to help him to assume his place in the *circle* of the Kingdom and the church which is called to manifest that Kingdom.

[We could also put it this way: the kerygma is the mode of *actualization*: the salvation acquired and promised is actualized in the present in which the word occurs. The kerygma could be viewed as the *point* at which God's reality intersects ours. The didache is the mode of *continuation*: salvation is the way of the Kingdom, the word which points out the way as a *line*—i.e., a point in

---

[224]Note: The word *modus* derives from the root *med-*, "to measure off." *Modus* means first of all "measure," then "mode" or "manner."

motion—along which life renews itself. The paraklesis is the mode of *concentration*: over and over it takes life in all of its situations and relates it to the center of the salvation which has come; the image for paraklesis is the *circle*, the line which unifies everything on one plane, relating it to the center.]

We said earlier that the structural modes are "the existentials" of *the forms in which the pastoral role is fulfilled*.[225] From the perspective of the fundamental structure, which is now clear, we must try to distinguish those forms in their several "uniquenesses."

The forms of pastoral role-fulfilment have only gradually become visible in the history of the church. In the New Testament we encounter a number of words which can be translated "preaching," but no word which could mean "catechesis" or "pastoral care." This is not to say that "catechizing" did not take place or that pastoral care was not provided.[226] But these activities were not yet institutionalized. The things which now take place in preaching, catechizing, and pastoring also took place then, but they were not yet abstracted from the entirety of God's coming in his word through the intermediary of human ministry; the interactions and communications which differed in terms of situation and focus had not yet been objectivized as differing and distinguishable forms of ministry. We must remember that this process is much less advanced even now than it sometimes appears. We speak of preaching, catechizing, and pastoral care; within the field of practical theology we have separate areas of study which occupy themselves with these differing forms of pastoral role-fulfilment. But the moment one starts defining the forms—i.e., setting off the boundaries of a phenomenon from that which is associated with it in the viewer's mind—it turns out that their contours are not all that clear.

[One person may call catechesis "proclamation";[227] but someone else may dispute it.[228] One person may call pastoral care a "special instance of preaching,"[229] and another may counter that it is an independent function of the church.[230] D. Ritschl claims that preaching is pure kerygma and that even direct exposition of Scripture should be kept out of preaching as such.[231] But according to

---

[225]See above, p. 40.

[226]One could probably say that Paul's daily discussions in the hall of Tyrannus in Ephesus (Acts 19:9) constituted a kind of catechizing. In Acts 20:31 Paul mentions an activity we would call pastoral care: ". . . remembering that for three years I did not cease night or day to admonish every one with tears."

[227]Cf. G. Bohne, *Das Wort Gottes und der Unterricht.*

[228]K. Barth, *CD*, I/1, p. 55: "Here Gerh. Bohne's book . . . appears to me to lack a certain needful sobriety." "As such, instruction of youth has to teach, not to convert, not to 'bring to a decision,' and to that extent not to proclaim."

[229]E. Thurneysen, "Rechtfertigung und Seelsorge," in *Zwischen den Zeiten* 6 (1928):210.

[230]A. D. Müller, *Grundriss der praktischen Theologie*, pp. 279ff. Müller develops his concept of pastoral care from the biblical image of Christ as the Good Shepherd who came that his sheep might have life in abundance and who gave his life for the sheep.

[231]D. Ritschl, *Die homiletische Funktion der Gemeinde*, p. 26.

H. Schreiner, preaching is marked by its *Textgebundenheit* ("strict focus on the text"). "The course of preaching takes its departure from a text and offers textual exposition, illumination, and clarification of its message."[232] H. Faber describes pastoral care as "all the pastoral work in which the pastor gives a conscious account to himself of the effect which his part in a conversation or his arguments will have in the psyche of the person or persons who at that moment are involved with him,"[233] but this definition also covers preaching and catechizing. The moment one starts defining concepts they become less clear than they are in current parlance. This may be an indication that the art of definition, in the sense of delimiting phenomena, is not very well possible. Every person defining the phenomena infuses his own views concerning the correct conception of preaching, catechizing, and pastoral care into his definition, but each is able to do this because all of us face the inescapable reality that distinguishing the phenomena is hampered by the impossibility of untangling one from the other and neatly lining them up next to each other.]

If we are to arrive at a clear view of the forms of pastoral role-fulfilment, and at such a definition of each of them that it offers a point of departure for the study of the problems connected with it, then we must build this essential and original unity into our definition. In other words, one will have to define the various forms as variants of one pattern—as the differentiated expressions of *one* basic form.

This basic form may be discovered by observing the specific character of the church's life in the apostolic era. That specific character is not that of an organization in which a number of functionaries were busy working for the benefit of the members; it is much more that it was an utterly unique fellowship in which every member was part of the whole.

[In his study *Das Problem der Urkirche* ("The Problem of the Primitive Church") O. Linton has pointed out that around 1880 there was a prevailing consensus on this problem. People approached it from the perspective of the religious ideal of democratic individualism. "To begin with, there was the devout person as a free Christian. He was the arch-datum of the Christian religion. He and his equals created the churches by joining together." Christians united for practical reasons; the church was not necessary for salvation. It is built from the bottom up. "The part precedes the whole; the entire concept of the church is atomistic."[234] In the more recent literature, continues Linton in his study which appeared in 1932, this consensus has been abandoned. Over against the atomistic-collectivistic idea of the church a very different one is being advanced. "The church does not originate from the fact of people uniting with each other; it does not arise from the action of individuals; it is there before the individual;

---

[232]H. Schreiner, *Die Verkündigung des Wortes Gottes*, p. 227.
[233]H. Faber, *Pastorale Verkenning*, p. 12.
[234]O. Linton, *Das Problem der Urkirche in der neueren Forschung*, pp. 7ff.

the individual joins that church. The church is a creation from above."[235] "The event of becoming a Christian is the process of being saved into fellowship. The Christian is saved out of cohesion with the world and its evil powers and into a new cohesion—out of isolation into the fellowship of the people of God."[236] We have referred to this unique trait earlier in connection with the *mutua consolatio*.[237] We now wish to consider the concrete effect of this idea in the common life of the ancient church.]

Hebrews 10:24 exhorts believers: ". . . let us consider how to stir up one another to love and good works." Immediately following comes the indication how this may be realized: ". . . not neglecting to meet together, . . . but encouraging one another" (v. 25). (Note the Greek construction!) By participating in the life of the church as it assembles,[238] one can take part in mutual paraklesis, stirring up one another to a life of love. We have here more than an exhortation to be faithful in church attendance in order to receive the necessary spiritual food. The point is: *The act of assembling together as a church is the basic form in which the body of Christ functions.* There is no room for doubt, says E. Schweizer, that in the apostolic era "the worship service is by far the main center of the church's life. . . . It is there that the church presents itself as the body of the Lord."[239]

We know only a few details concerning what happened in these assemblies. Still, the main facts are clear. It can be asserted, negatively, that these assemblies did not bear a "cultic" character; sacrifices, priests, sacred spaces, and holy hours were unknown.[240] People assembled out of practical necessity in the homes of believers, in a fairly informal atmosphere.[241] As D. Ritschl remarks, it was the assembling of Christians which made a worship service a worship service. With some oversimplification, one could say, says Ritschl, "that everything could be missing in a service, except the 'assembled congregation.' "[242] As Linton puts it,[243] people were "saved into a new cohesion"; the act of assembling, *synerchesthai*[244] was in itself the full-bodied expression and experience of this fact.

What we know of "the way things went" in the worship services fits into

---

[235]Ibid., p. 133.

[236]Ibid., pp. 151ff.

[237]See above, pp. 74ff.

[238]According to W. Schrage, *TDNT*, VII, 842, s.v. *synagōgē*, it is most natural to think of the congregation gathered for worship.

[239]E. Schweizer, *Gemeinde und Gemeindeordnung*, p. 201.

[240]R. Bultmann, *Theology of the New Testament*, I, 114-15.

[241]It must be remembered here that Paul has serious objections to what Moule calls the "chaotic informality" (*Worship in the New Testament*, p. 63) which prevailed at Corinth (I Cor. 14:33, 40).

[242]D. Ritschl, *Die homiletische Funktion der Gemeinde*, p. 32.

[243]See above.

[244]According to C. Schneider, *TDNT*, II, 684, s.v. *erchomai*, the word in I Corinthians 11:17 "is a technical term for the coming together of the Christian congregation."

this picture whenever people come together: "each one has a hymn, a lesson, a revelation, a tongue, or an interpretation" (I Cor. 14:26; cf. Col. 3:16). Says Moule: "It is worthwhile to notice how far removed this sort of gathering was from most modern types of worship with a single leader and the rest comparatively passive."[245] No specific type of preaching prevails. "The tendency was to allow a diversity of ways, not yet governed by custom or precept, in which the word of Christ could dwell richly in the church assembly (Col. 3:16), honoring it as the Word of the living Lord."[246] The main interest lies in the word of the Lord, but no one has exclusive right to bring it. The word occurs in the magnetic field of a church gathered with Christ by the power of the Holy Spirit. In an atmosphere of *mutuum colloquium*[247] God comes in the modes of kerygma, didache, and paraklesis:[248] in the assembly which is assembly in Christ and in the Spirit the actuality of salvation is proclaimed, the way on which one can walk "in newness of life" is pointed out (Rom. 6:4; cf. Gal. 5:25), and the life of every member, in his or her contingent situation, is related to the center of the life of the entire called-out people of God—the salvation which has appeared in Christ. All this could be called preaching, or catechesis, or pastoral care. It is all these simultaneously or, rather, *it is the fundamental form of the subforms which in time particularized themselves, each of which*, be it in different ways, *is shaped in its fundamental structure by the modes of kerygma, didache, and paraklesis.*

Preaching

The central mode of preaching is kerygma. When the church has come together concretely "in one place"[249] to express that it is one body in Christ, the proclamation occurs which is constitutive for this unity. Salvation is shouted out: "Behold, now is the day of salvation"; "Today, if you hear his voice, harden not your hearts." The Heidelberg Catechism views preaching as the administration of "the keys of the Kingdom" (Lord's Day XXXI). The preacher in the church is another Eliakim who received authority[250] to "be a father" to the people; as minister in the palace, bearer of "the key of the house of David," he is to be

---

[245]C. F. D. Moule, *Worship in the New Testament*, p. 62.

[246]R. Stählin, "Die Geschichte des christlichen Gottesdienstes von der Urkirche bis zur Gegenwart," in K. F. Müller and W. Blankenburg, *Leiturgia: Handbuch des evangelischen Gottesdienstes*, I, 7.

[247]Doerne, *RGG*, III, col. 438, s.v. *Homiletik*.

[248]C. F. D. Moule, *Worship in the New Testament*, p. 65, also uses these concepts to describe the "occurrence" of the word in its diversity in the assemblies of the primitive church.

[249]Cf. the use of *epi to auto* in Acts 2:1, 44, 47; I Corinthians 11:20; 14:23 against the backdrop of the manner in which Paul uses it in I Corinthians 7:5, where it stands for the conjugal act. One could say that *epi to auto* refers to an external togetherness as the expression of an inner unity. The words as used in Acts 4:26 (=Ps. 2:2) can be understood in the same way.

[250]Hebrew *memšālâ*; cf. the use of this word in Genesis 1:16; Psalm 136:9.

a steward of the royal possessions and doorkeeper to the palace (Isa. 22:21-22). This is the typical image of the kerygma: authoritative proclamation, actualization of salvation in the present by speaking and listening; the announcement of the continuing validity of that which happened "once for all" to those who hear it now. We noted earlier that kerygma belongs not only in the missionary situation but also in the established church.[251] We made the point then that the kerygma must take place in the church, particularly because it has never been "now" before and because the person to whom the word comes has never before been *this* person. Every day anew, experiences, problems, worries, expectations, aspirations, and weal and woe in great diversity come to and over a person from within her world and by confrontation with them from within herself. All these things make her the person she now is and make the present in which she lives a unique moment of life: it has never been like this before and she has never been like this before. Then the kerygma comes: the word of the Kingdom, which is and remains different, which is truly *new,* which cuts through all the fear and hope, all the plans and calculations of *this* person *now.* However it may be with her, she is confronted by salvation; salvation confronts her, confronts *this* person—now. Her life, the life of *this* person *now,* again stands at the starting point God has made, is implicated again in salvation, *is now "in Christ."*

And then it begins: the person who is called through the kerygma is placed on the road she has to go in discipleship. It is the road of the church which has to perform the service of the Lord in confessing the name and doing the work of God. It is not as if believers will see salvation light up all in a flash; but they do get a lamp for their feet and a light upon their pathway (Ps. 119:105). They are called into life *in order really to live.* So, next to the central mode of kerygma which strikes the dominant note in preaching is didache, teaching oriented to the continuity of living in salvation.

No further argument is needed to prove that paraklesis rightfully belongs in preaching. Already in the primitive Christian church, according to Doerne, *"logos paraklēseōs"* (Heb. 13:22; Acts 13:15) "became the typical phrase for congregational preaching."[252] It seems questionable whether the passages quoted offer sufficient ground for this unqualified pronouncement. But there can be no question whatsoever that preaching in the church always has to be timely and relevant, in the sense that it comforts people in their present distress, admonishes them concretely for ongoing sin, raises the spirits of the fainthearted, corrects them when they go astray, strengthens them when they falter, restores them to their place in the community. To say that the mode of paraklesis must codetermine the structure of preaching implies that it must be concrete.

Helmut Thielicke has given a fascinating account of the emergence of the ancient error of docetism in the church of our day—not in Christology this time, but in anthropology. "Now we speak of man in an abstract general way, as if

---

[251]See pp. 48ff.
[252]Doerne, *RGG,* V, col. 530, s.v. *Predigt.*

he had only a phantom body";[253] people speak of "man," isolating him from his "world." But no person can be abstracted from "his" world; he is always "in situation." "To be 'in situation', however, can only mean that I stand in vocational, economic, political, erotic, and other relationships to others."[254] The person who is not really addressed in his situation will eventually say: "That sermon did not include me."

The mode of kerygma means: This person "counts" in the preaching because it is made plain to her that she "counts" in the gospel: she is in Christ. The mode of paraklesis means: This person "counts" in the preaching because it addresses her contingent condition: this person—this concrete person in her particular situation—is in Christ and with an appeal to that fact is addressed with a view to her situation.

Catechesis

In catechesis didache is the central mode. After what we have said about didache it seems superfluous to belabor the point. In addition to didache, kerygma belongs to the fundamental structure of catechesis. This is implied in the very definition of catecheis. One could say: not only does God come in his word through catechesis; catechesis is also intense systematic reflection on that word. But the word of God is the form of the Lord's presence: he is always present with it. For that reason the only legitimate way of dealing with Scripture is to listen for and to God speaking. Even when the word of God is material for instruction, God continues to address us in that word. And when the gospel is unfolded as well as its implications made plain, the gospel remains *gospel*, the message of the *mᵉḇaśśēr*. Didache focuses attention on the way of discipleship, on the "from now on" of life in Christ, but that way begins in our exodus from sin and death in Jesus Christ: that "from now on" has its *terminus a quo* in the "once-for-all" of Christ's death and resurrection. The way can never be seen as the way of destination for this particular person when she does not know herself as a "called-out" one; the resolution of "from now on" can never elicit her interest when she was not herself implicated in the turning point of the ages. The way in which kerygma occurs in catechesis can be put aside for now; but the fact that kerygma occurs where didache really takes place seems to us, considering the nature and content of didache, incontrovertible.

Catechesis also embraces paraklesis. The fact that its structure is codetermined by paraklesis derives from the reality that God's coming in his word is his coming into the concrete existence of the person who hears it. No person, no young person, is an abstraction: she is what she is in her situation. She is touched by suffering, assaulted by inner doubts, and discouraged, troubled by sin and error. Didache teaches her the way; but she knew the way and sometimes lost it. She belongs to the church, is in the covenant, but sometimes isolates

---

[253]H. Thielicke, *The Trouble with the Church: A Call for Renewal*, p. 67.
[254]Ibid., p. 73.

herself from the fellowship or feels excluded. She longs for the sense of connectedness and then again experiences the bonds as oppressive. One cannot say
that in all these cases pastoral care is in order, in the sense of personal therapy.
In some cases perhaps, but in any case paraklesis belongs to catechesis with a
view to the special problems of being youthful at a certain time and in a specific
culture. In fact, paraklesis in the catechetical situation can be especially effective
and fruitful because of its direct connection with, and subordination to, the
central mode of didache. When a young person is confronted directly and personally with admonition or encouragement, she may get the feeling that someone
else is meddling in private matters or trying to curry favor. But in the paraklesis
which occurs implicitly or is in any case connected with the teaching, it may
become evident to her that the focus of the concern is to discover or to rediscover
the way which the called-out ones have to go as disciples of Jesus.

Pastoral Care

The central mode of pastoral care is paraklesis. Having said this, we must
immediately recall that paraklesis is a function particularly of the church as
fellowship-in-Christ. Assembling for worship and mutual paraklesis are both
expressions of being-the-one-body-in-Christ. Doing paraklesis, one could say,
is itself a matter of "coming together," and so an expression of oneness-in-
Christ, i.e., in his body, the church. In the ancient church paraklesis was practiced particularly in the church assemblies. In many cases it could be practiced
there; people knew each other; they met in a small, familiar circle. As the church
grows, there is a diminution of closeness; and as worship becomes more tightly
structured, mutual paraklesis has to be shifted to private dialogue or take place
in a small circle (e.g., the family). But even then it is a coming together,
synerchesthai, in the full sense of the word; the church is manifest there, and
Christ appears "in the midst of them" (Matt. 18:20). Even then there appears
the magnetic field which is the church gathered by the Holy Spirit—the power
sphere in which the word "comes to pass" and God is present.

This is not to be understood as if a pastoral encounter is a worship-service-
in-miniature and the conversation which takes place in it is a specialized instance
of preaching, as Thurneysen put it. In our opinion one must construe the relation
between preaching and pastoral care differently. What we now call a church
service and what we may call a pastoral encounter—at a home visit, by a
sickbed, or in a pastor's study, for instance—both originated in the coming
together, being together *epi to auto,* of the church in apostolic times.

That "coming together" is the fundamental form; and the structure of the
word-coming-to-pass in that fundamental form (kerygma, didache, paraklesis)
remains decisive for the particularized forms of preaching and pastoral care
which in time developed from the fundamental form. The differentiation consists
in the fact that in each form another mode is central: in preaching it is kerygma;
in pastoral care, paraklesis.

The content and purpose of paraklesis became clear to us when we discussed this mode. Now, speaking of pastoral care, we will highlight just one point from that discussion. "To comfort" in the Old Testament, as we saw earlier, is "to comfort out of sorrow." Paraklesis is liberating; it draws a person into the light. Paraklesis is never a matter of stringing together words which people have often heard before, or as Job puts it, "strengthening with the mouth" (Job 16:2-5); paraklesis is helping, redeeming deed.[255]

Paraklesis can be this deed because it is done "with an appeal to the mercies of God."[256] On them it leans; from them it proceeds; to them it restores the afflicted or erring person. But then, as a consequence, paraklesis can never be isolated from the mode of kerygma. Sometimes that needs to be strongly stressed: "Behold, now is the acceptable time; now is the day of salvation"; "Today, if you hear his voice, harden not your hearts." Paraklesis can run aground in a situation where it is not simultaneously intersected by the other reality of salvation, of the Kingdom, of the forgiveness which is offered. It is not true that pastoral care has then reached its culmination and become really pastoral.[257] It is true that kerygma, the presupposition of paraklesis, cannot always be the silent premise. Pastoral care, says H. O. Wölber, is "a purely human activity. We attempt to return the heart to the right place and the mind from the abysses before which we humans stand."[258] Job longed for that purely human activity, and many after him have longed for it, perhaps most at the time they had a preaching "pastor" sitting by them. But at the same time Wölber comments: "Basically we have to say: what has to happen in the pastoral care we extend to one another is the call to believe.[259] But that call is possible only when the possibility of appeal to the gospel is present or when the kerygma "comes to pass."

Paraklesis is directed to the contingent situation, the condition of being "now-and-such." In many instances its focus will be turned to the momentary and nonrecurring aspects of a situation; but most often attention will have to be given to the continuing and enduring. It will always have to be remembered that all of life is discipleship and every situation must be experienced in discipleship. For that reason didache, too, belongs to pastoral care. In some instances, the emphasis will even have to be put there. The boundary between teaching and pastoral care in general is fluid.

We shall now summarize our discussion of the forms of pastoral role-

---

[255]Viewed in this light the construal of the distinction between *pastoral care* as a ministry of admonition oriented to personal sins and the *diaconate* as a ministry of helping oriented to suffering seems to be incorrect. See P. J. Roscam Abbing, *Diakonia*, p. 261. We wonder whether what we call the "diaconate" is not a special concretization of the mode of paraklesis expressed within the form of pastoral care.

[256]We remind the reader of what we said about "the parakletic formula" (pp. 71-72).

[257]So H. Asmussen, *Die Seelsorge,* and the somewhat more nuanced Thurneysen.

[258]H. O. Wölber, *Tröste mich wieder,* p. 33.

[259]Ibid., pp. 31ff.

fulfilment. Out of the original and fundamental form of being together *epi to auto* (I Cor. 11:20; 14:23), *en ekklēsia* (I Cor. 11:18), the three derivative forms developed: that of preaching in the worship service; that of deliberate and more or less systematic teaching (catechesis), and that of the more incidental pastoral care. God's coming in his word through pastoral role-fulfilment occurs in all three forms. The fundamental form is always preserved in the sense that the "coming together" in each of the forms is a "coming together" as the church, which is one body in Christ. The modes in which the word occurs determine the structure of each of the forms, in each of which one of the modes is central.

In this study, we said, we shall limit ourselves in the main to the three forms referred to. This is not to say, however, that there are no other forms of pastoral role-fulfilment, or that there could not be any, and certainly not that these forms are bound to the classic structures of the worship service, the catechism class, or the pastoral encounter.

A variety of structures are conceivable in which the pastoral role could and does function: training camps, inter-, super-, and paraparochial groups and circles, as well as the difficult-to-define structures originating in and through the mass media.[260] Such structures bring into being a new set of structural and functional problems. We cannot enter now on a discussion of these specific problems. It seems to us that these questions can be squarely addressed only when we have a conceptual apparatus with which to treat the fundamental problems of pastoral role-fulfilment in general. The aim of this study is to explore only a few possibilities in that direction.

13. DYNAMIC MOMENTS IN PASTORAL ROLE-FULFILMENT

God's coming in his word through the intermediary of pastoral role-fulfilment has a *dynamic structure,* we have said. With that word combination we tried to indicate that this phenomenon has a stable pattern, a permanent fundamental structure, but that it still may not be conceived as something "object-like," something "object-ive." A *coming* occurs, a word "comes to pass," there is action in role-fulfilment, and all this assumes the fundamental form of

---

[260]H. Vogel, "Rundfunk und Fernsehen als Kommunikationsmittel der christlichen Wahrheit," *Evangelische Theologie*, 158ff., raises the question *whether* the mass media can serve the truth of God which is "personal, relational, and communicative." This question will have to be borne in mind as we search for answers to the question *how* this may be. Words like "radio audience" and "TV viewers"—the very terms suggest an isolation which is alien to the word-event—indicate the problem. [The reader may wish to pursue consideration of the impossibility, or near impossibility, or possibilities of presenting Christian truth through mass media by reading Martin E. Marty, *The Improper Opinion: Mass Media and the Christian Faith,* in the series Westminster Studies in Christian Communication. *Tr.*]

a *being together in interaction and communication*—every one of these concepts and all of them together are full of dynamics. This became plain also in the concepts we use to describe the structural modes: a proclamation is made (kerygma), instruction and guidance are provided (didache), one goes to another in his contingent situation to bring him back, to strengthen, to correct, to comfort, to admonish (paraklesis).

According to H. Jonker, practical theology has two basic principles. He takes his starting point from Hebrews 4:12 and 13. "The word of God is pictured here, not as a speculative datum, a human projection, or an existential expression, but as a saving reality which comes from the outside and addresses itself to human beings in the form of an urgent and penetrating message." God *deals* with us in his word. "This dynamic activity of the word of God is the first fundamental principle of Practical Theology." The second fundamental principle is expressed in the same text and that "by the fact that this dynamic actuality of the word of God addresses itself to human beings in the vivid concreteness of their totality as soul and body."[261] These two fundamental principles make practical theology a discipline which does not ask, in the first place, what and how a thing *is*, but raises questions like: What is happening and how can it happen?

In other words, practical theology is interested especially in something that is not tangible and cannot be "nailed down," because it is a *movement*. It is not a movement which comes to a stop somewhere down the line, but a movement which itself generates movement: a movement which addresses itself to human beings and then mobilizes them. If now we wish to have at our disposal a model that can help us face the questions which practical theology must address, then the element of a "motion-generating movement" must be given a distinct place in that model. It will have to be abstracted from the whole in which it is the very life, and not just a part.

With an eye to this goal we distinguish *dynamic moments*[262] next to the structural modes, but not of course apart from them. When the "dynamic actuality of the word of God addresses itself to human beings in their concreteness," when God enters into communication with them, then a magnetic field arises in which "lines of power" run. From within God's initiative arises a live relatedness between God and people—and then something *happens*. Sometimes it happens that one person says something to another and the other feels that after those words have been spoken, she is not the same anymore: she has been damaged, or enriched, for life. Such "a word" did not return "empty" to the speaker, like a boomerang which missed. The word God speaks never misses: it is a movement

---

[261]H. Jonker, *Woord en Existentie als Probleem der praktische Theologie,* inaugural address (Utrecht, 1959), p. 5.

[262]We speak of "moments" because this word carries with it the notion of "movement." [Lat. *momentum,* fr. earlier (assumed) *movimentum,* fr. *movere,* to move. *Webster's Third New International Dictionary. Tr.*]

which sets everything in motion: ". . . as the rain and the snow come down from heaven, and return not thither but water the earth, making it bring forth and sprout, giving seed to the sower and bread to the eater, so shall my word be . . ." (Isa. 55:10-11).

What then are those dynamic moments, those "lines of power" which run in the magnetic field where the word works? In other words, Of what movement is pastoral role-fulfilment the intermediary? In order to "nail that down" we must ask again: What is the word? Earlier we saw: the word a person speaks is the form in which that person betakes himself or herself to another in order to enter that person's thoughts, feelings, and experience. But the same thing can happen in still another way. The word must also have something specifically appropriate for this form of participation in the life of another.

The Hebrew concept *dābār* can illumine this specificity for us. According to Procksch, *dābār* is not to be taken in the indefinite sense of a saying but "as the definite content or meaning of a word." Everything has its *dābār*, that is, a background and meaning. The *dābār* concept turns out to have two main components which are theologically highly important. First, there is the dianoetic element: the *dābār* contains a thought which displays the meaning of a thing. "By its *dābār* a thing is known and becomes subject to thought. To grasp the *dābār* of a thing is to grasp the thing itself." But along with the dianoetic is the dynamic element. Every *dābār* is filled with power; everyone who receives the word and takes it in experiences this power.[263] Thinking along this line we can perhaps also say: The word has the power to clarify, by which understanding arises; and the power to influence, by which change occurs.

In the first instance we look at the word itself as referential: it denominates a reality. Something exists: a thing, a feeling, an opinion, a conception, or an image—and that something is then put into a word. What is the intent of verbalization? This: that another person to whom the word comes may begin to understand what has been turned into speech. The word-symbol uncovers for him the thing to which the speaker refers—at least to the extent that the speaker knows the thing and the symbol is apt and intelligible. If the knowledge of the speaker were complete and the aptness and intelligibility of the word-symbol perfect, the word would lead to complete understanding of a thing. The lie— the untruthful and perverted word—aims at obscuring or concealing a thing; it intends to deceive, to cause someone to live in a dream world full of specters, to lead a person into confusion. A true word, i.e., the word that is true and truly a word, seeks to clarify, to make transparent, in order that the other person may arrive at the most nearly perfect understanding of a thing.

When the word is truly word this element—the power to clarify in order to create understanding—is always present in it. This is true of all those familiar expressions which fill our existence to the rim: "Fine weather today!"; "Close the door, please!"; "Good to see you!"; "Did you hear the joke about . . . ?";

---

[263]O. Procksch, *TDNT,* IV, 92, s.v. *legō.*

etc., etc. Those "words," too, feed the understanding; they offer something the addressee needs to know at this moment, or an indication that the speaker wants contact, or a sign of interest in the other person. But their intention is not that they may continue to affect the addressee. For that reason one cannot make the unqualified judgment that the second element—the power to influence in order to effect change—is always present in them.[264] Some words attain their purpose just by being spoken. Still, this element is probably never totally absent. It sometimes happens that simple offhand words, spoken without any deliberate intent have a more lasting effect. When a person has heard a word and gained some new understanding, however trivial, that person is no longer exactly the same as before.

The word of God, too, aims to create understanding and change. God does not speak deceptive words; he never says anything offhandedly to pass the time. His word is truly word and word of truth. His word names his name: he helps us understand who he is, what he is for us; he thus makes us other people who may live in the knowledge of his name and who may call on the name. His word reveals the truth: he leads us out of our delusions into understanding and discernment of reality; he changes us so that we do not need to run our lives by what is deceptive and changing. The word of God actualizes salvation; he makes us understand that all things are new, and causes us to walk in newness of life. His word is the form of his presence: it is our prerogative to know him in his word and to live with him, drawing our life from his word.

These two dynamic moments in pastoral role-fulfilment—as intermediary of the word which creates understanding and change—we call the *hermeneutic moment* and the *agogic moment.* Later on we shall explain these terms more fully, but even at first sight their meanings may be clear: the word offers material for understanding and constitutes a "directive" address to other persons. These moments, as we have remarked, can only be conceptually abstracted from the modes of which they are the "power." This applies also to their mutual relationship: the *hermeneia*—the function of bringing to light and creating understanding— is simultaneously a process of leading to change, to living in the light;[265] the agogy—leading to change, the power to become new *in concretis*—is also an illumination and the opening of perspective. The distinction between the two moments does not, of course, imply a separation. We break them apart here only because—with a view to the one as well as to the other—it is necessary to investigate both the possibilities for, and the demands to be made of, pastoral role-fulfilment. In the model we are constructing (and a model, remember, is

---

[264]O. Procksch (ibid.) also says of the dynamic element that it does not always come to such clear expression as the dianoetic.

[265]Cf. G. Ebeling, *Theology and Proclamation,* p. 28: the exposition event is at bottom this, "that it brings men to the truth in such a way that at the same time it both reveals and transforms reality."

only an artificial construct of the real thing) these moments reveal the nodal points at which practical theology must address its questions to other disciplines.

14. THE HERMENEUTIC MOMENT

It would surely be defensible to consider the entire problematics of practical theology—and certainly the doctrine of pastoral role-fulfilment—as a hermeneutic problematic. The central theme of the doctrine of pastoral role-fulfilment is God's coming in his word through the intermediary of pastoral role-fulfilment. This role-fulfilment is therefore characterized as a ministry of the word, i.e., an essentially hermeneutic activity. If we now speak of "the hermeneutic moment" in pastoral role-fulfilment, it is not our intention to reduce this primary trait to a "mere" moment. Pastoral role-fulfilment is hermeneutic or it is not pastoral role-fulfilment, nor intermediary of God's coming. Nor can it be agogic if it is not primarily and continually hermeneutic.

From the preceding it will have become clear that by "hermeneutic" we do not mean to refer to the task of scriptural exposition. The word "hermeneutic" could suggest that; many people, when they hear of "hermeneutics," will think first of all, or exclusively, of "the doctrine of the exposition of Scripture," and then perhaps take the words "hermeneutic moment" as an indication of what one may expect from pastoral role-fulfilment, namely, that it clarifies the words of Scripture and does this in accordance with certain hermeneutic rules. We view this activity, however, as a *function* of didache, the second mode of pastoral role-fulfilment, not as a *moment,* i.e., a motion-generating movement, in the totality of that role-fulfilment.

If "hermeneutic" in this context is not a reference to hermeneutics, in the sense of the doctrine of scriptural exposition, then what does it mean? According to Gerhard Ebeling, the word "hermeneutic" has an additional, an even more primary, meaning. We offer here a summary of his explanation.[266] Hermeneutics—as "the theory of the exposition of texts"—is necessary because there are factors which hinder the proper understanding of texts. The language in which the texts are written may not be intelligible to us and has to be interpreted: that interpretation must occur in accordance with well-defined rules and cannot be done arbitrarily. By means of interpretation an understanding of the text is rendered possible. The text, the language, the word, in that case, is the object of understanding. But this is not the real function of the word. "The word is not really the object of understanding. . . . Rather, the word is what opens up and mediates understanding, i.e., brings something to understanding. *The word itself has a hermeneutic function.*" "The primary phenomenon in the realm of

---

[266]G. Ebeling, *Word and Faith,* pp. 305ff.

understanding is not understanding OF language, but understanding THROUGH language."[267]

According to J. Behm, "On the Greek view, one of the gifts proper to man is the creative gift of *hermēneia*" by which we human beings are able to share with each other the good things of life. To a special degree this gift belongs to the poet; he is interpreter of the gods.[268] The task of Hermes, messenger of the gods, is described as *hermēneuein*. "He was credited with the invention of the things which serve understanding, especially speech and writing."[269] In addition to this, *hermēneia* can mean exposition, translation, and commentary.[270]

When we speak of "the hermeneutic moment in pastoral role-fulfilment," we have in mind the first meaning of *hermēneia* and *hermēneuein*: that which serves understanding. *The word in which God comes to people is hermeneia, and when that word-event occurs in pastoral role-fulfilment, a power is at work which leads to understanding.*

It is important to note that, especially in the religious sphere, the word does not always function in that manner. We have seen that according to Procksch the Hebrew word contains a dianoetic element first of all and then also a dynamic element. In the primitive conception of language there is first of all, and virtually exclusively, a dynamic element; the function of language is "not to depict or to communicate, but to effect."[271] The cultic or magic formula does not have to be understood, cannot even be understood, and does not intend to lead to understanding; it effects blessing or curse on condition that it is pronounced in exact accordance with the rules.

The Old Testament also knows the power of cursing or blessing; and Yahweh takes protective measures for the deaf person who cannot offer verbal resistance to curses pronounced over him (Lev. 19:14; cf. Ps. 38:13-14). But the cursing or blessing of God is pronounced in intelligible language; they are both held before people in order that they may choose (Deut. 30:1, 11ff.), but with the appeal: therefore choose life, i.e., the blessing (Deut. 30:19). Yahweh did not speak in secret (Isa. 45:19; 48:16) but in a way that people could hear and know (Isa. 40:28). God's word is a clear, articulated word. When at Pentecost people begin to speak by the power of the Holy Spirit, the effect is that people are beside themselves with astonishment, not because they hear strange, supernatural sounds, but because they hear the apostles speaking *in their own tongues*, i.e., in their own native languages, of "the mighty works of God" (Acts 2:8, 11). The surprising thing about the word in which God comes is not that it hits us in numinous sounds but that it sounds ordinary and familiar. God speaks our

---

[267]Ibid., p. 318.

[268]J. Behm, *TDNT*, II, 663, s.v. *hermēneia*.

[269]G. Ebeling, *RGG*, III, col. 243, s.v. *Hermeneutik*.

[270]Cf. J. M. Robinson, "Hermeneutic since Barth," in J. M. Robinson and J. B. Cobb, Jr., eds., *The New Hermeneutic*, p. 6.

[271]Sløk, *RGG*, VI, col. 268ff., s.v. *Sprache und Religion*.

mother tongue. He comes into our homes, speaking where—as Fuchs remarks somewhere—"one does not speak so that people may understand but *because* people understand,"[272] where understanding occurs in a relationship which was there before. Fuchs says elsewhere: "What is it now that marks speech as speech? Not the mere act of giving names to things . . . , not mere information, but a special power of understanding to create understanding, in which one person causes herself or himself to be understood by another. . . ."[273] God does not first offer a morsel of information for us to understand; he offers himself for us to understand. He draws near to us, discloses to us his name and his truth so that we may live in his salvation and his fellowship. He addresses us in our mother tongue, in the language of home and confidential colloqui, in order that we shall know him as—what he is for us—our Father whose heart is warm toward us.[274] "My heart says to thee: thou hast said, 'Seek ye my face'; thy face, LORD, do I seek!" (Ps. 27:8) [translation of Dutch original, *Tr.*].

When God offers himself to us for understanding, this means that the person to whom he comes in his word also begins to understand herself or himself. Says Ebeling: ". . . it is the nature of the word to illumine that which is dark, to bring light into darkness. As such, if it is the Word which concerns all men unconditionally, it is able to show men the truth of what they really are."[275] God offers himself to us for understanding—and then the reality of the person to whom the word comes springs open. The Father speaks in our mother tongue; now we learn who we are; the light dawns: I am lost, but nevertheless God's child—he speaks to me, comes to me, and he expects I will come to him. The Lord Jesus calls this moment of illumination "coming to oneself" (Luke 15:17). To come to oneself is to become aware again of home and the Father, and to see clearly the misery into which one has plunged himself, the misery of the Father's child away from home. It implies "a shattering of all pseudo-strongholds, to the moment when man becomes aware of his inner self, and regards himself solely in terms of his real relationship to God."[276]

Martin Buber passes on a story told by Rabbi Hanokh: "There was once a man who was very stupid. When he got up in the morning it was so hard for

---

[272]E. Fuchs, "The New Testament and the Hermeneutical Problem," in J. M. Robinson and J. B. Cobb, Jr., eds., *The New Hermeneutic,* p. 124.

[273]E. Fuchs, "Das hermeneutische Problem," in E. Dinkler, *Zeit und Geschichte,* p. 364.

[274]When we say that God offers himself to our understanding, this does not mean that God's mystery is thereby decoded. R. Bultmann, *Jesus Christ and Mythology,* pp. 43-44, makes the point: ". . . to understand does not mean to explain rationally. I can understand, for example, what friendship, love and faithfulness mean, and precisely by genuinely understanding I know that the friendship, love and faithfulness which I personally enjoy are a mystery which I cannot but thankfully receive." "The fact that . . . the gracious God is my God remains forever a mystery . . . because it is inconceivable that he should encounter me in his word as the gracious God."

[275]G. Ebeling, *Theology and Proclamation,* p. 28.

[276]J. H. Bavinck, *An Introduction to the Science of Missions,* pp. 123-24.

him to find his clothes that at night he almost hesitated to go to bed for thinking of the trouble he would have on waking. One evening he finally made a great effort, took paper and pencil, and as he undressed noted down exactly where he put everything he had on. The next morning, very well pleased with himself, he took the slip of paper in hand and read: 'cap'—there it was, he set it on his head; 'pants'—there it lay, he got into them; and so it went until he was fully dressed. 'That's all very well, but now where am I myself?' he asked in great consternation. 'Where in the world am I?' He looked and looked, but it was a vain search; he could not find himself. 'And that is how it is with us,' said the rabbi."[277] The story makes us think of something Jesus said: "For what will it profit a man if he gains the whole world and forfeits his life?" (Matt. 16:26). The person who has the world by the tail, so to speak, or the person in the story ("very well pleased with himself, he took the slip of paper") has not yet found life. Sometimes—not always—it suddenly comes over us: "Where in the world am I? And what do I do with myself?" Sometimes we sense this "forfeiture of soul," this condition of being estranged from the Father, from life itself, from ourselves. It comes over us when we enter the magnetic field in which the word occurs. *Then God comes* to us—and when it happens a person comes to herself or himself. A person begins *to understand*: it is understanding of one's misery achieved through the gospel which is the word of life.[278] This understanding is life, C. Aalders remarks: "It has always been the secret of the true Christian posture that it knew *what it meant to be human*. And out of this understanding flowed all the expressions of life, without prejudice or compulsion. They arranged themselves into a meaningful coherence and bore the inimitable stamp of an inner assurance. Human creativity thus acquires the character of an answer to a higher calling."[279] "This marvelously enlightened knowing is one of the most characteristic properties of what Christianity has ever called 'faith.' "

It is only when God comes to us in his word that human understanding begins and this enlightened knowing has a start. But that coming of God is not a chance occurrence. He offers himself to us and causes us to understand ourselves where there is a coming-together in the Lord; where, through the intermediary of pastoral role-fulfilment, the proclamation of salvation occurs *hic-et-nunc* (kerygma), where "directive" wisdom is voiced (didache), and where persons are addressed in their actual situation and are led out of sin and sorrow by consolation and admonition (paraklesis).

Does it really happen? Massive scepticism and disillusionment about pastoral role-fulfilment in preaching, catechesis, and pastoral care are all around

---

[277]M. Buber, *Tales of the Hasidim (The Later Masters)*, p. 314.

[278]G. Wingren, *The Living Word*, p. 13: "Men understand themselves aright and receive true human life in the hearing of God's Word. The Word reaches the objective for which it was sent out only when it effects an entrance into men. Man reaches the spring out of which he can draw human life only when the Word of the Creator comes to him."

[279]C. Aalders, *Terug naar de Medicina Sacra*, pp. 36ff.

us—more than we can or need to detail here. Even when comments are mild criticism is implied: sermons are "fair,' catechism instruction "pretty good," a pastoral conversation "pleasant." It is as if a dim nightlight were burning, enabling a person to sit around in comfort. But no one entered a bright circle of illumination, no discoveries were made, and, worst of all, no one made gains in self-understanding. To put it in terms of the story told by Rabbi Hanokh: people became smarter about the things written down on a slip of paper: "This is here and that is there"—but no gains were made in relation to the question of life, to say nothing of the answers.

The task of practical theology is to study the questions connected with pastoral role-fulfilment and its function of leading people to understanding. A variety of problems announce themselves. We shall name a few, more or less at random. What does it mean "to understand"? Are there different ways of understanding and, if so, which are the most relevant from the perspective of pastoral theology? What route does the process of coming to understanding follow; how can it be started and guided? How can a word serve, or hinder, this process? What should be the structure of preaching, of instruction, of a dialogue, with a view to *hermeneia*? What is "language"; what does it mean "to speak"; what language should be spoken in certain situations and how should it be used? Practical theology can offer answers to these and similar questions only if it consults other disciplines. For that purpose it must formulate its questions in a way which makes them operational for those other disciplines.

It would take us outside the design of this study to continue this line of questioning. For us it is adequate to state that *hermeneia*—that which brings understanding—is one of the lines of power in the dynamic structure of pastoral role-fulfilment. In the following section our attention will be focused on the other dynamic moment—that of agogy.

15. THE AGOGIC MOMENT

The Word "Agogy"

A real coming to understanding implies, as we have already indicated, a process of change. This is impressively shown in the concluding words of Job: ". . . I have uttered what I did not understand. . . . I had heard of thee by the hearing of the ear, but now my eye sees thee; therefore I despise myself, and repent in dust and ashes" (Job 42:3, 5-6). God has caused Job to understand him and now Job is "in place"—he has become the person he is and is intended to be. When the subject is the agogic moment (the motive power generating change), we are talking about something other than the hermeneutic moment (the motive power generating understanding). In discussing the agogic moment, however, we bring into view another aspect of the same matter. The question is now: What must pastoral role-fulfilment be like, as intermediary of the coming of God in his word, if it is to serve God's purpose of making the people to whom he comes new people?

Before we concern ourselves in the next few sections with this question, we must make clear what we mean by the term "agogic moment"; in so doing we must also consider the problems which arise when the concepts "pastoral role-fulfilment" and "agogic" are in some fashion correlated. And finally, by way of concluding the part about pastoral role-fulfilment, we must say something about an issue which was persistently present in this part but which we have ignored till now, namely, that of the relationship between God's action and human action; in other words, the question about the nature of pastoral role-fulfilment as being *intermediary*.

First, a remark or two about the term "agogic moment." The use of the word "agogy" is of fairly recent date. Words like "pedagogy," "demagogy," and in lesser measure "psychagogy" have been known and current much longer. When S. Strasser makes the remark, "Some speak nowadays of '-agogy,' by which they understand the giving of help and guidance to people in general," his use of the hyphen before "agogy" indicates his reluctance to adopt a growing usage. The way in which this usage has come about is clear. Since the Enlightenment a variety of activities have arisen which aim to help adults achieve greater real maturity—so-called "education of the working classes," "adult education," "people's university." This work has a "pedagogic" character. No sooner do we use the word "pedagogic," however, than the question comes up whether it is correct. The word embraces the Greek word *pais* (child, boy), and if there is one thing of which we need to be aware, both with regard to practice and its theory, it is that we are dealing not with children but with adults. There may be an importat similarity between this work and what we call the nurture of children or "pedagogy," but there are also important differences. An obvious solution to the problem was to dissolve the compound "ped-agogy." This freed up "agogy" for use in new connections and served as an indication of what child-nurture and work that offers help and guidance to adults have in common. Next to pedagogy new compounds could be coined like "andragogy" and possibly also "gerontagogy."[280]

[A number of objections can be lodged against this procedure. There is first the history of the Greek word *paidagōgia*. That history is, in broad strokes, as follows. There was in Greek the word *agōgē*, derived from the verb *agein* whose central meaning is "to guide," "to lead"; *agōgē* refers to the concrete activity of guidance: the act of directing either a human being or an animal. In well-to-do Greek families a slave was given responsibility for the *agōgē* of a child. Initially he was something like a nursemaid: he took the child out and accompanied it to school; gradually he began to contribute to the upbringing of the child. Such a slave was called a *paidagōgos*, i.e., the one who is charged

---

[280]Cf., e.g., H. Hanselmann, *Andragogik*. [Hanselmann, whose sensitivities clearly predate the feminist era, proposes "andragogy" for adult education. *Tr.*]

with the *agōgē* of the child. Because many slaves had the same job, the fulfilment of this task was viewed as an independent phenomenon, called *paidagōgia*, which consisted in being a *paidagōgos*, and then also the giving of aid and guidance to a child. *Paidagōgia*—and the same applies to *dēmagōgia* and *psychagōgia*—is not a compound created by connecting *pais* and *agōgia*, but a development of *paidagōgos*. The word *agōgia* does not even occur in Greek. What this all comes down to is probably this: from the concrete tasks of a *paidagōgos* came the general notion of giving help and guidance to a child; it was not the case that a general concept of agogy arose from a variety of forms of guidance. This wasn't even possible: pedagogy and demagogy differ not only in terms of their object but are almost completely opposite in terms of content, the kind of *agōgē* each tends to offer.

If we now speak of agogy in general, it implies that we believe we can arrive at a general concept. However, it is not so general that it embraces both pedagogy and demagogy; it embraces pedagogy and "andragogy." The fact that "pedagogy" has been treated as though it were composed of *pais* and *agōgia* is a minor objection. More objectionable is the issue of the dissociation. There are various types of composite words. In the word combination "saddle horse" the first member qualifies the second: a horse can be a saddle horse or a draft horse. But—to remain in "pedagogic" context—a word of the type "kindergarten" is a different matter. A kindergarten is not a species of the genus "Garten," of which there would also be an "Erwachsenengarten." Composite words of this type do not specify but name a genus. This is not what originally happened with the word "pedagogy"—the *paidagōgos* was *agōgos*, guide, escort, or nurse for a child, but there were other guides as well—instead, pedagogy has been promoted to a word of the type "kindergarten." Pedagogy is not agogy applied to the child and her situation; the concept is altogether determined by its relation to the child.]

Despite these objections we still continue to speak of an "agogic moment." The choice of this term is somewhat of an embarrassment. We are concerned to point out something which can best be compared with pedagogy, but which is not pedagogical because it usually lacks the orientation to the child and her situation. What's more: in our use of the term "agogic moment" we do not mean the moment of "*agōgē*" (the act of guiding).[281] One could speak of "pastoral agogy" as a function to be fulfilled in the forms of catechesis or pastoral care, but we now have in view a motive force inherent in the coming of God in his word and therefore in its intermediary, pastoral role-fulfilment. It is a motive force which activates the person on whom it is focused, so that that person begins to change. Because of its original Greek meaning and the color it has by association with "pedagogy," the word "agogy" expresses well the nature of that force.

---

[281]*Agōgē* is pronounced ə'gōjē (*Webster's Third New International Dictionary*, p. 43).

Is There Room for "Agogy" in the Pastoral Role?

Because of the undeniable kinship between the concept "agogic moment" and "agogy," we must now comment on the issue of the relationship between proclamation (preaching, pastoral care) and agogy.

According to K. Fezer, a basic ambivalence is to be noted in the homiletic theories which have prevailed since Schleiermacher.[282] On the one hand, preaching is characterized as "missionary, pedagogical, and pastoral," and also "psychagogic."[283] According to this view, preaching is "a work done on behalf of the congregation." Here the individual sermon, by proclaiming the gospel, (ideally) always tries consciously and methodically, with a sure touch, to reach a clearly defined goal which lies not in the sermon itself but specifically in the religious consciousness of the congregation concerned. Over against this is the view that preaching must be "cultic," an expression of the religious life of the congregation, given in the form of an artistic presentation. At bottom, then, it is an activity not *for,* but *of,* the congregation.[284]

As one of the objections against the first point of view, Fezer mentions that here preaching is built upon "the religious-ethical imperfection of the congregation." Preaching is an activity, then, "which has a place in the Christian church not insofar as it is a Christian church but much more insofar as it is not yet a Christian church." A practical consequence of this would be that in this view it would be "impossible to establish that the call of the sermon would be equally binding for all members of the congregation." The most serious objection, according to Fezer, is that on this view the congregation becomes an object to the preacher and—at least for the duration of the sermon—is forced into passivity. After explaining his objection to the second view, Fezer points out that both conceptions suffer from the same basic error: a wrong focus on the anthropocentric.[285] Over against both conceptions he then lays down a concept of preaching which is "radically theocentric": "Preaching is the effort of a person, by means of free speech, to help work toward the end that God, who offers us his fellowship in the word of Scripture, may become communally present by the Holy Spirit to a circle of other people."[286]

[J. J. Stam also turns against both of these conceptions. The preacher "is not the educator of the congregation, nor the exponent of its Christianity. Thank God he isn't! He is a person called by God whose mandate it is to proclaim the Word of God. He is the sower of the Word, whose privilege and therefore whose duty it is to let God do with it what pleases him. God himself . . . is the real

---

[282]K. Fezer, *Das Wort Gottes und die Predigt,* pp. 28ff.

[283]Fezer mentions as representatives of this tradition Vinet, Nitzsch, Achelis, Baumgarten, Hering, Kleinert, Sachsse, Niebergall, Wurster, and Meyer.

[284]For this perspective Fezer lists Schleiermacher, Alexander Schweizer, Palmer, Bassermann, Krauss, Spitta, Smendt, and Eckert.

[285]K. Fezer, *Das Wort Gottes,* pp. 57ff.

[286]Ibid., p. 77.

Preacher by his Holy Spirit."[287] "Preaching is not intended to 'bring up' the members of the congregation—to help them along on the way to perfection. . . . The preacher is no pedagogue. . . . By means of preaching God places people in confrontation with himself. . . . Preaching is the 'severely merciful' effort of God to let people live."[288]]

In the field of poimenics as well people have raised their voices against every effort to link the proclamation of the word of God with "nurture." The essential mandate of the church, according to H. Asmussen, lies "beyond the pedagogue's task."[289]

[Asmussen makes a distinction between *Seelsorge* (pastoral care), which he describes as "the proclamation of the word of God to the individual,"[290] and *Seelenführung*, as "the deliberate education of the congregation."[291] *Seelenführung* is "a matter of the law"[292] and as such "alien work" to a pastor.[293] In *Seelenführung* the pastor acts as a specialist in religious affairs;[294] its purpose is to create a public opinion "appropriate" for the church.[295] But pastoral care is proclamation of the gospel. *Seelenführung* occurs especially in giving advice; in pastoral care the reference is exclusively by way of proclamation to the faith and the means of grace. "If it were true that advice had a genuine place in pastoral care, then it would also be true that righteousness comes from the law."[296]]

In the Netherlands Du Boeuff and Kuiper most emphatically expressed themselves against tying pastoral care with *agogy*.

[They distinguish three types of "intervention" in the inner life of another. *Psychotherapy* is a medical activity; it is "never anything other than an effort to make a new adjustment possible and to give the organism a chance to heal itself."[297] *Pastoral care*, the second form of intervention, is "an individualizing proclamation of the Word, in which the emphasis lies on the inner relationship of a person to God and which is directed to the entirety of a person's existence."[298] Finally there is *agogy*, which is "to give guidance" as an educator or parent-figure does it. "Agogy aims to perfect the human personality; to exert influence governed by ideals or normativity."[299] Pastoral care always runs the risk of degenerating into agogy.[300] The reason is, among other things, that

---

[287]J. J. Stam, *Rondom de Preek*, p. 24.
[288]Ibid., pp. 69ff.
[289]H. Asmussen, *Die Seelsorge*, p. XI.
[290]Ibid., p. 15.
[291]Ibid., p. 43.
[292]Ibid., p. 59.
[293]Ibid., p. 70.
[294]Ibid., p. 59.
[295]Ibid., p. 46.
[296]Ibid., p. 33.
[297]C. W. du Boeuff and P. C. Kuiper, *Psychotherapie en Zielzorg*, p. 25.
[298]Ibid., p. 27.
[299]Ibid., p. 29.
[300]Ibid., p. 36.

"agogy really suits all of us best. Every human being is by nature work-righteous."[301]]

P. J. Roscam Abbing views "the ministry of the church" as three-dimensional. The first, the apostolate, fulfils the ministry of proclamation; the second, the pastorate (or pastoral care), fulfils the ministry of exhortation and admonition; the third, the diaconate, has the calling to help.[302] This admonition "has nothing to do with the activity of leading and influencing, the agogy, which Dr. Du Boeuff and Dr. Kuiper rightly reject; it has nothing to do, that is, with the rectilinear imposition of a fixed form or ideal on a person."[303]

A study committee of the Dutch Reformed Foundation for Public Mental Health, appointed "for the study of the definition of and the mutual relationship between psychotherapy and pastoral care," also reports on the relationship between pastoral care and agogy.[304] The report says that, if by agogy one understands "action in terms of a certain norm-concept," "such agogy will not be put in a position of unbearable tension with a biblical practice of pastoral care only if it is expressly evangelical in orientation. Should a therapist make an appeal in terms of a certain norm—*in this case the law of God*—without the presupposition of the work of Christ and his continuing presence in the life of the believer, then this appeal, this agogy, becomes an abstract legalistic affair. Pastoral care is in essence evangelical." "The danger exists that agogy could become a human 'bonum'—guidance toward a balanced, liberated, nonfrustrated life which could do without the gospel." This agogy can be compared "with the lighting of a tiny lamp for someone which would block his access to the real light." Still, the study committee does not mean to say that "within the boundaries of pastoral care there is no room for any agogy at all." But then it understands agogy as "life-direction in the total sense of the word." There is room for this agogy because "To proclaim is not just to 'announce'; there is a 'directive' element in it. By its very nature—since it occurs in the midst of life—pastoral care is always agogic, directive—guidance in a certain direction."

The report leaves the impression that, as far as the problem of the relationship between pastoral care and agogy is concerned, it has tried to bring about an integration of two differing concepts—concepts which differ so basically because they proceed from a different notion of what constitutes the essence of pedagogy. Such an attempt seems meaningless: mutually exclusive points of view cannot be integrated. Nevertheless, the relevant chapter in this report is of some importance for practical-theological reflection. It is of some importance because it opens the way to another understanding of agogy, which can be fruitful both for the theory and the praxis of pastoral role-fulfilment.

---

[301]Ibid., p. 147.

[302]P. J. Roscam Abbing, *Diakonia*, p. 261.

[303]P. J. Roscam Abbing, *Over de Verhouding tussen Zielzorg en Psychotherapie*, p. 312; cf. Roscam Abbing, *Diakonia*, pp. 350ff.

[304]The Report *Over de onderlinge Verhouding tussen Psychotherapie en Zielzorg* was submitted in 1954 and published in 1956.

Objections to the Linkage

To make this clear we should make a quick survey of the background of the problem under discussion. Two ideas play a role in the resistance to the linkage between pastoral role-fulfilment (in preaching and pastoral care) and agogy. Both were expressed in a line we quoted earlier: "Agogy aims to perfect the human personality; to exert influence governed by ideals or normativity."[305] In other words, (1) to educate or nurture is an effort toward the realization of an ideal of personality in an actual person; (2) this education or nurture takes place in the atmosphere of law.

W. Jentsch, in his study of educational thought in ancient Christianity, characterizes the Greek and Roman notions of pedagogy as anthropocentric. "The point everywhere . . . is to elevate the naturally human onto a higher but still human level." "Everywhere the 'higher' human being, as an attainable ideal, is central."[306] Education must help people learn to go the way of *paideia*—a concept which, in Scheibe's pointed definition, refers to "a state of mind in which a person by his self-forming effort has finally become authentically human since soul and spirit have developed themselves to their full potential."[307] Over against this clear pedagogic goal, says Jentsch, there is no equally clear biblical equivalent. With reference to the Old Testament he remarks: "If one can speak in general of a pedagogic goal in the Old Testament, it can only be that the individual covenant-member may grow further into Israel's state of being bound to the LORD."[308] The Old Testament ideal for bringing up children is strictly theocentric, or really "Yahweh-centric." "The bond with Yahweh—that is the dominant note in Old Testament thought on pedagogy." Viewed from the perspective of method, the Old Testament idea of upbringing lies "altogether under the spell of the correctional process." "It must often have been a harsh, even an inhuman, process."[309] In the thinking of the rabbis the Torah comes in the place of Yahweh; "the nomocentric takes over from the theocentric." "In the place of God-centered pedagogical thinking has come a man-made orthodoxy or a legalistic religious pedagogics."[310]

Two lines of thought about nurture converge in the New Testament: "The more Old Testament notion of 'discipline' (to constrict)—hence a negative keynote!—and the more Greek notion of 'form-educate' (to unfold)—hence a positive keynote!"[311] In the New Testament both of these concepts come to stand in a special coherence and polarity because both are related to the gospel. "They fall under its criticism and are newly formed by it."[312] The New Testament has

---

[305]See p. 103.

[306]W. Jentsch, *Urchristliches Erziehungsdenken*, p. 82.

[307]Scheibe, *Die Pädagogik im XX Jahrhundert*, p. 13.

[308]W. Jentsch, *Urchristliches Erziehungsdenken*, pp. 93ff.

[309]Ibid., p. 109; cf. p. 86: "The word most often used for *bring up* is *jsr pi* = discipline, correct."

[310]Ibid., pp. 138ff.

[311]Ibid., p. 147.

[312]Ibid., p. 152.

not developed as evangelical pedagogics but it has set the theme for an "evangelical" nurture. "It is convinced that the Lordship of Jesus cannot come to a halt before the department of pedagogy. With the demand for *paideia kyriou* (Eph. 6:4) in the question of nurture, it clothes the central confession of primitive Christianity in concrete form: *kyrios Iēsous Christos* (Phil. 2:11; I Cor. 12:3)!"[313]

In the picture Jentsch has drawn of the anthropocentric nurture of the Greeks and of Jewish nurture as declining toward the nomocentric, one sees in profile all the errors which arouse the opposition of those who are out of sympathy with a linkage between pastoral role-fulfilment and agogy. "Preaching is not intended to 'bring up' the members of the congregation—to help them along on the way to perfection," we heard Stam say. The concept of "nurture" implies for him the idea of leading a person to perfection. And this is no illusion of his.

It would take us too far afield to trace the development of pedagogical thought in the nineteenth century. Schaller has pointed out that Rousseau's real discovery is the concentration of pedagogic action on people as people. This is worked out further in neo-humanism; the educational ideal becomes the "formation" of "personality" (Von Humboldt). Present-day pedagogics, says Schaller, remains faithful to its humanistic origins "when it puts everything in the service of personality-formation, while passing off the most diverse notions of personality—harmonious, Christian, democratic, Bolshevist, moral, etc.—as the goal of the undertaking."[314]

[The literature the author cites next reflects especially the struggle of German Christians to resist nurture which is ideologically conditioned. There is a marked parallel here with the objections raised against linking pastoral work with agogy. The danger of pastoral agogy is that the pastor will *use* the word of God in forming Christians of a desired stripe rather than *serve* the word of God as God's way of reaching people. *Tr.*]

People tend to *use* the material in the educational program. A teacher, e.g., may teach in such a way that she tries to make pupils the kind of people they ought to become according to her lights. Preaching and pastoral care which seek to be "pedagogical" run the danger of becoming unfaithful to "the cause," i.e., the word in which God wants to speak, because they do not *serve*, but *use*, the word. One runs into this when a pastor is always intent on arousing in his people a "sensus catholicus" or on leading them to a "Reformed lifestyle" or on forming in them an "orthodox" or a "liberal" mind-set. One encounters it also when in his preaching and pastoral care he pursues the ideal of "militant Christianity" or "a piety detached from the world" or whatever other ideal of being Christian there may be.

Directly related to this is the objection that an agogic type of preaching and pastoral care will be less than evangelical and in fact legalistic.

[Here again there is a parallel with a tendency in the pedagogical school

---

[313]Ibid., pp. 202ff.
[314]Schaller, *Die Krise der humanistischen Pädagogik,* pp. 12ff.

of Herbart. The governing slogan is "education by instruction" or educative instruction. At the core is the idea that to instruct the mind is to construct the mind.[315]]

The analogy in hyperagogic pastoral care and preaching is that the pastor acts as the person "who knows" and communicates that knowledge freely to others. He acts with the expectation that the knowledge so communicated will make a person the person he or she ought to be. G. Ebeling has pointed out that Luther linked "law" and "reason" closely together. "A human word which springs from human reason has the character of a law-word."[316] In general, one can say that where knowledge, in the sense of possessing and utilizing correct concepts, is considered determinative of being, the person who thinks he knows, and feels called to impart his knowledge, will try to bring others under the sway of that knowledge. The "clear concept" is for him the "correct insight" and a "binding truth." Such a preacher or pastor tends to call a spade a spade; he draws a set of clear lines; he offers concrete advice on a variety of issues; he calls "the shots"—you know where he stands. But in all this he causes the weight of his ideas and insights to rest heavily on the lives of the people entrusted to him.

It cannot be denied that resistance to the linkage between pastoral role-fulfilment and agogy is legitimate for these reasons. If agogy aims to refashion other people after the ideal image of the agogue by laying down norms and giving prescriptions, then the separation between the two cannot be radical enough. But the question is: In posing the issue like that, have you captured the agogic in its true nature?

The Traditional View of Nurture

We have pointed out a number of times that reflection on nurture in the Christian world tends to follow two lines. Actually both come together in one word, *paideia*, which acquired a double charge. The Greek notion of *paideia* is anthropocentric; it aims to describe the glory toward which a freely developing human being is traveling: the *humanitas* or *cultura*, as the Latin equivalents have it. The *paideia* concept which derives from the Septuagint and the New Testament conveys the notion of discipline, a notion one can perhaps best describe in the famous words with which Francke, the great pedagogue of Pietism, summed up the task of nurture: "It is a matter of the greatest consequence that the natural self-will be broken."[317] Already in the earliest period of the Christian era one can observe these two motifs controlling pedagogical reflection. On the one hand, Christian thinkers believed they were able to take over the grand ideals

---

[315]G. Compayré, *Herbart and Education by Instruction*, p. 46.

[316]G. Ebeling, *Erwägungen zur Lehre vom Gesetz*, pp. 279ff.

[317]Quoted in J. von den Driesch and J. Esterhues, *Geschichte der Erziehung und Bildung*, I, 303.

of Hellenism: Is not Christ the great Pedagogue and at the same time the ideal model of mankind?[318] But they knew people better than the Greeks did; they knew of sin, which makes *paideia* in this sense impossible. For that reason they wedded the optimistic *paideia* ideal of the Greeks with the severity of the *paideia* practice of Israel. Again, it would take us too far afield to trace the development of pedagogic thought in Christendom, but it is crystal clear that this view of nurture consistently controlled thought and speech about it.

Around 1930 theology in Germany began to deal critically with the fundamental questions of pedagogy and focused its energies, as Frör formulates it, especially on the pertinent separation of the redemptive action of God in word and sacrament from the traditional leveling of the gospel into a culturally formative power and a Christian ideal for education as well as from the interhuman domain of nurture. In order to accomplish this separation theologians resorted to the schematism "law and gospel."[319] Nurture is necessary but it is a work of the law, a "worldly work." G. Giese puts it like this: "That which Christ brings people: Salvation, eternal life, the kingdom of God that has come with him and is in the midst of us (Luke 17:21), all that cannot be the object and goal of nurture; for nurture is always a human affair which leads on human roads to 'worldly' goals with human means."[320] One can speak then of "law and gospel" in the way of the Lutheran tradition, or of "gospel and law" in the manner of Barth; in either case the result remains the same: nurture is never viewed as coherent with and flowing from the gospel, the word of God's acquittal which renews life. Many of the theologians we have cited see the dangers of an anthropocentric-idealistic and legalistic Christendom of nurture; they do not see the possibility of a radically different approach to the phenomenon of nurture which would make it possible to get past the problematics which occur here.

The traditional view of nurture could be reproduced as follows: Nurture consists in the action of a nurturer in relation to a nurturee; this action is oriented toward a pedagogical goal and motivated by the intention to reach it. The actions in question are matters such as a parent-to-child conversation; personal address in the form of admonition, encouragement, or instruction; punishment, praise, or reward.

This view is clearly illustrated by a remark we once heard in a conversation about bringing up children: "Sometimes I say to my children: 'Watch it, boys, or I may have to start bringing you up.'" The person who made the remark meant: In dealing with my children, deliberate, conscious, and emphatic acts of nurture are an exception; I resort to them only when the situation requires special intervention. What the father of a large family said about his youngest child is in the same vein: "When he grew up I did not do much to bring him

---

[318]In this connection cf. W. Jaeger, *Early Christianity and Greek Paideia*.

[319]K. Frör, "Die theologische Lehre von Gesetz und Evangelium und ihre Bedeutung für die Pädagogik," in *Glauben und Erziehen: eine Festgabe für Gerhard Bohne*, p. 97.

[320]G. Giese, *Erziehung und Bildung in der mündigen Welt*, p. 68.

up; I can't say that the result was so much the worse for it." In both instances the words "bring up" were synonymous with the description we gave of them. In neither case was this kind of nurture or upbringing deemed very important, while in both instances we were convinced that we were dealing with good "nurturers."

"Begetting Life"

Perhaps we have met people who had chosen a certain style of bringing up their children. T. Litt, in his discussion of the fundamental problem in pedagogy, first published in 1927, has pointed out that one sometimes hears in the slogan "Let them grow" a protest against an excess of schoolmasterly zeal.[321] On the other hand, the parent figure is often viewed as the one "who knows where the goal lies; he knows the way by which one may reach the goal, and because of this advantage leads the way for the one who lacks this knowledge." According to this view, to "bring up" is to "lead."[322] Both of the parent figures we quoted a minute ago seem to be of the first type. They are not strong believers in the importance of laying down rules, of leading, and of offering prescriptions. Experience has made the parent somewhat sceptical of deliberate pedagogical intervention (the father of the large family); the parent does not view himself as being called constantly to intervene in the life of a growing person, as the one who knows and has authority (the first parent quoted).

It appears that something else is at work. S. Strasser believes that if one is truly to get the subject of nurture in clear focus a third category has to be introduced, a prepedagogical category which is "a more elementary unity, in which the two poles can be found back, still undifferentiated."[323] Strasser begins by positing two givens: (1) in nurture we aim at *human* life; and (2) we are dealing with the life of *immature human beings*. But then a third "given" urges itself upon us: Human life is begotten by human beings. It is by procreation that the nurturing situation is made possible. There is "something that precedes *all* forms of nurture, also the nonexpress, the wordless, the unintentional." And that is the begetting of life. "Is it not true that all forms of nurture are finally made possible by the act of procreating life, and helping it to do well and to grow, a life which the parents view as theirs?"[324]

It may be true, as M. J. Langeveld claims, that "in every morally acceptable adult-child relationship the nurture-relation is germinally present";[325]

---

[321]T. Litt, *Führen oder Wachsenlassen*, p. 17.

[322]Ibid., p. 20. For Litt himself "Führen" vs. "Wachsenlassen" (to "lead" vs. to "let grow") is not a dilemma. He views them as polarities, in which the claim of the one may not negate the claim of the other.

[323]S. Strasser, *Opvoedingswetenschap en Opvoedingswijsheid*.

[324]Ibid., pp. 23ff.

[325]M. J. Langeveld, *Beknopte theoretische Paedagogiek*, p. 32.

this does not mean, however, that it is a given of every random relationship of adults to children. Most parents will spontaneously demur if someone else begins to concern himself pedagogically with their child *apart from them*. They know that the life of their child has its origin in their lives. If all is well they will acknowledge this child in his uniqueness and individuality; at the same time they know him as "life of their life." This must not be taken only biologically (however dangerous it is to make sharp distinctions here). The knowledge of this life as life of their life is total: here is a person who is there because they were there (together)—a person who exists in unbreakable coherence with their joint existence. They are the procreators of this life, but because "life" is more than its biological functions—breathing, blood circulation, etc.—because "life" is being human in freedom and responsibility, they remain the *auctores* of this life. *Auctor*—originator, producer, builder—must be understood in its original sense: one who promotes the prosperity, increase, or existence of anyone or anything (from *augeo*). Parents are the "promoters" who, in virtue of their responsibility for starting a life, strive to make it grow and increase in strength; they help the life that started in biological processes really to come fully alive. "To beget life" is not a self-contained act; it is a sequence, albeit not one which continues at will or *ad infinitum*. It is not an act which results in well-rounded "being," but one which leads to a self-continuing "becoming." When the child arrives, the full-fledged person is not yet there—but to "beget life" is to beget the life of a person. It therefore implies responsibility for this life until the person can function independently as a spiritual being.

So then, to be a nurturer is not to do things whose intention it is to guide the child in the right direction. It means: *as procreator of this life to take part in the development of this person*. Whoever as procreator of a life is responsible for that development is a nurturer—at least should be a nurturer—even when he or she does not deliberately "nurture" in the sense of the examples we gave. What began at the moment of procreation continues uninterruptedly until this person is a person indeed.

[One could put a question mark behind this word "uninterruptedly." Langeveld rightly remarks that a good deal of interaction between adults (e.g., parents) and children is not strictly nurture. "One does the child a favor, takes the child for a walk, etc., etc., not in order to nurture the child but because one loves the child and enjoys the child's company." True, the interaction can at any moment turn into nurture (Langeveld calls the normal interaction a "pedagogically preformed field"), but "finally every nurture-relation, on being completed, turns back into a relation of interaction." That is to say, when the adult and the child coexist in one field of interaction, the purposeful and goal-conscious action of the adult toward the child which one calls nurture is not always present; it is in fact rather infrequent, even incidental. The father in our first example was conscious of this fact; he even warned half-jokingly: "Watch it, or I may have to start bringing you up." It was normal for him simply to be in one space with his children and not—intentionally or directly—to nurture them. Says Emil

Brunner: "The father who prays with his children and reads the Bible does not act toward them as educator but as 'priest.' . . ."[326] The connection in which he makes this remark is immaterial to us, but the meaning is clear: the father, when he prays with his children, goes to God with them and is not aiming to educate or nurture them. But does he not *in fact* educate them? Strasser quotes from an article by F. Vander Meer: "When I think . . . of real prayer, I do not in my mind's eye picture a definition or an orderly school-mass, . . . but I see my dad, sitting in the pew of our old Waterstaatskerk between Hofstra and myself; I see a posture, an air of surrender, a kind of exaltedness, which I experienced as a little fellow, pint-sized next to the winter coat of my enormous father; it was a state in which even then I wanted to share and which I still haven't forgotten. . . ." "One could," says Strasser, "call this the begetting of religious life." In all probability what is done in this atmosphere, without any pedagogic intent, will generally do most for a child: a walk in which the idea of the walk was the main thing; a talk which was simply a talk between two persons; a posture, a disposition which shone through again and again; all these things work toward the end that a little breathing bundle of flesh becomes a living person. Speaking of Vander Meer's story, Strasser also says: what happened there may be best illustrated with an ancient symbol: *fire which is ignited by fire.* It is important to remember that fire is not concerned to spread itself; it does not plan, makes no decisions, prepares no actions. It is simply the nature of fire to ignite other fires. Just so, it belongs to the nature of life to diffuse itself."[327] It is like the act which one can call, in the real sense of the word, the "begetting of life." It is not done *in order to* raise life. Those who perform that act are intent upon the act itself, aiming simply to give themselves to each other and to receive each other in that act. They *live* in the act and they *experience* themselves and their love in it. Then, when it turns out that what they did and experienced was "the begetting of life," they experience a meaning which goes beyond their immediate intent. The father does not pray in the presence of his children in order to educate them in prayer—the thought alone is repugnant. But by living his real life before the eyes of his children and in openness toward them, he is the *auctor* of their life.]

In this atmosphere nurture takes place; in this connection it comes up. It is not exhausted by purposeful, goal-oriented actions: speaking, instructing, punishing, counseling, etc. Sometimes it comes to this; sometimes it ends up in this. But real nurture is not *doing*; it is much more a mode of *being*, namely, a state of being child-oriented, attentive, and loving, in the ordinary human context. To nurture is not to aim at *something*: the formation of that child, her development, his good conduct, a desired disposition, etc. It is to aim at *some-*

---

[326]E. Brunner, *Das Gebot und die Ordnungen*, p. 497. [I have not been able to find this statement in the English translation: *The Divine Imperative, Tr.*]

[327]S. Strasser, *Opvoedingswetenschap en Opvoedingswijsheid*, pp. 33ff.

one: that child, that person in process of becoming, that life in process of unfolding.

[It is clear that, approaching the subject of nurture in this manner, we cannot do a thing with a pronouncement like this: "Nurture is necessary because people are sinners. Without the help of nurture they must succumb to neglect in their sinfulness."[328] The words may be true in context, but they say nothing on what the pedagogical "thing" is about. True, one has to deal with sin in the nurturing situation—where does one not? But human beings do not come to nurture another because of sin; they nurture because in the context of their lives another life is in process of becoming which is dependent *on them* for that process.]

We talked about nurture, pedagogy. If we now speak of agogy in a broader sense, one that embraces a certain relationship between one adult and another, the issue is much different. "Nurture"—of a child by parents—is part of the continuum of begetting a new life. That connection is missing where parents entrust a part of that nurture to others—in a school, say—or in an agogic situation between adults. In the reference to the school situation we deliberately spoke of "entrusting to." Parents do not give up their child to a teacher; they entrust the child to the teacher and trust that teacher to be responsible for part of the life of that child. Something like this happens in an agogic relationship between adults. A person does not turn herself or himself over to another; nor does a person come to another as the consumer of "the product" of nurture, so to speak; a person turns to another in trust in order to let her take part in the process of her development. For an agogic relationship to be effective, trust and the ability to trust are essential. In other words, a relationship can be agogic only when the possibility exists of entrusting oneself to some other person who is willing to bear responsibility for the humanization of this person. One can also say that authority is essential; not in the sense of physical, psychic, intellectual, or hierarchical "superiority," but authority in the sense of actually being an *auctor*: a "promoter of the prosperity" of a life in process of becoming which trusts, and has been entrusted to, the promoter.

Christianus est in fieri ("To Be a Christian Is to Be in the Making")

Nurture, and agogy in general, is part of the order of begetting and promoting life. This "order" or connection has received all too little attention in the discussion on the relationship between pastoral role-fulfilment and agogy. Stam has said: "Preaching is not intended to 'bring up' the members of the congregation . . . ; preaching is the . . . effort of God to let people live."[329] A dichotomy is intended between "educating" people and "letting them live."[330]

---

[328]O. Hammelsbeck, *Evangelische Lehre von der Erziehung*, p. 137.
[329]See above, p. 103.
[330]The intent is to *cause* them to live, or to bring them to life.

This dichotomy may appear to occur in practice, but then the nurture in view is not nurture. If nurture operates in the order of begetting and promoting life, then one has to say the opposite. God comes in his word through the intermediary of pastoral role-fulfilment in order to bring people to life; this means, simply, that there is an agogic moment in pastoral role-fulfilment.

After what we have written about God's coming in his word, and the modes of that coming, this assertion needs little explanation. Not that we intend to say: the pastor is an agogue when he acts in the forms of preaching, catechesis, and pastoral care—even though this may be true, especially in catechesis and pastoral care. But this: In the entire phenomenon of God's coming in his word through the ministry of pastoral role-fulfilment there is a power which moves people. God's coming to a person means: to bring that person to life. That life is *real* life; not a life which is static, complacent, arrived; but a life which is in movement, underway, in a process of being renewed every day (II Cor. 4:16). God's coming to a person in his word creates a relationship between God and that person, a mutuality which is intensely dynamic, and in which the divinely adopted person, as part of and in coherence with the body of Christ, is led to full maturity, "to the measure of the stature of the fulness of Christ" (Eph. 4:13).

A clear example of what happens in this relationship is given in Paul's letters. Over and over Paul strongly emphasizes the objectivity of salvation: what has occurred in Christ for us and with us but apart from our contribution—we have died, been raised, been made to sit in heavenly places; we have been reconciled with God, justified, and sanctified. That is the indicative of begetting life, of communicating salvation, of setting people into relationship with God through the Spirit. But on the basis of this indicative Paul never fails to assert the imperative: be renewed, seek and mind the things which are above, put on the new man.[331] The intent of this imperative is not to mandate believers to realize salvation themselves, not to demand an addition to what God has done in Christ. The person who has been placed in fellowship with God now lives in what one might call a *relatio auctifica*—a relationship of the same nature as that between parents and their child.[332] In virtue of their responsibility for begetting this life, and in pursuance of their initial act of begetting it by which the relationship arose, they now promote the process by which the child comes to fulness and independence of life. They do this by nurturing her, i.e., by being "human" with the child in orientation toward the goal of the child's being fully human:

---

[331]H. N. Ridderbos, *Paul: An Outline of His Theology*, pp. 253ff., offers an exposition of the terms "indicative" and "imperative" as expressions of the phenomenon that "the new life . . . is at one time proclaimed and posited as the fruit of the redemptive work of God in Christ through the Holy Spirit—the indicative; elsewhere, however, it is put with no less force as a categorical demand—the imperative."

[332]*Auctificus*, derived from *augeo*, literally *growth-promoting*.

[For an extensive and outstanding study of the parent-child relationship between the apostle Paul and his converts as *relatio auctifica*, cf. W. P. De Boer, *The Imitation of Paul*, esp. pp. 145ff. *Tr.*]

they interact with the child, they instruct and admonish the child, they issue commands to the child at the point in time when the child can understand a command and can handle the relation to a "commander" and a command. The relationship between God and a person called by him to life in Christ is analogous. In this relationship God is *auctor* (growth-promoter) of life in process of becoming. God makes that person a new person in the sense that this person's life in its totality is conformed to the image of Christ—but he does not do it by way of a word of power. "To be a Christian is to be in the making," says Luther in his commentary on Romans 12:2. God treats the liberated person as really free. For that reason God's coming to a person over and over includes the call "repent," or as Paul has it: ". . . be transformed by the renewal of your mind, that you may prove what is the will of God, what is good and acceptable and perfect" (Rom. 12:2).[333] *"Metamorphousthe"* —God requires the continual transformation of a person; but from the imperative it is evident that in his relationship to a person he only intends to promote that person's full humanization as *ho tou theou anthrōpos* (II Tim. 3:17).

God comes to a person in his word. That is, he comes near to a person in order to interact with that person. He comes to reveal his name—in the way a child may know her father and mother, so the new "man" may know God— and this knowing is life (John 17:3). He comes to reveal his truth, i.e., his truthfulness and his perfect trustworthiness, so that a person can entrust herself to him. He comes to actualize salvation, i.e., at bottom to make people authentic, *human* as he intended. God comes in the kerygma—the proclamation: "Now it starts!" God comes in the didache—the way of life lies open and he guides a person on it. God comes in the paraklesis—in the confusions of our situation he makes his appearance and reorients us toward salvation. In all these ways and situations God moves toward people in order to change them: "And we all, beholding [or 'reflecting'] the glory of the Lord [the God who comes to us in his word and became incarnate in Christ], are being changed into his likeness from one degree of glory to another; for this comes from the Lord who is the Spirit" (II Cor. 3:18).

Ut veritas moveat ("In order that the Truth May Persuade")

Pastoral role-fulfilment finds its meaning in being intermediary for this movement. This reality poses an enormously significant problem for practical theology: *If God comes in his word to establish a relationship with a person, a relationship focused on the realization of the life of this person, and God uses an interhuman relationship for this purpose, then what must be the nature of the role-*

---

[333]J. Behm, *TDNT,* IV, 759, s.v. *morphē:* "The paradoxical *metamorphousthe,* which echoes Jesus' call for repentance, . . . has in view the responsibility of Christians for the change becoming and remaining effective. Its concern is the new moral life in the Spirit as an obligation: 'Become what you are!' "

fulfilment in that [interhuman] *relationship, for it to be serviceable to the divinely intended "relatio auctifica"?*

Augustine already occupied himself with this problem. In his treatise about hermeneutic and homiletic questions he quotes Cicero ("a certain orator") who said: "An eloquent man ought to speak in a way which 'instructs, pleases, and persuades' (his auditors)."[334] Commenting on II Timothy 2:14 ("avoid disputing about words"), he himself remarks: "The person who avoids disputing about words . . . aims by means of his words to bring about that the truth may be clear, pleasing, and persuasive."[335] One could say that Augustine is talking about the dynamic moments in the form of the preaching. The truth must do something to the hearers, and the preacher's role is to see to it that the truth is served in its own activity. To this end Augustine borrows from the treasury of classical rhetoric some pointers which are important for the preacher. These pointers seem to us less important if not useless.[336]

[Classical rhetoric takes us into the atmosphere of psychagogy. K. J. Popma remarks that a statement by Socrates ("rhetoric is a form of psychagogia") possibly represents a fierce criticism, namely, that "in rhetoric people do not offer rational argument, but they generate moods. The audience is swept unconsciously into an emotional state which causes it to agree to the position defended by the speaker. But all this has nothing to do with sound argumentation or truth." "Psychagogia, the art of spiritual seduction, is a method of affecting emotionality: this emotionality is given a certain set, and that mind-set which is produced in me in spite of myself and almost without my noticing it, seduces me into making the decision which the speaker wanted."[337] Certainly Augustine did not endorse psychagogy in this sense; he does see in the tears of his auditors, which spring into their eyes when they hear "grand" speech, a sign that they are about to change, but he does not deliberately aim at such "successes." The souls of the auditors must be moved "not that they may know what should be done, but to do what they already know they should do." But by appealing to rhetoric he has left the door open to psychagogy, "the art of spiritual seduction," which already had free access to the practice of the church.]

Those who along with Augustine are convinced that only the truth must be clear, pleasing, and persuasive will see possibilities other than those available

---

[334]Augustine, *De Doctrina Christiana* IV.27. "Ita dicere debere eloquentem, ut doceat, ut delectet, ut flectat."

[335]Augustine, ibid. IV.61: "qui non verbis contendit . . . id agit verbis ut veritas pateat, veritas placeat, veritas moveat."

[336]In fairness it must be said that Augustine was clearly aware of the relative value of classical rhetoric. One can use it but over against all rhetorical formalism in which the words themselves are the thing, he asserts that one "must love the truth in the words, not the words" (". . . in verbis verum amare, non verba").

[337]K. J. Popma, "Psychagogia," in *Christelijk Middelbaar Onderwijs* 22 (1941-42): 83.

to Augustine when they occupy themselves centuries later with the same problematic.

In the following sections we will search for an answer to the question what pastoral role-fulfilment should be like in order that the truth may be persuasive (*ut veritas moveat*). Our point of departure will be that—since the issue is change and growth—the persuasion takes place in a *"relatio auctifica,"* i.e., a relationship which is agogic in character. This relationship is open to research, for it is between people: God comes in his word *through the intermediary of pastoral role-fulfilment.*

In this last statement a problem knocks on our doors for attention, the question, namely, as to the nature of this being intermediary and of the relationship between pastoral role-fulfilment and the action of God by the Holy Spirit. The moment we speak of the agogic moment in pastoral role-fulfilment the biblical image of "the sower" suggests itself to us. Earlier we quoted J. J. Stam to the effect that the preacher is "the sower of the Word, whose privilege and therefore whose duty it is to let God do with it what pleases him. God . . . is the real Preacher by his Holy Spirit."[338] If that is the truth, one can indeed still speak of pastoral role-fulfilment; and practical theology still has a large area for reflection on this role-fulfilment. But it does become a question whether practical theology can then still conceive a methodology of pastoral role-fulfilment. Should it attempt to think through a methodology, would it not then occupy itself with things which it *may,* and therefore *must,* leave to God?

16. THE HOLY SPIRIT AND PASTORAL ROLE-FULFILMENT

A Prior Practical-Theological Question

H. Jonker, in the introduction to his study on "live preaching," raises the question "whether theoretical reflection and confrontation with the actual situation are required and useful for preaching that is alive and relevant. Does not the word of God go its own sovereign way? Is it not the Holy Spirit who illumines the preacher and brings his auditors to faith and confession? Is it not possible that with all our theories we will hinder the development of our preaching?"[339]

Such questions, when addressed to the subject of pastoral role-fulfilment, do not always have the same background. Sometimes they arise from superficiality and indolence; sometimes from reverence for the mystery of God's work to which our Lord refers in a parable— "the earth produces of itself (*automatē*)" (Mark 4:28). W. J. Berger leans toward the first possibility when, in his obser-

---

[338]See above, pp. 102-03.
[339]H. Jonker, *Actuele Prediking*, p. 17.

vations on what he has seen and heard at seminaries in the United States, he states: "While I am writing this, it occurs to me how far removed we in the Netherlands still are from insight into pastoral care. We coast along too much on the strength of a supernaturalistic mentality: with God's grace we'll make it. The objection to pastoral care that has a scientific basis is increasingly that it is 'training'—something that has nothing to do with pastoral care."[340] On the other hand, E. L. Smelik remarks that pastoral conversation and preaching are not in the final analysis objects for scientific study because the essential element in both is "the proclamation of the Word which is not of us but of God." This opinion has nothing to do with a "supernaturalistic mentality" or with indolence, but everything with the modesty which is appropriate for the theologian. In the first instance it is a matter of refusing to begin the journey; in the second an acknowledgment of the limits set for the practical theologian by the object of his study. That object is not what people do but what God does through the human intermediary. At the close of Psalm 77 we read: "Thou didst lead thy people like a flock by the hand of Moses and Aaron" (Ps. 77:20). Pastoral role-fulfilment could not be characterized in better words. The question concerning the relationship between leading the flock of the Lord and the "hands" he uses is a fundamental problem for practical theology.

This problem is inescapable especially when the agogic moment in pastoral role-fulfilment comes into focus. We have already explained what we meant by "the agogic moment": a motivational force, a change-producing power aimed at persons, the begetting and promoting of life. Hearing such phrases one would be inclined to say: the reference is to the Holy Spirit—and indeed the reference is to the Holy Spirit. Nevertheless, the subject is the agogic moment in *pastoral role-fulfilment*, which is the role-fulfilment of human beings. Is it possible now to bridge the gap between the work of the Holy Spirit and the action of human beings? We will inquire into other disciplines to see what they can teach us concerning the agogic moment in pastoral role-fulfilment—but can they tell us a thing about what is basically the work of the Holy Spirit? In all this we hope to make a modest contribution to the methodological discussion of pastoral role-fulfilment in its various forms—but can one speak of "methodology" in the face of the work of the Spirit who blows where he wills?

"I Believe in the Holy Ghost, the Lord and Giver of Life"

However important these prior questions are for practical theology, it is no less clear that the answers cannot be expected from within that discipline. This fundamental problem in practical theology—the possibilities and limits of theoretical reflection on pastoral role-fulfilment—is a problem in pneumatology. We can only suggest a number of points of view which in our opinion are

---

[340]W. J. Berger, *Op Weg naar een empirische Zielzorg*, p. 65.

important but find ourselves in the unfortunate situation that, as H. Berkhof has it, "pneumatology is a neglected field of systematic theology."[341] This applies in particular to the themes which are important to our study. According to Berkhof, theology, when it dealt with pneumatological issues, "was far more interested in intellectualistic and speculative subjects than in those which could help the church and her members to see their role in God's great design."[342]

However this may be, one cannot say that the ancient creeds of the church cut off access to reflection on this matter. The Apostles' and Nicene creeds do not focus on speculative issues, but place the confession of the Holy Spirit in the context of God's grand design: they speak in one breath of the Holy Spirit, the church, and the life to come.

With a view to the problematics which occupy us here it is important to note first of all that the church confesses: "I believe in the Holy Ghost, the Lord . . ." (Nicene Creed). The church knows that in dealing with the Holy Spirit it has to do with God *personally,* with whom one stands in the relationship of person to person. G. Friedrich offers a clear impression of how people often thought and spoke about the Holy Spirit: "By spirit people often, in animistic fashion, mean a power which comes over a person, seizes that person, enabling him to do unusual things; or they mean, in sharp contrast to this and in rationalistic fashion, the 'spiritual' capacities which are at the disposal of people for the performance of an action that is related to their special responsibility."[343] Even where people subscribe to the orthodox confession of the Holy Spirit, neither the one nor the other interpretation is rare. Often one senses the feeling that the work of the Holy Spirit is something you wait for, and that when the Holy Spirit works in a person to bring her to faith in Jesus or to renew that person and cause her to participate in the work of God, he does this outside the boundaries of a person's consciousness. The Creed, however, speaks clearly of a relationship which is mutual—*the relationship of faith.*

One could raise the question whether this manner of speaking agrees with the way the New Testament speaks of the relationship between the Holy Spirit and people. We have in mind statements saying that the Holy Spirit *fell* on people (Acts 10:44); that the Holy Spirit *came on* them (Acts 19:6); that God has *sent* the Spirit of his Son into our hearts (Gal. 4:6); that people *receive* the Holy Spirit (John 20:22; Acts 8:15, etc.; I Cor. 2:12); that God *gives* the Holy Spirit (Luke 11:13; Acts 5:32, etc.; Rom. 5:5; II Cor. 1:22; I Thess. 4:8); that people *are filled* with the Holy Spirit (Luke 1:15, 41, 67; Acts 2:4; 4:8, 31; 9:17; 13:9, 52); that they are *full* of the Holy Spirit (Acts 6:3, 5; 7:55; 11:24); that the Holy Spirit *dwells* in them (Rom. 8:9, 11; I Cor. 3:16; I Cor. 6:19; II Tim. 1:14); and that their bodies are *temples* of the Holy Spirit (I Cor. 6:19). Given these expres-

---

[341]H. Berkhof, *The Doctrine of the Holy Spirit,* p. 10.
[342]Ibid., p. 109.
[343]G. Friedrich, "Geist und Amt," in *Wort und Dienst,* p. 61.

sions, it sometimes seems that one loses her personhood over against the Holy Spirit; then again that the Spirit is a "thing" which enters into a person's existence.

It must be remembered that each of these expressions aims to tell us something about a reality which cannot be adequately described but only referred to, now from one perspective, now from another. In any case, none of these words says that there is no distinction between humans and the Spirit. They do in fact indicate clearly that it cannot be said that a person "absorbs" the Spirit or that the Spirit "fuses" with a person. The Spirit remains the Spirit; humans remain humans. All together these words refer to the reality of an entirely unique, intersubjective relationship. The unity which originates when the Spirit fills a person is a unity of two beings who are very closely associated and who in their intertwinement are most fully themselves.[344]

In this context it is important to notice the way in which Paul speaks about the church, and its members, as the temple of God in which the Spirit dwells (I Cor. 3:16; 6:19). From these statements it is clear that the Holy Spirit is a Person but it seems that over against him the human person sinks away; she is no more than a temple, a dwelling place of the Spirit. The context shows, however, that this is not the intent of the statements. In I Corinthians 3 Paul uses the image of the temple to underscore the church's holiness, which confers on it a large responsibility. In I Corinthians 6 he applies the same truth to the members of the church. When persons become temples of the Holy Spirit, then even their relation to their bodies has become new; those persons are no longer their own but the Lord's and must so live that they do not sin against their own bodies but glorify God with them. In II Corinthians 6 Paul uses the same image again: "For we are the temple of the living God" (v. 16). But that definitely does not mean that a person is depersonalized by the reception of the Holy Spirit and has become a "space" in which God takes up residence. Paul immediately adds a number of Old Testament quotations which speak clearly of a very close, intersubjective relationship. The indwelling of God turns out to be the highest intensification of God's association with his people: "I will live in them and move among them, and I will be their God, and they shall be my people. . . . And I will be a father to you, and you shall be my sons and daughters . . ." (vv. 16, 18).

The reality referred to in the image of indwelling becomes more clearly visible in Ephesians 3:14ff. Here Paul recounts how he prays that God may grant believers "to be strengthened with might through his Spirit in *the inner man,* and that Christ may dwell in your *hearts* through faith." *Ho esō anthrōpos* (v. 16) and *kardia* (v. 17) are used synonymously here; both refer to "man himself insofar as he enjoys self-awareness, as he thinks and wills and feels,"[345] in the

---

[344]P. A. Harlé, "Le Saint-Esprit et l'Eglise chez saint Paul" [in *Verbum caro* 19, No. 74 (1965)], pp. 13ff., quotes Congar who with reference to terms like "dwell in" speaks of an "intersubjective ontology."

[345]J. Behm, *TDNT,* II, 699, s.v. *esō.*

deepest and most personal core of his existence. Again, the Spirit does not depersonalize, but rather enhances the unique individuality of a person. This means that Christ makes his dwelling in a person, in the heart, i.e., where he is entirely himself, a person, an acting subject. Christ dwells in us "by faith"— i.e., the relationship created by his indwelling is no other than a *faith-relationship*.

Now it is true that in Ephesians 3:17 Paul does not speak about the Spirit who dwells in a person, but of Christ. It is clear, however, that the reference again and again is to the same reality. Apparently, in the picture of indwelling, the names "God," "Christ," and "Holy Spirit" are interchangeable.[346] This fact alone makes it even clearer that the relation to the Holy Spirit, as with God and Christ, is a relation of person to person. The more recent discussions concerning the Holy Spirit place strong emphasis on the fact that Paul often identifies *pneuma* and *kyrios*,[347] making pronouncements which culminate in the statement: "Now the Lord is the Spirit" (II Cor. 3:17). "The Spirit," says Käsemann, "is the earthly presence of the exalted Lord. . . . The Risen One manifests himself, together with the power of his Resurrection, in the Spirit."[348] In how far one can speak here of identification, and what the nature of this identification may be, are questions we do not have to take up.[349] For us it is enough that the relationship between a person and the Holy Spirit poured out upon that person and with whom the person has been filled is a relationship with the risen Lord and with him who raised Jesus from the dead. By pouring out the Holy Spirit the Lord fulfils his promise that he will not leave his disciples desolate (John 14:18); that he will be with them to the close of the age (Matt. 28:20). "To receive the Holy Spirit" means to be placed in the lasting fellowship of the Lord, a fellowship which a person can only experience in faith, i.e., in personal trust and obedient self-dedication.

Pentecost — The Beginning of the Future

With a view to the problem which occupies us at this point—the problem of the relation between God's action and human action in pastoral role-fulfil-ment—we must now try to get a clearer insight into the new reality in which the church and believers live as a result of the Holy Spirit's outpouring. G. Ebeling

---

[346]A clear example of this occurs in Romans 8:9-11, where the references are successively: you are in the Spirit; the Spirit of God dwells in you; someone has the Spirit of Christ; Christ in you; the Spirit of him who raised Jesus from the dead dwells in you; the Spirit of God dwells in you.

[347]Cf. E. Schweizer, *TDNT,* VI, 418ff., 433ff., s.v. *pneuma*; H. Berkhof, *The Doctrine of the Holy Spirit,* pp. 21ff.; H. N. Ridderbos, *Paul: An Outline of His Theology,* pp. 86ff.

[348]E. Käsemann, *RGG,* II, col. 1274.

[349]D. Holwerda, *The Holy Spirit and Eschatology in the Gospel of John,* p. 66, says with reference to II Corinthians 3:17 that this statement "does not express an ontological identity but an identity based upon the functions performed by the Spirit."

points out that in the self-understanding of primitive Christianity the experience of the Holy Spirit was almost the key signature of its existence. "If one had asked a Christian what then was really new in Christianity, he would not have put forward a new doctrine, but he would have referred to the new reality of the Holy Spirit."[350] Receiving the Holy Spirit meant receiving the "firstfruits" of the eschaton (Rom. 8:23), which gift as such is the guarantee or earnest of the inheritance to be expected (Eph. 1:14).[351] The future of the Kingdom of God which had come in Christ had started for them,[352] and they knew themselves called out of darkness into God's marvelous light (I Pet. 2:9). This could create the impression that the signature of the Spirit meant for them that they were alienated from the world of men and women and from the whole of creation itself—and in fact something like that can be observed throughout the history of the church.

[At the very moment a person becomes conscious of having received the Holy Spirit, the inclination often arises to withdraw into enjoying the salvation received, to leave the world behind and to forget the larger creation. This is true not only of various sects but also of the church. H. Berkhof outlines clearly the situation in which pneumatology existed for centuries: "In Roman Catholic theology, the Spirit is mainly the soul and sustainer of the church. In Protestant theology he is mainly the awakener of individual spiritual life in justification and sanctification. So the Spirit is either institutionalized or individualized. And both of these approaches are conceived in a common pattern of an introverted and static pneumatology."[353]]

Reading the New Testament, one is forcibly impressed with the fact that people receive the gift of the Holy Spirit in order that they may be able actively to participate in the movement which leads the creation to its culmination. Abraham Kuyper has pointed out that the proper work of the Holy Spirit is to lead the creature to its destiny, to cause it to develop according to its nature, to make it perfect.[354] All the work of the Holy Spirit, including his work in leading the church and renewing people, takes place in this perspective. Pentecost does not simply mean that a few people received the firstfruits of the eschaton—it means that the new heaven and the new earth have begun. For that reason the

---

[350]G. Ebeling, *The Nature of Faith*, p. 103.

[351]Cf. II Corinthians 1:22 and 5:5.

[352]P. S. Minear, *Images of the Church in the New Testament*, pp. 133ff., summarizes a number of New Testament statements with reference to this aspect: "Reference to the Spirit is always thoroughly eschatological. Wherever the Spirit moves there is detected God's new creation of the new humanity. Wherever the powers of the Spirit draw men within the realm of God's Kingdom, there the new age comes. This life-giving Spirit makes men sons of God and sharers in God's eternal glory and life."

[353]H. Berkhof, *The Doctrine of the Holy Spirit*, p. 33.

[354]A. Kuyper, *The Work of the Holy Spirit*, translated by H. De Vries, p. 21. Cf. T. F. Torrance, "The Epistemological Relevance of the Holy Spirit," in *Ex Auditu Verbi*, p. 277.

outpouring of the Holy Spirit takes place in the presence of people "from every nation under heaven" (Acts 2:5), who hear the apostles speak, "each in his own native language," of "the mighty works of God" (Acts 2:6, 8, 11). The Spirit as the gift of the end time (Acts 2:17) is given to people in order that they may receive power to be witnesses to the Lord and his Kingdom "to the end of the earth" (1:8), and preach the gospel "to the whole creation" (Mark 16:15).[355] In the Spirit comes the God who acts, makes history, and brings it to his goal; in the Spirit comes the Risen One whom God has made "both Lord and Christ" (Acts 2:36), who is "a life-giving spirit" (I Cor. 15:45)—and thus people are taken up into the fulfilment of God's plan. In the order of the Spirit's actions "mission has a logical priority," says H. Berkhof;[356] an "introverted and static" pneumatology is by definition no pneumatology. To speak of the Holy Spirit in keeping with the revelation concerning him is to speak of the Holy Spirit in terms of movement and relatedness to the whole of creation.

"To Each One Individually"

Mission has logical priority in the order of the Spirit, as we noted earlier; this does not mean, however, that the Holy Spirit does not work in the church and believers. To be sure, the story of Pentecost emphasizes missions. But the Epistles refer frequently to the "intra-ecclesiastical" work of the Holy Spirit. The Holy Spirit involves the church in the completion of God's plan for his creation; it is also the Spirit by whose agency the church can so function as is needed to carry out its God-given responsibility. Furthermore—as we observed when we discussed the mode of kerygma—a certain mission also takes place, in a sense, *inside* the church; those "inside" can move outward and become part of the "outside," with the result that in the church *one* has to speak to the *other* in the power of the Holy Spirit.

Not that there are only a few "bearers of the Spirit" in the church. At Pentecost not a few, but *all* were filled with the Holy Spirit (Acts 2:4). The desire of Moses is here fulfilled: all the Lord's people become prophets and the Lord puts his spirit on them (Num. 11:29; Acts 2:17-18).[357] This is not to say that all receive the Spirit individually; the church, the body of Christ, receives the Holy Spirit and the individual receives the Holy Spirit by virtue of belonging to, and incorporation with, the body. Luke begins the story of the Spirit's outpouring by saying that all the believers were together *epi to auto* (Acts 2:1); the

---

[355]The reference is to the whole of humanity. Cf. W. Foerster, *TDNT*, III, 1000, s.v. *ktizō*.

[356]H. Berkhof, *The Doctrine of the Holy Spirit*, p. 30.

[357]Cf. H. R. Boer, *Pentecost and Missions*, p. 115: "The minister of the gospel is not, as was the Old Testament prophet, an individual bearer of the Spirit, nor is he seized by Him on occasion for some specific purpose. He has the Spirit, not occasionally but always, and not alone but in common with all the members of the body of Christ, for the Spirit dwells in the body and informs all its members."

fundamental form of "the living church assembled" is there,[358] and then the Holy Spirit comes on all who are there. H. N. Ridderbos, referring to the Letters of Paul, remarks: "Being in-the-Spirit is . . . not in the first place a personal, but an ecclesiological, category."[359] Whoever has been incorporated by baptism into Christ, and so into his body, participates *as such* in the Spirit, who is the Spirit of Christ and of his body.

With a view to the issue which occupies us here it is important to look at this matter from still another point of view. The individual participates in the one Spirit by virtue of belonging to the body of Christ. This also means that the Holy Spirit manifests himself in a diversity coextensive with the varying members of the body. In I Corinthians 12:7 Paul speaks of the manifestation of the Spirit given to each member of the church individually for the common good. However one interprets the genitive in *tou pneumatos*,[360] it is plain that Paul means to say that common participation in the Spirit does not mean that the individual sinks away in the collective; on the contrary, in relation to the others and in view of the special function she has with regard to the whole, the individual has her own significance. It is "one and the same Spirit who apportions *to each one individually* as he wills" (I Cor. 12:11) "gifts that differ according to the grace given to us" (Rom. 12:6; cf. Eph. 4:7). Without directly mentioning the Holy Spirit, Paul makes the same point emphatically in Ephesians 4:16: From Christ, who is the head, "the whole body, joined and knit together by every joint with which it is supplied, when each part is working properly, makes bodily growth and upbuilds itself in love."

For this personal share in the manifestation of the Spirit in the church Paul introduces the concept of *charisma*.[361] Charisma is the gift and power of the new aeon. Says E. Käsemann: "It is . . . individuation, the specific share in the grace given with baptism to every Christian and, because a gift ever obligates, because the Spirit makes alive, and Christ lays the foundation for obedience, simultaneously a specific share in ministry (I Cor. 12:4ff.). [. . .] As every Christian has been given the Spirit (Rom. 8:9), so also has he been given his special charisma, and that as a concrete calling (I Cor. 7:7, 17)."[362] Paul offers a number of charisma catalogues, namely, in Romans 12:6-8, I Corinthians 12:8-10, 28-30, and Ephesians 4:11; their purpose is not, however, once and for all to fix the charismata present in the church. Paul's intent is simply to say that

---

[358]See p. 86 for the term *epi to auto*, esp. n. 249.

[359]H. N. Ridderbos, *Paul*, p. 221.

[360]According to F. W. Grosheide, *The First Epistle to the Corinthians*, p. 410, the question whether the genitive is subjective or objective can be left undecided because in this instance it makes little difference.

[361]As parallel concepts one can mention *charis* (II Cor. 9:8; I Cor. 3:10; I Pet. 4:10; John 1:16), *pneumatika* (I Cor. 12:1; 14:1); related, though not synonymous, are *pneuma* as used in I John 4:1 and I Corinthians 14:32, *dona* (Eph. 4:8), and *dōrea* (II Cor. 9:15). In I Corinthians 12:4-6 Paul puts *charismata*, *diakoniai*, and *energēmata* in a series.

[362]E. Käsemann, *RGG*, II, col. 1275ff., s.v. *Geist*.

these charismata exist and that they display great diversity, "a diversity, however, which must find its harmony in the unity of the body and its general well-being."[363] The church manifests itself in the New Testament as the *charismatic* church, i.e., it is a living complex of mutually complementary and supporting ministries, which have been assigned to the church and in which every member can function with the gift given to him or her, in service to one another and the church as a whole. The overall purpose of the gifts is that the church may actively participate in the work of God by the Holy Spirit, a work which is oriented to the completion of God's creation.[364] Surveying what we have said so far about the Holy Spirit and his manifestation in the church, we believe we can summarize it best in the words with which Karl Barth begins his discussion of the third section ("I believe in the Holy Ghost") of the Apostles' Creed: "We are concerned with man who participates in the act of God, and moreover participates actively. Man belongs to the Creed. This is the unheard-of mystery which we are now approaching."[365] The nature of human participation in the action of God will be the concern of the following section.

The Participation of Humans as Such

It must be emphatically stated at the outset that our concern here is genuine participation. Often the participation of humans in the work of God by the Holy Spirit is pictured in a way which excludes the human dimension as such. One encounters this view in two forms. On the one hand, reference is made to human participation as something that appears on the scene after God by his Spirit has already done the essential work immediately.[366] On the other, human participation is viewed as more apparent than real: the Holy Spirit takes possession of a person who then becomes an instrument of, and base of operation for, the Other. It is Another who speaks through the person's mouth. E. Brunner describes this second aberration as one of "being-possessed" and makes short work of it: "To be led by the Spirit of God is not to be possessed. On the contrary, it is to be liberated from possession, from the alien domination of evil. Man

---

[363]H. N. Ridderbos, *Paul*, p. 447. G. Friedrich, in *Wort und Dienst*, p. 83, believes that the charismata can be divided into six groups: 1. The gifts of *apostolate*, in which all charismata coexist; 2. of *proclamation*; 3. of *service*; 4. of *church leadership*; 5. of *special powers*; 6. of *prayer*.

[364]With reference to the dynamic structure of the church the idea of a functional differentiation in groups of ministries (*taxeis*) is important.

[365]K. Barth, *Dogmatics in Outline*, p. 137.

[366]As typical of this trend we quote here a few lines from S. O. Los, *Moderne Paedagogen en Richtingen*, who writes in reaction to Paul Natorp: "It is not the parent-figure who produces in a child a sense of personhood and community, for that is the work of God in regeneration and conversion. Neither is spiritual maieutics the work of humans, but the work of the Holy Spirit whom Christ has acquired for his own. We parent-figures come on the scene in second place in order, by our formative efforts, to create in the child a knowledge of, and feeling for, culture."

only becomes himself through the operation of the Holy Spirit."[367] We do not of course deny that the way in which the Holy Spirit works in a person, or through an interpersonal relationship, remains incomprehensible to us,[368] but one thing is very clear: the work of the Holy Spirit never takes place at the expense of our essential humanity. On the contrary, it finds its central focus in restoring the human person to her freedom and responsibility.

[This is true of the entire work of the Holy Spirit. An illustration of this is the way Paul arrives at the admonitions in his Letters. They follow, not as an appendix to the message of salvation, but as a direct outflow. Says O. Cullmann: ". . . in Primitive Christianity ethics without theology is absolutely inconceivable. All 'Ought' rests here upon an 'Is.' The imperative is firmly anchored in the indicative. We are holy; this means that we should sanctify ourselves. We have received the Spirit; this means that we should 'walk in the Spirit.' "[369] According to Cullmann, the polarity between the indicative of proclamation and the imperative of parenesis produces a field of tension "between the already fulfilled and the not yet fulfilled." It seems to us that this is saying too little. In Christ salvation has come; by faith we participate in it. The salvation granted to us embraces much, but it can be put in a few words all of which refer to the same reality: righteousness, life, peace, freedom. Take now the last word as indicative of total salvation in Christ: Whoever is in Christ is a free person— "everyone who commits sin is a slave to sin; . . . if the Son makes you free, you will be free indeed" (John 8:34-36). Two modes of life are possible: being a slave or being free, or—as Paul puts it—walking according to the flesh or walking according to the Spirit (Rom. 8:4-5; cf. Gal. 5:13ff.). To be free in Christ implies the calling to be free indeed (Gal. 5:13)—i.e., to "walk by the Spirit and not to gratify the desires of the flesh" (Gal. 5:16). E. Kamlah construes the tension between indicative and imperative, not just as that between the "already fulfilled" and the "not yet fulfilled," but much more and more essentially as that between Spirit, freedom, and action on the one hand, and "flesh" or the principle of compulsive self-indulgence on the other. In Philippians 2:12-13 Paul demonstrates in a few words what life in the state of salvation, i.e., in freedom, means. It is God who works in the believer both the willing and the doing (*theos . . . estin ho energōn*); that is the indicative of the freedom which has been bestowed. That freedom consists in being a free human being, a being who is not driven, whom no one uses, but who is able both to will and to work. In this indicative the imperative is implied: work out your own salvation (*kater-*

---

[367]E. Brunner, Dogmatics, III: *The Christian Doctrine of the Church, Faith, and the Consummation*, p. 13.

[368]T. F. Torrance, in *Ex Auditu Verbi*, p. 278, remarks: ". . . in his mode of Being and activity as Spirit He hides Himself from us." H. R. Boer, *Pentecost and Missions*, p. 102, says it is characteristic of all the work of the Holy Spirit "that only its actuality, never its manner is evident."

[369]O. Cullmann, *Christ and Time*, p. 224.

gazesthe); to that end the person in Christ, the person in the Spirit, has been made free.]

It is from this perspective that our problem is illumined. The gift of the Holy Spirit, the *charisma* granted to a person, enables her in freedom, *as a human being*, self-motivated and self-activated, to participate actively and creatively in God's work. Torrance, speaking of the Holy Spirit in connection with our knowledge of God, says: "God reveals himself to man . . . in the medium of the creaturely existence to which man belongs in space and time and uses the sign-world of interhuman communication in order to communicate himself to man."[370] This is true; only it can be said more forcefully: In revealing himself God not only makes use of "the sign-world of interhuman communication"— words of languages people speak and understand; he reveals himself through the intermediary of interhuman communication, by words people speak and acts people perform. No one can speak the word of God by himself; what applies to the "prophecy of Scripture" applies to all kerygma, didache, and paraklesis: ". . . no prophecy ever came by the impulse of man, but men moved by the Holy Spirit spoke from God" (II Pet. 1:21). But to speak for God one must have received a special charisma, i.e., authority (*exousia*[371]) and power[372] (*dynamis*[373]). But this is all given to human beings, enabling them *as human beings* to speak the word of God and do the work of God. "That which is proclaimed is indeed the word of God but it is 'God's word from our perspective.' [. . .] The fulness of grace proves itself precisely in the fact that God takes people, together with their full responsibility, into his service."[374] The Spirit does not "use" people. He enters, as O. Weber puts it, into "correspondence" with people,[375] or as K. Barth has it: "To receive and have the Holy Spirit has nothing whatever to do with an obscure and romanticised being. It is simply to receive and have direction. To be or to walk in Him is to be under direction, and to stand or walk as determined by it."[376] The person who by faith remains in fellowship with the Spirit; who allows herself in her entire existence and conduct to be led by the direction of the Holy Spirit; who in the responsibility of faith lives in this freedom, can and may relate herself to other people in such a way that on that interhuman level the word of God comes to pass.

---

[370]T. F. Torrance, in *Ex Auditu Verbi*, p. 289.

[371]W. Foerster, *TDNT*, II, 566, s.v. *exestin*: "it denotes the power which decides, so that it is particularly well adapted to express the invisible power of God whose Word is creative power."

[372]In sending out the Twelve (Luke 9:1) Jesus gave them *dynamin kai exousian*, words which can also describe the charisma.

[373]W. Grundmann, *TDNT*, II, 284, s.v. *dynamai*: "Words deriving from the stem *dyna-* all have the basic meaning of 'being able.' "

[374]E. Schweizer, "Die neutestamentliche Gemeindeordnung," in *Evangelische Theologie* 6 (1946-47): 338ff.

[375]O. Weber, *Foundations of Dogmatics*, II, 237.

[376]K. Barth, *CD*, IV/2, p. 362.

[The importance here of *human* participation as such, of God's making use of the qualities which come into play on the interhuman plane, appears from the fact that Paul, in his theology of the charismata, makes *love* central. After arousing believers to strive after the highest gifts, he shows them a still more excellent way (I Cor. 12:31), the way of love. That way is not other than the one of the charismata; in I Corinthians 13 Paul pictures love as the preeminent charisma. Whatever charismata a person may possess, unless they function in the context of the first and greatest charisma, that of love, she is nothing and her charismata are without significance.[377] No more than other charismata is love a human possibility; it exists only as a reflection of the love of God. E. Brunner expresses it in a striking image: "God alone shines in his own light . . . we are *planets* which can only shine in a borrowed light."[378] Love is a charisma in the full sense of the word, a manifestation of the Spirit in human existence. But that does not mean "it" loves in us in the way that "it" rains; we love; to love is for us to will and to do, or love cannot be love. The person who loves must be free, herself, a Person. So Paul says: "Make love your aim" (I Cor. 14:1). Romans 12, after an exposition of the charismata, makes an appeal to believers to love. In I Corinthians 13:4-7 Paul offers what one could call an "operational definition" of love. Here "the concrete significance of what love is is not expressed in lofty generalities, but pointed out in the concrete relationships of man to man."[379] To love is to be patient and kind, not jealous or boastful, not arrogant or rude, not insisting on one's own will, not irritable or resentful; love does not rejoice at wrong, but rejoices in the right, bears all things, believes all things, hopes all things, endures all things. Love so understood must inform all interhuman relationships. The reason is not just that this is how one ought to relate to the other members of the church. The operational definition is given in the context of instruction concerning the charismata. Only in these relationships can the charismata function; the Spirit can manifest himself in these relationships only where people practice their humanity in relation to each other in this fashion.]

The Human Being — An Instrument?

We believe that we can now begin to answer the question: How, in pastoral role-fulfilment, is the human action related to God's?

Says Calvin: "When we say that the Holy Spirit uses an external ministry as an instrument, this is what we mean: Both in the preaching of the word and in the ministry of the Sacraments there are two ministers, each of whom has a distinct office. The external minister administers the word that resounds, as well

---

[377]Cf. E. Stauffer, *TDNT*, I, 52, s.v. *agapaō*: "In 1 C. 13 it is brotherly love which gives value and content to all other action or gifts."

[378]E. Brunner, *The Divine Imperative*, p. 164.

[379]H. N. Ridderbos, *Paul*, p. 298.

as the sacred signs which are external, earthly, and perishable. The internal minister, i.e., the Holy Spirit, acts independently, internally, in order by his hidden power to effect communion with Christ, by one faith, in the hearts of whomever he wills. This communion is an internal matter, heavenly and imperishable."[380] The *minister externus* can speak the word and administer the sacraments—even to the point where if we hear God's ministers it is "just as if he himself spoke"[381]—but it would remain without effect were it not for "The Spirit as the inner teacher by whose effort the promise of salvation penetrates our minds, a promise that would otherwise only strike the air or beat upon our ears."[382] Not that the action of the external minister is unimportant. Paul shows in Ephesians 4:4-16, says Calvin, "that the church can be kept intact only if it be upheld by the safeguards in which it pleased the Lord to place its salvation."[383] "When God willed to call Paul to the knowledge of himself and to engraft him into the church he does not address him with his own voice but sends him to a man. . . ."[384] God uses the ministry of humans ". . . only that through their mouths he may do his own work—just as a workman uses a tool to do his work." God uses the ministry of other people to exercise us in humility. If he spoke directly from heaven it would be no wonder if we accepted his word. "But when a puny man risen from the dust speaks in God's name, at this point we best evidence our piety and obedience toward God if we show ourselves teachable toward his minister, although he excels us in nothing."[385]

These quotations, we know, are not adequate for the purpose of reproducing Calvin's position precisely. But that is not now our object. Pronouncements like the ones quoted here have begun to live a life of their own in Calvinistic churches; they have deeply influenced the mind of these churches on the relation between God's action and that of people in his service. One can hear it said over and over in these churches that the minister of the word, the *minister externus*, can do no more than convey an external word to the ears of people; God himself must apply it to their hearts by the Holy Spirit, the *doctor internus*. It would appear that after a mere human being has brought the external word, the Holy Spirit must do the really effective preaching in the people's hearts. On this view one cannot really speak of an active and creative participation of human beings in the word of God. A human being is no more than an Aeolian harp whose strings can only be stirred into music by the soft breezes of the Spirit;[386] he or she is not the harp player.

---

[380]J. Calvin, *Summa Doctrinae de Ministerio Verbi et Sacramentorum* (*Corpus Reformatorum*, IX), 774-75.

[381]J. Calvin, *Institutes*, IV.i.5, p. 1018.

[382]Ibid., III.i.4.

[383]Ibid., IV.iii.2.

[384]Ibid., IV.iii.3.

[385]Ibid., IV.iii.1.

[386]The metaphor is that of A. Kuyper, who asserted in his Stone Lectures that Calvinism was such a harp, "absolutely powerless" "without the quickening Spirit of God" (*Calvinism*, p. 199).

After what we have said about the relationship between the Holy Spirit and the believer, which is an intersubjective relationship, and about the charismata by which God gives to human beings *as such* the authority and power to do his work, it needs no further demonstration that we reject this point of view. The outpouring of the Holy Spirit and the bestowal of charismata do not reduce a human being to the level of an instrument by means of which God, as the only really acting Subject, can do his work.[387] The Holy Spirit takes "the puny man risen from the dust" (Calvin) and makes him really what he is intended to be: almost divine, crowned with glory and honor (Ps. 8:6)—and in that wonderful freedom he may serve God in his coming to people in accordance with the gift given him.

Synergism?

In pastoral role-fulfilment a human being is a subject—not depersonalized, but restored to fulness of personality. Sometimes the term "synergism" is used to characterize the relation between human and divine action.

[Roscam Abbing uses the term cautiously and with some reservations. After positing that in order to reach the world God makes use of the church's ministry, he says that the Reformers, when it came to the Christ-church relationship, knowingly taught "a certain 'synergism,' if one may use that term." He points out emphatically that the theological locus in which "cooperation" comes into view must be kept carefully in mind. It makes a substantial difference whether "human cooperation is discussed in Pneumatology or in Christology." Saying "yes" to the first is not inconsistent with saying "no" to the second.[388]

A. A. van Ruler expresses himself much more forcefully. Speaking of the offices of the church, he says that though in the long run they make themselves redundant they nevertheless remain constitutive for the church. He then continues: "In any case: only then will it be completely 'catholic' when God is not alone and unilaterally at work, but when God and man are at work together, in synergism that is total. This synergism, this reciprocity, is characteristic for the work of the Spirit." In Christology this cooperation is excluded by definition. "But the work of the Spirit consists by definition in the fact that He makes the human partner a full co-participant." "The full catholicity of the Christian religion brings with it that God and man stand pneumatologically in a synergistic relationship." The reciprocity, according to Van Ruler, is theonomous; but that does not imply heteronomy. In the Spirit there is no hierarchical relationship

---

[387]This statement is not in conflict with Acts 9:15. Instrument (*skeuos*) used as metaphor for a human being expresses (1) God's radical superiority over man, and (2) the idea of a purpose for which he ordains a person. The expression *skeuos eklogēs* (Acts 9:15) is elaborated in Acts 22:14 in nonmetaphorical categories. From this passage it is clear that the image of "instrument" does not imply the depersonalization of the man Paul. Cf. C. Maurer, *TDNT*, VII, 358ff., s.v. *skeuos*.

[388]P. J. Roscam Abbing, "De Kerk en haar Dienst in de Wereld." in N. vander Linde and F. Thijsen, *Geloofsinhoud en Geloofsbeleving*, pp. 281ff.

between God and man. Humans are not under God, nor are they next to him; they are over against him in the sense of being before his face. In the same vein Van Ruler warns "that we must not speak docetically about the Holy Spirit and be extremely careful with the category of immediacy. . . . For then the Spirit becomes the magician's wand with which we conjure all the problems off the table. . . . The Spirit does not exclude but emphatically includes the creature. . . ."[389]

The intent of Roscam Abbing and Van Ruler—with which we are in full agreement—is clear. They reject the idea that in one way or another the human subject participates actively and creatively in the acquisition of salvation; but they state with emphasis that the divinely called person does participate actively and creatively as subject in the work of God by which he makes salvation known and communicates it to people. Humans can do this as God's partners by the indwelling of the Holy Spirit.[390] Still, we believe it is incorrect to use the term "synergism" here. This "model" does not seem useful in resolving the question of the relationship between God's action and human action in pastoral role-fulfilment.

Our reasons for rejecting the term are as follows. First, "synergism" is a polemical term; it was used only by the opponents of a certain point of view. One can declare himself against "synergism" but by definition no one can say he is for it.[391]

Second, it is not very well possible to place a pneumatological synergism next to a christological synergism. When the Roman Catholic Church speaks of human cooperation in the process of justification, the reference is not to the natural man but to man as he has become by God's grace, i.e., by the Holy Spirit. In other words, synergism in soteriology has a pneumatological foundation.

Third, the focus of the Reformation's polemic against synergism is not on the idea of cooperation as such but on the idea of the human capacity to receive grace—the idea of a natural disposition to salvation enabling humans to cooperate in acquiring salvation. Van Ruler believes that we "must be extremely careful with the category of immediacy" with regard to the work of the Holy Spirit, but he might well apply such caution to the term "synergism." Consider these quotations from a Roman Catholic author: "An activity becomes pastoral in a formal sense when it indirectly cooperates with grace, by the use of human means, in order to bring forth *better* fruit in individuals and communities," and

---

[389]A. A. van Ruler, *Reformatorische Opmerkingen*, p. 76; for earlier quotes, see pp. 102ff.

[390]Ibid., pp. 102ff.

[391]One might be tempted to appeal to I Corinthians 3:9 (*theou gar esmen synergoi*) for justification for the use of the term. But here the reference is not to "synergism," however understood, but to ministry (cf. 3:5). The exact meaning of the expression is not clear. Grosheide (*The First Epistle to the Corinthians*, pp. 82-83) says it refers to "people who work together in God's service" and not to "people who work together with God." [See the RSV: "For we are fellow workers for God." *Tr.*]

"the pastor as shepherd reveals himself as the one who *goes before* his flock, and prepares for the direct working of the Spirit."[392] From these statements it is clear that the category of *immediacy* and the idea of *synergism* belong to the same world of discourse. Synergism means that a human being is able, in virtue of his natural potential, to contribute a share next to God's share of salvation. In Christology and soteriology this is excluded; but certainly no less in pneumatology. What a human being does, e.g., in pastoral role-fulfilment, is not a preparation for, or the completion of, what God himself does immediately. Still less is it a second element, equivalent to God's part, in God's coming to people. God *and* man do not cooperate in one fashion or other. *God* acts. It is he who comes into the lives of people to actualize salvation (the mode of kerygma), to offer guidance on the way (the mode of didache), and to reorient people toward salvation in the concreteness of their lives (the mode of paraklesis). But he does it by taking people into his service and by equipping them with the Spirit-given charisma, i.e., with authority and power to do his work.[393]

Pastoral Role-Fulfilment: Field of Tension in Which the Word Works

We have tried to show that neither the image of humans as instruments nor that of cooperation between divine and human action offers us a suitable model for depicting the relationship between God's action and that of humans in pastoral role-fulfilment. By speaking of pastoral role-fulfilment as *intermediary* of God's coming in his word we may not be much clearer, but we do believe that this term offers us a way of approaching the issue at stake which is more promising. There are five reasons why we hold this opinion.

First, the term "intermediary" shows that pastoral role-fulfilment, which is a human activity, does not exist by itself. It has its meaning, foundation, and goal in the action of God.

Second, the action of God, whose intent it is to cause people to live in redemption, is not something which happens apart from them, or something by which they are swept along, but is God's *coming to* them.

Third, God's coming is not an appearance "in naked majesty," as Torrance puts it;[394] salvation, says Rossouw, is "a living word-relationship of personal

---

[392]A. Godin, S.J., *De menselijke Relatie in de pastorale Dialoog* (translated from the French), pp. 22, 79.

[393]It should be mentioned that Karl Barth, *CD*, IV/3/2, p. 600, believes the notion of cooperation, used to describe the manner in which humans as subjects participate in the work of God, had better be avoided, especially because it is burdened by the term "synergism." Says he, ". . . the fact remains that the Christian . . . does participate as subject, and indeed as an active subject, in the action of Christ and therefore in the history of salvation, doing things with Christ even if not . . . effecting them." According to Barth (p. 601) the term "service" or "ministry" is best fitted to give expression to the matter at stake.

[394]T. F. Torrance, in *Ex Auditu Verbi*, p. 289.

communion."[395] God comes in his word; i.e., God enters into relationship with a person, addresses the person, deals with him "in the second person."

Fourth, God comes to people *in his word,* not in words. The church has always known this when it referred to Holy Scripture as "the Word of God" and insisted on the singular in the face of a multiplicity of books and words. When God comes in his word, it does not mean that one will hear a series of pronouncements. The *dicta Dei* together form but a relatively small part of the book which the church calls the "word of God." The word of God is not the sum of all the words of God; it is an extremely complex concept which embraces words of God but also material addressed to God—human answers, questions, complaints, objections, even protests and challenges.

[To gain insight into the complexity of the concept "word of God," a person will do well to take another look at the book of Job or the prophecies of Jeremiah. Especially Jeremiah can serve as a model. On the one hand, there is God who comes to the nations and especially to his people. On the other, there are the nations. Finally—apparently both on the one hand and on the other—there is Jeremiah himself. God has put words in his mouth and Jeremiah says them—sometimes with all the passion of his dedicated soul, sometimes with disgust and even under protest. At times he interrupts God, or turns away from him and curses the day of his birth which has resulted in his lonely life between God and other humans. And that whole tension-filled book of Jeremiah is the "word of God." So, in the same way, is the whole of Scripture.]

The word of God is the expression of God's relatedness to living people, to whom he draws near, to whom he reveals the name "I AM," to whom he discloses truth as reality present and actual, for whom he realizes redemption—a complex and dynamically moving reality.

Karl Barth has applied the christological analogy to Scripture: Scripture is not divine only nor human only, nor is it a mixture of the two, nor a *tertium quid* between them, "but in its way and degree it is very God and very man, i.e., a witness of revelation which itself belongs to revelation, *and* historically a very human literary document."[396] J. Barr thinks that the unity of God and man in the incarnation is not an adequate analogy for the Scriptures as the word of God.[397] The inadequacy he signals is "the neglect or underemphasis of the element of human response behind the Scriptures." The witness to the word of God which Scripture gives is a witness in the form of a response to that word. This response is also a witness of sorts, but not just that. "All response cannot be subsumed under proclamation; buying is not a form of selling." With an

---

[395]H. W. Rossouw, *Klaarheid en Interpretasie,* p. 248.

[396]K. Barth, *CD,* I/2, p. 501.

[397]J. Barr, review of *The Authority of Scripture,* by J. K. S. Reid, in *Scottish Journal of Theology* 11 (1958): 86ff.

allusion to one of Barth's favorite images[398] he says: "The finger of John the Baptist should be given a rest." "Scripture is answer as well as address." The Bible is "in essence . . . Word of Israel, Word of the Church." A purer analogy is "the relation of the Spirit of God to the People of God." Barth's way of applying the christological analogy creates the impression that the authority of Scripture rests on its divine character. But Barr says with some emphasis: "The human character is the bearer of Revelation, the *human* word is the word that has authority. The human scripture is true Man, or rather is true Israel, speaking or writing its historical literary document which is in its own particular form the witness to, and response to, revelation." The valuable component in Barr's views, it seems to us, is that he clearly shows that the concept of the word of God as dynamic reality implies the tension-filled relationship to the human beings addressed and responding. The word of God does not exist by itself; it "exists" when there are ears to hear and a heart that has not grown too fat to listen (Isa. 6:10; cf. Matt. 13:14-15).

Fifth, pastoral role-fulfilment is intermediary of God's coming in his word as dynamic reality. It does not mean that humans function as "loudspeakers" through which God's words resound, or as commentators who explain God's words, or as applicators who make them relevant to people and their situations. In pastoral role-fulfilment the word of God must come to pass—must realize itself in relation to the people to whom God seeks to come. So *pastoral role-fulfilment is the field in which God and man are brought together in a relationship of tension in which the word occurs which brings people to understanding and change.* Once we view pastoral role-fulfilment as intermediary of the encounter with God, then the role of the pastor is twofold. He participates in the action of God who comes. He also participates in the existence of the people to whom God comes. This duality comes out clearly in the kerygma, didache, and paraklesis which the pastor brings as ambassador of Christ (II Cor. 5:20). The kerygma is the proclamation of salvation in the "now" of the lives of the people addressed; for the pastor this means that he must be present in the "now" of the people to whom the word comes. The didache is the voice which points the way; for the pastor this means that he has made the problem of the direction of a person's life his own problem. Paraklesis is the consolation and admonition of God which reorient people toward salvation in the concreteness of their situation; for the pastor this means that he knows the concreteness of the situation of these people by participation in it.

The methodological problematics of pastoral role-fulfilment can now be described: How should the pastoral role be fulfilled? How should the pastor relate himself to the God who speaks and to the person whom God wills to encounter, if the pastoral role is to be intermediary for God's coming in his

---

[398]It is the finger of John the Baptist pointing to the Lamb of God, depicted in a painting of the crucifixion by Matthias Grünewald. Cf. Barth, *Das Wort Gottes und die Theologie,* p. 79: "This is the hand which is documented in the Bible."

word? One cannot reply to the questions which arise in this problematics with a simple reference to the Holy Spirit. The Spirit's way of working is by authorizing and empowering people *as human beings* to serve God in his coming. The Spirit does *not* make human deliberation and action *superfluous*; he makes it *possible* by conferring freedom and responsibility to that end.

In the previous section we dealt with the agogic moment in pastoral role-fulfilment: By the intermediary of the pastoral role God comes to enter into a relationship with persons in which these persons are led into the realization of their full humanity. Pastoral role-fulfilment, dependent as it is on the action of God which it aims to serve, can thus be viewed from the perspective of an agogic relationship. In order to gain insight into it from this perspective we must now enter the field of agogics.

III. The Agogic Factor

1. INTRODUCTION

In the previous part we observed that pastoral role-fulfilment is the intermediary for God's coming in his word. In the interhuman relationship into which the pastor ventures when fulfilling his role there arises a field of tension in which God and the person to whom he would come are brought together in mutuality. What happens in this field of tension can be viewed in various ways; in any case, *one* of the aspects of what transpires is that of *change* in the person thus encountered. This means that the field of tension arising as a result of pastoral role-fulfilment can be viewed as an agogic situation. Our premise is that this way of viewing pastoral role-fulfilment can help us discover points of view which are important for the formation of theory concerning pastoral role-fulfilment and, from that vantage point, for the training and formation of the pastor as well as for pastoral praxis.

In this part we shall attempt, by way of expanding on what was said in Part II, section 15, to define what is specifically agogic. The number of pages devoted to this project, and the issues which will come up, may suggest at first blush that we are venturing far beyond the confines of a practical-theological study and are engaged in something other than merely consulting another discipline with a view to the formation of practical-theological theory. A broad consideration of the question concerning the specifically agogic was forced on us, however, because we could not fully endorse any of the current theories. We are in the process of finding our own way—but we do want to share with our fellow students how and where we searched for answers, who helped us find them, and how they did it. Anyone familiar with the problematics treated in this part will notice that we have placed severe limits on ourselves. Subjects not relevant to practical theology are not discussed; but it must be granted in the same breath that in this book the relevance of many matters touched upon is not made explicit.

2. ORIENTATION BY REFERENCE TO POINT ZERO

J. W. van Hulst, in his analysis of pedagogics, remarks that a person reflecting on the nature of nurture "must realize that the subject has been around for a while. We cannot return to Point Zero and act as if no one ever committed thoughts to paper on the subject before."[1] This observation is undoubtedly correct: one cannot occupy herself with the so-called "pedagogical question" and act as if pedagogical reflection starts with her.

Still, something must immediately be said on the other side of Van Hulst's concern: reflection on the problematics of pedagogy consistently calls for orientation to the pedagogical Point Zero. What the pedagogues have put on paper is not the reality the pedagogues examine and reflect on. In the books one can find theories concerning that reality and images of it; but what one does not find in pedagogical works is the reality of a child growing into maturity or of parents involved in some way in that process. And that reality is one's Point Zero.

One could, of course, say something like this about every discipline. Still, we believe, now that we are talking about pedagogics, that it is important to say the obvious: In this discipline the danger is not imaginary that practitioners will ascribe more content to abstractions from reality than to reality itself. We shall try to demonstrate the truth of this assertion with an example.

[Fischer once made the statement: "The eternally naive multitude of educators whom we call parents are neither picked nor trained for this task; but it must be said that in virtue of their love, faithfulness, devotion, and patience, they are superior in their labor to the entire mass of 'state-of-the-art' pedagogical experts."[2] W. Linke, who quotes this statement, agrees with it but has reservations: "Fischer's words are correct on the assumption that the parents are cultured folk who in spite of their lay ideas on pedagogics fulfil their parenting role, if not perfectly, at least with heartfelt devotion and in principle correctly."[3] We shall read both statements as though they were one argument of which Linke is the author. The starting point for this argument is the discipline of pedagogics. Glancing ahead one sees the professional educators who use the insights of this discipline in their work. Glancing backward one glimpses the parents. "Parents" is what we call them, but in view of our starting point we should call them "preliterate" educators—"the eternally naive multitude"—dilettantes with lay ideas on pedagogy. The fact that they may do their job well, even "in principle correctly," if certain conditions are met, is not due to, but in spite of, their lay pedagogy, which serves them as a crutch. They have something else: the inspiration of love, faithfulness, devotion, and patience, something which is perhaps even a shade more important (see Fischer).

---

[1] J. W. van Hulst, *De Beginselleer van Hoogvelds Pedagogiek*, p. 161.
[2] Fischer, *Erziehung als Beruf*, p. 2.
[3] W. Linke, "Grundformen erzieherischen Verhaltens," in *Erziehung zur Menschlichkeit: Festschrift für Eduard Spranger*, pp. 293ff.

But should one take one's point of departure in the reality of the life of parents with their children, one would reason very differently. One could, for example, using as much of Linke's and Fischer's language as possible, reason like this: We observe that parents, under the inspiration of love, faithfulness, devotion, and patience, with the help of common sense and their knowledge of the child, and other factors as yet unknown, are able to help their children in their human development. We also observe that not all parents are capable of this, the failure being due, it seems, to a cause which lies mostly in themselves. We have arrived at these observations by a systematic study of parents living with their children. This systematic study takes place in a scholarly discipline which we call "pedagogics." By means of a more precise analysis of the reality referred to earlier we discover, in the lives of parents living with their children, a number of phenomena which, it seems certain or at least probable, are directly interrelated. We gather these interrelated and mutually dependent facts together in a concept and call it "nurture." From the perspective of pedagogics we can now call the parents "nurturers"—just as in another science they might be called "mammals"—and the activities which are directed toward the children's development into maturity we can call "to nurture." Having advanced this far, we can, with the help of experiences we have had in our study of this reality and on the basis of insights and convictions we have gained in other areas, say a few words about the way this nurture should be conducted. The theory so constructed will be especially useful to those whose task it is secondarily to help the child in her development: the professional "nurturers"—the people in child guidance clinics as well as those who teach pedagogics. It is our hope that despite the fact that they derive their inspiration mostly from theory—pedagogics in the narrow sense—they will nevertheless fulfil their task "in principle correctly." If these nurturers and educators have not had real parents who have helped them to become "cultured folk," we can only despair of it.]

We now return to our point of departure. As to "the nature of nurture" we must remember that a lot has been written on it. But we must also remember that in pedagogics it is not enough simply to bandy about the old established concepts. If one is about to consider the question of the nature of nurture, for instance, one should first raise another, namely, whether this very formulation of the question is not perhaps the reason why so much that is important remains hidden. We speak of "nurture"; but we soon become aware that nurture is a concept gained by reflection on what parents do with their children and by abstracting from that reality. Such a concept may be of help in our study of reality; it is a stencil-like grid which we put on top of the reality to be studied and which makes it possible to get some details into sharper focus. But it has the side effect of covering up other things which are essential to an understanding of nurture and which should perhaps be studied first.

When we orient ourselves, not to the concept of nurture, but to Point Zero of the reality of the lives of parents living with their children, we observe at least three sets of phenomena which bear on the child's movement toward human maturity. *One*: the child lives and grows up in a situation which contains much more than responsible parents and in which parents do not always act from motives which are in keeping with their responsibilities as parents. Focusing on the growth of the child, we notice that this development takes place in a world as big as life. The complex of influences which affect the child from all around we call "contextual influence." *Two*: Parents as well as others turn to the child in a given situation and with an eye to the child's well-being in that situation address him or her, calling for attention, giving encouragement, or offering correction. This address is incidental; it is not deliberately nurturant; and it is related to the momentary well-being of the child. This complex of phenomena we call "equihuman address." (*Note*: The word "equihuman" is a coinage which will be explained on p. 159.) *Three*: interwoven with both of these complexes is another set of phenomena directly and intentionally related to the development of the child—not so much to the child's momentary needs as to her overall growth. This, then, is what is usually called *nurture*.

Anticipating the sections to follow and by way of introducing a specific terminology, we wish to introduce a distinction between "nurturing" and "nurture." By *nurturing* we mean the actions of the nurturer which are intentionally and directly related to the development of a growing person. By *nurture* we mean the sum of events occurring between the nurturer and the person being nurtured, whether pedagogically intended or not, insofar as these events serve the development of the growing person. So in *nurturing* the reference is to concrete actions; and in *nurture*, to a quality of life in which the nurturer and "nurturee" share.

3. CONTEXTUAL INFLUENCE

Is Nurture Necessary?

M J. Langeveld asserts that for pedagogics "the concept that a human being is 'animal educandum,' the animal that needs to be nurtured because it is an 'animal educabile'—an animal inclined toward, and dependent on, nurture—is absolutely constitutive."[4] "One of the most fundamental features of our image of man is that the human being is a being which nurtures, is nurtured, and is dependent on nurture," says he.[5] It must be remembered that when Langeveld speaks of nurture he has in mind the deliberate influence which the adult exerts on the nonadult in order that the nonadult may become "of age."[6]

[In another passage Langeveld makes a distinction between "nurture" and "humanization." A human being, he argues, is not born as a human being;

---

[4]M. J. Langeveld, *Beknopte theoretische Paedagogiek*, p. 155.
[5]Ibid., p. 158.
[6]Ibid., p. 28.

initially he or she is no more than a young one of the race which bears the name "Homo sapiens."[7] "Even by rudimentary contact with that which is human, the young get the opportunity gradually to identify themselves with the species-specific forms of behavior which they find in their environment. They start in fact to display postures and movements; the choice of, and preference in, foods; the formation of ties and the experience of being thrust out and tieless; the assumption of symbol-systems in their elementary forms; the handling of tools, etc., etc." The merely humanized ones are "the persons who still had a chance to catch the main features of humanity by copying them from their environment."[8] Humanization is really infrahuman; it teaches only the human basics which "hold the possibility of leading to culture through being nurtured."[9] "In the absence of nurture the humanization process remains stuck in its most rudimentary form."[10]]

One can summarize Langeveld's position by saying that a human without nurture—in the sense of deliberate, goal-oriented formation—is not human. R. C. Kwant, however, remarks: "In a primitive world, the 'field' of meaning, and therefore of human action, is still primitive and simple. Children, because they imitate, are naturally taken up in the world of meaning surrounding them and a deliberately organized process of nurture is hardly, or not at all, necessary. Children are educated through participation in the circumambient life of adults."[11] That is to say, in some cultures there is no need for programmatic nurture. This reasoning is not easy to defend, simply because it is hard to support it with empirical data.[12]

Nevertheless, it is possible in theory to create a hypothetical situation in which deliberate and regular nurture is missing. As a way of getting the actual phenomena into sharp focus, such an exercise may have its value. F. D. E. Schleiermacher, who distinguishes two forms of nurture, namely, the reinforcement of what is positive in the growing person and his environment and counteraction against the negative, asserted that counteraction needs to be undertaken only against those elements in the growing person which block her own true development—"on condition that the various moral spheres have been brought to moral completion and individuals have their proper influence on the younger

---

[7]M. J. Langeveld, " 'Humanisering' mede in verband met 'opvoeding'–'cultuur,' " in *Gedenkboek voor Prof. Dr. Ph. A. Kohnstamm*, p. 153.

[8]Ibid., p. 156.

[9]Ibid., p. 154.

[10]Ibid., p. 155.

[11]R. C. Kwant, *Sociale Filosofie*, p. 91.

[12]Considering, e.g., the initiation rites of "primitive" peoples, it would seem that they believe "programmatic nurture" to be very necessary. Even things like "schools" are present, if one may apply the following criteria for the presence of a school: methodical intervention, a teacher with a special educational mandate, and a complex of educational happenings organized in a separate space away from the usual intergenerational setting. Cf. E. Weniger, "Zur Geistesgeschichte und Soziologie der pädagogischen Fragestellung," in H. Röhrs, *Erziehungswissenschaften und Erziehungswirklichkeit*, p. 353.

generation according to the intent and in the spirit of their communities." The level of counteraction can be reduced to the extent that harmony between the community and the individual is increasing. Nurture will then be increasingly a matter of positive reinforcement. However, the more the total environment is imbued with moral habit and custom, the less intentional and methodical the reinforcement needs to be. All has become custom. "Given that this situation can be maintained, the influence on the younger generation can be nothing other than the formative outflow of custom, which can exist without special theories and methods. . . ." "On the assumption of absolute perfection, nurture as a special activity can cease to exist."[13] Schleiermacher could come to this position because he was aware of the fact that factors other than direct nurture influence the growing person, a homogeneous community life being particularly influential. Schleiermacher believes that only deliberate influences can be called "pedagogical." The criterion is intentionality. At the same time he asserts that "unintentional influences" can also effect what nurture intends.[14] This last claim would appear to be indisputable. Every person analyzing her own growth into adulthood will encounter elements which cannot be traced back to the intentional formative influences of a nurturer or educator. It is even probable that forces working counter to the intentional efforts of a nurturer or by way of negative reaction to them helped give shape and direction to the process.

Nurture Plus Something Else

Increasing awareness of the significance of "unintentional influences" has led—approximately a century after Schleiermacher gave the lectures from which we quoted—to the distinction between *intentional* and *functional* nurture. Krieck, who became the theoretician of Nazi education, very one-sidedly stressed the importance of functional nurture. He saw nurture as a "fundamental function of community": "all are educators of everyone else all the time."[15] A person is inducted into membership in a nation by her connectedness with the organism of that nation.

[Bollnow, who does not lapse into the one-sidedness of Krieck, still believes that the notion of functional nurture is of immense significance for pedagogics. "By this term is meant the nurturing influence which occurs without conscious pedagogical intent and as a matter of course in a well-ordered society."[16] Abraham further elaborates the distinction between intentional and functional nurture. In addition to the intentional nurture of humans he sees a functional nurture exerted by humans and by things. In functional nurture we can distinguish again between that exerted unintentionally by an individual and that ex-

---

[13]F. D. E. Schleiermacher, *Pädagogische Schriften,* pp. 63ff.
[14]Ibid., p. 111.
[15]Krieck, *Philosophie der Erziehung,* pp. 3ff.
[16]O. F. Bollnow, *Pädagogische Forschung und philosophisches Denken,* pp. 230ff.

erted by a social structure—an industry or business, for instance—in which a growing person participates and is influenced.[17]]

One cannot claim that this development in pedagogical thought has made it any easier to talk about the relevant reality. Terminological confusion abounds.[18] Still, this development is important. As long as people focus their attention exclusively on intentional nurture, and maintain the grand assumption of what Herbart called "the fundamental concept of pedagogics," namely, "the educability of the nurseling," the issue of the humanization of a person appears to be quite plain. The scenario then goes like this: there is a child who, within the limits of its bent, of course, can go in almost any direction; there is an educator who knows the goal toward which this child must grow; the educator so molds the child that he or she arrives at this goal. Apart from the difficulties which may arise in a developmental process—through mistakes made by the educator or interference from undesirable outside influences—the process runs along fairly straight lines. But then the whole story turns out to have been more complicated. An unintentional influence as well as an intentional one proceeds from the nurturer, and the former is at least as effective as the latter. Other people exert influence either as individuals or in the configuration of a group or organization. People exert influence, but so do things. To this we may add: some influence is more or less continuous, and focused on the process of a person's development and formation; other influence is incidental and contingent, focused on a person's existence as it is at a given moment or in a certain situation.

That is to say, even if intentional nurture did not take place, the growing person would still be subject in the process of her development to contextual influence. Were this to happen in a society which, as Schleiermacher pictured it, had reached absolute perfection, so that all influence was simply the "outflow of custom," then this contextual influence would bring about more than "humanization" (Langeveld); it would be enough to lead a person to full-fledged and authentic humanity. We are, however, far removed from such an ideal situation. Much influence is not conducive to the development and formation of a growing person. Much influence is possibly quite conducive, but still creates problems because it interacts with other influences or hinders their effect.[19] In any case, contextual influence is not of one spirit or direction, but polyvalent.[20]

---

[17]K. Abraham, *Der Betrieb als Erziehungsfaktor,* pp. 20ff.

[18]W. Brezinka, *Erziehung als Lebenshilfe,* p. 59, refers to a number of terms which have been current to denote the phenomenon later called "functional nurture": adjustment, assimilation, socialization, etc.

[19]Reference has sometimes been made to "secret coeducators," meaning in particular the press, radio, television, advertising, and propaganda. Cf. J. Rudert, "Die unkontrollierte Erziehung," in *Erziehung Wozu?,* p. 82.

[20]W. Brezinka, *Erziehung als Lebenshilfe,* p. 244, mentions "a chaos of interlocking influences." J. H. vanden Berg, *Metabletica,* pp. 46ff., has referred to the problematic nature of this situation: "Every step a child takes in the direction of adulthood is a step into the fog of polyvalences."

These circumstances make it necessary to pay deliberate and rather systematic attention to the maturing person with an eye to her development and formation. With regard to this development, however, contextual influence has a kind of logical priority, with the result that an adequate concept of nurture can be formed only when the phenomenon of contextual influence, in its functional uniqueness, has been brought into clear focus.

The Concept of Socialization — Is It Pedagogically Useful?

Especially W. Brezinka has recognized the necessity of this approach to the problematics of pedagogy. "It is necessary in today's world," says he, "for the theory of nurture to give more intense consideration to the background of unintentional effects which proceed from the social and cultural environment. Every deliberate plan of nurture which does not take account of these unchecked influences builds on a foundation of sand."[21] In this context Brezinka speaks of "socialization and nurture."[22] According to him, nurture is but a small part of the mass of influences which affect the growing person. In the social environment "habits" arise which work as predispositions. By growing up within a certain society and culture a child becomes an adult stamped by, and adapted to, that society and culture.

We are convinced that the discipline of pedagogics must study this phenomenon of contextual influence. It does not, however, seem advantageous for this discipline to introduce the concept of socialization into its conceptual vocabulary. Brezinka's orientation derives from Child, who views socialization as a "process by which an individual, born with behavioral potentialities of enormously wide range, is led to develop actual behavior" which agrees with the norms which are dominant in the group to which he or she belongs.[23] There are many other definitions of the concept,[24] but they are all intended to summarize those phenomena which jointly bring into being the "well-adjusted" person who fits into the society in which she lives. The focus of this concept is especially the common *effect* of all those phenomena; neglected in the concept are the intrinsic differences between the phenomena. This is not a defect. One can create various abstractions, depending on the focus one chooses. The choice of focus depends on the mode of observation appropriate for a given discipline. Socialization is a concept appropriate for the disciplines which are interested in societies and their cultures and in people as members of those societies and participants in those cultures. One of the questions which occupy the disciplines

---

[21]W. Brezinka, *Erziehung als Lebenshilfe,* p. 57.
[22]Ibid., pp. 48ff.
[23]Ibid., p. 52; I. L. Child, "Socialization," in G. Lindzey, *Handbook of Social Psychology,* p. 655.
[24]Often "socialization" is more broadly defined, but the thrust remains the same. Cf. D. Krech and R. S. Crutchfield, *Elements of Psychology,* p. 608, where socialization is described as "the process whereby socially determined factors become influential in controlling the behavior of the person."

of sociology, cultural anthropology, and social psychology, each with an agenda and framework of its own in which the problem functions, is, briefly, this: Why do individuals within societies, cultures, and subcultures show such striking similarity in all their behavior and even in their basic attitudes? Do biological factors play a role in this? Is a person genetically disposed to be an American, or a German, or an Ethiopian; to be a school teacher or a bureaucrat; to be Roman Catholic or Presbyterian? One certainly cannot ignore the genetic factor, many scholars say, but it is increasingly clear that it does not explain everything or even the most important data. Kluckhohn tells this story: "Some years ago I met in New York City a young man who did not speak a word of English and was obviously bewildered by American ways. By 'blood' he was an American as you or I, for his parents had gone from Indiana to China as missionaries. Orphaned in infancy, he was reared by a Chinese family in a remote village. All who met him found him more Chinese than American. The facts of his blue eyes and light hair were less impressive than a Chinese style of gait, Chinese arm and hand movements, Chinese facial expression, and Chinese modes of thought."[25] The "typical" Dutchman, the "typical" bureaucrat, the "typical" intellectual, even the "typical" man or woman, is not born that way; he or she as "typical" Dutchman, etc., is the result of a process which a person with a certain bent and certain potentialities undergoes in a certain society and a certain culture, where she is molded by influences which are typical for that society and culture. A human being who, granted, is more than raw material in the early stages, but who can develop in any number of directions, is pressured by a variety of influences into congruency with the culture in which she has to be a functioning person.

A conceptual summary of all this, viewed from the perspective of the effect which the phenomena bring about, is that of socialization. Checking out the phenomena summarized, one finds a variety of "unintentional influences," but that is not all. Price-Williams describes "socialization" as "the training of an individual towards certain sets of values which are dominant in any society."[26] Watson defines the process as "a socio-psychological process whereby the personality is created under the influence of the educational institutions."[27]

---

[25]C. Kluckhohn, *Mirror for Man,* p. 25. Cf. R. Benedict, *Patterns of Culture,* p. 26: "An Oriental child adopted by an Occidental family learns English, shows toward its foster parents the attitudes current among the children he plays with, and grows up to the same professions that they elect. He learns the entire set of cultural traits of the adopted society, and the set of his real parents' group plays no part." K. Lewin, *Resolving Social Conflicts,* pp. 35ff., gives examples of the permanent characteristics of German, Italian, English, and Russian nationality. That these characteristics are cultural and not racial is "shown by the fact that children taken from one country to the other will quickly and thoroughly adopt the characteristics of the people in the new country."

[26]D. Price-Williams, "Cross-cultural Studies," in B. M. Foss, *New Horizons in Psychology,* p. 408.

[27]Watson, *Dictionary of Sociology,* p. 298, s.v. "Socialization Process." Watson observes: "It is a process centered fundamentally around the school, the base of all educational efforts and aims."

Again, the concept of socialization is clearly a summary of phenomena which require the special attention of pedagogics. But this does not mean that the concept is serviceable for the discipline of pedagogics.[28] The aim of socialization is a state in which the social dimensions of a person are developed. This is an important enough matter but not pivotal in the discipline of pedagogics. One might say that the socialization concept is a step in the direction of answering a question like: How does a child born in America become American? Or: How did this person who is a public official become a typical public official? But in pedagogics the first question is this: How can this child become the person she is by temperament and she should be in her world? Or: How can this person be and remain himself as a public official?

[When we doubt the usefulness of the socialization concept for the formation of pedagogical theory, this does not mean that we opt for an individualistic approach to pedagogics. The old conflict between an individualistic and a social approach to the subject is passé, now that it is generally accepted that to be human is to be human-in-community. We only intend to underscore that the typical function of pedagogics is to view the human person from the perspective of humanization, since it is up to this discipline to suggest what human beings should be in terms of their responsibility as human beings. The adoption of the socialization concept could be a reason why pedagogics, by forcing itself into an inappropriate framework, should fail to fulfil its proper function.]

Personality Formation: The Dialectics Between a Person and Her World

Where other disciplines speak of socialization, pedagogics must speak of personality formation. The elements it would gather up in this concept are probably to a high degree the same as those which fall under the umbrella of socialization. The perspective within which they are arranged, however, differs. By personality formation we mean the process by which the personality is formed. It is not our intent to immerse ourselves in the many theories of personality which are current, nor to favor one or other of these theories. The first would take us too far afield, and for the second we do not have the competence. What is more, psychologists themselves state: "We are not in a position at this stage of psychological knowledge to accept or reject any of these theories in

---

[28]T. Wilhelm, "Sozialisation und sozial Erziehung," in G. Wurzbacher, *Der Mensch als soziales und personales Wesen*, p. 146, rejects the notion that socialization is the all-embracing process of human maturation in which, then, nurture is one element. We agree with Wilhelm's intent, but believe he is mistaken in viewing the concept outside of the appropriate context. Some disciplines dealing with socialization can place nurture alongside other modes of influence; only, pedagogics is not one of them since its focus is on the "specifically pedagogical."

toto."[29] We have to limit ourselves to an outline of a few points of view which, we hope, will turn out to be helpful in finding our way through the problematics which occupy us.

[Words like "personality system" and "personality" are derived from the word "person." In his study of the word De Wilde points out that it is an "embattled" one. It appears, however, that "different ethnic groupings have chosen the symbol of the face or the head, as the most striking and, individually, the most characteristic part of the human body, to denote the typically human and the humanly typical. This role has now been fulfilled during the last two thousand years in Western Europe by the precious and indispensable word *person*."[30] *Person*, then, means "an independently acting being with a unique and specific nature."[31] Zuithoff describes *person* as "the ontic core of the personality, . . . a specifically human mode of being, a point of departure for further development and self-realization"; *personality* is "the partially realized human being in process of realizing itself." In view of the many definitions offered for the words "person" and "personality,"[32] the nonspecialist has to make an arbitrary choice; we shall stay in the vicinity of Zuithoff's attempts at definition.]

At birth we encounter a human being as a coherent set of potentialities; we shall call this the *original system* formed by a complex of genetic and congenital dispositions. The "who," "what," and "how" of the future of this human being are primarily determined by the composition of the original system. This original system is as it were the Point Zero of the development of a certain person. But it is a Point Zero full of potential. Says R. C. Kwant: "The newborn child is taken up in a pre-canalized field of existence in which the meaning of things has to a large extent already been established."[33] This child now enters a history which becomes her prehistory. She not only exists with the endowment of her biological heredity, the psychosomatic potentialities of her original system, but from the moment of birth she shares in the social heritage of the sociocultural system of the family, group, and nation to which she belongs.[34] As a

---

[29] D. Krech and R. S. Crutchfield, *Elements of Psychology*, p. 628 (1961 edition). C. S. Hall and G. Lindzey, *Theories of Personality*, pp. 554ff., affirm the existence of a "theoretical multiplicity." They believe that an attempt at synthesis or integration of personality theories is not right at this stage and would not be conducive to further inquiry.

[30] A. de Wilde, *De Persoon*, p. 18.

[31] Ibid., p. 17.

[32] G. Allport, in *Personality*, lists fifty descriptions of personality from a variety of authorities. According to him, a brief description of personality could be given in the phrase "what a man really is." Cf. C. S. Hall and G. Lindzey, *Theories of Personality*, p. 262.

[33] R. C. Kwant, *Sociale Filosofie*, p. 144.

[34] Cf. R. M. MacIver and C. H. Page, *Society*, p. 119: "The term *social heritage* was used . . . to signify the 'knowledge and expedients and habits' which are socially, not biologically, transmitted, being handed down from generation to generation through social participation and education."

participant in that system she is at once much more than she is in her original system: there is for her a mother tongue enabling her to communicate with others and to think for herself; there is a quantity of acquired knowledge and insight available to her; there are tools which she can use and which will expand and refine her work potential.

The question is: How must we understand the relationship between the biological heredity of the original system of the person and the social heritage in which she participates by virtue of being taken up into a socio-cultural system? Is it true that a person has something of her own and then gets something additional?[35] It seems to us that it is all somewhat more complicated. Says Fuller: "Heredity is a capacity to utilize an environment in a particular way."[36] The question how a person becomes the person she is meant to be depends in the first place on her capacity to utilize the opportunities offered by her world. That "capacity to utilize" is in itself a very complicated set of factors, but for the moment we shall assume that it is identical with the psychosomatic dispositions of the original system. Assuming the existence of such a thing as a special (hereditary) "aptitude for music," it is clear that a person who is absolutely devoid of this aptitude, though she lives in a world where all the facilities for becoming a musician are present, will never be one. The condition for participating in this part of her social heritage is missing. But even the person who does have the aptitude has no guarantee that she will ever become a musician or even a musical person. Langeveld offers an example. Here is someone with an "aptitude for music." In a culture which boasts musical instruments and conservatories he may get to be a musician. But as a Papuan, chances are that he will become a skilled birdhunter.[37] What is all too hastily called an "aptitude for music" is actually "an aptitude for X" where X stands for a number of forms of actualization of which music is one. Only *in a certain context* is it "aptitude for music"; in general it is a capacity to make use of those givens of the world in which the learner lives which correspond with this aptitude or—to put it in the language of chemistry—a capacity to react to those elements in the system for which this aptitude has affinity. One can view the same phenomenon from the side of the world in which the learner lives. Says Fortmann: "A culture selects and realizes only a few of the human potentialities present in every newborn child. All the others are left unused."[38] One has to assume that there are people who are born centuries too late or centuries too soon; or people who have as their world a world in which their specific potentialities can find no possibility of realization or application.

---

[35]Some such view seems to lie behind a statement like this: ". . . what we start with as human beings—our original nature—and what we acquire in the course of a lifetime are the components of personality" (A. D. Ullmann, *Socio-cultural Foundations of Personality*, p. 5).

[36]Quoted by A. L. Knutson, *The Individual, Society, and Health Behavior*, p. 54.

[37]M. J. Langeveld, *Kind en Religie*, p. 91.

[38]H. M. M. Fortmann, *Wat is er met de Mens gebeurd?*, p. 7.

It is possible, therefore, to view the original system of a person and the system of the world in which she grows up as two mutually related magnitudes which exist in an intersubjective relationship. In order to discover the specific nature of the process of personality formation, we must take still another step and observe that in the duality of these systems there is a functional unity. With reference to heredity and environment Knutson remarks: "These are not two distinct forces influencing one another in any systematic way. Rather, there is a continuous transaction between two interdependent force constellations."[39] Lewin is even more emphatic: "The development of experimental psychology shows more and more that a person and what might be called his psychological environment cannot be treated as separate entities but are dynamically one field."[40] The term "psychological environment" approximates what in phenomenological psychology is called a "situation," i.e., "a complex of meaning relationships in which a person is placed, and at the same time one which is constituted by this person."[41] The world in which a person lives, to the extent that it exists significantly for her, is more than an "outside" world; it is *her* world. This is not to say that a person cannot be estranged from it or threatened by it. But this does not diminish the fact that this world is her world; this is how she knows it, this is how she experiences it: as something strange or remote or hostile to her, but as such it is still, and even more emphatically, *her* world. For this reason it does not help much to try to convince a person who experiences her world as hostile that it is in fact a fine and friendly world, or that she is taking too dark a view of it. This kind of talk is not relevant to the actual world she lives in.

This insight into the functional unity of a person and her world is of great importance in view of the need to distinguish the specific nature of the process of personality formation. This process is not an immanent and autonomous development. Neither is it a process of actualization by which the potentialities present in the original system respond to stimuli coming from the outside—a process of cause and effect. Perhaps this unique process could be designated as being "dialectic": the person in process of becoming is involved in a continual dialogue with her world. It involves a relationship which is not instrumental or mechanical but direct and dynamic.

[Many theories of personality stress the role which events in infancy play in the process of personality formation. Special attention is given to the method of feeding (breast or bottle), weaning, and toilet training. Krech and Crutchfield point out that in general the outcome of a given practice is impossible to predict. "The point seems to be that it is not the precise form of the practice that is significant, but the particular meaning it has for the infant. The 'same' practice

---

[39] A. L. Knutson, *The Individual, Society, and Health Behavior,* p. 54.

[40] K. Lewin, *Resolving Social Conflicts,* p. 174.

[41] J. Linschoten, "Nawoord," in J. H. vanden Berg and J. Linschoten, *Persoon en Wereld,* p. 247.

can be quite different psychologically, depending upon the manner in which it is carried out and the emotions engendered."[42] So it is not the objective occurrence which shapes the direction of the process of personality formation, but the manner in which the events are perceived and experienced. The secret lies in the dialectic between a person and her world.[43]]

So the process of personality formation is not one in which a person is involved as object; it is not a process determined in its course and dynamics by the world in which she lives. Cultural anthropologists have correctly pointed out that the process of socialization and personality formation is socio-culturally conditioned—we have already referred to it. But this must not give rise to the notion that a person *becomes* what the world makes of her. We must not allow a socio-cultural determinism to take the place long occupied by biological determinism. A human being is more than, and especially different from, a number of autonomous or dependent potentialities: she is a person who has her history with the self in dialectic with her world. In that history her personality formation occurs; in other words, in that history she realizes herself.

Says Langeveld: "In the world of all that lives nothing is less a biomechanical process than the development of a human being. Everything depends on how a person handles the biological occurrences; on the one hand, he is subject to them insofar as they happen to him; on the other he has to assimilate them, place them in the course and plan of his life . . . at which they cease to be biomechanical phenomena."[44] What Langeveld here posits with reference to a person and her psychosomatic constitution also applies to her relationship to the socio-cultural environment. Fortmann makes the point that the influence of culture on a person has long been viewed as one-way traffic. "A child passively undergoes the habits of her environment and socialization can be reduced to the acquisition of reflexes." But this would not explain the occurrence of rebels.[45] And rebels occur in every culture, even the so-called primitive cultures.[46] "Rebels and conformists can . . . exist because each of them assigns meaning which constitutes the pre-eminently human dimension. Humans create their own world; choose their own mode of existence. A human being takes what comes to her out of her world and *does* something with it: interprets, accepts, rejects, or

---

[42]R. Krech and R. S. Crutchfield, *Elements of Psychology*, pp. 629ff.

[43]Cf. H. Gerth and C. Wright Mills, *Character and Social Structure*, p. 148: "The human biography results from the interplay of inner features of character previously given and acquired, with the external world of man and nature, and with hopes and fears, demands and expectations of the future. We call this interplay 'experience.' . . ."

[44]M. J. Langeveld, *Beknopte theoretische Paedagogiek*, p. 12.

[45]H. M. M. Fortmann, *Wat is er met de Mens gebeurd?*, p. 8.

[46]R. Benedict, who strongly emphasizes cultural conditioning, remarks: ". . . no anthropologist with a background of experience of other cultures has ever believed that individuals were automatons, mechanically carrying out the decrees of their civilization" (*Patterns of Culture*, p. 220).

changes it."[47] Vander Horst remarks that, given this approach, new light is shed on an old antinomy, that between heredity and environment, constitution and culture. "A person is never helplessly bound to her constitution or culture, but has the freedom to work with them; it is human to want to manage and so to maintain a measure of freedom." The kind of constitution or culture a person has is secondary to the question of whether a person will master them."[48]

The question may arise whether in this context it is proper to ascribe so much value to the fact that in every culture rebels and nonconformists occur. Rebels and nonconformists are typically, as the words indicate, deviants and as such exceptions. Should they not be viewed as failures and freaks rather than as proof for a theory whose tendency is to stress the freedom of people in process of becoming persons? One can further raise the question whether the conception we have just advanced in quotations from Langeveld and Vander Horst is not in itself an outflow of a certain type of personality formation which is heavily culturally conditioned? Are these people not the typical representatives of what D. Riesman called the "inner-directed type"? Or are we speaking of the relatively rare "autonomous" personality type which occurs, according to Riesman, as much in cultures of "tradition-direction" as in those of "inner-direction" and "other-direction": "people capable of transcending their culture at any time or in any respect"?[49] In other words, are we here forming a culturally conditioned theory about "the rule" on the shaky foundation of the "exception"? It seems to us that our knowledge of persons and personality formation is still so elementary that an adequate and scientifically responsible answer to our question, and the problematics implied in it, cannot yet be given.

We would like to address a few more remarks to the issue. One may not infer from what was said about the freedom of human persons that the ego in a person is an agency which sovereignly takes its place above or against heredity and environment. Vander Horst calls the inner ego "the core, the inner vitality, the unremitting propulsive drive from within."[50] This description may suggest that somewhere within a person is an "I." Such a conception seems incorrect. We have referred to a "personality-system"; that, too, is an abstraction or a concept. The "ego" is a conceptual summary of the same reality viewed from a different perspective. There is not an "ego" in the person but there is a human person who, depending on what one wishes to find out, can be viewed from a variety of other perspectives, and is an "I-sayer."

We would rather say that the human person is spirit, i.e., a being who relates and orients herself. The "I-saying," spiritually functioning person relates herself to her self and her world. She does not develop her personhood apart from what comes to her in that world, nor is her development determined by

---

[47]H. M. M. Fortmann, *Wat is er met de Mens gebeurd?*, pp. 8ff.
[48]L. vander Horst, *Anthropologische Psychiatrie*, I, 48ff.
[49]D. Riesman, N. Glazer, and R. Denney, *The Lonely Crowd*, p. 282.
[50]L. vander Horst, *Anthropologische Psychiatrie*, pp. 48ff.

what is within and without. The process of personality formation takes place in the storm and stress of relating oneself in various ways and directions, and it forms a personality that is uniquely one's own. This is not to deny that it can be meaningful to view a human being as a self-realizing organism or as a socio-culturally conditioned mechanism; each of these models can serve as a means by which one tracks down certain traits or elements in the extraordinarily complicated process of personality formation. But for the discipline of pedagogics, which studies people from the perspective of their full maturational development as human beings, it is necessary to recognize clearly the relativity of these models and to remember that they are not specifically oriented toward those aspects of the process which are most relevant for pedagogics. In contemplating the process of personality formation the practitioners of this discipline must ask: How does the growing person orient and relate herself? How does she function spiritually in relation to herself and her world?

In the heading of this section we refer, not to environment or milieu or "Umwelt," but to context. The context of a sentence or a word is the setting in which it functions; that setting is a dynamic whole. A word or a sentence acquires its meaning, color, and value from that context. But it also contributes meaning to the totality of that context. One cannot block out the context in order to have the plain sentence left; one cannot block out the word or the sentence in order to have just the context left. Now persons and their worlds have a similar dynamic context: they contribute their meaning to that of the whole by deriving their meaning from that whole, and vice versa.

The discipline of pedagogics finds its starting point in the fact that people function in their contexts—in the dynamics of relating to their world as their situation. In this connection pedagogics must pay attention to the influences which issue from outside people; it views them as *contextual*, i.e., as forces which work in the unitary dynamic field of people and their world, hence as questions and answers with which people have to deal in their dialectic interactions with their selves and their world, interactions which make up the process of personality formation.

Contextual Influence and the Authoritarian Personality

We should like to make clear the importance of the subject of this section with an example chosen as well with a view to what we shall say later in our discussion of how people function as spiritual beings.

[In the last few decades social psychologists have devoted a fair amount of energy to the study of a certain type of personality, usually called *the authoritarian personality*. Of fundamental importance is the so-called Berkeley research done under Adorno in the framework of a number of projects initiated by the American Jewish Committee. The report on this research appeared in

1950.[51] The central hypothesis, which was supported by the results of the research, was "that the political, economic, and social convictions of an individual often form a broad and coherent pattern, as if bound together by a 'mentality' or 'spirit,' and that this pattern is an expression of deep-lying trends in his personality."[52] The research began with a study of the anti-Semitic mind. It became apparent in this study that extreme anti-Semites exhibited not only an aversion to Jews, but a predominant anti-Semitic ideology rooted in a number of variables, such as "stereotypy; rigid adherence to middle-class values; the tendency to regard one's own group as morally pure in contrast to the immoral outgroup; opposition to and exaggeration of prying and sensuality; extreme concern with dominance and power . . . ; fear of moral contamination; fear of being overwhelmed and victimized; the desire to erect social barriers in order to separate one group from another and to maintain the morality and the dominance of one's own group."[53] If this is correct, the authors reasoned, then anti-Semitism is not an isolated phenomenon but a particular example of control by an ethnocentric ideology.

So they came to a second phase in their research. It led to the following conclusion: "Ethnocentrism is based on a pervasive and rigid ingroup–outgroup distinction; it involves stereotyped negative imagery and hostile attitudes regarding outgroups, stereotyped positive imagery and submissive attitudes regarding ingroups and a hierarchical, authoritarian view of group-interaction in which ingroups are rightly dominant, outgroups subordinate."[54]

After a third phase, which did not entirely lead to solid conclusions, it was clear to the researchers "that anti-Semitism and ethnocentrism were not merely matters of surface opinion, but general tendencies with sources, in part at least, deep within the structure of the person." The question arose whether it would be possible to penetrate directly the underlying forces working in the personality.[55] To meet the challenge, an F Scale (Fascism Scale)[56] was designed. The final phase of the research consisted of clinical investigations in which the personality structure of some two thousand persons was determined by means of interviews and psychological tests—after first testing them on their prefascist tendencies with the aid of the F Scale. From these studies it became

---

[51]T. W. Adorno, E. Frenkel-Brunswik, D. J. Levinson, and R. N. Sanford, *The Authoritarian Personality*.

[52]Ibid., p. 1.

[53]Ibid., p. 100.

[54]Ibid., p. 150.

[55]Ibid., p. 223.

[56]The instrument was so called "to signify its concern with implicit prefascist tendencies" (ibid., p. 224). J. Weima, *Psychologie van het Antipapisme*, p. 20, issues an important caution: "The personality at issue here is not always, however, fascist, but may also be antifascist, communist, catholic, or liberal. It is better, therefore, just to limit oneself to the observation that the authoritarian personality shows relevant traits which can be noted in many fascists, past and present, and which manifest themselves vividly and concretely in the ideology of fascism."

clear that the high scorers on the F Scale displayed a markedly different structure from that of the low scorers. The *authoritarian syndrome,* as it was called, showed the following traits: "the desire to present oneself as very strong and important; admiration for authority and authorities and an excessive tendency to submit to authority; viewing every social structure as a purely hierarchical one; seeing all social processes as power struggles; the evaluation of people in black-and-white categories as good or bad, strong or weak; the strong tendency to conform to conventions and to submit to the collective; the glorification of the in-group and the rejection of the out-groups; and very often, a fatalistic view of life."[57] To this can be added that the research Weima did in the Netherlands showed a connection "between the authoritarian syndrome, or posture of socio-centric prejudice, and a less personal attachment to religious values."

As an illustration—though somewhat dated—of the authoritarian personality one thinks of these lines by Samuel Butler (1612-80) from *Hudibras* (1662):

> *For his religion, it was fit*
> *To match his learning and his wit;*
> *'Twas Presbyterian true blue;*
> *For he was of that stubborn crew*
> *Of errant saints whom all men grant*
> *To be the true church militant;*
> *Such as do build their faith upon*
> *The holy text of pike and gun;*
> *Decide all controversies by*
> *Infallible artillery;*
> *And prove their doctrine orthodox*
> *By apostolic blows and knocks;*
> *Call fire and sword and desolation,*
> *A godly, thorough reformation;*
> *Which always must be carried on*
> *And still be doing, never done;*
> *As if religion were intended*
> *For nothing else but to be mended.*
>   (Part I, Canto I, II, ll. 189-206)

---

[57]M. Albinski, *De Onderwijzer en de Cultuuroverdracht,* p. 9. Compare this description of the authoritarian syndrome with the description of an authoritarian ideology as found in the handbook "The U.S. Klans, Knights of the Ku Klux Klan," quoted by J. W. Vander Zanden, "The Klan Revival," *The American Journal of Sociology* 15 (1959-60): 458: ". . . we invite all men who can qualify to become citizens of the invisible Empire . . . to share with us the sacred duty of protecting womanhood; to maintain forever the God-given supremacy of the White Race; to commemorate the holy and chivalric achievements of our fathers; to safeguard the sacred rights, privileges and institutions of our government; to bless mankind and to keep eternally ablaze the sacred fire of a fervent devotion to a pure Americanism."

That someone knows the gospel is no guarantee against becoming an authoritarian personality; Albinski's research among teachers in the Netherlands showed that especially church-related folk most frequently scored high on the F Scale.[58]

A number of questions remain regarding the genesis of the authoritarian personality. It need not be doubted, however, that contextual influence plays a large role. "It does not make much sense," says Weima, "to charge isolated aspects of the nurturing situation with responsibility for the development of the authoritarian syndrome. *It is the nurturing situation as a whole which affects the child; the atmosphere of the family* in which the child grows up and in which she interprets her various experiences *is decisive*." An expression like "the atmosphere of the family" may sound a touch too vague to be useful, but it seems plausible that it holds the key to the process of personality formation. Bollnow devoted a study to this neglected concept; in it he speaks of the "pedagogical atmosphere," by which he understands "the entire complex of human attitudes and emotional conditions which exist between the nurturers and the child and form the background for all nurturing behavior."[59] He has in mind "the total makeup of a person which exerts a steady and steadying control in the whole of her life, sustaining and shaping all the individual behaviors."[60] From the Berkeley research we now quote a few sentences which offer a hint of the atmosphere in which both the high scorers and the low scorers on the F Scale grew up.

— "In general the fathers of the unprejudiced men seem to have spent a great deal of time playing and 'doing things' with their sons." (P. 361)

—[With reference to a low scorer whose father had an interest in art:] "From all our evidence it seems likely that many of the fathers of our prejudiced men would have considered such an interest, in themselves or in their sons, as effeminate or 'sissy.' "

— "The unprejudiced man did not as a rule have to submit to stern authority in his childhood; in his later life, therefore, he neither longs for strong authority nor needs to assert his strength against those who are weaker." (P. 365)

— "There is evidence that the high scorers tend to come from families tending toward 'father-*domination*' and the low scorers from families tending toward 'mother-*orientation*.' " (P. 370)

---

[58]In the Berkeley research the link was less clear although it did show "that people who reject organized religion are less prejudiced than those who accept it" (T. W. Adorno, *The Authoritarian Personality*, p. 220). In the Lapeer research the high scorers turned out to be Roman Catholics, members of "fundamentalist Protestant sects," and regular church attenders (cf. D. Stewart and T. Hoult, "A Social-Psychological Theory of the Authoritarian Personality," in *The American Journal of Sociology* 65 (1959-60): 275ff. See also M. Argyle, *Religious Behaviour*, pp. 87ff.).

[59]O. F. Bollnow, *Diè pädagogische Atmosphäre*, p. 11.

[60]Ibid., p. 107.

—"Prejudiced subjects tend to report a relatively harsh and more threatening type of home discipline which was experienced as arbitrary by the child." (P. 385)

—[With reference to high scorers:] "Family relationships are characterized by fearful subservience to the demands of the parents and by an early suppression of impulses not acceptable to them."

—Parents of high scorers were marked by "the lack of an internalized and individualized approach to the child, . . . as well as a tendency to transmit mainly a set of conventional rules and customs. . . ."

—[With reference to low scorers:] "One of the most important differences as compared with the family of the typical high scorer is that less obedience is expected of the children. Parents are less status-ridden and show thus less anxiety with respect to conformity and are less intolerant toward manifestations of socially unaccepted behavior." (P. 387)

—". . . the unprejudiced subjects on the whole received more love and feel basically more secure in relation to their parents." (P. 388)

We now wish to pass along some of the relevant data from the research of M. Rokeach which relates directly to this admittedly impressionistic sketch.[61] He, too, concerns himself with the atmosphere in which the authoritarian personality tends to develop. According to him, the Berkeley research is too much oriented toward content in its questions and method of inquiry. So he made a study of the general properties held in common by all forms of authoritarianism, which he calls "dogmatism" and which is characterized by a closed belief system. In this study it became evident that in their childhood years the low scorers were much less troubled by neurotic symptoms (thumb sucking, nail biting, temper tantrums, nightmares, sleepwalking) and stopped wetting their beds at a much earlier age. The connection of this behavior with the atmosphere of "security and confidence, gratitude and love, patience and hope"—with a healthy atmosphere of nurture, that is—is obvious.

Rokeach's research offers yet another significant datum. To the question which persons outside the restricted family circle were influential in the lives of growing children there were divergent responses. The high scorers and middle group referred especially to clergy and scout leaders; the low scorers indicated they had been influenced by a variety of persons and groups. This information seems to support the theory concerning the genesis of the authoritarian personality proposed by Stewart and Hoult. They hold that the authoritarian personality is characteristically able to play only a limited number of social roles and has

---

[61]M. Rokeach, *The Open and Closed Mind,* investigations into the nature of belief systems and personality systems. "The *belief system* is conceived to represent all the beliefs, sets, expectancies, or hypotheses, conscious and unconscious, that a person at a given time accepts as true of the world he lives in. The *disbelief system* . . . contains all the disbeliefs, sets, expectancies, conscious or unconscious, that, to one degree or another, a person at a given time rejects as false" (p. 33).

little capacity for imagining the roles fulfilled by others. According to them, the data show "that authoritarianism is most likely to appear among people who are reared in *established* social surroundings that inhibit the development of role-taking and role-playing ability." The authoritarian syndrome may be found especially among "(1) the less educated, (2) the aged, (3) the rural, (4) members of disadvantaged minorities, (5) of the more dogmatic religious organizations, (6) of lower socioeconomic strata, (7) social isolates, and (8) those who have been reared in an authoritarian family environment." We may suppose that the person who grew up within a narrow circle and with little diversity in social contacts easily failed when he had to play new social roles, and therefore regressed to more familiar and acceptable roles. He will also have difficulty understanding the way in which roles are fulfilled in other groups and to empathize with members of other groups, "and therefore he tends to reject such groups, to feel hostility toward their members, and to rationalize his own failures by projecting blame on outgroups and their members."[62] It seems to us that this explanation of the rise of authoritarian personalities need not take the place of a psychoanalytic explanation but can be an important complement to it. In general, to revert back to our own vocabulary, one could say that the authoritarian personality is the result of the "dialectics" of a person and a world in which there were few opportunities for really dialectic interactions. In this world the growing person gets to know only a small variety of models of behavior. The rules for correct behavior in his socio-cultural system are strictly laid down; deviation is punished and rebellion crushed. He is allowed little space for exploration, and when he seeks it out he is pulled back. It is his job to appropriate what "we" know, to comply with what is valid "among us"; he must keep himself uncontaminated by "the others" whose modes of thought, action, and life are "different." His experience takes place in a circumscribed, even a closed, world. His context is that of the restricted and exclusive "we": "we whites," "we Aryans," "our people," "we workers," "we of this area," "we Reformed," "we Catholics." His induction into life is little more than induction into the "we-group" [the wee group?], the "we" of race, or club, or clan.[63]

All this can be made explicit in direct and intentional "nurture." But this implies that it was all implicit in his world. There is an atmosphere which precedes all action, the atmosphere of the exclusivistic we-feeling, which shapes the action. It instinctively raises barriers against everything which is experienced as a threat to one's own way of life; it is defensive against what comes up out of the growing person whose dialectic with her world is nonconformist.]

From this example—the genesis of the authoritarian personality syndrome—it is clear how extremely important to pedagogics the concept of contextual influence really is. We have found now that what is done intentionally

---

[62]D. Stewart and T. Hoult, "A Social-Psychological Theory of the Authoritarian Personality," in *The American Journal of Sociology* 65 (1959-60): 274ff.

[63]J. Weima, *Psychologie van het Antipapisme*, p. 17, uses the term "sociocentrism."

and directly to a growing person does not determine who and of what kind she will be; of primary influence is what happens in the dialectics between *this* person and *her* world—which is the situation in which the early years are embedded and the process of personality formation takes place.

We shall indicate later what we believe the significance of the preceding section to be for a concept of nurture.

4. EQUIHUMAN ADDRESS

A Breakthrough in Pedagogic Thought

The process of personality formation occurs in the dialectics between the growing person and her world. A person becomes a person in the context of *her* context. Before it treats nurture as such, therefore, pedagogics has good reason to give every consideration to contextual influence. But something else has logical priority over nurture. In a sense it is an element in the spectrum of contextual influences, but it is marked by a certain intentionality and focus without being, in the strict sense, nurture. In general we can describe this element as follows: in the world of the growing person are others who approach and address her simply as one human being relating to another without any strictly pedagogic intent. This address comes to expression in a variety of ways; e.g., as correction, comfort, encouragement, advice, or appeal.

O. F. Bollnow in particular has studied these phenomena, which he has called "inconstant formative processes."[64]

[Bollnow points out that after 1945—"after so many sincerely meant efforts at nurture had hopelessly failed"—serious doubt arose about the possibility of nurture. The classic theory of nurture had been "the pedagogics of steady continuity": the basic idea is that a person, responding to the influences that bear down on her, moves by gradual steps toward a relative form of maturity. This conception still prevailed after the idea of gradualism—no leaps—had been given up in the natural sciences. It is time, said Bollnow, for pedagogics to consider the question of whether "continuity is a necessary presupposition of *all* nurture."[65] In order to answer the question Bollnow turns to the philosophy of existentialism. Not that it is his intent to construct a pedagogics based on this philosophy; his point of departure is pedagogics and its problems; but he does want to know what pedagogics can learn from the impulses of existentialist philosophy. This philosophy has developed a view of man "in which there is no continuity at all." This view of man now serves Bollnow as a model. He uses

---

[64]O. F. Bollnow, "Das veränderte Bild vom Menschen und sein Einfluss auf das pädagogische Denken," in *Erziehung wozu?*; "Die Ermahnung," in *Erziehung zur Menschlichkeit*; and *Existenzphilosophie und Pädagogik*.

[65]O. F. Bollnow, *Existenzphilosophie und Pädagogik*, p. 19.

it as a heuristic principle helping him to track down forms of nurture other than those which have been long recognized. Bollnow believes that existentialist philosophy can alert us to forms of nurture which have always existed but which classic pedagogics has overlooked and cannot place, with its exclusive bias toward gradualism.[66] Bollnow's reason for turning toward existentialist philosophy is probably that this philosophy, as Köhler puts it, "includes the experience of human failure. It has developed against the background of the shattering events which twentieth-century man has experienced." Nevertheless, it does not degenerate into pessimism but affirms human freedom to make decisions. For that reason it can save pedagogics from optimism without driving it into pessimism.[67] Existentialist philosophy denies the continuity of human existence. People exist merely in the moment, and therefore cannot be subject to gradually formative influences: the person of today is different from the person of tomorrow. But in the present moment of his existence he can be addressed and freely make his own decisions. With the help of this model new forms of relating spring into view, especially those modes of address which are focused on a person in his present moment. Bollnow lists exhortation, admonition, command, appeal, alerting, counseling, information, and encounters. The clearest example of the "inconstant" forms of nurture is admonition, the most commonplace form in the group.[68] Admonition, says Bollnow, does not enjoy high ratings in public opinion. It does not accomplish much, so runs the consensus, and the educator who resorts to admonition feels it as a pedagogical defect that she cannot prevent the development of a situation in which she has to resort to it. But why is resort made to it over and over? Is that sheer weakness or is something else at work? Bollnow is persuaded of the latter. Admonition is "heightened warning." Someone has failed; a debt has been incurred. "Admonition is addressed to a being who has the property of being able to fall culpably short of what may be expected and of having the ability, with a new effort, to make good the difference."[69] Admonition is a reminder of what might have been, but wasn't, realized; it is an address to persons who are free to decide their course of action and can still shape their futures by their choices.]

We have reproduced some snatches of Bollnow's thought because he appears to have made reflection on "the pedagogical question" a new adventure. His greatest merit, it would seem, is that he has broken up a firmly established pattern of pedagogical thought.

[This is most strikingly evident when he speaks of "risks and failure in nurture." Given the technical conception of nurture (nurture is a vocational act of guidance), or the opposite conception of organic development ("let 'em grow"), failure is either a mistake in the guidance offered, or a defect in the "material,"

---

[66]Ibid., pp. 21ff.
[67]H. Köhler, *Theologie der Erziehung*, pp. 169ff.
[68]H. Schaal, *Erziehung bei Kierkegaard*, p. 122.
[69]O. F. Bollnow, "Die Ermahnung," in *Erziehung zur Menschlichkeit*, p. 177.

or a disturbance in the process of development. But a pedagogics which is aware of "inconstant formative influences" realizes that the possibility of failure is anchored in the very essence, one might say the very dignity, of nurture itself. For at the core of the process a free being encounters another free being with certain expectations and from the beginning the first must take into account the freedom of the second, a freedom which fundamentally escapes prediction and calculation. Viewed from this core, admonition is a "richly helpful appeal to the freedom that is unfolding." This is even clearer in the category of "calling attention to." H. Schaal, in his study of nurture in Kierkegaard, shows how Kierkegaard sums up all his work in the phrase: "Calling attention to the religious dimension without reference to any authority."[70] Beyond that Kierkegaard does not dare to go; neither is it possible. "That which alone has weight for Kierkegaard, that which alone constitutes the essence of nurture for him, is the experience of the claim of the Absolute which alone has binding force. . . ."[71] "Calling attention to" is ". . . the dialectical moment of essential (because divinely initiated) nurture."[72] As such "it lies beyond all pedagogical planning and action."[73] But this is not to say that the category is not important for pedagogics. "To call attention to," like the appeal or the admonition, is "a form of address to the inwardness of a person."[74] Next to organized pedagogical action, this, too, can and must be done; and as a result of this vertical transaction nurture, now no longer a merely horizontal process, again becomes "an event."[75]]

This breakthrough, we have said, has made pedagogics a new adventure. In any case, it enables us to assume a more critical position toward a traditional concept of nurture and to focus on Point Zero of pedagogical reflection: the reality of the growth of a human being. In our opinion Bollnow, under the sway of the impulses of existentialist philosophy, has not gone far enough in that direction. We ask: How does the reality of the growth of a human being look? This is what we have seen so far: there is a context which exerts continual influence upon her. There is also what we think of when we hear the word "nurture": a somewhat systematic, continuous influence upon the growing person exerted by people who are responsible for her growth into maturity. But "inconstant formative influences" (Bollnow) also bear directly on the growing person: the nurturer's address, which is incidental and existential. But what in these "inconstant formative influences" is now the essential component from a pedagogical viewpoint? It is not, we believe, their "inconstancy." Commenting on the existential category of encounter, Hauschildt has remarked that "the event

---

[70]H. Schaal, *Erziehung bei Kierkegaard*, p. 25.
[71]Ibid., p. 17.
[72]Ibid., p. 110.
[73]Ibid., p. 111.
[74]Ibid., p. 114.
[75]Ibid., p. 16.

of encounter unfolds its formative power in a field of encounters."[76] One could say the same about all forms of nurture embracing an appeal to inwardness and responsibility: in themselves they are incidental and focused on the existential "now." But they do not occur in isolation; they occur to the growing person in one field of experience and together reveal something to her of how she is viewed by significant others. One of Bollnow's emphases has been that admonition presupposes that the person being admonished has the possibility of self-determination; the very aim of admonition is self-determination. This is even more strongly the case with other categories of address—in counseling, in "calling someone's attention to," in making appeals. In counseling the counselor is completely at the disposal of the decision-making process of the other. In the counseling situation a person is called to make her own choice between the available options. The "encounter" is an "inconstant event" which "shakes up" a person; i.e., the encounter breaks through the line of development and implies a new beginning which the counselee herself has to make.[77]

Now in all this—and it seems to us we are about to touch on an aspect which is extremely important for the humanization process—the growing person again and again encounters forms of treatment which are alike. Two things can be said of those forms of treatment. *One*: they consist in address (Dutch *aanspraak*), in admonition, in exhortation, or in confrontation in a counseling setting, and such forms of relating are all directed to a person with the intention that she may know that she is being spoken to as *agent,* and that she may begin to take responsibility for the behavior in question. It is as if, out of the context of her developing life, in each of these forms of address, something comes to her which is clearly focused on her as a person, something uniquely aimed at her. Through these forms of address she comes to the discovery: I am somebody; I myself am somebody; I am I. *Two*: This address is typically "equihuman."[78] It seems to us that in saying this we have come upon an important preagogic category whose meaning needs to be more closely explored.

The Recognition of One's Equals (Dutch evenmens)

We have noted earlier that, as Strasser observed, the begetting of life precedes all forms of nurture.[79] Were one to neglect this prepedagogical category one could not see clearly what nurture is. To this another element must be added. People who procreate life procreate a life which, however directly bound up

---

[76]K. Hauschildt, "Wachstum im Glauben," in *Glauben und Verstehen,* a Festschrift for Gerhard Bohne, p. 244.

[77]O. F. Bollnow, *Existenzphilosophie und Pädagogik,* p. 99.

[78][The word "equihuman" is a coinage used as the semantic equivalent of the Dutch word *evenmenselijk.* I know of no existing English equivalent. The word implies a preethical presumption of equality between persons not usually thought of as equals. *Tr.*]

[79]See p. 109.

with their own, is *new*. The newborn baby *has* a name, the family name, but is also *given* a name, a *proper* name. The proper name individualizes the newborn in the midst of those who bear the same family name. The newborn is called and destined to be independent—to a dignity and responsibility which is uniquely her own. Those who have begotten the new life and should function as its *auctores* (growth promoters) need to acknowledge the unique personal dignity of the newborn as well as their being of "one flesh" with her. She is their child but at the same time their *evenmens,* i.e., their "equal in the quality of being human."

[We deliberately refer here to the "equihuman" and not to the "fellow human." The latter term has a special significance which is not here under discussion. Karl Barth has called "fellow humanity" the basic form of humanity. *"The* humanity of human being is this total determination as being in encounter with the being of the thou as being with the fellow man, as fellow humanity."[80] This being in encounter, this fellow humanity, consists concretely in that one looks the other in the eye; there is mutual speech and hearing; there is mutual assistance—all of it done on both sides with gladness, not reluctantly or neutrally but from the heart.[81] The recognition of the other as equal is implied. For the experience of "fellow humanity" this recognition is in a sense a condition. I can look the other in the eye, talk with, listen to, and assist the other, only if I recognize her in her freedom and uniqueness as my equal on the level of her humanity. The child, too, is equal to those who are responsible for her human-ization. This statement is not a contradiction in terms. "Our lives consist in the process of becoming. What constitutes my life is not something I am from the start but something I become in the course of time," says R. Guardini.[82] But a person can become human in the full sense only if she is recognized in her humanity—spoken to and held accountable for that humanity. Parents and chil-dren have practically always done this; it was only when people thought and talked about children *apart from this direct association* with them that the rec-ognition was hard to come by.

Alexander Pope's condescending lines suggesting the vanity of childhood are typical of the way children have been viewed for centuries.

> *Behold the child, by Nature's kindly law,*
> *Pleased with a rattle, tickled with a straw;*
> *Some livelier plaything gives his youth delight,*
> *A little louder, but as empty quite. . . .*
> From *The Essay on Man* (1733), Epistle II, Part VI, ll. 275-78

M. J. Langeveld, who has repeatedly complained that neither philosoph-ical nor theological anthropology, nor even pedagogics, has given attention to

---

[80]K. Barth, *CD*, III/2, pp. 222ff. The quotation is taken from p. 247.
[81]Ibid., pp. 266ff.
[82]R. Guardini, *Grundlegung der Bildungslehre*, p. 9.

childhood *as a mode of being human*, stated that from ancient times on people have reflected on childhood but only "as a stage to be overcome. As quickly as possible the child should cease to be stupid. The child was a lovely creature, of course, a future citizen and hence a means to political ends, and the like. But what was the child herself?"[83] Without that question, the question concerning the humanness of the child, there can be no real association with the child or even nurture. The question is *still* urgent. J. Fangmeier[84] remarks that, of late, interest in the child has increased. Much is being done for the child, and many disciplines—each from its own angle of vision—study the young person. "But that is no guarantee that justice will be done to the child as a human being or to human beings as children. 'The anthropology of the child' no longer means the one-sided elevation of the child, which was for a period of time a necessary reaction to the violence done to him, but now it focuses on the *integration* of the child. What of the integration of the *child*?"]

We have called "equihuman address" a preagogic category. By that we mean that *all action toward a human being with a view to his or her humanization has its starting point in dealing with a particular person as a human being*. A human being is never—not even as a child—only an object which can be taught, commanded, spoken *to*; he or she is always an equal who is and has to be himself or herself an agent, and as such has to be spoken *with*.

In Part II, section 15, we noted that both in practical theology and in the discussion surrounding psychotherapy opposition has arisen to agogy. Agogy, it was said, may have its place, but it has no role to play in pastoral or in psychotherapeutic contact. This opposition seems to be mistaken; but it is entirely corect if it is directed against an agogy which is not rooted in human-to-human address; an agogy in which only the nurturer knows the rules and fails to see the other as *an* other but only views her as one whose life must be shaped by the nurturer's goals and fashioned in accordance with her ideals. Such a situation is not normal. The real humanization process is different: in it the nurturer "forgets" she has to nurture; in it human-to-human talk is the rule.

[*Situation*: Mother asks 12-year-old Tom to please keep an eye on Gregory, who is just out of his playpen, while she is in the kitchen. She does not say this to Tom in order to teach Tom a lesson, but only because someone has to watch little Gregory. When mother returns to the living room and finds that Tom has had his nose in a book and never looked up, and that Gregory has emptied the sugar bowl and grabbed the scissors off the table, she says to Tom: "Why didn't you do what I told you?" She says this because she finds Tom clearly guilty of negligence and holds him accountable. This sort of thing happens all the time. Without consciously wanting to "bring up" their children, parents make demands of them, confront them with expectations, call their attention to things, admonish them—*as humans to humans*. Whatever "nurture" may be, it is normal for it not

---

[83]M. J. Langeveld, *Studien zur Anthropologie des Kindes*, pp. 1, 106.
[84]J. Fangmeier, *Theologische Anthropologie des Kindes*, pp. 4ff.

to be a reversal or cancellation of the human-to-human relationship. When the equihuman relationship is real, conscious nurture takes place in the form of equihuman treatment.]

The Nurturer as Equal to the Nurturee

Next we wish to examine more closely a number of elements in this category of "equihuman address." It implies, in the first place, that the nurturer is equal to the nurturee.[85] F. Blättner, in his discussion of Socrates, remarks: "The dialogue is something essentially Socratic: The epic poets pictured great events; the Sophists used the lecture-form; but here is one who asks questions, one who knows the pain of the unresolved issue. He does not raise questions simply to enlarge upon and polish what he already knows; no, he asks questions of others in order to confront his own ignorance."[86] In contrast with the Sophists, Socrates, by his questions, put himself at risk. But by this method he was able to get people to search for wisdom and virtue. He, the man who was everybody's equal, became an educator so great that a society lost in the illusion of having the answers had to condemn him as the corrupter of the young. We have already referred to another great educator—the apostle Paul—who, though he was conscious of having authority as an apostle of the Lord, knew himself an equal of other believers. He longed to meet the believers at Rome in order "to impart some spiritual gift"; but no less for the encouragement and admonition which he would receive from them, as one believer among others (Rom. 1:11-12). According to J. H. vanden Berg, one of the conditions of dialogue is the asymmetry of the speakers.[87] This applies to every relationship if it is to be a life-promoting relationship; perfect equals have nothing to share with each other. There is a typical asymmetry in relationships like that between nurturer and nurturee, teacher and student, pastor and parishioner. But this does not mean that the person who is the growth promoter in each of these relationships does not appear as equal in the qualities which express and make for humanity. If this equality were not present and presupposed, there would be no sense in speaking of asymmetry. The term refers to a disparity which exists on the basis of a fundamental and essential equality.

---

[85]We speak of nurturer, nurture, and nurturee without having said what we understand by "nurturing" and "nurture"; and we have said that "equihuman address" is a preagogic category. We use these terms partly because we have no other, partly because other terms would sound artificial and affected and perhaps unintelligible. By nurturer we mean an *auctor* in a *relatio auctifica* (for these terms, see pp. 110, 112-14).

[86]F. Blättner, *Geschichte der Pädagogik*, p. 17. The picture of Socrates presented here agrees with what Van Peursen has said of "real communication": "to influence one's fellow human by the manner in which one oneself proves to need the fellow human in order, in this special interhuman relationship, to be oneself"; "Communicatie," in M. Kamphuis, *Om de Leefbaarheid van het Bestaan*, p. 206).

[87]J. H. vanden Berg, "Het Gesprek," in J. H. vanden Berg and J. Linschoten, *Persoon en Wereld*, pp. 153ff.

[In recent years Carl R. Rogers has mentioned the significance of the equihuman in another typically asymmetrical relationship, namely, that of counselor and client. His terms are congruence and genuineness, or realness and transparency on the side of the therapist. His concern is "a realness in the counselor which is deep and true, not superficial." Rogers' conviction is "that personal growth is facilitated when the counselor is what he *is*, when in the relationship with his client he is genuine and without 'front' or 'facade.' " In research into the therapeutic process as it occurred in the treatment of schizophrenia, Rogers found his hypothesis confirmed: "The individual therapists in our research program who seem to be most successful in dealing with these unmotivated, poorly educated, resistant, chronically hospitalized individuals, are those who are first of all real, who react in a genuine, human way as persons, and who exhibit their genuineness in the relationship."[88]]

Rogers refers to a specific relationship, the therapeutic. The equihuman in this relationship means that the counselor will react to his client in genuine human fashion and allow his client to participate in what he experiences in the relationship, even though he would reveal his own imperfections.[89] In other typically asymmetrical, growth promoting relationships the growth promoter will experience and express his equality in accord with the nature of the relationship. But always the idea is this: the nurturer in a nurturing relationship or the pastor in a pastoring relationship will be present as equal and not as the representative of perfect knowledge, an inviolable order, or the absolute truth. One must always remember that in each of these relationships—in some more than in others—a person has to deal with the strictly and specifically personal life of another human being. This takes place with a certain purpose and in a certain functional relationship; nevertheless, the fact remains that one person must admit another into the sensitive regions of his or her life. Speaking of a sick visit—in this case, of one friend or acquaintance with another—Vanden Berg remarks that the visitor must put herself in the place of the patient but that the patient "can allow this only when she, on her part, will have permission to put herself in that of the visitor."[90] One cannot simply say that the same thing applies to the functional relationships which are typically asymmetrical. Equality is constitutive for the relationship between friends. In the relationships between nurturer and nurturee, therapist and client, and pastor and parishioner, the functional inequality is constitutive. Rümke's well-known saying "maximal empathy without loss of objectivity"[91] applies absolutely to all relationships. But both are human, a fact which is not accidental but essential for the relationship. The

---

[88]Carl R. Rogers, "The Interpersonal Relationship: The Core of Guidance," in R. L. Mosher, R. F. Carle, and C. O. Kehas, *Guidance*, pp. 50ff.

[89]Ibid., pp. 51ff.

[90]J. H. vanden Berg, *Het Ziekbed*, p. 28.

[91]H. C. Rümke, *Psychiatrie*, I, 342. [Or more literally: "maximal closeness without loss of distance." *Tr.*]

humanity of the growth promoter in the relationship creates the field in which what needs to happen can happen.[92] A robot cannot be pastorally or psychotherapeutically active. In these relationships the humanity of the growth promoter serves the healing or the reorientation of the humanity of the other. *The growth promoter who does not enter the relationship as equal, does not enter the relationship; he not only does not come close to the other; he cannot even maintain distance: he is simply not there.*

The Nurturee as Equal to the Nurturer

The first element in the category of "equihuman address" is that the nurturer is the equal of the nurturee. Related to this is a second element, namely, that of the presence of the nurturee as an equal.

[M. Buber, in his addresses on education, asserts that over against will to power as the principle of the old education, Eros has been posited as the principle of the new. He believes this to be wrong. Both the will to power and Eros are passions of the soul. "Eros is choice, choice made from an inclination. This is precisely what education is not."[93] The "essence of education," he explains, begins with "the experience of the other side." Buber brings out the significance of this concept by means of two examples. One man strikes another. The moment the striker hits the body of the other he receives in his own body the impact of the blow. For the space of a moment he experiences the common situation from the other side. Now what will he do? He has two possibilities: "either he will silence the soul or his impulse will be reversed."[94] Another example: A man caresses a woman, who lets herself be caressed. Then he feels the contact from two sides—with the palm of his hand still, but also with the woman's skin. By this experience of the other side he arrives at "inclusion"—"the complete realization of the submissive person, the desired person, the partner, not by the fancy but by the actuality of being." This "inclusion" is not the same as "empathy." The importance of empathy for nurture, psychotherapy, and pastoral contact has often been referred to; it is the act of transposing oneself into the "space" of the other. But, says Buber, this involves the exclusion of one's own concreteness. Inclusion is its opposite: "it is the extension of one's own concreteness, the fulfilment of the actual situation of life, the complete presence of the reality in which one participates." Inclusion involves, as an element, the fact that this one person, without forfeiting anything of his own, at the same time lives through the common event from the standpoint of the other.[95] Real education takes place in the relation of inclusion. Concretely, this means for the educator: "Without the action of his spirit being in any way weakened he must

---

[92]P. T. Hugenholtz, *De Psychagogie of reëducatieve Behandelingsmethode*, p. 33.
[93]M. Buber, *Between Man and Man*, p. 94.
[94]Ibid., p. 96.
[95]Ibid., p. 97.

at the same time be over there, on the surface of that other spirit which is being acted upon—and not of some conceptual, contrived spirit, but all the time the wholly concrete spirit of this individual and unique being who is living and confronting him. . . ."[96] We need not follow Buber's expositions of education as a dialogic relation. Our intent is merely to call attention to the concept of "experiencing the other side" and the notion of "inclusion," both of which may help us understand better the category of "equihuman address."]

In equihuman address the person being addressed is concretely present as the equal of the person speaking. Words of admonition or encouragement or inspiration or advice are not just addressed to a person; they are not just about her; they enter her existence. But this can occur only if she is so present to the speaker that she can open her existence to his words. Words, intended as personal address, tend to run off our backs if we do not recognize ourselves in them. Everyone has had the experience that a sermon, or an admonition, or a pastoral word, made no impression. It just did not touch one. One of the causes of this nonoccurrence was always that we did not see ourselves in the words. They remained alien to us because we were not included as equals in the formation of the thoughts and words of the speaker. They were not, in Buber's words, spoken from the relation of inclusion. The address was aimed at our problems, our defects, our needs, but stood in no relation to ourselves.

Eric Erikson, in his book on the young man Luther, devoted a few pages to the psychoanalysis of young people. According to Erikson, young people are continually concerned to affirm themselves and to receive affirmation. When they get into trouble and need psychotherapeutic help, one has to remember this. With young people one cannot follow the "orthodox" analytic practice of letting the patient lie on a couch while the analyst positions himself out of sight. "They want to face you, and they want you to face them. [. . .] When suddenly confronted with such a conflicted young person the psychoanalyst may learn for the first time what facing a face, rather than facing a problem, really means."[97] "Facing a face" is a fundamental condition for success, not just in a therapeutic relationship, nor just in the relationship with young people, but in any relationship intended to be growth promoting.

[It is necessary to note here that it is not easy to indicate concretely what this implies. Especially in the theory of psychotherapy attention has been given to the questions which come up here. We have the impression—as outsiders—that a path is becoming visible on which adherents of different schools can travel. It has often been observed that psychotherapists of different schools, holding to mutually exclusive theories and using radically different techniques, nevertheless all have results. In view of this reality a consensus is growing that in psychotherapy the relationship between the therapist and the client is what counts. Says J. H. Dijkhuis: "The unfruitful discussions concerning which ther-

---

[96]Ibid., p. 100.
[97]E. H. Erikson, *Young Man Luther*, p. 15.

apeutic therapies should be preferred have given place to an analysis of the conditions which the therapeutic relationship must meet.[98] This is not to be considered a victory for encounter theory in psychotherapy. The accent lies not so much on encounter—according to Buber encounter is possible only by grace[99]—but on the process of interaction between therapist and client, a process which can be directed, conducted, and afterward analyzed. The process of interaction is typically a process between humans; it is necessary, therefore, when all depends on the process, that the therapist perceive and acknowledge the other as an equal.[100]]

In pedagogics, and certainly in practical theology, much less attention has been given till now to the problematics of the interhuman. In any case, the pedagogical and pastoral situations are *naturally,* as it were, situations in which the concern is "facing a face, rather than facing a problem." Even when in this situation "something" of the other person is in focus, by that token the person of the other is at once involved; i.e., the person in process of becoming or, as Luther had it, "the man of God" who is always in the making. But neither pedagogics nor practical theology can be satisfied to confess this "with the mouth" and then do business as usual. It is urgently necessary, especially in practical theology, that methods be developed with the help of which it will become possible to get to know the other person in her uniqueness and current experience of reality, in order that the real process of interaction may get under way.

The Nurturee as a Person with a Unique Responsibility

Finally we turn to a third element in the category of equihuman address. It is the point at which this preagogic category touches directly upon the agogic.

We remind ourselves that the "inconstant formative influences," of which Bollnow speaks, have the character of a specific appeal in concrete situations. Call to mind, for instance, the word of admonition. Admonition is an intense reminder of something which is of basic significance for a person's behavior in a given situation, and it confronts that person and her behavior with that of which she is reminded. Counseling provides a person with new data and new insights with which she now has to deal. We saw earlier that the process of personality formation occurs in a dialectic between the person and her world. In the equihuman dialogue something out of that world is brought out and lifted up for examination, a possibility of restructuring that world is offered, and a

---

[98]J. H. Dijkhuis, *Het Proces van de Interactie tussen Psycholoog en Cliënt*, p. 20.

[99]M. Buber, *I and Thou*, p. 11. "The *Thou* meets me through grace—it is not found by seeking."

[100]Cf. J. H. Dijkhuis, *Het Proces van de Interactie . . .* , p. 18: "The process of interaction occurs in a situation in which information is exchanged back and forth, the partners entertain expectations toward each other, the relationship is emotionally charged, personal affinities play a role, and the human dialectic between the two partners is always a condition."

new response to that world is expected. This is to say that inherent in equihuman address is the recognition of the other *as someone called and entitled to give an account of his or her actions*.

Hugenholtz points out that "society in general" does not accept the image of a human who is completely determined by heredity or environment. "The code by which society lives, the laws by which it is regulated, proceeds from the possibility of choice between good and evil. They ascribe this possibility of choice to the *I* of a person and so declare the *I* to be an addressable and responsible entity." The *I* demands that it be held responsible.[101] According to Hugenholtz this can be said only of the adult. Were this true, it would mean that this element is missing in the equihuman form of speech. This in turn would imply that the category of equihuman address should not be called a preagogic but a postagogic mode of speech. On this issue we wish to submit a few [parenthetical] remarks.

[*First*: we note that Hugenholtz places the concept of responsibility in the moral sphere: he speaks of the possibility of choice between good and evil. That, in the concrete situations of every day, is an important choice to make. But the elective activity of a person not only functions in a choice between moral alternatives; to choose is to take one's position over against many different possibilities. It is one of the fundamental activities of the life whose premise is the ability to experience oneself in freedom and responsibility.

Second: The child, too, regularly positions herself over against a range of possibilities. From the candy jar she picks her sweets; from the playroom closet she chooses a toy or a puzzle. At school, when doing arithmetic, she makes a choice from the options known to her. When conflicts arise in class or among friends, she chooses sides. Reading a book or watching a TV show, she picks her hero or heroine. In a tense situation she opts for a certain form of behavior. In the process all kinds of factors—of temperament, upbringing, and momentary circumstances—play a role; factors, too, of which the child herself is not conscious. Often it seems as if "it chooses" in the child, the way "it rains" outside; sometimes that is close to being true. But anyone who regularly deals with children knows that choices are not made by a self-operating mechanism in the child. One may notice that even young children do not know how, or dare, to choose. Sometimes when the choice is difficult they say in advance that it is hard to choose because they are afraid they'll regret the choice later. Perquin says that children tend to follow a subjective heteronomous morality that must develop slowly into a subjective autonomous morality; "they are tied to the value judgments of their environment."[102] It is a question whether one may speak here

---

[101]P. T. Hugenholtz, *De Psychagogie of reëducatieve Behandelingsmethode*, pp. 11ff.

[102]N. Perquin, *Pedagogiek*, p. 231. Here is a typical example of the heteronomous morality of a child: At the very moment that one of my children—a 5-year-old—was hurling imprecations at his little brother, I entered the room. I admonished him, to which he reacted by saying: "I did not know you were here." When I tried to explain that this was no excuse, he said: "Honest—I *really* did not know you were here." The child knew he had done something "wrong" but that meant to him "something dad won't allow."

of heteronomy. It is probably more correct to say that the child, when making choices, in whatever situation—in the absence of experience of her own and also to avoid getting into an unsafe isolation—will orient herself to the value judgment of "significant others"—i.e., others who are significant to her in a specific situation.[103] This does not mean that the child neglects to make choices; the changes in orientation—now the parents, then the sibling, now the teacher, then the class, then the rascals on the playground—themselves point toward the activity of choosing.

Third: we must always bear in mind that the elective activity of a child is the activity *of a child*. Like the adult the child is responsible in the measure of his "response-ability." This responsibility is not an abstract one, but the concretely human "response-ability" of this person. If in doing sums for which he is not ready the child opts for a wrong approach; if in a problem situation which calls for the experience of an adult the child opts for inappropriate behavior; if he—still unfamiliar with the idea of the objective economic value of a thing— trades in his scooter for a bag of marbles, he is not responsible for his choice. Says Janse de Jonge: "Accountability rests on the possibility of conversation conducted between two agents, whatever their standing."[104] This implies that accountability is determined, and hence limited, by the possibility of mutual confrontation in a given situation. The child is responsible to the extent that he can understand and answer and "give reasons" in a situation of choice and accountability. But this immediately means that he is called and entitled to answer for himself at his level of human maturity. Even the "minor" is not entirely without "say." Being "of age" is always a relative thing; the child is "of age" in the measure he is conscious of his conduct in a given situation.

We may therefore infer that equihuman address is possible in the relationship between an adult and a child. The asymmetry in this relationship *pre* supposes equality in being human. The nurturer must always be aware that the child is not a choice-making machine but a human being who in his choices is beginning to function mentally and who must be taken seriously in this capacity. Only if the child is treated with respect will his ability to function mentally get past the level of rudimentary reflexes and to the level of a full-fledged human response. With a view to a conversation between a nurturer and a nurturee Strasser remarks: "Conversation includes affirmation and nonaffirmation. It is clearly the case that if the nurturer were to affirm everything the child said this kind of utterance would not deserve the name 'conversation.' "[105] This applies not only to the conversation with words; life-in-community between adult and child includes affirmation and nonaffirmation; it is an ordinary human, i.e., an equihuman, life.]

---

[103]These are by no means always the parents; in dress choices, for instance, the peer group soon takes over.

[104]A. L. Janse de Jonge, *De Mens in zijn Verhoudingen*, pp. 52ff.

[105]S. Strasser, *Opvoedingswetenschap en Opvoedingswijsheid*, p. 52.

This acknowledgment of the other as a person called and entitled "to give an account" is an important element in the preagogic category of equihuman address. When this acknowledgment is missing as a starting point for an agogic relationship, then that relationship cannot be growth promoting. *The person who cannot actually acknowledge the core of the life he is called to promote, cannot in his relationship to another be of any positive significance.*

One of the most tragic stories in contemporary history is the life story of the Hiroshima pilot Claude Eatherly. After World War II Eatherly felt called to oppose the spirit of adoration for war heroes, which is dangerously close to the glorification of war and violence. He then tried to make clear that a person like himself was guilty of murder. But his distress of conscience was dismissed as pathological, his feelings of guilt as abnormal. In order to unmask "the hero of Hiroshima" and to demonstrate that atomic warfare not only brings about physical destruction but also demoralizes people, Eatherly turned to petty crime— never to his own advantage, however. [He forged a check for a small amount and paid the money into a fund for assistance to the children of Hiroshima. *Tr.*] Gunther Anders, whose correspondence with Eatherly forms the text of a book,[106] writes about him to one of his judges. "Ever since Claude has seen the dreadful result of the Hiroshima mission, his whole life has consisted of his futile attempt to understand what he considers his 'guilt' and to make this guilt clear to other people. All his partly 'nonsensical' and 'criminal' acts result from his frustration: he took recourse to deeds which are, at least, recognized as criminal acts in order to prove to his fellow men that he is not as innocent as they think him to be. *While ordinary people are guilty on account of their deeds, he committed the deeds in order to prove his guilt.*"[107] No one can deny that the matter at issue here is very complex. No one can say: indeed, the Hiroshima pilot is in fact guilty of mass murder. Everyone who breathed a sigh of relief when the bomb was dropped must take his place next to that pilot. The point which concerns us now is that his sense of guilt was simply viewed as pathological. Some lines from T. S. Eliot's play *The Elder Statesman* come to mind:

> *You think that I suffer from a morbid conscience,*
> *From brooding over faults I might well have forgotten.*
> *You think that I'm sickening, when I'm just recovering!*

This was precisely what Eatherly experienced. Having been made a part of the war machine, he fell into a collective compulsion. Afterward he tried to reclaim his own humanity by claiming his right to be held accountable for what he had done as part of the machine. But at a time when individual noncombatants were exhorted to acknowledge their part in a collective guilt, he was denied the right to bear his part in it as a personal debt. His sense of guilt was viewed as

---

[106]G. Anders, *Burning Conscience.*
[107]Ibid., p. 64.

sickness; his deed was called a "self-imagined wrong." The people who so judged—therapists and judges—were the ones whose duty it was to help him recover his humanity.

It is not possible to offer a monocausal explanation of this phenomenon which in its disastrous effects is at least the equal of the Hiroshima bomb. But one of the factors, certainly, which have helped to bring about this menacing situation is Freudian psychoanalysis.

[J. H. vanden Berg, reflecting on Freud's psychology, has this to say: "In Freud's work both the word and the concept 'responsibility' are lacking. One cannot expect anything else. The person who believes himself one-sidedly to be genetically determined will find a quick excuse for his activities. He is exculpated. He is justified by reference to his past which brings him to his acts of commission and omission."[108] According to Frankl, there is in psychoanalysis an "endeavor not to accept the validity of the humanity of the other person, and to rob him of his human dignity. What happens here is the devaluation of the *Thou* into an *It*."[109] Human dignity, says Frankl, consists in "being responsible," the fundamental principle of human existence.[110] The American writer O. Hobart Mowrer has turned with special ferocity against the psychology of Freud. It is his contention that we must view him, not as a Messiah, but as a "Deceiver";[111] gradually we are discovering "how thoroughly misleading and destructive"[112] his theory is. Under the influence of Freud's doctrine psychologists have come to believe "that human beings become emotionally disturbed, not because of their having *done* anything palpably wrong, but because they instead *lack insight*." The highly prized insight is that the client has in fact been too good. He has within him impulses . . . which he has quite unnecessarily inhibited.[113] A neurosis, says Freud, stems from a too severe superego. The neurotic is not sinful but sick; he is the helpless, innocent victim of the "sins of the fathers" who bound him so strenuously that he could not live by what he wanted.[114] Over against Freud's "impulse theory" Mowrer posits his "guilt theory." His hypothesis is that in neurosis it is "actually the individual's conscience that has been repudiated and 'repressed' rather than his 'instincts.' "[115] "For several decades we psychologists looked upon the whole matter of sin and moral accountability as a great incubus and acclaimed our liberation from it as epochmaking. But at length we have discovered that to be 'free' in this sense, i.e., to have the excuse of being 'sick' rather than *sinful* is to court the danger of also

---

[108]J. H. vanden Berg, *Psychologie en theologische Anthropologie*, p. 22.
[109]V. E. Frankl, *Homo Patiens*, p. 29.
[110]V. E. Frankl, *Medische Zielzorg*, p. 24.
[111]O. H. Mowrer, *The Crisis in Psychiatry and Religion*, p. 136.
[112]Ibid., p. 148.
[113]Ibid., p. 41.
[114]Ibid., pp. 48ff.
[115]Ibid., pp. 83ff.

becoming *lost.*"[116] This is bound to have consequences for psychotherapy. If sin is again taken seriously, the sinner must be helped to accept his guilt and sinfulness. Only then will the possibility of radical reformation open up for him.[117] Remarkably, now that psychologists have begun to realize this, they must worry about theologians and clergymen. Mowrer makes repeated reference to the fact that pastoral counseling has in his judgment a clear tendency in the direction of the dangerous theories of Freud. To the question "Has evangelical religion sold its birthright for a mess of psychological pottage?" he gives an affirmative answer. Not that he finds this development so strange; he refers sadly to "the strange affinity of Protestant Christianity and Freudian psychoanalysis."[118] This "affinity" would make an interesting study,[119] which we will not now undertake. The important point for us is that Mowrer clearly shows the extent to which a certain psychology, and pastoral praxis which allows itself uncritically to be shaped by it, can be a threat to people's humanity.]

Because this threat is always present, it seemed necessary to focus attention on the preagogic category of equihuman address. A given relationship cannot be growth promoting, or genuinely agogic, if the person called to be growth promoter (*auctor*: parent, nurturer, seminar leader, supervisor, pastor, therapist) does not relate as equal to the other-in-the-relationship. He acts irresponsibly if he does not recognize the other in his own "response-ability."

The category of equihuman address is not specifically agogic. Reference to the one does not imply reference to the other. In the remainder of this part we shall try to uncover the connection between the two. But this much should be established by now: agogy as an interhuman process can be agogy only if the agogue understands and practices a basic human-to-human posture and approach, i.e., "equihumanity." This preagogic category, which is directly connected with the category of "the promotion of life" we discussed earlier, is decisive for every form of nurture as well as for the whole of it.

5. NURTURE AS COUNTERPOINT IN THE PROCESS OF PERSONALITY FORMATION

The Concept of Nurture: Its Critical Function

In 1942 the S.D. (*Sicherheitsdienst*, 1933-45) in Germany composed a report on the opinions of ordinary Germans concerning the S.S. (*Schutzstaffel*: special protective services). The report mentions that some feared that "the education of armed S.S. men in ruthlessness" also served to make them willing

---

[116]Ibid., p. 52.

[117]Ibid., pp. 53ff.

[118]Ibid., pp. 159ff.

[119]To do it well the student would have to have more openness to the ideas of Paul, Calvin, and Luther than Mowrer himself evidences.

to turn against their fellow citizens.[120] Anyone reading this as a decent human being will sense within him a spontaneous protest against the use of the word "education" or "nurture" in this context.[121]

If now we try to find an answer to the question "What is nurture?" we cannot ignore realities like the ones referred to in the preceding paragraph. Perhaps a discipline like sociology or cultural anthropology could afford to be more tolerant here. One can examine what "nurture" is in a given society or culture and how it is provided for. One can take certain constants having to do with the guidance, training, and instruction of growing persons and gather them under the umbrella-concept of "nurture" without making specific value judgments about the aims of this guidance, training, and instruction. But the discipline of pedagogics cannot act this way. It is a discipline aimed at the praxis of nurture. *Its concept of nurture must fulfil a critical function and be able to serve as standard for the business of nurture.* One cannot simply and matter-of-factly, as Litt has remarked, "abstract the phenomenon of 'nurture' from its own inner reality the way one lifts the phenomenon of 'magnetism' or 'electricity' from its context. . . . Only he can say what nurture is who has some notion of what nurture is intended to do."[122] Not everything which bears a certain formal resemblance to nurture can be called by that name. Pedagogics must ask: What are the aims of the process? Its aims and focus must fall within the boundaries of its concept of nurture.

The Plurivalence of Contextual Influence

Earlier we spoke of the process of personality formation: A human being becomes a human being in the dynamic field of his original system—genetic and congenital—and his world. He does not become human in a vacuum but in his unique situation. Included in this situation are the nurturers, i.e., the people who know themselves responsible for the "humanization" of this person, with their whole life and in all their actions insofar as the growing person experiences them.

[It seems important to put it that way. One often encounters the idea that nurture does not begin until the nurturers abstract themselves, as it were, from the situation of the growing person and address him directly, e.g., in giving direction, in teaching, in putting on pressure, in punishment and reward, in special inducements, etc., with the somewhat explicit intent of influencing his human development; it is the idea that nurture coincides with the act of nurturing.

---

[120]*Der Spiegel,* January 23, 1967, p. 56.
[121][The English word "nurture" (Dutch *opvoeding*; German *Erziehung*) is less inclusive in meaning than the original here. In this section I will assume that "education" can be subsumed under this heading. *Tr.*]
[122]T. Litt, "Das Wesen des pädagogischen Denkens," p. 103; published as an appendix in *Führen oder Wachsenlassen,* pp. 83ff.

Earlier we quoted Langeveld, who viewed the day-by-day association between parents and children as a "pedagogically preformed field."[123] This implies that not all dealings between parents and children constitute acts of nurture. Elsewhere Langeveld remarks that it is possible to act toward the child "in a capacity other than that of nurturer." A father takes his son for a walk simply because he is eager to talk with him a bit. So he talks about the fact that once there was a Napoleon and that isosceles triangles still exist and that Uncle John has purchased a new car. "One can also use such information . . . in education when offering it to the student as material. By doing this one places it under the laws of the educational situation. Offering material for learning is certainly not the same as letting the pupil be."[124] True enough. But it cannot mean that education begins only when one starts offering information. In any case, it is not true that only when the posture of letting the pupil be—in the pedagogically preformed field of mere association—passes into the deliberate act of education by offering information has the child's situation at last become significant for his or her humanization. Suppose the child on his walks with his father, or in conversations which he witnesses, keeps hearing him speak with adoration of a variety of "Napoleons" and keeps hearing that today Uncle John, and yesterday the next-door neighbor, has bought a new car and that now Mr. Johnson will also probably buy one—*that* affects the child. Perhaps it affects him more than the presentation of material about Napoleon in the learning situation. Says Martin Buber: "A hidden influence proceeding from the educator's integrity has an integrating effect on the pupil."[125] This influence can be positive or negative; in any case, this especially is what influences the child: the involuntary contextual coexistence of the older person—particularly parents—with the growing person.]

In the section on contextual influence we referred to the origination of the authoritarian personality syndrome. One cannot simply say that parents, still less that parents alone, are responsible for the formation of such a syndrome in their child. In numerous cases influences from beyond the family circle will play a role. It is highly possible that among the children of one family there will be "high scorers" and "low scorers" on the scale; it is probable that psychosomatic dispositions will also play a role. Still, the example shows not only how significant direct pedagogical action is but also how important to the child the parents with their whole way of life and ways of dealing with the child are. J. A. Stalpers writes that "young children, in search of ways of acting and thinking, follow the simplest and most obvious way, namely, that of imitating the people in their environment. Imitating solutions to problems is less troublesome than

---

[123]M. J. Langeveld, *Beknopte theoretische Paedagogiek*, p. 42. In our opinion N. Perquin (*Pedagogiek*, p. 42) is right in taking a further step when he calls this day-by-day association between parents and children not just a "pedagogically preformed field" but a "highly important element of nurture by itself."

[124]M. J. Langeveld, *Studien zur Anthropologie des Kindes*, pp. 14ff.

[125]M. Buber, essay on "Education," in *Between Man and Man*, p. 90.

inventing them, certainly for the very young child. . . . Nurture comes to a large extent from the fact that the child has the opportunity to hear the same opinions and value judgments again and again and to see resort being taken to the same solutions to problems over and over. Life in a tradition is implicitly nurture."[126] One must not believe, however, that this adaptation to a given culture is limited to socially acceptable conduct. Research has shown that the aggressive behavior of role-models leads to aggressive behavior in those who witness their behavior. Here, too, example is more powerful than precept.

[On the basis of their research Bandura and Walters say that middle-class parents who as a rule use only physical violence in punishing their children usually achieve a different effect than they intend. They offer this example: "If a parent punishes a child physically for having struck a neighbor's child, the intended outcome of the training is that the child should refrain from hitting others. Concurrently with the intentional training, however, the parent is providing a model of the very behavior he is attempting to inhibit in the child. Consequently when the child is thwarted in subsequent social interactions, he may be more, rather than less, likely to respond in a physically aggressive manner."[127] It is also plain that parents who try to teach their children not to solve their conflicts by resort to physical violence have still less success than the parents already referred to, if in all their behavior they offer proof that they prefer this method above all others.]

In the preceding section we already encountered the phenomenon of *imitation*, which plays such an important role in the process of personality formation. Sometimes this idea is distinguished from *identification*. This concept was introduced by Sigmund Freud, who meant by it the immediate experience of unity with parents which is fundamental for the life-situation of the child.[128] By this immediate experience of unity with the parents—especially by identification with the parent of the same sex—the child takes over the basic features of the parental life-style and internalizes their commands and prohibitions. Identification, in distinction from imitation, is defined as self-orientation to another person to whom one has a strong emotional attachment.[129] By this orientation toward another a child takes over the values and attitudes of the other in a way which makes them seem self-evident. This phenomenon of the inner appropriation of norms, by way of identification with persons who are the bearers of these norms, is called internalization. Not only moral norms but also expressive

---

[126]J. A. Stalpers, *Zelfbehoud, Aanpassing, en Cultuur*, p. 66. We agree with the author in substance but do not think it is appropriate to use the word "nurture" in that sense. His usage is not unlike the confusing expression "functional nurture."

[127]A. Bandura and R. H. Walters, *Social Learning and Personality Development*, p. 69.

[128]Cf. C. S. Hall, *A Primer of Freudian Psychology*, pp. 74ff.

[129]A. Bandura and R. H. Walters, *Social Learning and Personality Development*, pp. 89ff., believe that the distinction is of little importance "since essentially the same learning process is involved."

norms which refer to emotional relations to persons and things, as well as cognitive norms, are internalized.[130] These matters, so far from being petty, go to the roots of what is typically human. The basic patterns of human functioning—how she thinks, judges, and relates herself to others and things—are shaped by way of her identifications; that is to say, they are shaped by processes of learning which for the most part are not deliberately initiated or systematically guided by nurturers but which start and operate "naturally" simply because a person in the period and situation of growing up sees others who are significant to her function as human beings.

Many problems, which we cannot discuss here, are associated with the concept of identification. We refer to it because it points to a reality which is pedagogically of the greatest importance. It is this: not only, and not even in the first place, is the child affected by the pedagogically intentional actions of a nurturer. The nurturer lives his own life in part within the child's field of observation—an area which is larger than its field of vision. And the process of personality formation which the child experiences is a process in which the entire existence of the nurturer, as perceived by the child, is a codetermining factor.

Nurturers often ask: "What shall I do?" And, granted, it is important to know how a person should act in general or in a specific nurturing situation. But a more fundamental question is always relevant, even when the question how to act pedagogically is raised; and that is the question What kind of person should I be? What is the content of my life, and what is the shape I give to it? The nurturer must be thoroughly aware of this: in the whole of my existence I function for my child, this human being in process of becoming, as a model; my child, this person in process of becoming, is so bound up with the whole of my existence that her process is a process of *becoming what I am*. Nurture is a concept which embraces more than acts of nurturing. The concept of nurture has to do, in the first place, with the phenomenon that here is a person to whom a child is entrusted, who knows and accepts the responsibility which comes with the child, and who in that awareness is conscious that the whole of what she *is* as a human being affects the child's process of *becoming* human. In other words: "Nurture" means among other things that *a person lives her life in the awareness that her life as it takes shape in concrete existence may be either life-producing or life-corrupting for the person growing up in her shadow*. So then the question "What is the impact on our children of our married life?" is more typically pedagogical than "How do I tell my children about sex." "Does my child see truthfulness modeled in me?" is more pedagogical than "How can I make Johnny stop telling lies?" "What is the impact on my children of the way I view and exercise authority?" is more pedagogical than "How can I get my children to show respect for authority?"

---

[130]F. J. Stendenbach, *Soziale Interaktion und Lernprozesse*, pp. 179ff.

Nurture as Something Other than a Complement to and Reinforcement of Contextual Influence

But more than the life of parents shapes the context of a person's development—we already pointed that out in the section on contextual influence. Much of that influence is of positive value for the process of personality formation in general. Brezinka, as we pointed out, saw in this influence the "supporting ground" for intentional nurture, and Bollnow spoke of it as the "ground floor" on which to build the superstructure of intentional nurture.[131] This brings us to a problem of great importance for the determination of the concept of nurture. Is it in fact possible to view the relationship between contextual influence and intentional nurture as a relationship between foundation and superstructure? Is nurture a *complement* to this influence? Or is the relationship quite other?

First of all, we wish to point out that contextual influence is clearly very ambivalent, certainly in a society like our own of which it cannot be said, in the words of Schleiermacher, that all has become "custom." When people speak of "functional nurture" or "pedagogically significant reality," they have in mind all those factors which, as they impinge upon the growing person from the side of society and culture, have a positive influence on her humanization. The objection to such an abstraction is that one cannot return to concrete reality with it. We know that there are good influences and bad—but in the situation itself it is hard to say which are good and which are bad. Furthermore, not only is contextual influence ambiguous as a whole; some concrete influences are ambiguous in themselves, having a positive and a negative side, while other influences have a positive effect on one personality and a negative effect on another. This situation offers many challenges to the praxis of nurture, but few clear points of contact. And in practice it is very difficult to show what kind of complementary direction should be given by intentional nurture.

Second, one of the most important effects of contextual influence is the socialization of a person. Growing up in society, the maturing person adapts to his social context and its culture. Such adaptation is necessary[132] but then as part of the whole process of personality formation.

[*Summary*: Schleiermacher depicts two extremes: (1) Nurture should fit youth for life in the state as it is. (2) Nurture should confer the drive and intent to improve society at all points. To him these are the foci of the ellipse of nurture. Ideally, nurture would be such as to produce youth who were disciplined both for life in society and for vigorous participation in the improvement of society.[133]

Should pedagogics adopt the socialization concept of sociology, which

---

[131]O. F. Bollnow, *Pädagogische Forschung und philosophisches Denken*, p. 231.

[132]J. A. Stalpers, *Zelfbehoud, Aanpassing, en Cultuur*; the central theme of this study is "self-preservation through adaptation" (p. 252).

[133]F. D. E. Schleiermacher, *Pädagogische Schriften*, pp. 31ff.

embraces nurture, the danger would be that it would help bring about a state of affairs in which the growth of the maturing person was restricted by the actualities of the existing socio-cultural status quo. Wilhelm is rightly concerned about this. It is very dear of sociology to grant nurture a place in the socialization of a person by allowing the individual to internalize the role expectations of society, he says, but pedagogics cannot be content with this assigned field of operation.[134] Pedagogics is not satisfied with a socialization process whose only aim is a stabilized relationship between society, culture, and person. "The dimension of pedagogics is not the perpetuation of society but the continuation of history."]

It would not be difficult to adduce examples from the history of nurture which show that the focus on the preservation of society and culture often stood in the way of an address to human beings as beings who live in history. What concerns us is that a similar tendency can be observed in "religious" and in "Christian" culture.

[W. E. Oates points out that this kind of nurture is not in fact nurture but conditioning. "The legalists of the Old and New Testament tended to fall into the priestly tradition of scribes who perpetuated a fixed law for all behavior. A child was to be conditioned in every detail of his growing life to depend upon the exactitudes of the law. [. . .] Even in the Christian tradition this type of psychology took root as early as the work of the Judaizers, and was firmly established by the time of Tertullian, who developed rules of behavior that he aptly called 'molds' for Christian lives. Today this type of behaviorism is seen in the confusion of morality with spirituality which characterizes much of both Catholic and Protestant fundamentalism."[135]]

In a situation like the one just described nurture is complementary to and supportive of a process by which the growing person is adapted to, and fitted into, the existing socio-cultural context. The result of this kind of nurture is the polished conformist or the frustrated nonconformist forever in revolt in an effort to come to terms with his past. In either case we are left with the counterimage of the human being as God intended him or her, i.e., the person who relates himself or herself to self and the world in freedom and responsibility.

Nurture Correlates with the Dialectics of the Process of Personality Formation

In order to get the relationship between contextual influence and nurture in clear focus, one must not—as in the concept of socialization—view nurture as one of the forms of environmental influence; nor as an intentional complement to, or specification of, functional influence; but rather as a dialectic or, even better, a contrapuntal relationship. The first melody in the process of personality

---

[134]T. Wilhelm, "Sozialisation und soziale Erziehung," in G. Wurzbacher, *Der Mensch als soziales und personales Wesen*, p. 134.

[135]W. E. Oates, *The Religious Dimensions of Personality*, p. 293.

formation is the contextual influence which plays upon the original personality system. People used to speak of the "ethnic character" which would be discernible in an individual who had been raised in a certain society and culture. Later there was repeated reference to a "basic personality," a socio-cultural pattern of personality of which the individual in a given society and culture would be a variant. Objections have rightly been lodged against both concepts. Still, in the midst of, and *beneath,* all the diversity, people who have been raised in the same social and cultural situation show some similarity—something a person does not lose even when he opposes, or breaks with, that society and its culture. Contextual influence is inescapable and its effect cannot be eliminated. The important thing is that the growing person not be abandoned to contextual influence.

We noted earlier that for the process of personality formation it is characteristic that the growing person is caught up in a dialectic between himself and his world. His humanization is a dialectical process: the person-as-spirit realizes himself in receptive and responsive openness and encounter with what comes up out of himself and his world, and in a responsible assimilation of this material. Not only does he become human by this dialectic; rather, *in* this dialectic he is active in becoming human. Nurture is not exactly "the assimilation of experience," as De Klerk would have it,[136] though this assimilation ties in directly with the process of nurture. We can say that in the process of personality formation nurture provides the "countermelody." It functions as *punctum contra punctum*; i.e., over against the primary melody of contextual influence it has its own independent role (in music the tones of the countermelody themselves constitute a melody); but it is at the same time attuned to it. Nurture may not be determined by contextual influence; nevertheless, concretely it is dependent on the nature and quality of the actual contextual influence, with which it must make some kind of harmony.

While contextual influence always tends toward conformity with others, nurture aims at bringing out the uniqueness of the person. This *becoming* oneself lies on a continuum, however, with an increasingly vivid process of *being* oneself. Nurture entails an appeal to growing persons, not just to undergo influences, but to assimilate them, and so to be oneself. We have talked in a previous section about equihuman address as a preagogic category. In equihuman address the focus is not on the future of the person-in-process but on the present of the person who *is,* and who has his freedom and responsibility. Inherent in nurture is the future perspective; it aims by definition at what is in process of being realized. *But structurally nurture is determined by the equihuman dimension*; the growth-promoting relationship *(relatio auctifica)* realizes itself in recognizing the humanness of the person being nurtured—i.e., his equality in dignity as a human being. In this relationship a person relates to a maturing fellow human in such a way that his process of personality formation will occur in the dialectics of

---

[136]L. de Klerk, *Beginnende Volwassenheid,* p. 136; cf. pp. 21, 138.

contextual influence *and* personal assimilation of the influences that impinge on him.

Nurture Focuses on the Quintessence of Being Fully Human

From this perspective we can now define the real aim of nurture.

[Mention is often made of the "goal" of nurture. We would rather not use that term. It is too suggestive of a fixed point which has to be reached. It will become evident later that one cannot, in the context of nurture, speak of such a fixed point. Nurture does not culminate in a fixed state of affairs; it is focused on humanity in process of becoming. When we speak of the "aim" or "focus" of nurture, we have in mind the process to which day-by-day nurture is related; not some stable point of culmination at which nurture is aimed.]

In the literature of pedagogics frequent reference is made to *maturity* as the goal of nurture, both in the sense of the point at which it aims and in the sense of a point at which it ends *(terminus ad quem)*. Perquin offers this definition: "Nurture is the help given by persons responsible for the development of a child in order that the child may reach maturity."[137] For Langeveld the issue is so self-evident that it does not need to be argued: "The goal is maturity"; "the primary and natural destiny of man."[138]

We object, however, to using this term to describe the goal or aim of nurture. Maturity, as Wijngaarden remarks, is a biological and psychological, but not an anthropological concept.[139] Maturity is a time phase in the psychosomatic development of a person.[140] Perquin summarizes nurture as "guided growth." He comments: "The word 'growth' is in fact taken over from biology and this has disadvantages. . . . The same difficulties adhere to words like ripeness, maturity, 'getting big,' etc. As a matter of course we use the term as a metaphor."[141] This is hardly enough justification for the use of such terms. It was hurtful for pedagogics in the past to work with biological analogies and models.[142] The use of a term like "growth" could take it right back into the danger zone. The situation as far as the word "maturity" is concerned is more complex. This word is more detached from its rootage than "growth." To us a mature person or adult is one who is no longer a child. In legal terms it means he or she is marriageable, entitled to vote, competent to sign contracts; in psychological terms a mature person is one who is passing into or through a life phase. One could say that if no mishaps occur in the development of a person,

---

[137]N. Perquin, *Pedagogiek,* p. 38.

[138]M. J. Langeveld, *Beknopte theoretische Paedagogiek,* p. 56.

[139]H. R. Wijngaarden, *Hoofdproblemen der Volwassenheid,* p. 221.

[140]Ibid., p. 64. He roughly stakes out maturity as the time between the eighteenth and forty-second year.

[141]N. Perquin, *Pedagogiek,* p. 37.

[142]T. Wilhelm, "Sozialisation und soziale Erziehung," in G. Wurzbacher, *Der Mensch als soziales und personales Wesen,* pp. 126ff.

he will automatically become an adult. He will turn twenty-one and enter upon
the rights that go with being of age; the boy and the girl become a man and a
woman. Is that the goal of nurture? No one will say that it is. Nurture is much
more concerned with a person's *being* mature: that he knows his rights and
responsibilities and can assume the burdens and joys of being man or woman.
But this is not all; in the instance of child nurture this is not even primary. It is
the case only where being mature is viewed as the "apex of being human." But
this, says Pöggeler, is a distortion. "The truth is that every life phase, when it
unfolds in accord with its meaning, is in itself fully valid."[143] This is true of
childhood; we have already observed that the concrete recognition of this truth
is the condition of all nurture. For that reason it is not enough, nor is it on
target, to say that nurture's goal is to guide the child to maturity. It aims at a
human being for whom the *full validity* of life, no matter what the phase, implies
a continuing, and ever-to-be-renewed, mandate. Nurture's arrow points to the
future, but "future" must not simply be understood as something temporal. The
future is the open horizon of one's present identity—the perspective of the living
person in process of self-realization.

The question is: What do people mean when they speak of maturity as the
goal of nurture? According to Langeveld, maturity has a relatively closed, ordered, and static character, in contrast with the change-oriented mind-set of
youth. In maturity, too, one may observe dynamic tendencies, but the overall
dynamics of the adult evidence more continuity, purposiveness, and self-limi-
tation; in short, "responsible self-determination."[144] Perquin is less formal: "We
speak of maturity in a strict sense when real independence has been attained and
a person is capable of taking his own position; when he can assume responsibilities which require unselfish orientation toward others or 'the' other; when he
has discovered those values which require independence and self-surrender."[145]
The expression "maturity in the strict sense" is remarkable; Perquin also speaks
of signs which show that a period of life has been concluded but not "that true
spiritual maturity has been reached."[146] Apparently the latter is maturity "in a
strict sense." This implies that not all maturity is authentic.[147] It would seem
that whoever is mature is an adult, but not every adult is mature. This sounds
like banter, but it is hardly that. Both in Langeveld and in Perquin, maturity is
defined as a boundary fixed by age ("the adult in years") and at the same time
as the ideal on which the practice of nurture is focused ("true spiritual matu-

---

[143]F. Pöggeler, *Der Mensch in Mündigkeit und Reife: eine Anthropologie des Erwach-
senen*, p. 146.

[144]M. J. Langeveld, *Beknopte theoretische Paedagogiek*, p. 43.

[145]N. Perquin, *Pedagogiek*, pp. 52ff. This coincides in part with young adulthood—
twenty-five to forty—whose main feature, says H. C. Rümke, is "the ability to function
in ordered, stable connections" (*Levenstijdperken van de Man*, p. 86).

[146]Ibid., p. 53.

[147]Something similar must be in Langeveld's mind when he speaks of people who
are "adults in years."

rity"). So two concepts meet in the term "maturity"; two concepts which are related but must still be strictly distinguished. The theoretical consequences will certainly be felt in the elaboration of pedagogical theory; the first idea is bound to interfere with, and contaminate, the second.

Wijngaarden's approach has the potential for bringing greater clarity. He views maturity as a period in a person's life and raises the question: In the period of maturity, what are the typical life challenges and problems?[148] He describes the central challenge as acceptance, concretized in four dimensions: (1) acceptance of self; (2) and (3) acceptance of others and *the* other; and (4) acceptance of a meaning in life.[149]

[In a later critical comment Wijngaarden dissociates himself from the concept of "life acceptance" because it carries an anthropological judgment into the description of a developmental phase. The life challenge of adulthood, says Wijngaarden, should be described in strictly psychological terms as "a conscious choice of attitude toward self, the others, the other, and the meaning of life."[150]]

If now, in determining the aim of nurture, one wishes to speak of "adult-hood," one could say (with a variant of Perquin's definition): Nurture is the help given by persons responsible for the development of a child which leads the child to the ability, as an adult, to fulfil the life mandate of an adult. But then why speak of "adulthood"? The life challenges enumerated by Wijngaarden are not so strictly limited to the period of adulthood that they must be regarded as typical for this phase of life. One can also find them in Maslow's list of the essential marks of the "self-actualized personality";[151] and they display a good deal of similarity with the criteria for mental health at which Jahoda arrived in his synthesis of a number of current definitions.[152] Referring to these criteria Fortmann remarks that mental health is a "limit-concept only rarely completely realized."[153] According to Maslow, the future is present in the self-actualized personality in the form of ideals, hopes, goals, calling, destiny, etc. This future, in the sense of the open boundaries of one's present contingent existence, is realistically present in the life of a growing person. It is characteristic for the process of personality formation that in the dialectics of the self with one's world one is experimenting with the future. Sometimes one can observe that at a given moment a child is already "mature." It would be better to say that the child is displaying conduct which we notice with more frequency and greater continuity

---

[148]H. R. Wijngaarden, *Hoofdproblemen der Volwassenheid,* p. 72.

[149]Ibid., p. 74. Cf. J. Goldbrunner, *Realisation,* pp. 79ff.

[150]H. R. Wijngaarden, ibid., p. 222.

[151]Cf. D. Krech and R. S. Crutchfield, *Elements of Psychology,* p. 628.

[152]M. Jahoda, *Current Concepts of Positive Mental Health.*

[153]H. M. M. Fortmann, *Opdat zij Gezond zijn in het Geloof,* p. 22. Jahoda lists these criteria: (1) an attitude of self marked by acceptance and trust; (2) the capacity for growth and the actualization of one's own possibilities; (3) integration; (4) a realistic attitude toward one's environment; (5) a degree of personal autonomy; (6) the capacity to master life's circumstances.

in the adult but which as such is more typically *human* than adult because it shows the essence of what it means to be completely human. The adult may approximate it more closely, and at more points, than the child; but for the adult, too, it remains future, in the sense referred to; a future toward which the adult, too, should continue to move.

One can give a number of names to this quintessence and none will say it all. If we are to describe it in terms which are pedagogically useful, we can perhaps best speak of it as *the ability to function spiritually on one's own.* By *nurture* we then mean: *everything which happens in the field of tension between the nurturer and the growing person which is directed toward this person's ability to function independently as a psychospiritual being in his own world.*

The Human Being as Spirit

We shall now try to make plain how the phrase "the ability to function mentally on one's own" is intended to be understood. The word "mental" (or "spiritual") in particular tends to call forth misunderstandings and questions.

[From the course of our discussion so far it is clear that the word "spiritual" should not be understood in the very narrow sense of "relating to the religious dimension." But that still leaves enough ambiguity. In *Webster's Third New International Dictionary,* there are no fewer than 25 entries under the word "spirit." Should one limit herself to the use of the word in philosophy, even then the difficulties are not resolved. "So many and so various have been the attempts to delimit the word 'spirit' (or 'mind') in the history of philosophy that it is impossible to give a simple definition of its essence."[154] Against that background it is hardly possible to make naive references to "spirit" (or "mind") or to leave undefined the phrase "to function mentally."]

One can hardly speak of "spirit" without evoking the triad body–soul–spirit. By way of this association we run the risk of losing ourselves in the problematics of what G. C. Berkouwer calls the "composition" of man.[155] Nurture, we said, is directed toward a person's ability to function mentally. Does this mean that nurture has nothing to do with body and soul? Or does it mean that it is aimed at "spirit" (or "mind") as the highest faculty in a human being—the "leadership principle," as Goethe called it—what makes a human being human and offers direction and guidance in all of her existence? This, let it be said emphatically, is not our intent. Nurture's concern is with human beings. And a human being, as G. Ryle pointedly puts it, is not "some sort of committee or team of persons,

---

154W. Wieland, *RGG,* II, col. 1286, s.v. *Geist.* [Note: When the words "spiritual" or "mental" occur in this translation the indulgent reader is asked to hear in them a description of persons as *psychospiritual* beings. *Tr.*]

155G. C. Berkouwer, *Man: The Image of God,* p. 38.

all laced together in one skin,"[156] or a "ghost-ridden machine"; the human being is a human being—"a tautology which is sometimes worth remembering."[157] *By "mind," then, we do not mean one of the "components" of a human being; but the human being in her totality and, especially, her unity.*

Then why not simply say that nurture is aimed at the humanity or humanization of a person? The trouble is that this statement is far from simple. Whatever the merits of a composite view of man—is he soul and body? soul-spirit-and-body?—resort to these distinctions arose from the very strong sense that man is a complicated being. One word does not say it all; one simple concept does not contain it all. The human being of flesh and blood, visible and tangible, is also the human being who feels and thinks, loves and strives. Does this mean man is composed of parts? In our time people are beginning to realize that this composite view does not correspond to reality. Man is *not composed of* body, soul, and spirit; man *can be viewed* as an organism in which chemical and physical processes occur—as body; or as a center of thoughts, feelings, decisions, etc., which are only objectively observable in behavior—let us say, as mind. Ever more clearly people are beginning to see that the object in view in the differing perspectives is never *something in* man but the one human being. Says C. A. van Peursen: "As the natural sciences advance today and our understanding of the human organism advances with them, it becomes more and more evident that what we regard as the 'higher' spiritual and intellectual reaches of human life—love, enjoyment of the arts, religious experiences and so forth— simply do not occur apart from glandular activity, metabolism, and much more besides."[158] From this point of view, what we call "memory" is something like a system of chemical reactions. One has to transpose man into another field of inquiry to see why and by what means he remembers some things and not others; how the process of absorption and retention operates in the memory; how a person uses the material retained, etc. In one field of study one sees chemical and physical processes at work, in another the psychic. But the reference is all the while to processes in the one human being, processes which presuppose and support one another and interlock; better still: the reference is to one occurrence which, viewed from within differing fields of inquiry, turns out to be accessible in very different ways, and then reveals very different aspects. These aspects are so different, in fact, that the temptation to separate them and to allow the

---

[156]G. Ryle, *The Concept of Mind*, p. 190.

[157]Ibid., p. 81.

[158]C. A. van Peursen, *Body, Soul, Spirit: A Survey of the Body-Mind Problem*, p. 61. Translation by H. H. Hoskins. Paul Tillich, *Die verlorene Dimension*, pp. 72ff., believes the matter at stake here can be approached better by the metaphor of "dimension" than that of "level." " 'Levels' can exist independently of one another; this metaphor does not offer promise of a resolution of the body-soul problem; only when body and soul are understood as dimensions of one and the same reality does the nature of man become intelligible" (p. 76).

indivisible unity of the human being to fall apart in two or three pieces is constant.[159]

Van Peursen observes that the "body" and the "soul" are "models, static representations, objectivizations which somewhat make plain—but at the cost of a measure of distortion—what a human being is as subject, as I-sayer, who is always dynamically directional and intentional, never completely objectifiable in her psychosomatic existence."[160] And in another place: "The unity of soul and body becomes apparent . . . the moment we begin to look at both in the context of the concrete man, of his mental orientation."[161]

We observed earlier that nurture occurs within a dynamic relationship between two concrete persons who are each other's equals. One is not an object to the other—the nurturee is not an object for the nurturer to manipulate; in nurture two subjects, two agents, two persons are related to each other in the totality of their psychosomatic existence. One person in that relationship, the developing person, is caught up in an extremely important process, the process of personality formation by which she acquires her own identity. If that process is to have the desired outcome, then that developing person must be allowed to be an agent in the process; the dynamic core of the process must be formed by the dialectic with the self and her world. Nurture, which relates, as countermelody, to the *cantus firmus* of contextual influence, finds its meaning in stimulating the developing person and supporting her in this dialectic; i.e., in affirming her as a human agent by acknowledging her as a human agent. In order then for pedagogics to do justice to the fundamental structure of nurture, it must place "man-as-mind"[162] at the focal point of its attention; this is "no abstraction but the concrete person as she manifests herself bodily."[163] "Man's character as 'mind' [or 'spirit'] is that of an orientation from within his world as its context . . . ; 'mind' here denoting not so much *what* man is as a given entity as *how* he is apropos of his being-as-man. . . . Mind as intention, as the directional aspect of being, signifies orientation."[164] This orientation, says Van Peursen, is typical for our humanity. "By orientation I do not mean an instinctive, almost self-evident adaptation to the world about us, but . . . the conscious sense of having

---

[159]G. Ryle, *The Concept of Mind*, pp. 15ff., shows that basic to "the double-life theory" is the error of viewing dissimilar categories as similar. Ryle lists a number of examples of such category mistakes; e.g., a child observes the parade of a military division; battalions, companies, and sections are pointed out to her; then she asks: When is the division coming? She supposed all the while "that a division was a counterpart to the units already seen."

[160]C. A. van Peursen, *Christelijke Encyclopaedie*, III, 438ff., s.v. *Lichaam en Ziel*.

[161]C. A. van Peursen, *Body, Soul, Spirit*, p. 168.

[162]We are now adopting Van Peursen's terminology as defined in *Body, Soul, Spirit: A Survey of the Body-Mind Problem*.

[163]Ibid., p. 150.

[164]Ibid., pp. 180-81. [In these quotations the word "mind" occurs where one might expect "spirit." The Hoskins translation does, however, have the strong endorsement of Dr. van Peursen; cf., p. VI. *Tr.*]

to find a direction: the sense of wonder, the questioning, the search for pointers and norms, in short, human existence as it is manifest in consciousness, a sense of normativity, deliberation, tools, culture, philosophy, daily experience, social praxis, language, and the like. This orientation is not an optional function; on the contrary, without orientation a human being ceases to be human."[165] "If then we want a model for what is intimated by 'mind' we must think of it as resembling not so much a thing—a something-or-other—as an actuation, a moving."[166]

We have made extensive reference to Van Peursen because in these quoted sentences we find precisely defined what we wanted to say, in our description of nurture, with the phrase "the ability to function as mind." For all nurture has its focus here: the human being as one who *orients* herself, *defines* herself, *relates* herself.

[Hendrikus Berkhof observes that the secret of Jesus' humanity does not lie "in what we usually view as the characteristic inventory and real essence of humanness. That secret lies in his relationship to the world which surrounds him: to God, to his fellow humans, to nature." This presses us toward the conclusion, says Berkhof, "that for us, too, the essence lies in the fact that we are called to enter into certain relationships."[167] The highest and at the same time the most fundamental relationship is the relationship to God.[168] Pannenberg has pointed out that traces of the influence of this mark of biblical thought about man can be detected in the whole of modern anthropology.[169] The big difference between man and animal, as has often been shown, is that man is "open to the world" whereas an animal is "bound to its environment." But "to what is man really open? To begin with, . . . he is open to constantly new things and fresh experiences, while animals are open only to a limited, fixed number of environmental features that are typical of the species." The openness which characterizes man is not, however, openness only to a bigger world than that of animals, as if human beings differ only in degree. " 'Openness to the world' means that man is completely directed into the 'open.' He is always open further beyond every experience and beyond every given situation."[170] Man is characterized by "chronic need" and "infinite dependence" which presupposes something outside himself which is beyond every experience of the world. This entity upon which man is dependent in his infinite striving we call "God."[171] It seems questionable whether this way of formulating the issue is correct; whether this can be said in any way other than "confessionally," i.e., as response to God's

---

[165] C. A. van Peursen, *Filosofische Oriëntatie*, p. 250.
[166] C. A. van Peursen, *Body, Soul, Spirit: A Survey of the Body-Mind Problem*, p. 166.
[167] H. Berkhof, *De Mens Onderweg*, p. 27.
[168] Ibid., pp. 32ff.
[169] W. Pannenberg, *What Is Man?*, p. 12.
[170] Ibid., p. 8.
[171] Ibid., p. 10.

address to man.[172] The fact that man orients, determines, relates himself in openness, has been a mark of humanity since and because God called him to it when God gave him a place and a mandate (Gen. 2:8, 15). This being so, man's humanity must show itself in the functioning of the mind, and nurture must be directed toward this functioning.[173] Reflecting on the situation and future of education, P. J. Idenburg remarks: "The essential dimension of our humanness is that we humans move forward and wish to become what we can be. A human being *chooses*, thus showing that she exists in responsibility for herself. In that activity she is unique, irreplaceable, different from animals and things, and shows her dignity as a human being. . . . Another feature of this essential dimension of one's humanness is the aspect which points to others. . . . All nurture, whether in or outside of formal education, will have to be 'arrowed' toward the development of the essential dimension. All else that can be experienced, learned, and practiced in the nurturing process receives its meaning only against this background."[174]]

Thus "mental functioning" is meant to refer to the actualization of a person's essential humanity. How is a person human? In this, that in her connections, in relations with people and units of people—as in the family, groups of friends, a team of workers, as a citizen—in relation to things, institutions, values and concepts, etc., etc., she will determine a position in which she can be and relate in freedom and responsibility. In the next section we shall have a closer look at the structure of this human interactivity.

Nurture's Aim: Self-Reliance

We have said that nurture aims to help bring about the ability of a person to function independently in her world. The word "independent" needs further discussion. What we have in mind is "self-reliance," which does not exclude a degree of dependence. What Wijngaarden has said on this in the framework of psychotherapy is also our view: "A person is qualified by dependence, his-not-being-able to grow and develop without others. To become mature means to grow by steps toward self-reliance, to arrive at the place where one chooses one's own positions with regard to the relationships in which one functions. *Self-reliance* is the criterion for me, not independence."[175] So what we have in mind

---

[172]One thinks of the opening chapter of Augustine's *Confessions*: "Thou hast made us for thyself and our hearts are restless until . . ."

[173]Concerning the significance of this for education, see N. Perquin, *Algemene Didaktiek,* p. 13. [The reader may wish to refer to N. Wolterstorff, *Educating for Responsible Action,* Ch. 2, "Humanity alone God has *graced* with responsibilities" (p. 7). *Tr.*]

[174]P. J. Idenburg, "Op het Keerpunt der Onderwijsgeschiedenis," in *Gedenkboek voor Prof. Dr. Ph. A. Kohnstamm,* pp. 76ff.

[175]H. R. Wijngaarden, "Gesprekstherapie," in *Nederlands Tijdschrift voor de Psychologie en haar Grensgebieden,* N.S. 16 (1961): 425.

with the phrase "mental independence" is not spiritual autonomy but the strength to be oneself in essential contexts.

Second, when we speak of nurture's aim being independence, the emphasis derives from a fundamental conviction that the nurturing process is directly related to the process of personality formation. The person who is "somebody," and is called to be "somebody," actually becomes "somebody," acquires an identity in her dialectic with her self and her world. The process of personality formation implies that a person, by trying to be self-reliant, to be "somebody" in various situations, arrives at self-reliance, and finds her own place where she can function in accord with her own potentialities and responsibility. These personal potentialities and this personal responsibility must, therefore, always be the focus of pedagogical attention. *Nurture*, which in its fundamental structure is determined by the category of equihuman address, is aimed toward the *provisional, experimental self-reliance of the growing person*. It appeals to awakening self-reliance and so evokes it. For the practice of nurture, this point of view must have important consequences: A kind of nurture, or any single nurturing action, which fails to lead the growing person to this mental self-reliance, or fails to offer the opportunity to practice it—i.e., the opportunity to experiment, to try things, to test commands or suggested solutions by oneself—is by definition no nurture at all. The distinction between nurture and mere training is marked by the recognition and the call to mental self-reliance.

Nurture's Focus: The Human Being in Her Own World

Finally, in seeking to describe nurture and at the risk of sounding redundant, we wish to point out that it is aimed at a person's being able to function mentally on her own *in her own world*. The addition is not superfluous. Schools are often accused of ignoring the things which are important in the world of the developing person and of burdening her with all kinds of things which may be weighty outside her world but meaningless inside. Such criticism can be cheap; it may even stem from a pragmatistic and, at bottom, banal idea about the purpose of education. The world of a growing person is a world in process of becoming—an open world. Education or nurture dare not lock a human being up in the circle of the momentary and the immediate. Education's or nurture's purpose is to open up the world for a person and a person for that world, so that her world may grow larger and richer and she may grow in relation to the world. But, then, that opening-up process must really occur. If the intent of an admonition escapes the nurturee because it evokes nothing in her;[176] if a given word of direction simply does not make sense because it ignores her needs or abilities; if she is being taught an answer to a question which was never hers—then, no matter how dedicated the nurturer may be, the process of learning has not gotten

---

[176]Note: to "admonish" a person is to remind her forcefully of something which seems not to have been remembered.

underway. In such situations the nurturee is abstracted from her world; i.e., she becomes somebody who is not really there.

In other words, nurturing, in order that it may serve the cause of nurture, must situate itself in the world, the expanding world, of the growing person. If she must believe somehow that what is taught her will be good for something sometime, she will learn nothing. The growing person's growth consists in the "dialectic" with her world. Whatever stays outside the dialectic because it has no bearing on her world or on her being in the world will have no influence on her process of personality formation.

The problem of making sure that nurture hits home and touches the person *in her world* shows up as a problem only when nurturers deliberately set out to nurture, whether in or out of school. As long as nurture is just part of day-by-day association the growing person will simply be a person-in-her-world. But as soon as nurture becomes intentional, the growing person is transposed into the role of nurturee. She is, then, a person who doesn't yet know, a person in the learning process, a person still underway—and we may easily overlook the fact that she already is a person, with numerous connections with the outside world, by which she transcends what she is inside her own skin.

Formal and Material Nurture — A False Dilemma

An important question which our description of nurture raises is this: Is this conception of its aim not too formal?

[L. de Klerk lodges a similar objection against Margaret Mead, who in her book *Coming of Age in Samoa* comes to the conclusion that in the complex society of the West young people should much more be taught *how* to think than *what*. De Klerk disagrees: ". . . because as an adult a person must also know what he thinks and why he chooses as he does. . . . A person has to choose from among very specific concrete options and he does this on the basis of what he has personally assimilated and accepted."[177] In light of what De Klerk says, and with reference to our description of nurture, one could ask: Does nurture transmit, and does the growing person receive, anything which adds to her personal value inventory? This is a question on which we wish to comment further.]

First, we speak of *nurture* as a process which occurs in the dynamic field of the relationship between a nurturer and a growing person. The process proceeds by way of concrete interactions: the nurturer does something, says something, shows something, is something and somebody in relation to the growing person. The entire life of the nurturer is present in those interactions. By imitation, identification, and simply listening to what the nurturer tells her, the growing person begins to share in what constitutes the life of the nurturer: his

---

[177]L. de Klerk, *Beginnende Volwassenheid*, p. 43.

opinions, convictions, ideas, attitudes, etc. But all of this acquires the quality of nurture only if the growing person can come to a dialectic confrontation with those opinions, convictions, ideas, attitudes, etc. This is what we wish to underscore in our definition. With regard to both ordinary human-to-human contact with the growing person and to deliberate attempts at nurture, one's concept of nurture has a critical function. In our opinion, it seems possible, with the help of the concept we formulated, sharply to define those qualities in ordinary contact or in intentional nurture which actually do help the nurturing process. The nurturer may pass on to the nurturee ever so much good and worthwhile and even necessary information, but if he does not thereby help the growing person toward self-reliance in her mental functioning, it has not helped at all. In this context we wish to repeat De Klerk's words: "A person has to choose from among very specific concrete options and *he does this on the basis of what he has personally assimilated and accepted*" (italics ours, author); i.e., on the basis of what he, by personal reflection and selection, has been able and willing to appropriate for himself from, *inter alia*, the personal values of the nurturer. A person who is really human does not "think" the thoughts of "the fathers," does not repeat the choices of "the father"—but he thinks and chooses for himself in freedom and in terms of his own responsibility, either "in fellowship" with the thoughts and choices of the fathers or in deviation from them.

Second: What Margaret Mead has said about education has also been said by others about the modern situation in general. Says Nieuwenhuis: "If nurture for a concrete situation becomes impossible because that situation as such is no longer predictable, then nurture will have to aim at *adaptability*. This aim implies a focus on what all kinds of possible situations have in common. That is, nurture will have to become more general, more abstract, and, ethically, more deliberately principled in nature."[178] This situation is very clear in the area of training and educating people for technical enterprises. "The world of labor," according to Idenburg, "is more and more moving away from the traditional job concept." "The ideal of having 'the right man in the right place' had to yield to a demand for people whose personality structure and range of abilities are not fixed but who know how to adapt themselves to the diverging and changing needs of the production process."[179] The modern technical situation demands a functional adaptability—the ability rapidly to adjust to another job situation. But this certainly applies to more than the technical environment. Our time is rightly described as one of rapid social and cultural change. Not only is the rate of change rapid; more important is the fact that what modern physics discovered in its field applies increasingly to our society and its culture; i.e., reality does not *exist* but *happens*. Social and cultural change in our time does not mean that we are moving toward another way of living in society and toward a new set of cultural

---

[178]H. Nieuwenhuis, *De Taak van de Opvoeder in deze Tijd*, pp. 5ff.

[179]P. J. Idenburg, "Op het Keerpunt der Onderwijsgeschiedenis," in *Gedenkboek voor Prof. Dr. Ph. A. Kohnstamm*, p. 72.

patterns, but manifestly toward a society and culture whose permanent mark is change, a society in which only discontinuity is the pattern. So it is not just the case that the situation in which the growing person will have to live as adult is unpredictable. That could mean a handicap for the growing-up process. But in fact it is predictable that the young person of today will be an adult in a situation which is caught up in a process of permanent change. For education and nurture this implies the mandate to help young people become persons oriented to change as a continuous process.

Third: One division of pedagogics, namely, didactics, manifests a clearly visible shift in thinking about the problematics of this polarity between the formal and the material.

In a critical review of the educational theories which have been promoted in the last century and a half, W. Klafki asserts that two large clusters may be distinguished, namely, "material" and "formal" theories. Whereas the representatives of the "material" school of thought took their position on the object side of the educational process and were "curriculum centered," the adherents of the "formal" theories took their stand on the subject side and were "child centered."[180] The *material* education theories, whatever their internal differences, agreed in this: They all sought to define the essence of education in terms of an objective content. In the *formal* theories, content served a "functional" goal; it served as material, namely, for shaping and developing the *functions* of the growing person, e.g., her ability to observe, think, and evaluate; her esthetic sense and ethical appreciation. Or content served a "methodical" goal; as exercise-material by which to learn to use the *methods* of learning and so have the skill to acquire whatever knowledge the life situation demands.[181]

The grand premise of the formal, and especially the functional, theory is that a person is able to transfer abilities acquired in one field to another, from one content to another. So the opinion has been defended that the study of mathematics and classical languages shapes and strengthens the ability to think logically; even that memorizing pieces of prose, series of numbers, and nonsense words strengthens the memory. The question is whether such a transfer of learning actually takes place. Since the beginning of the century this question of "the transfer of learning"[182] has been one of the most important issues in the psychology of learning. The results of the studies made, beginning with the basic research done by Thorndike and Woodworth in 1901, are not favorable for the formal theory of learning.[183] According to Hillebrand, two conclusions can be drawn from all the research: "One cannot assume a general concomitant exercise

---

[180]W. Klafki, *Studien zur Bildungstheorie und Didaktik*, p. 27.

[181]Ibid., pp. 33-36.

[182]An overview of the research done is given by H. Ellis, *The Transfer of Learning*.

[183]Cf. ibid., p. 63: "An early study by Thorndike and Woodworth (1901) critically examined the notion of formal discipline and failed to find any substantial evidence in support of it. For about twenty-five years following their classic study, a number of investigations were conducted with little or no support for the doctrine resulting."

of faculties, but need not doubt the fact that under certain conditions a transfer does take place."[184] The conditions are that the student must have aptitude and interest in the field of study on which his activity as a learner is focused—say, mathematics or classical languages—and also that the instruction is such that it furthers a tendency toward conceptual clarity, insight into general principles, and the habit of mental discipline.

Hillebrand's conclusion agrees with what we have said about the human being as mind and its functioning. The human being as mind is the human being who orients, determines, and relates himself. There would be no concept of the "mind" if there were not something vis-à-vis the mind. One can speak of the mind and its functioning only when there is something over against the mind in relation to which it functions: something she thinks about, something about which she makes a judgment, something to which she relates herself, something with which she enters into a dialectic interaction. One can function mentally only on condition of "knowing." Mental functioning is not just a formal operation, then, but it has content, and that content is one which belongs to the personal value inventory of a human being. To learn to function as mind (one could call it formal education) is at the same time to acquire a personal value inventory (one could call it material education). But by saying this we transcend the dilemma which has so long been posited in didactic theory. Klafki says very well, in our opinion, what education as dynamic occurrence is: "It is the embodiment of processes in which the contents of a material and spiritual reality disclose themselves; and, viewed from the other side, this process is nothing other than the self-opening and the being-opened-up of a human learner to those contents."[185] It is this two-sided opening-up process—which has an objective, material aspect as well as a subjective, formal aspect—on which real education is focused.

In essence this is the issue in all of nurture. In the dynamic field of human maturation, which is defined by the poles of the growing person and her world, a person opens up to reality and reality to a person. Nurture aims to serve this mutual opening-up process. Martin Buber has spoken of nurture or education as effected by "the selection of a world" by one who mediates it to another. The educator educates himself to be the effective vehicle of the constructive forces of the world.[186] Without wanting to endorse the whole of this description we do resonate to a part of it. For in nurture there is the one who intermediates between the growing person and reality; it is the reality in relation to which the growing person must begin to function mentally. In his person the educator represents reality, namely, in his "selection" from it, which consists in his knowledge, experiences, and the insights he thinks he ought to share with the growing person and in which he allows the growing person to participate by the life he leads in

---

[184]M. J. Hillebrand, *Psychologie des Lernens und des Lehrens*, p. 85.
[185]W. Klafki, *Studien zur Bildungstheorie und Didaktik*, p. 43.
[186]M. Buber, *Between Man and Man*, p. 101.

the face of this growing person. Thus he influences the growing person. The critical question is this—and obviously it is the central agogic question: Is this "selection" and is this influence, both the unintentional and intentional, such that the growing person is led by it to the ability to function mentally as a self-reliant person in her world? When this question is not, in one fashion or another, the question which guides the educator/nurturer in regular self-scrutiny, there can be no true nurture. All that remains, then, is unexamined contextual influence, to which the growing person is abandoned. Or worse: the conditioning is a caricature of nurture (think of the "education" of the S.S. police in Nazi Germany), foreign to any sense of nurture.

6. AGOGY AND CHANGE

From Pedagogics to Agogics

Starting with the reality of the growing person—Point Zero of the child in her openness—we tried to determine the nature of nurture. By this method we have arrived at a concept which can play a critical role in relation to the praxis of nurture and which offers perspectives for the development of new theories in the interest of that praxis. This, however, is not the aim of this study. Our concern is not now the problems arising in the field of nurture and education; our concern is a question in practical theology, namely, that concerning the agogic moment in pastoral role-fulfilment. For this we need to know what is the "specifically agogic" and we proceeded on the assumption that our view of the answer to that question would be clearer once we knew what nurture is.

The threat that hangs over our head, now that we are about to leave the arena of pedagogics, is that some would stop us at this point and rob us of all that we have found. The argument is that the moment you start talking about adults you must let go of all thought of "nurture."

[In a previous section we observed that the same objection was lodged from within practical theology, but now the protest comes from another direction. Vanden Berg comes on very strong: "With an air of self-evident logic which is simply frightening experts advance the notion that nurture is proper for the whole of life, from the cradle to the grave."[187] "Adult education" is a contradiction in terms; it signifies the "infantilization of the adult" and cultivates a "lasting immaturity." Perquin, who came to the conclusion that nurture is "the help offered to the child by persons responsible for the child's development," tells us that only nonadults can be the objects of nurture; strictly speaking, only "normal

---

[187]J. H. vanden Berg, *Metabletica*, pp. 110ff. In the school of adult-education theorists there is a growing awareness that education is "not a preparation for life" but "a continuous life-long process" (cf. A. J. M. Hely, *New Trends in Adult Education*, pp. 56ff.).

nonadults" are eligible.[188] Langeveld calls adulthood "the end of nurture."[189] "We reject any definition of nurture so broad that it includes adults as persons for whom the effect of these influences is intended";[190] "adult education is something essentially different from nurture."[191]]

The question is whether we can do anything with what we have learned so far about nurture, now that we return to the issue of the agogic moment in pastoral role-fulfilment.

We believe we most certainly can. Langeveld points out that as one passes into adulthood, self-education takes the place of participation in the nurturing process. There is an essential difference between the two. "Self-education is undertaken completely on one's own; the active participant in the nurturing process is, finally, subject to the authority of the nurturer." But then he adds: "Undoubtedly, self-education is the nearest analogue to active participation in the nurturing process."[192] We believe that more than an analogy is involved between them, but it is clear at any rate that if we use certain insights derived from the area of pedagogics to flesh out our understanding of the pastoral role as it relates to adults as well, Langeveld will not stand in our way. The warnings couched in the objections to adult education can still be taken seriously. There *is* a real danger that adult education, or "agogy" in another connection, will lead toward the "infantilization of the adult." Ten Have rightly stresses that the point is not to work *for* but to work *with* adults. "One can speak of education in a real sense only when the other person cooperates and is viewed, not as an object of our action, but as co-agent."[193] We would comment with some emphasis, however, that this also applies to the education of the child. Treating the other person, be that other child or adult, as an equal in the quality of being human is fundamental in all nurture, we have said. Nurture occurs in a relationship between two agents. In that relationship one of the agents is bearer of a specific, i.e., pedagogical authority and thus the pedagogical relationship does have an aspect of authority. But it is still a relationship between two agents. The very notion of authority implies equihumanity. J. Waterink writes: "Authority belongs to him who has the right of 'say-so.' But among humans only that person has authority who has won the inner consent of the other. Without this inner bond authority turns into coercive power."[194] The exercise of coercive power over somebody else absolutely excludes a focus on the self-reliant mental activity

---

[188]N. Perquin, *Pedagogiek*, pp. 38, 87, 91.

[189]M. J. Langeveld, *Beknopte theoretische Paedagogiek*, p. 42.

[190]Ibid., p. 28.

[191]Ibid., p. 44.

[192]Ibid., p. 82.

[193]T. T. ten Have, *Vorming*, pp. 22ff.

[194]J. Waterink, *Theorie der Opvoeding*, p. 92. [For an illuminating discussion of authority, especially in the family, as well as of the different kinds of authority which are exercised, cf. L. Smedes, *Mere Morality: What God Expects from Ordinary People*, pp. 67ff., 260. *Tr.*]

of the other. The denial of the essentially human calling to be free and responsible can never be of benefit to the process of humanization—not in the case of adults, and no more in the case of children. Real nurture only occurs if the child—to use the word Ten Have used with reference to adults—is viewed as "coagent"; rather, if the child be viewed as an equal-in-relationship who is destined and called to be herself in freedom and responsibility. This is not to say that a child nurtures or educates herself; it does mean that the nurturing process finds its meaning in, and directs its energies toward, this: that the child begins to function mentally with increasing independence, also toward the nurturer and his influence.

[It would be a mistake to find in these statements an ideology of nurture attuned to this "age of the child." To show that we have not fallen prey to some prevailing ideology, we wish to approach the subject of "the nature of nurture" from a somewhat different angle. All nurture, not only what is called education, intends to set in motion a process which, from a formal point of view, is a learning process. If nurture does not lead to learning it is a mere boxing of the air. The intent of all future-oriented nurture is not that the growing person should cease to grow but that she should change; not that she should only appear to have changed but that she should arrive at a different orientation and a different way of functioning than was possible before the nurturing action occurred in her life. One can call such change "learning." Learning, according to Van Parreren, is "a process with durable results by which a person can originate new activities or alter activities already in his repertoire."[195] Learning occurs in all kinds of situations and throughout one's life. One can say a person learns every time an event becomes an *experience*. Educative action explicitly intends to lead people to specific experiences which bring about durable changes, at one point or another, in the way her personality functions. The goal and criterion of all agogic action is that it makes learning possible, i.e., that it facilitates having such experiences. Of such learning Klafki says—with special reference to education but in a way that is applicable to all learning in an agogic context—"Such learning does not consist in a student's simply taking over the material offered him. . . . It is much more a free, spontaneous mental transaction by which the learner follows from start to finish the structure of a perception or the steps of a skill and appropriates it."[196] The word "dialectic," which we used earlier to indicate the essential interaction operative in the process of personality formation, again comes to mind. The process of personality formation is a process of learning; and all learning which takes place in that process—e.g., learning at school—follows the laws of that process. Prins says it clearly: "Learning is an active, creative, expressive, and intentional procedure by which the student selects from the potential elements of his environment those which fit into his developmental structure, are compatible with his developmental level, and agree

---

[195]C. F. van Parreren, *Psychologie van het Leren*, I, 17.
[196]W. Klafki, *Das Fischer Lexikon*, part 36, p. 63, Pädagogik, s.v. *Didaktik und Methodik*.

with his needs."[197] To learn is to select; it is not a process of addition, but one of recognition, evaluation, acceptance, and rejection. To educate is to help the learner; it is to focus one's activity and attention on "the active, creative, expressive, and productive participation of the student."]

Now the adult placed in the position of a lifelong nurturee may be infantilized—everyone involved in adult education of some sort should take note of this. But it seems hard to maintain that anyone helping an adult in his dialectics with himself and his world is doing something essentially different from what any nurturer does with a child. In both cases one directs his energies toward the same process, the process of working for durable change. In both cases one relates in human-to-human fashion to another who must be active and creative himself and function as coagent in the relationship if anything of consequence is to happen to him. In both cases one encounters the other as a person in process of becoming—i.e., becoming himself. Each of these situations can be viewed as a special case of agogics; the insights gained in previous sections help to put in perspective the specifically agogic element which applies equally in both situations.[198] We would describe this specifically agogic element as the change in the mental functioning of persons (x) in virtue of their active involvement (f) in a relationship which is directed toward producing this change (y). Expressed in a formula it comes to this: $x = f(y)$. The keyword, obviously, is *change*. To discover the nature of the specifically agogic we must first consider this central notion.

Change

In his introduction to a book about social change Martindale states that the theory of social change is the weakest part of sociological theory. This, in his opinion, is an intolerable situation, "For man is a bird of passage. To be sure, at times he rides with his head tucked under his wing, asleep on the lifting waves, and on occasion he feeds along the eroding shores of time, stopping to rest on a gray rock or a marine-worm-weakened, weathered piling. But surely he is most fully himself when he lifts his wings and speeds along the buffeting winds of change between the revolving seasons of his spinning-top world as it whirls about his dying star."[199] These lyrical words give vivid expression to something which is typical for man and human society: In the stormwinds of change a human being is most himself. A society whose structures are unalterable and inside whose structures a change of position has been made impossible

---

[197] F. W. Prins, *Wisselende Aspecten in de Didaktiek*, p. 22.

[198] Cf. B. Morgan, G. E. Holmes, and C. E. Bundy, *Methods in Adult Education*, p. 14: "The same general principles apply to adult education that govern education at other levels."

[199] Martindale, Introduction to G. K. Zollschan and W. Hirsch, *Explorations in Social Change*, p. XII.

for its members has an inhuman face. A culture frozen stiff in its own acquired crystalization, and no longer able to reform itself under the impulse of a new inspiration, is moribund. The historian J. Romein, in an essay with which he concluded his lifework, offered his reflections on the central problem of the history of culture: the problem of continuity and change. In this treatise he remarks: history is duration in process of change and change which endures.[200]

"It is hard to picture what there would be if there were either only 'duration' or only 'change,' but it would certainly not be what we call history."[201] These words apply especially to man, whose very existence is history and in history. In the dialectics of remaining himself and at the same time changing, his humanity is actualized. This process is the fundamental condition for the life of the individual—as it is for the life of his society and culture.

A variety of very different interests, each with its own form of intervention in the life of man, converge in a common focus on change. Following a conference of psychotherapists and pastors dealing with this theme, W. Bitter concluded: "Not only in pastoral care and psychotherapy in general, but in all other areas of the study of man as well, one always encounters at last the observation: A solution of urgent problems is possible only through a complete renewal of the individual person." And the people who make a thorough study of the problems of society as a whole arrive at solutions "which are realizable only through changing the individual first."[202] In the opinion of many people, the different disciplines and professions whose interest and activity are especially aimed at change cannot be satisfied with incidental encounters.

[L. K. Frank, in a book called *The Planning of Change*, refers to the danger of "the fragmentation of the helping professions." He goes on to say: "I personally believe that each discipline and profession needs the awareness, the insight, the understanding of all the others so that it will recognize in each patient, client, and situation what the other disciplines and professions can help to reveal and to deal with."[203] The modern helping professions referred to are psychotherapy, social work, and counseling, but one may also think of the older professions "such as medicine, law, teaching, and the clergy."[204]]

The change aimed at by each of the different professions must be viewed as a special instance of change-in-general.[205]

---

[200]J. Romein, "Duur en Verandering in de Geschiedenis," in *De Nieuwe Stem* 17 (1962): 615ff.

[201]Ibid., p. 627.

[202]W. Bitter, *Die Wandlung des Menschen in Seelsorge und Psychotherapie*, p. 5.

[203]L. K. Frank, "Fragmentation in the Helping Professions," in W. G. Bennis, K. D. Benne, and R. Chin, *The Planning of Change*, pp. 43ff.

[204]W. G. Bennis, K. D. Benne, and R. Chin, *The Planning of Change*, p. 9. N. Sanford mentions as examples of change-oriented institutions "schools, training programs, hospitals and clinics, correctional institutions, therapeutic relationships, the family" (*Self and Society*, p. 293; cf. p. 40).

[205]Cf. N. Sanford, *Self and Society*, p. 311.

But it does not stop here—with the focus on changing the individual. A new discipline is growing whose object of study is the phenomenon of "planned change" in general, change which may occur in the individual personality system, the face-to-face group, an organization, a politically or ecologically determined society.[206] An effort is made in this discipline to arrive at a general theory of change. "Planned change" means "a conscious, deliberate, and collaborative effort to improve the operations of a system, whether it be self-system, social system, or cultural system, through the utilization of scientific knowledge."[207]

It does not seem altogether correct to extend the boundaries of the field to be investigated quite this far. The reason one can do this is that one uses the umbrella concept of systems in which deliberate and systematic change is effected. True, a personality system and a socio-cultural system, and the processes which occur in them, are largely comparable. One can even, as in cybernetics, track down analogies between a personality system, a group system, an organic system (like a body or plant), and a mechanical system (like an engine). It will deepen one's insights in each of the systems compared. But then one must realize that one is only talking about a *system*, i.e., a model of a given reality, not the reality itself. The model may be useful, but it represents reality only in part. The reality, of which the personality system is an abstraction, is the human being as mind. It is this reality which the educator or nurturer addresses, whether the nurturer operates in the family, in the school, or in adult education, whether she is a psychotherapist, a social caseworker, or a pastor relating to an individual or a group. In each of these situations the dominant concern is human beings in their mental-spiritual functioning; in each of these settings there is an explicit or implicit focus on change in that functioning, in virtue of a relationship, however qualified. Certainly here is an area of research and reflection which will benefit all the helping professions.

Conversion and Change

The question now is whether the pastor in his role-fulfilment can profit from this development. No one can deny that pastoral role-fulfilment in kerygma, didache, and paraklesis aims at change; but this is not to say that this change can be put in the same category as the changes the educator, the psychotherapist, and the social worker aim to produce. Does not the pastor aim at a change which in theological language has to be called "conversion," and is not conversion in a category by itself?

The psychology of religion, especially in its early years, made an intense

---

[206]Cf. R. Lippitt, J. Watson, and B. Westley, *The Dynamics of Planned Change*, pp. 5ff.

[207]W. G. Bennis, K. D. Benne, and R. Chin, *The Planning of Change*, p. 3; R. Lippitt, J. Watson, and B. Westley, *The Dynamics of Planned Change*, p. VI, refer to "professional guidance" rather than to "scientific knowledge."

study of conversion.[208] But, as H. Bavinck has pointed out, the psychology of religion is in the nature of the case powerless to penetrate the inner core of conversion; it can only observe the external phenomena, but cannot get through to the point where the finite touches, and rests in, the infinite. The psychology of religion brings with it the danger of "destroying the very thing it is studying by robbing it of its own character."[209]

In reflecting on these objections—which also touch on our concerns—one must remember what the psychology of religion actually aimed to study. That was not conversion, however defined, but the human being in whose life the signs of what, in a certain religious context, is called conversion are manifest. Benson describes it as follows: "The classic pattern of religious conversion is that of an adolescent or young adult abandoning his former self-seeking and pleasure-loving ways of existence and professing a new loyalty to Christ or God. Such conversion took place during mass religious meetings in which the influence of crowd psychology on the individual's decision was prominent."[210] What actually happens in this pattern between God and the person or the person and his God, or, in Bavinck's words, what happens at "the point where the finite touches the infinite," is not for psychological research to determine. But this is not only true of religious phenomena; it is true of every phenomenon, when it is studied from a particular scientific perspective, that only certain aspects can be captured. From a psychological point of view, conversion, or what outside of psychology bears the name "conversion," can be observed only as human behavior; as a result, however, one may discover, not everything but still a great deal of information concerning this phenomenon. The psychology of religion has demonstrated this through its research.

[There is, e.g., the finding that conversion, including the dramatic "experiential" conversion, in general turns out to be the climax of a long process.[211] This is not to say that conversion is a predictable development; it does mean that it is to be understood in terms of the history of the individual concerned; in terms, i.e., of the dialectic of duration and change which is of the essence of that history. It has also become evident that the life-manifestations of a conversion are codetermined by the kind and mode of influence which led to the conversion. H. Carrier, S.J., summarizes a study of conversions in mission fields as follows: "The same orientation of preachers brought in their train conversions of very different types: perhaps a crisis culminating in a profound

[208]We have in mind the well-known studies of E. D. Starbuck, *The Psychology of Religion*; W. James, *The Varieties of Religious Experience*; and R. O. Ferm, *The Psychology of Christian Conversion*. The last-mentioned offers a summary of the research (pp. 19ff.).

[209]H. Bavinck, *Gereformeerde Dogmatiek*, IV, 592; cf. 114.

[210]P. H. Benson, *Religion in Contemporary Culture*, a study of religion through social science, p. 496.

[211]C. G. Jung mentions this in connection with the conversion of St. Paul (*Psychological Types*, pp. 575, 577-78).

spiritual rebirth; or a brutal shock obtained by a systematic attack on the emotions."[212]]

In such results, which we mention only by way of example, nothing of the (religious) essence of conversion even surfaces. What does become visible is that conversion, however it may be viewed theologically, shows resemblance to what we can generally call "a change of personhood." This in turn enables practical theology to discover things which as a theological discipline it cannot discover for itself but which may be of great consequence for the formation of theory which helps the pastor in his role-fulfilment.

Practical theology can journey outside its own boundaries and ally itself with agogic science, however, only if first it has been able to arrive at a sound formulation of its questions. So it first has to provide a theological definition of "conversion."

Karl Barth has said that "conversion" is a term which, for all its doubtful associations, we cannot avoid.[213] The word immediately conjures up associations with the atmosphere of revivalism and conversion movements whose importance one need not deny in order to believe that it is not the atmosphere in which the church, ideally, spends its life. Add to this that the problematics surrounding conversion do not now seem to be at the center of the church's attention. J. H. vanden Berg, in his discussion of the psychology of religion in its early stages, makes this point: "In our day conversion as an abrupt religious development is exceptionally rare; even as a less abrupt turn in a human life it is infrequent. The religious problems of those who are now growing up tend to be rather different."[214] In the experience of pastors today, conversion will not be a frequent topic of conversation, and when it is mentioned, it may not have the same meaning it had in an earlier day.

The remarkable thing is that in this respect our situation is somewhat comparable to the time whose written deposit we find in the New Testament. In the preaching of the prophets of the Old Testament the summons to conversion was central. In the time in which John the Baptist and Jesus appeared, this call was also issued. "In those days Israel spoke much of conversion, radical change, and penitence. One could even say that Pharisaism was a penitential movement." This conversion had become a matter of externals, however. The Pharisee, says Schniewind, "offers his conversion to God as an achievement and under those conditions God takes lightly the sins of his own. This is how the Pharisee fails to bring forth fruit that befits repentance (Matt. 3:8)."[215] When John the Baptist

---

[212]H. Carrier, S.J., *Psycho-sociologie de l'Appartenance religieuse*, p. 61. The reference is to R. Allier, *La Psychologie de la Conversion chez les Peuples non civilisés*.

[213]K. Barth, *CD*, IV/2, p. 560.

[214]J. H. vanden Berg, *Psychologie en Geloof*, p. 31. P. H. Benson, *Religion in Contemporary Culture*, remarks: "The phenomenon of religious conversion was once much more conspicuous than it now is" (p. 496).

[215]J. Schniewind, *Die Freude der Busse*, pp. 22ff.

speaks of conversion he utters a familiar call. But he gives it a very different meaning: he summons people to "a change from within."[216]

It is striking that the writers of the New Testament, in contrast to those of the Septuagint, preferred *metanoein* over *epistrephein*, which is the equivalent of the Hebrew *šûb*. The reason for this choice is undoubtedly the radicalization of the call for conversion issued by John the Baptist and Jesus. Says Klijn: "It turns out that the writers of the New Testament, in selecting a word for conversion, did not choose the word for a more external turnabout but the word which signifies a 'change of mind.' Not only must a person's attitude change; he must become another person."[217]

What it means in this context to become another person, from a practical-theological point of view, is a question of great importance. One can say, of course, that we are talking of a miracle of God, the miracle of rebirth, but this is only a partial answer to the question and should not hold back the search for a fuller answer. It cannot be for nothing that the *summons* to conversion is heard over and over in Scripture, that change is commanded, and that humans are *called* out of a state of sin and death into a new life. We explained earlier that in God's coming to man through his word, human salvation is actualized. We observed that this actualization does not occur automatically but by way of *hearing*, the hearing in faith of the person addressed.[218] We have also seen that pastoral role-fulfilment is intermediary for God's coming in his word; the miracles which God would do for a person occur in the situation of an interhuman relationship. But as we saw, this means that human action—the whole human inventory—is relevant to God's action.[219] Practical theology, then, if it is to be helpful to the pastor in his role-fulfilment, must go as far as possible in its attempts to understand what God does through the intermediary.

It strikes us that the verb *metanoein* offers us a key to understanding.

[Schniewind would have us be cautious at this point. In the first place, says he, at the time when the New Testament was formed, "the original meaning of the word *meta-noia* had been long forgotten." Second, Jesus spoke Aramaic. He did not use the word *metanoia* but took up the proclamation: "Repent! Return to God!"[220]

In reply we would say that if *metanoein* does not, as such, say anything essential about conversion, the evangelists' choice of this word over the obvious alternative *epistrephein* becomes inexplicable. One has to believe that the Gospel writers chose this word to bring out that the intent of John the Baptist and Jesus was different from that of the Pharisees when they spoke of repentance and conversion. This is even clearer from what Paul, who rarely uses

---

[216]J. Behm, *TDNT*, IV, 1001, s.v. *metanoeō/metanoia*.

[217]A. F. J. Klijn, *Wat weten wij van Jezus van Nazareth*, p. 88.

[218]See above, II, 7, pp. 34ff.

[219]See above, II, 16, pp. 124ff.

[220]J. Schniewind, *Die Freude der Busse*, p. 20.

metanoein/metanoia, says in Romans 12:2, where he virtually offers a description of *metanoeite*:[221] "Be transformed by the renewal of your mind."

According to Barclay, *metanoia* is the word for "penitence" or "repentance." "The meaning of *metanoia* is clear; it means an *after-thought. Meta* is *afterwards* and *noia* is a *thought*. . . . Originally and by derivation, *metanoia* simply meant the condition in which a man had second thoughts about something." It means a change of mind—an altered judgment on something. "So then *metanoia* comes to involve not only a new judgment on some previous action, but also regret and sorrow for it."[222] This explanation strikes us as arguable. *Metanoia* can have the meaning Barclay attributes to it, but it is certainly not—in classical Greek or in the New Testament—the only possible one. "In compounds the preposition *meta* can have many different meanings ('after,' 'with,' 'around,' etc.) which can often be present at the same time, thus giving rise to a certain ambiguity."[223] Because *metanoein-metanoia* is used in the Gospels for the Old Testament *šûb*—to turn about—one will have to think not of "second thoughts" but of a reversal of the action of *noein,* of the *nous.*

Pohlmann, for whom *metanoia* is "the central concept of Christian piety," is right when he says that the word, in the Gospels, expresses a new beginning in life.[224] The question then becomes to what action *noein* refers. Clearly *noein* refers to the action of the *nous.* According to Pohlmann, *nous* is the natural man, "the man of reason," who shows a tendency to think he is big and God small.[225] *Nous* means "self-righteousness."[226] *Metanoia,* then, is "a break with the rule of *nous* and an unconditional recognition of the Godness of God."[227] Listening to Pohlmann one gets the impression that he, proceeding from the correct idea that in the cry *metanoeite* God aims at the transformation of the *nous,* has made *nous* the inclusive category for the human impulse toward self-aggrandizement which opposes God. Checking out the places where the New Testament uses the word, however, one does not find anything which points in that direction. Certainly one finds nothing of the sort in the Gospels, where *nous* occurs only once, in Luke 24:45.

According to R. Bultmann, *nous* expresses that "being man means being a specific self that is the subject of its own willing and doing." The term does not mean "the mind or intellect as a special faculty, but the knowing, understanding, and judging which belong to man as man and determine what attitude

---

[221]H. Lietzmann, *Römer,* p. 109, speaks of a heightened *metanoeite.*

[222]W. Barclay, *Turning to God,* a study of conversion in the Book of Acts and today, p. 48.

[223]J. Behm, *TDNT,* IV, 976.

[224]H. Pohlmann, *Die Metanoia als Zentralbegriff der christlichen Frömmigkeit,* p. 39.

[225]Ibid., p. 40. "Where *nous* rules, the question arises: Who is the greatest?" (p. 43).

[226]Ibid., p. 42.

[227]Ibid., p. 48; cf. p. 74: "*Metanoia* is Yes to the absoluteness of God and No to the absoluteness of man."

he adopts." The *nous* is by no means only contemplative, but includes "the taking of a stand."[228] Admittedly, the *nous* can turn toward the bad; ontologically, it can turn in either direction. "Man's volition is not an instinctive striving but is an understanding act of will which is always an 'evaluating' act and therefore necessarily moves in the sphere of decisions between good and evil."[229] The English language is incapable of reproducing in *one* word what is expressed in the Greek word *nous*. Gaugler refers to it as a "multileveled" word which one may not narrow down to a choice of one possibility—say, thinking. The word can signify "sense, mind, insight, intellect, a capacity for reflection; also that which results from such reflection, thoughts, decisions, goals, plans; also that which determines the attitude of the will."[230] H. N. Ridderbos, in his commentary on Romans, remarks: "In the religious usage of Paul *nous* refers not only to the faculty of knowing, but to man himself in his deepest conscious inner self, as the place where, on the one hand, he relates to God, and as where, on the other, his life-manifestation is determined."[231]]

It strikes us that *nous* is the word for what in the previous section we called "the human being as mind"—*the human being in the act of orienting, determining, and relating himself.* Conversion, in Paul's words, consists in a person's setting his mind in another direction (cf. Col. 3:1-2).

This change of direction in the functioning of the mind does not stand by itself, but relates to what may be considered the central occurrence in the Kingdom of God, the secret of renewal, or, in another phrase, the secret of "the new." When John the Baptist and Jesus Christ call people to conversion, this call is directly related to the kerygma, the proclamation of the Kingdom of God. Paul's paraklesis in Romans 12:2—"Be transformed by the renewal of your mind"—is "integral to the great changeover of the two world aeons. Christians, as those who are in Christ Jesus, do not simply stand in the old aeon, but also paradoxically, at the same time, already in the new and 'future' aeon. Already now, therefore, they have to take account, quite practically, of the radical transformation which this new aeon brings with it."[232] Says Paul in effect: "Be what you will become in the age to come."[233] In Jesus Christ the Kingdom of God is revealed; in him, too, the secret of that Kingdom, the secret of conversion, is revealed. The Lord refers to it every time he opens his mouth and acts. "Blessed are the poor in spirit. . . . Blessed are those who mourn. . . . Blessed are those who hunger and thirst for righteousness" (Matt. 5:3-4, 6). "The blind receive their sight and the lame walk, lepers are cleansed and the deaf hear, and the dead are raised up, and the poor have good news preached to them" (Matt.

---

[228]R. Bultmann, *Theology of the New Testament*, p. 211.
[229]Ibid., p. 213.
[230]E. Gaugler, *Der Römerbrief*, II, 235.
[231]H. N. Ridderbos, *Aan de Romeinen*, pp. 42-43.
[232]E. Gaugler, *Der Römerbrief*, II, 234.
[233]H. Lietzmann, *Römer*, p. 109.

11:5).[234] "For judgment I came into this world, that those who do not see may see, and that those who see may become blind" (John 9:39). Says the poet Remco Campert in a poem entitled "Credo":

> I believe in a river
> whose current flows upward
> from the sea to the mountains.[235]

So the movement of the Kingdom can be characterized by saying that it is the opposite of what is expected in this aeon—a world in reverse. Whoever is called to that Kingdom is called to participate in the movement of that Kingdom. When God turns to a person, it means not only that this person must turn once-and-for-all to God; as Karl Barth says, conversion is a movement which extends over the whole of life. "It is neither exhausted in a once-for-all act, nor is it accomplished in a series of such acts. . . . It becomes and is the content and character of the whole act of his life as such."[236]

It is upon this continuing movement, this new mode of Kingdom existence, this conversion, that pastoral role-fulfilment is focused. When God comes in his word through the intermediary of this interhuman relationship, then *kerygma*, which proclaims the new aeon as reality for everyone who hears it, is there; then *didache*, which points out the way of the Kingdom, which is the way of Christ, is offered; then *paraklesis*, the address to persons in their situation of need given on the basis of, and with an eye to, their being called to discipleship, takes place. But this is only to say that the pastoral relationship as intermediary of God's coming aims at change, a change which is realized in a person's actually functioning mentally and spiritually as a new person in all the concrete situations of his daily existence. Being a "change agent" is one of the aspects of the many-sided pastoral role.[237] It makes sense, therefore, to pay attention to the "planning of change" within the framework of practical theology.

A Changing of Attitudes?

We now return to our description of the specifically agogic, which we have viewed as *"the change in the mental functioning of persons in virtue of their active involvement in a relationship which is directed toward producing this change."*

By speaking of "change in mental functioning" we have deviated from the language typically used at various training centers. In these circles one hears regularly that their aim is a change of attitude. Initially we believed, too, that

---

[234]H. M. M. Fortmann, *Wat is er met de Mens gebeurd?*, p. 16, correctly states that these words are to be understood as "the announcement of a new mode of existence."

[235]R. Campert, "Credo," in *Vogels vliegen toch.*

[236]K. Barth, *CD,* IV/2, p. 566.

[237]The term "change agent" is used to designate the person who gives professional guidance in a process of "planned change."

with the concept of "attitude change" we would be on target in terms of the problematics which occupy us in this book. In the course of our study, however, we have discovered that this is not the case, even though much of what has been learned over the past few decades concerning change and "attitude change" is of great importance for the practice of agogic work.[238] To demonstrate this importance, as well as to explain our preference for the expression "change in mental functioning," it is imperative that we make a few remarks about "attitude" and "attitude change."

    According to Paillard, the word "attitude" derives "from the late Latin *aptitudo*, designating an aptitude understood as a natural disposition to accomplish certain tasks." In physiology "attitude" has acquired a meaning which lies close to the original, namely, that of "a way of holding the body."[239] The term was taken over in psychology. Just as the body assumes a certain posture with a view to fulfilling a certain task—like climbing a stairway or catching a ball— the psyche has a tendency to do something similar. It has been remarked that subjective orientation plays an important role in observation. When a starved person, for example, is shown an unclear picture through a tachistoscope, he sees something like food in it. This subjective orientation affecting a person's powers of observation was initially called an "attitude."[240]

    Against this background one must understand the term as it is used in social psychology, where "attitude" has become one of the most pivotal concepts. In this discipline researchers encountered the fact that people show a tendency to react to the same object—a person, a group, or an idea—with the same type of behavior in different situations. Someone is anti-Jewish or not; highly values scholarship or not; is hot-eyed for money or not; loves fast cars or not; adores classical music or not. This tendency to react to things with the same kind of behavior is so strong that the experiences people have in certain relationships tend to be quite alike. Some people have only bad experiences with authority figures, while others have only good experiences with them. There are Protestants who have never met a Catholic whom they could trust; there are others who think that in matters of honesty Protestants could learn a thing or two from Catholics. There are men who are confirmed every day in the conviction that a woman behind the wheel is a danger on the road; the experience of other men is consistently that only women are "gentlemen" drivers.

    The question is: Why do different persons display this constant, but quite divergent, behavior, and why do they constantly have these divergent, and even opposite, experiences with the same object? Is the factor which determines this

---

[238]For a comprehensive introduction to the literature, see E. E. Davis, *Attitude Change*, and M. Jahoda and N. Warren, *Attitudes*.

[239]J. Paillard, "Les Attitudes dans la Motricité," in H. C. J. Duyker, *Les Attitudes*, p. 8.

[240]In French psychology this is still the case; in Germany the word is *Einstellung*; English-language psychology currently speaks of "mind-set."

constant type of behavior located in the object or in the subject who reacts to it? At first sight one is inclined to answer: in both. Mr. A. is unsympathetic toward Catholics, only knows unfavorable things about them, would love to help confine their influence, and has only bad experiences with them. Now Mr. A. is not one who easily dislikes another person and it is not in his nature to work against another. Only, a Catholic affects him, so to speak, as a red flag affects a bull. One could say: the stimulus which produces this response in him proceeds from the object. But that cannot be the whole story. Mr. B, who like A is a Protestant, and who is of the same character type as A, has a similar background, and has had just as much contact with Catholics, reacts very differently: his experience is that on the whole Catholics are very fine people and wherever possible he would like to work with them. So the source of the difference must lie in the subject. The question is: What makes the subject act as he does? Ostensibly, all there is to see in the picture is the given object, on the one hand; the manifest behavior of the subject, on the other. It is clear that the behavior of the subject is related to the stimulus of the object. But there must be a factor in between which gives the stimulus an effect creating this behavior. In technical terms: it must be assumed that between the independent variable—the stimulus—and the dependent variable—the response—there must be an intervening variable. This variable is hypothetical and can be inferred only from the response. It is this inferred factor which social psychology calls an *attitude*.

There are many definitions of attitude, but according to Davis they agree in general on two major points which he summarizes in this definition: An attitude is "an inferred factor within the individual which involves a tendency to perceive and react in a particular manner toward some aspect of his environment."

There is, first, the matter of "the inferred factor." The word "attitude" has found its way into popular usage. That is not at all strange: the same things which the social psychologists infer from certain patterns of behavior, we also infer in everyday life.[241] We observe, for instance, that the moment someone hears about France she gets excited and wants to talk of nothing else, and we say: "She is a Francophile." We observe that someone else can never get interested in a given cause and always has negative things to say about it, and we say: "It does not appeal to him." So when we, who already draw these inferences, discover that social psychology has developed a concept for this procedure, we begin to use it in everyday life. The remarkable thing is that we then go beyond scientific usage. Says Brown: "Quite simply, an attitude is a concept used by the social psychologist in order to explain without complicated references to individual psychology . . . what happens between stimulus and response to produce the observed effect."[242] Newcomb calls it a "shorthand" way to say

---

[241] T. M. Newcomb, *Social Psychology*, pp. 120-21.
[242] J. A. C. Brown, *Techniques of Persuasion*, p. 37.

something that is quite complicated.[243] Ask a social psychologist whether an attitude "exists" and he will answer that he has never seen one. He can operate with the idea; it saves him the telling of a long tale; but he knows that an attitude does not exist in the sense that a person exists, not even in the sense in which a conception or a mental image exists—it is simply "a concept used by a social psychologist," no more than a theoretical construction.[244]

Second, we must notice that the attitude of a person has reference to "some aspect of his environment." That can be anything: religion, the church, art, classical music, authority, marriage, the use of creamery butter, the World Council of Churches, professional football, one of my children. One can never speak of "the attitude" of a person; at most, of "an attitude."

One must remember two more things when speaking about "attitude." The first applies to the composition of an attitude. One group of authors defines attitude as "an enduring system of three components centering about a single object: the beliefs about the object—the *cognitive component;* the affect connected with the object—the *feeling component;* and the disposition to take action with respect to the object—the *action tendency component.*"[245]

Whenever one speaks of an attitude, then, three sets of things are always at stake. A person has favorable or unfavorable ideas about an object; positive or negative feelings; the tendency to go into action in favor of or against that object. It has been shown that change in one of the components brings about change in the others; e.g., if the affective relationship of a person to an object changes, then he tends to accommodate his thinking about that object as well. One can also put it like this: an attitude is not just a belief, a feeling, or a state of readiness to act with reference to an object; it is *an organization of the entire personality system in one relationship or another.*

An attitude may be more peripheral or more central but it always concerns an orientation of the entire person toward an object.

It is not surprising to learn, then, that attitudes do not occur in isolation. Carrier describes attitude as "a disposition or a structuration of personal dynamism orienting behavior either positively or negatively with regard to a psycho-sociological object."[246] It is clear from this description that attitude is a property of the whole personality system.[247] Attitude research continues to confirm this

---

[243]T. M. Newcomb, *Social Psychology,* p. 119.

[244]The same is true of concepts like "character," "personality," the "subconscious," etc., all of them concepts about which there is a tendency to think too "realistically."

[245]D. Krech, R. S. Crutchfield, and E. L. Ballachey, *Individual in Society,* p. 146.

[246]H. Carrier, S.J., *Psycho-sociologie de l'Appartenance religieuse,* p. 46.

[247]Cf. T. M. Newcomb, *Social Psychology,* p. 119: "Attitudes . . . represent persistent, general orientations of the individual toward his environment." In later publications Newcomb uses orientation as equivalent for attitude; cf. his "An Approach to the Study of Communicative Acts," in A. P. Hare, E. F. Borgatta, and R. F. Bales, *Small Groups,* pp. 132ff.

finding. Attitudes, it turns out, tend to come in clusters. If someone has an attitude X, it is statistically probable that he will also have attitudes Y and Z. This is something one may observe without research. Talk with someone whom one has not met before about, say, "the youth of today." He turns out to have a very distinct attitude on the subject. Once you have discovered it, you are not surprised by what he believes on the subject of authority, and one can even predict with some confidence what his attitude will be to the problem of co-determination of policy in a factory, the politics of apartheid, and—once you know what church he belongs to—his attitude toward church life in general and toward several current problems in particular. Van Veldhoven remarks: "Attitudes are not independent psychic elements but they are structured in larger wholes."[248] Research like that of Adorno, to which we have referred earlier, has clearly shown this. Social psychology can, on the basis of this research, offer generalizations which are important for the formation of its theory and further research. But one can never approach an individual with a generalization. In addition, one must be on guard, as Katz warns, against "the great error of oversimplification—the error of attributing a single cause to given types of attitude."[249] Attitudes may serve very different functions: "the same attitude can have a different motivational base in different people."[250] Two people may have the same attitude but they do not necessarily hold it for the same reason. In linguistics, a word does not mean anything apart from its context. The same can be said of an attitude. Not everyone who is opposed to "women in office" is conservative; not every advocate of movie censorship is intolerant. The entire knowing, emotionally involved, and volitionally active person in all the complexity of a personality system shaped by past history and present dynamics is present in an attitude. Against the background of this history, and from within the perspective of the present motivational direction, an attitude makes sense; and one understands the reasons why this person is in "a state of readiness" with regard to this object.[251] That is to say, it is not possible to "take the measure" of a person at a glance.

Having said this much, we can now formulate our objections to the use of the concept of attitude in an agogic context.

First, the concept has been formed from the vantage point of the social psychologist who uses it in his research as a "theoretical tool." In agogy one needs helps in approaching the concrete individual.

Second, people do not have attitudes in general, but attitudes in relation to

---

[248]G. M. van Veldhoven, *Attitudes van Meisjes in Militaire Vrouwenafdelingen*, p. 45.

[249]D. Katz, "The Functional Approach to the Study of Attitudes," in E. P. Hollander and R. G. Hunt, *Current Perspectives in Social Psychology*, p. 342.

[250]Ibid., p. 343.

[251]These words form the core of one of the best-known descriptions of "attitudes," the one of G. W. Allport in C. Murchison, *Handbook of Social Psychology*, p. 810. Cf. G. W. Allport, "Attitudes in the History of Social Psychology," in M. Jahoda and N. Warren, *Attitudes*, pp. 15ff.

this and that object. If in "the planning of change" people intended only a change in a specific behavior, then—apart from the other objections—the concept of attitude would be useful. Ter Hoeven, for instance, remarks: "In trying to influence people's actions, you must first influence their attitudes." He has in mind matters like persuading orchard keepers to dig up unproductive fruit trees, changes in eating habits, introducing immigrants to the organizations of the big city.[252] In advertising, too, the concept of attitude would be useful. But in agogy one is not concerned primarily with the actions of a person but with that person as a whole in the whole of his existence. A change of attitude at one point or other may be important from an agogic point of view but then only in a larger context. And that larger context is not the sum of a person's attitudes.

Third, essential to the concept of "attitude" is its constitution, including cognitive, affective, and action-oriented components within one system. The system seeks equilibrium, but one cannot say in an individual instance in which direction the process of achieving equilibrium will run. Nor can it be predicted what corrective influence would be exerted by the other components should one of them be affected. Will not a play on the cognitive component elicit a reaction from the affective component in a direction opposite of the one intended? Will a stimulation to action cause inner tensions in the system? And what will that do to the system? These are questions which turn up over and over in every agogic relationship; the fact that they do, however, is an indication that one's agogic attention should encompass the person, and only, incidentally, attitude (a) or (b).

Fourth, there is a bond between the various attitudes of a person; they are parts of a personality system. When "attacking" one attitude, do we know what that means for the system? In earlier times one heard of "a conversion from sin to virtue." This could be disastrous. A person changes in one area; he may lose his wastefulness or his greed; but the result may be an impossible person.

A report of a UNESCO conference on "attitude change in intergroup relations" concludes: "The real question that we have to ask in this connection is therefore not so much which are the techniques for changing given attitudes, but rather if it is at all possible to educate children so that they will not yield to an excessive conformism, but think for themselves. Is it possible to introduce methods of education which will lead children and young people to display some independent thinking and not blindly to follow the norms and patterns of behavior of their society, whatever they may be?"[253] In other words, what we are after, in the first place, is not that "good" attitudes replace "bad" ones; more important by far is the change by which a person arrives at a sound orientation and the ability to function well all around. One can view an attitude as a solidified movement: someone has acquired a durable attitude to a given object. Perhaps he should be brought to another attitude. This would mean eventually that one congealed form of his movement had taken the place of another. From

---

[252]P. J. A. ter Hoeven, *Houdingen in Beweging*, p. 9.
[253]UNESCO, *Attitude Change in Intergroup Relations*, p. 37.

an agogic point of view this new form is not so important, but the basic change toward movement is. C. R. Rogers says that it is possible for a person to move "from a fixity or homeostasis through change to new fixity. . . . But much the more significant continuum is from fixity to changingness, from rigid structure to flow, from stasis to process."[254] At the end of a good psychotherapeutic process "the person becomes a unity of flow, of motion. He has changed; but what seems most significant, he has become an integrated process of changingness."[255] Changingness, in Roger's idiom, has its own connotations on which we do not need to comment. But even apart from them the concept is significant for a correct view of the agogic process. This process is only secondarily aimed at change at this point or that, but primarily at the ability to function well in a variety of relationships.

Change toward Objective Realism[256]

We can define the ultimate focus of the agogic process more clearly with the help of the category of *objective realism*. This category assumes a central place in the anthropology of Hengstenberg. By objective realism he means "that attitude which turns to an object for its own sake, without regard for its utility. . . . That person is objectively realistic who comes to an 'existent' as he would have the 'existent' come to him; views it as it, being viewed, displays itself to the viewer; deals with it and values it in accordance with its own integrity and design—in total abstention from all high-handedness."[257] "Objective realism is conspiring with the object."[258]

["Objective realism" is one of several basic attitudes or ways of relating to objects. The opposite attitude is nonobjectivity (*Unsachlichkeit*). The nonobjective attitude of a person consists in his inner rejection of the demand or claim which an object or another person makes on him. A person then turns away from the dynamic sense of a thing.[259] An instructive example of nonobjectivity is the lie. "The true definition of a lie is not consciously to tell an untruth, but to abuse trust. . . . Since I know that the other person trusts me I tell him something which makes him useful to my purposes."[260]

The category of objective realism is also used in the characterology of Künkel. By character Künkel understands "the system of determinations present

---

[254]C. R. Rogers, "A Process Conception of Psychotherapy," in W. G. Bennis, K. D. Benne, and R. Chin, *The Planning of Change*, p. 363.

[255]Ibid., p. 373.

[256][The expression "objective realism" (Dutch *zakelijkheid*; German *Sachlichkeit*) needs to be heard as a term for a fundamental spiritual and mental attitude, and not as a description of any particular philosophical tradition. *Tr.*]

[257]Hengstenberg, *Philosophische Anthropologie*, p. 9.

[258]Ibid., p. 12.

[259]Ibid., p. 123.

[260]Ibid., p. 32.

in the subject which shapes his conduct."[261] This system may be oriented in two ways: toward the "I" or toward the "we," the latter being "objectively realistic." To be objectively realistic, in Künkel, is "to be in accord with the requirements of a situation." "An objectively realistic mode of relating to a person is to be 'personable' and to a loved one, loving." "Indifference, insensitivity, coldness, fanaticism, rage, and various forms of 'cramp' are always 'I' centered."[262] Such modes of behavior serve only the realization of the "I"-ideal—"the preservation and the protection of the precious self."[263]]

Hengstenberg points out that in these categories one is concerned with a "fundamental disposition," the "archphenomenon of a basic orientation" which cannot be reduced to something else. In the references to "objective realism" and "nonobjectivity" we are addressing the very ABC's of spiritual and mental functioning which is determinative for all that follows in the conduct and life-manifestation of a person. The "I" and the matter at issue (the "other") are always there. That "other" may be a person, a thing, an idea, a fact, a circumstance, a task, a question—everything that impinges on us from without and with which we must come to terms. Nearly always a variety of behavioral options are available to us, but the fundamental disposition in accord with which we function as human beings is decisive in any case. We can practice a disciplined *realism:* turn toward the "other" in openness, whatever it is; try to decode the language of that "other"; discover the peculiar properties and values of that other; and then answer the question which comes to us in that other. We can also be *nonobjective:* close ourselves off from the other; deny by prejudice the actual manifestation of that other; deprive that other of the opportunity to be what it is in itself—and, before we have heard the question of that "other," pronounce our domineering word. The nonobjective person is he who, in terms of his own thinking, imposes an alien system of coordinates on the other and so subjects it to himself. The "other" in essence eludes him. "The attitude of domination, which transforms a person and his mind into the lord of his fellow humans and other 'affairs,' is the strongest barrier against gaining a true insight into people and affairs."[264] The objectively realistic person, on the other hand, is a questioner and a listener; the genuine questioner asks the "affairs" (German *Sachen*) themselves to speak in response to the question: "Who, then, are you?"[265]

[In a previous section we viewed the personality system which Adorno calls "the authoritarian personality." One cannot simply say that this is the profile of the person who lacks "objective realism"; still less, that its opposite—to be found in the common factor uniting the low scorers on the F Scale—is the

---

[261]F. Künkel, *Einführung in die Charakterkunde*, p. 147.
[262]Ibid., p. 7.
[263]Ibid., p. 9.
[264]F. Schulze, *Pädagogische Strömungen der Gegenwart*, p. 91.
[265]Ibid., p. 97.

image of the "objective realist." But we can say that the duality between objective realism and its lack is basic to the two types of personality system.]

The person who, out of fear for himself and the "other," dares not give himself to that other and to himself, and who therefore is incapable of a real relationship, is never free, never really bound, never in correspondence with reality or "affairs."[266] For him there is no third possibility over against harshness and sentimentality, fanaticism and the absence of principles—the possibility of coming to terms with reality in freedom, openness, and responsibility.

It is on finding this possibility that all agogy is focused. In our attempts to define nurture's aim we called it "the ability to function spiritually and mentally on one's own"; and in our description of the specifically agogic, as "change in spiritual and mental functioning." But in terms of the basic issue at stake, it can all be captured in the category of objective realism. That person is capable of functioning mentally and spiritually on his own; that person is a *changing* person—i.e., not fixed in one mental posture—who is "objective," open to the language of the "other," whatever it is, and who deals with that other, *as* it is. For that "other," one can substitute whatever in the human world appears to him. It may be a mathematical or language problem to a school child; or another child who enters her life; it may be a wife to a man; a black man to a white man; a painting to a visitor at the museum; a disease to a sick person. In all these instances and situations a person only then realizes his humanity—its potentialities and their destination—when he turns resolutely toward the matter which comes to him in a given situation. And *agogy* can be defined as *help in achieving that objectivity; help in understanding the matter before him; help in learning to hear and to answer.*

[At this point a misunderstanding may arise to which we need to pay attention. According to Klafki, for all the diversity of opinion which exists with respect to the concept of "education" (German *Bildung*), there appears to have developed a consensus at one point: "Only then can we say that the concept of *Bildung* is still valid as a basic category in pedagogics when it includes in its view of man that attitude which we designate as responsibility and accountability."[267] He then correctly points out the danger of one-sidedness which an emphasis on accountability brings with it. *Bildung* must also include what can be appreciated as the counterpole: "play and leisure, freedom from obligations and commitments, and reflection . . . an interest in knowledge and truth for their own sake."[268]]

When we speak of the agogic moment in pastoral role-fulfilment, we view this action as a dynamic field in which movement is begun in the direction of change toward objective and self-reliant spiritual and mental functioning. Pastoral role-fulfilment is not primarily an agogic situation—and one should not

---

[266]Cf. D. Bonhoeffer, "The Structure of Responsible Life," *Ethics*, pp. 194ff.
[267]W. Klafki, *Studien zur Bildungstheorie und Didaktik*, p. 46.
[268]Ibid., p. 49.

therefore call the pastor a "nurturer" or "educator." His role-fulfilment lies in being intermediary for God's coming in his word. But that coming brings with it a force which moves a person by calling him into movement; there is in God's coming a kind of *agoge*. When in the kerygma the Kingdom of God is proclaimed to this person as a present reality; when in didache a new way of life is pointed out; and when in paraklesis a person is addressed in his own situation on the basis of the salvation which has appeared in Christ and with a view to its coming appearance—all rigidity has to go. The Kingdom of God is a new state of affairs; the new way is really "new";[269] and therefore it can only be expected that the person to whom God comes in his word will be drawn into a process of change involving the very form of his existence, a process which has its starting point in the renewal of his *nous,* the center of spiritual and mental functioning (Rom. 12:2). *As intermediary of God's agoge pastoral role-fulfilment is agogic; it relates God's re-creative initiative to the concrete existence of a human being.*

Unhindered Receptivity

In his role-fulfilment the pastor has to deal, as does all agogy, with *human functioning in three relational dimensions* in which objective realism must concretize itself. In this context we shall discuss successively unhindered receptivity, pure discernment, and creativity.

When a matter comes to a person it is necessary, first, that the person be objectively receptive. "What is it?" "What does it mean?" These are the questions with which his relations to that matter begin. Not that pure receptivity is identical with objectivity. It is a question whether humans are capable of real objectivity—in any case, they are not photographic plates. It would take us too far afield to enter at length on what the psychology of observation has told us about that issue, but a few things may be mentioned.

First, we must be aware that in our observations we humans are always selective. When a mother sits in her house while her child is playing on the street, she could listen to a great number of noises: the squeals of streetcars and the low roar of cars, the footsteps or the voices of pedestrians, the exclamations of playing children—but in fact she has ears only for the sounds uttered by the infant in her playpen. When suddenly the sound of her child crying rises in the midst of all other sounds, she hears it instantly. A driver of a car is theoretically able to see all sorts of things on the street: the cars passing by, the houses on both sides, pedestrians on the sidewalk—but out of that assortment he selects only the stimuli that are important to him: the sound of a horn coming from behind him, the movement of a child chasing a ball, the color of the traffic light. Selective perception is a necessity: a person who hears everything, sees every-

---

[269]Cf. J. Behm, *TDNT,* III, 449, s.v. *Kainos: "Kainos* is the epitome of the wholly different and miraculous thing which is brought by the end-time of salvation."

thing, and notices everything can hardly pay attention to what is important to him.

A second point of importance is that in our perceptions we not only receive certain selected impressions but also influence them. Says M. Mulder: "We do not see things objectively as to size, distance, and form." Research showed that people tend to underestimate the size of objects in proportion to the personal value they represented. "The degree of familiarity with an object, and its emotional connotation, proved to exert much influence on the perception of its size, distance, and form. . . . The emotional relationship between observer and observed object proved able to determine the manner in which a person viewed 'his' object."[270] But other factors are present as well. Gerth and Wright Mills offer a remarkable example: "Moral and social taboos, as well as interests and skills, pattern our perceptions. If the members of a group believe that children should not resemble certain relatives, it is unlikely that within the group any such resemblances will ever be remarked. The Trobriander, Malinowsky has indicated, will not see resemblances between female parent and children, nor between two brothers. These resemblances are taboo and it is an insult to say that they exist. These social norms may, in time, be internalized and actually block out the perception of resemblances."[271] Along the same lines is the effect of prejudice on observation. In one research project in the United States a number of persons were shown cartoons of a white person who demonstrated hostility toward minority groups. Two-thirds of the people tested misunderstood the drawing; many of them completely reversed its meaning. The most important correlate to understanding or misunderstanding proved to be, not someone's I.Q., but the predisposition to understanding, i.e., holding or not holding prejudices against blacks. The findings of Allport and Postman in their experiments in the psychology of rumor were also striking. Test persons were shown a picture of a white with something like an open razor in hand, talking with a black. The response was: "A Negro has a razor in his hand." So the objective fact was not reproduced, but rather the stereotypical image.[272] Perhaps we are dealing here with a phenomenon which can be viewed as a degenerate form of selective perception which is normal and necessary—what Künkel calls "tendentious apperception," "the colored glasses, consisting in the fact that each person accepts only those sense impressions which relate to his goals, and assimilates only those impressions which correspond to his goals."[273] A falsification of reality takes place in tendentious apperception because people first make a biased

---

[270]M. Mulder, *Mensen, Groepen, Organisaties*, p. 235. [On factors affecting one's perceptions, see also J. H. vanden Berg, *Things: Four Metabletic Reflections. Tr.*]

[271]H. Gerth and C. Wright Mills, *Character and Social Structure*, p. 71.

[272]G. W. Allport and L. J. Postman, "The Basic Psychology of Rumor," in E. E. Maccoby, T. M. Newcomb, and E. L. Hartley, *Readings in Social Psychology*, p. 57.

[273]F. Künkel, *Die Arbeit am Charakter*, pp. 28-29.

selection of the material of observation and then assimilate it in biased ways, and so try to maintain the world image with which they are comfortable.[274]

Künkel clearly indicates the point at issue here. That a person is selective in his perceptions and that in his observations he reinterprets reality does not mean that he is deficient in pure receptivity. On the contrary, we have already seen that the typically human consists precisely in that, in coming to terms with reality, the human "creates" his own world. The child's world is different from the world of the adult; the world of an artist differs from that of the businessman; the world of every individual differs from that of every other individual. The same reality can have different meanings for different people because one relates to that reality differently from the way another relates to it. The question is only: Does that reality "intend" to have the significance it has for somebody; is justice being done to the "matter" of that reality?

We intentionally speak of "doing justice." It seems to us that the idea to which we referred in the phrase "objective realism" is embodied in the Hebrew term *ṣᵉdāqâ* as it is used in the Old Testament. *Ṣᵉdāqâ*, according to Schrenk, "represents an extraordinarily rich and varied group of concepts." But above all it is a relational concept. "A man is righteous when he meets certain claims which another has on him in virtue of relationship."[275] Vriezen says: "*Ṣaddîq* is somebody or something that is as he or it should be; the meaning of the word is *'real,' 'pure,' 'true,'* that which agrees with the end to which it has been created, that which inwardly, fundamentally corresponds to its external appearance and therefore actually fulfils the function for which (he) it exists."[276] The meaning of the word comes out with characteristic force in what Proverbs says of the *ṣaddîq*: "A righteous man has regard for the life of his beast," i.e., he knows its nature. This is pure receptivity. The nonobjective, i.e., unrighteous, person thinks: A beast is only a beast. He is not open to "that other" which comes to him in an animal—he is boss of his cattle and that is it. The righteous sees the otherness and is concerned to maintain its integrity.

The example from Proverbs causes us to ask whether, in the interest of a purer receptivity, we do not need another mode of observation, another way of relating to reality, than the one to which our cultural-historical situation has disposed us. One could reproduce the sense of Proverbs 12:10 like this: "The righteous person has a heart for his beasts." Even then, however, the notion of knowing is present, the knowing that arises from a commitment of the heart. But has this way of knowing not been largely lost to the typical modern? Fortmann reminds us of the complaint of many young people with regard to religious reality: "It does not get to me; it does not turn me on; it leaves me cold." He remarks: "Something must be wrong with our cultural climate, and with the way the Message is presented, to occasion such complaints. The change in cultural

---

[274]F. Künkel, *Einführung in die Charakterkunde,* p. 12.
[275]G. Schrenk, *TDNT,* II, 195, s.v. *dikē.*
[276]T. C. Vriezen, *An Outline of Old Testament Theology,* p. 389.

climate clearly has to do with the reduction of things to a scientific formula.
. . . It means . . . the atrophy of our capacity to grasp the multidimensionality,
the richness, the wonder, of things. The religious problematics of modern man
goes back, at least in part, to a defect in his experience of what is."[277] In his
large work on religious observation, that is the central theme. He points out that
the people who populate the Book of Acts were different from modern West-
erners. They walked in the midst of wonders; they expected and experienced
things which lie completely outside our world of experience. They experienced
the nearness of God. Apparently they allowed other thought forms next to the
scientific; they still "had an organ for reading nonscientifically verifiable meaning."[278] In his reproduction of Guardini's ideas on that subject he continues:
"What is lost is the capacity to 'see' the spiritual in the material. . . . The
proper relationship between the powers of the soul has shifted: abstract intellect
and the utilitarian will have overshadowed everything; the capacity for the vital
view, the 'concrete encounter,' on the other hand, has shrunk."[279] Again, what
is lost is the "consciousness which is marked by an openness to the significance
which the world has for me here and now; in other words, a knowledge 'in the
first person.' "[280] It is a matter of "hearing" and "seeing" which is more than
a "mere act of observation." True observation is always "the recognition of a
context of meaning. That meaning eludes the eye of objectivizing science. But
I can find it."[281] "The righteous knows—literally, is knowing—the nature of his
beasts." That was said in a culture in which "the atrophy of our capacity to
grasp . . . the richness of things" had only just begun. In the stage in which we
find ourselves now this capacity of "knowing" has become almost completely
impossible—perhaps we have it still in relation to animals, but it seems to elude
us in relation to things, to people also, and to ourselves.

But something else may be even more basic than that to which Fortmann
refers. According to Buytendijk, nurture which aims to be Christian is "nurture
in humility." Following the tradition of Christian mysticism, he views humility
as the essence of the Christian faith.[282] Humility is the opposite of the proud
attitude which consists in "twisting all the capacities and powers of the soul
around the 'I'—toward *self* value in one's *own* eyes. . . . Comprehension in the
sense of spiritual possession is the highest ideal of pride." Humble reflection is
very different. "In it, not comprehension, but seeing, *in*sight, is the decisive act
of the soul. The soul's concern, then, is truly to see things, . . . not in our own
light, or in our forms, but in their immediacy, in their natural unity and embed-

---

[277]H. M. M. Fortmann, *Aan de Mens nabij*, p. 13.
[278]H. M. M. Fortmann, *Als ziende de Onzienlijke*, I, 13ff.
[279]Ibid., I, 296.
[280]Ibid., II, 272.
[281]Ibid., IIIa, 250.
[282]F. J. J. Buytendijk, *Erziehung zur Demut*, p. 23.

dedness; not to comprehend them but tenderly to apprehend them; not to take them in but to lose oneself in them."[283] We have hardened our hearts, says Buytendijk, not only to the spiritual world but to the most common and simple things, and cannot see them in their own worth.[284] A definite practice, soul exercises, are needed to bring a person to an attitude of humility.[285]

One may ask Fortmann whether his judgment of the process of "de-animation," desacralization, and objectification—a process which originates in Jewish-Christian monotheism and continues in rationalistic science—is not too negative. One may believe that too much romanticism lurks in Buytendijk's views.[286] The issues with which they confront us are no less important. Is it not true that as a result of socio-cultural developments—so says Fortmann—and our pride—so Buytendijk—we have been robbed of a possibility of relating to the world, have suffered damage to our objectively realistic, well-attuned receptivity, and can no longer be "righteous" in our all-around human functioning? The Berkeley research confirmed the hypothesis that one of the elements of the authoritarian syndrome is "antiintraceptiveness."[287] By intraception is meant "the inclination to adopt a subjective, psychological, human approach to personal and social problems."[288] The antiintraceptive person thinks it is nonsense to try to put himself into the feelings of another; he even closes himself off from his own feelings. He is afraid of silence and reflection; he wants to be a realist, "objective" and "practical." Antiintraceptiveness in its extreme form found collective embodiment in National Socialism. "An important feature of the Nazi program was the defamation of everything that tended to make the individual aware of himself and his problems. . . . This general attitude easily leads to a devaluation of the human and overevaluation of the physical object; when it is most extreme, human beings are looked upon as if they were physical objects to be coldly manipulated."[289] To what extremes antiintraceptiveness can lead may be seen in the burning of "degenerate art" and in the manner in which "the final solution of the Jewish problem" was accomplished. Nothing is left here of the righteous, whose concern is to stand by to protect the integrity of each person, animal, or thing; in large-scale realism one observes here the truth of the second member of the parallelism in Proverbs 12:10: "The mercy of the wicked is cruel"—and cruelty is nothing other than the fear which keeps a person from being open toward himself and his own feelings, and toward the other whose existence in his world is a question to which he is an answer.

National Socialism made visible the disastrous consequences which the

---

[283]Ibid., p. 27.

[284]Ibid., p. 83.

[285]Ibid., pp. 23, 96.

[286]Notice, for instance, his glorification of the life which is far removed from the corrupting influence of the centers of culture (ibid., pp. 28ff.).

[287]T. W. Adorno, *The Authoritarian Personality,* pp. 465-66.

[288]Ibid., p. 44.

[289]Ibid., p. 235.

absence of a disciplined receptivity can have. But something similar may be seen in numerous instances around us. Families break up if people do not try to come to a real understanding of themselves and the other; churches split when people are not open toward the legitimate concerns of one another; people perish in loneliness because there is no one to see or listen to them. Within the circle of the life of the individual a lack of pure receptivity is also damaging. Some Christians never learn to pray because they never learned to listen; never learn to read the Bible because they have never learned to be humbly open to its contents; people "burn out" in their work because they have not understood its intent; human energy congeals in discontent or dies out in despair because people are not receptive to the call of the moment; human potentialities remain un-realized because people are blind to opportunities for actualization.

It requires no argument that, in view of his responsibility for the indepen-dent functioning of the growing person, every nurturer must address himself primarily to the development of pure receptivity. This will call for systematic exercises in observation[290] and learning to know "in the first person." In agogic work with adults this attention to the ability to understand the human possibilities must also be primary.

[At adult seminars it is relatively immaterial what the thematic focus is. It may be woodworking, a problem in world politics, modern literature, or human relations in industry, leisure time activity, or sick visiting—it may be anything that makes up the world of a person or group of persons. The primary aim must always be to work toward a realistic receptivity which corresponds with the object or situation under study: What is wood? What purpose does it serve? How does one deal with this particular piece of wood? What does it mean to be sick? What does it mean that a human being—always more than just a patient—is sick? Etc.]

At this point of receptivity one must expect serious difficulties: distortions in people (prejudices, tendentious apperception, haste, and shallowness), resis-tance to genuine openness (fear of self, of the other, of that other, of risk). Were this not the case, that fact alone would be an indication that this kind of spiritual formation was hardly, or not at all, necessary. For independent functioning, the flow of "changingness," begins here: in the renewal of receptivity toward things, situations, people.

For pastoral role-fulfilment it is of great importance that the pastor see clearly that, from the perspective of the agogic moment, his first responsibility is toward the other person in the pastoral relationship. We cannot reduce all the difficulties in a church or in the life of an individual in it to just one thing. Doubt, traditionalism, absolutism, dualism between faith and life, indifference, fanaticism, lack of trust—and whatever else one may meet—are each of them very complex things which, in turn, differ from person to person. But at the

---

[290]See the chapter on "die Übung des sinnlichen Beobachtens," in Buytendijk, *Erziehung zur Demut,* pp. 79ff.

core of all these phenomena is always a blockage, an inability or refusal really to understand, to understand "in the first person." The pastor must always be alert to that blockage, that inability or refusal to understand, in the different forms of his role-fulfilment. The question then becomes, not: Do I tell the other concretely enough what his situation is? but: Do I help the other recognize his own situation? Not: Do I offer a satisfying explanation of a part of Scripture? but: Can the other person tell from my behavior how this Bible passage is intended to be understood? Not: How do I bring two people who are living in conflict with each other to a peaceful resolution of their difficulties? but: How can I help them to the point where they are really willing to try to discover each other and explore themselves? Not: How can I encourage this person before a major operation? but: How do I bring this person to the point where she is open, in faith, to all the things which are now relevant?

Pure Discernment

In receptivity a person develops an initial relationship; the real moment of relating comes in the relational dimension of *pure discernment,* the distinguishing choice in which a person determines his relationship to an object. Merely to mention this notion is to touch upon theological, philosophical, and psychological problems which we must set aside. Says P. Kohnstamm: "The only standpoint that is tenable in the practice of nurture is that which acknowledges a person's freedom under law which limits this freedom; i.e., the person who acts can alter the outcome of events by positing an incalculable and hence unimaginable 'novum' (a decision of the will) within the space offered by the laws which restrict and the regularities which bind the will."[291] What is designated "the providence of God" may not in any case be viewed as a suspension or restriction of that freedom. God's action in the life of a human being qualifies this creaturely freedom as a *given* one, which as such is a mandate which the person has to fulfil in dependence on God. God never makes a person an object; instead he calls him to be a subject. We can indeed speak of a degree of restriction of this freedom by factors outside and within a person—even without reference to a violent deprivation of a person's freedom or to an inner condition in which a person no longer enjoys self-mastery. This relative limitation of personal freedom is due, in the first place, to the circumstance that a person functions as part of a socio-cultural system which embraces many different individuals. This system molds him not only in his external behavior but also in his inner disposition. "The Oriental," it is said, thinks differently from "the Westerner" and has a different set of values, a different expectation of life. We may ignore for the moment the question whether one is entitled to such easy generalization. The intent of the example is plain: there is a connection between the spiritual

---

[291]P. Kohnstamm, *Persoonlijkheid in Wording,* p. 67.

and mental functioning of an individual and the socio-cultural system in which he belongs. This connection may be positive, but it may also be negative;[292] it remains undeniable. The personality system, too, contains factors which actually limit a person in his freedom to determine himself. One may think, first of all, of the factor of temperament; next, of all that moves him from within: instincts, needs, wishes, goals, etc. All this tends to canalize his possibilities of choice and motivates him, a priori, to make certain choices.

This is not yet to say, however, that self-determination is a fiction. It must be noted, first of all, that one can only speak of the self-determination of a particular, concrete person. That person does not exist apart from his own personality system. He is what he is within that specific socio-cultural system, which is more than a framework that surrounds him but is what it is partly because he is a part of it and his humanity is real and concrete in its web. He is what he is with his temperament, his history, and his individual motivation. It is *that* person—not people in general—who is called to self-determination in true discernment. *The freedom of a human being is the freedom of the very complicated unit which is this person.*

Second, what is given in and around this person, hence what belongs to the components of this individual, what constitutes him a particular person, is *not* given as *an act of fate.* It may predispose him; it causes him to incline in one direction or another; it motivates, i.e., it moves him, but it does not inescapably coerce him. Sometimes a person will let his temper control him, but on other occasions we can tell that he does control himself; sometimes a person goes at a thing impulsively, guided by instinct, but at other times we see her act with careful deliberation. This need not mean that a person contains an agency which places itself against or over the whole—but apparently the person as a whole, the I-sayer, is able to structure the constituent parts of her life in varying ways.

But there is something else: every time a person faces the necessity of choice, the system is different from what it was before. In the entire complex of givens which constitute this concretely existing person there appears a new datum, "that other," in relation to which she now has to make a determination. That fact is not just another object outside of her. It has come to her in her world—as a question, a task, a challenge, or, in other, more general terms, as "that perceived other." This means that the dynamic field of her humanity— i.e., the person and her world—has changed. And the activity of choice is a function of this changing field; one can also say that self-determination is the restructuring of the system—a system which had already been changed by "that other." And because the entire dynamic field has now changed, when the restructuring occurs, everything can begin to move. Needs which never played much of a role in the self-determination of a person may now come to the fore;

---

[292]The reader will remember what we remarked about the nonconformist and deviant who show up in every culture.

expectations and goals which were never an important motivating factor in her activity of choice may now become dominant.

When we refer to pure discernment, we must keep this last-mentioned reality firmly in mind: That other, as "perceived other," also participates in a person's process of choice. This implies that the purity of one's discernment depends, first of all, on the purity of one's receptivity. If I have not purely received "that other," I cannot make a pure self-determination with respect to that other—I can then only make a self-determination based on an unrealistic picture of that other. If I perceive a thing with bias, the road to an objective judgment is closed off and I can no longer do justice to that other.

This fact has important agogic consequences. Consider—even though our focus on pure discernment does not bear specifically on this topic—the issue of moral nurture, the nurture which directs its attention at ethical self-determination. It often happens that nurturers put heavy emphasis on the norms which must guide people in their moral self-determination. And it must be readily granted: attention to these norms is entirely proper. A human being is not as God, knowing good and evil (Gen. 3:5); he may not structure his world nor determine his relations from within himself and on his own terms. His ordering activity must consist in dovetailing himself into an order which transcends him, and true norms are expressions of that order. But the ordering of his world by self-determination must take place in relation to "that other." That is to say, moral nurture cannot merely make known the norms for certain situations and then stop. A person must relate to the matter which comes to him in "that other" in accordance with that norm. This involves more than attention for the norm.

By implication Paul offers a picture of this one-sided emphasis on norm-oriented nurture when he addresses "the Jew" who boasts of knowing God's will and approving what is excellent because he is instructed in the law (Rom. 2:18). That is not enough. For that reason he prays for the believers at Philippi that "your love may abound more and more, with knowledge and all discernment so that you may approve what is excellent" (Phil. 1:9-10). What it comes down to, then, is *to dokimazein ta diapheronta*, the careful determination of what is essential in a concrete situation,[293] what the heart of the matter is. What needs to be discerned is "the will of God" (Rom. 12:2); one must try to learn "what is pleasing to the Lord" (Eph. 5:10), which means, what God asks of me in this situation. In order to make this determination the whole person must be involved. "Intelligence, discernment, attentive observation of the given facts, all these now come into lively operation . . . the whole apparatus of human powers must be set in motion when it is a matter of proving what is the will of God."[294]

---

[293]According to O. Cullmann, *dokimazein* is "the key to all New Testament ethics" (*Christ and Time*, p. 228). It denotes "the capacity of forming the correct Christian ethical judgment at each given moment." See also D. Bonhoeffer, "Proving," *Ethics*, pp. 161ff.

[294]D. Bonhoeffer, *Ethics*, pp. 163-64.

According to Paul, *epignōsis* — "reflective inquiry"[295] — as well as "sensual perception,"[296] "feeling" for the situation, is needed to ascertain what the will of God, the right choice, is in any given situation. Moral nurture must aim to teach people to engage in reflective inquiry and an open, sensitive weighing of the situation. But Paul goes deeper still: he prays that love may abound with knowledge and all discernment; a person must be able to love if in a given situation he is to discern the heart of the issue. A person must not so much learn to know the law and the norms; a person must learn to "prove and approve what is excellent" (*dokimazein ta diapheronta*), an action which includes a vital and sensitive knowledge of the norm.

What we said of moral nurture applies to nurture in general.[297] In all of his spiritual-mental functioning a person must ever plumb the best way to go. Whether it concerns the solution to a math problem, the reading of a book, the choice of a profession, picking a candidate in an election, the approach to a technical problem in one's profession, a person's conduct in the home, the drawing up of a contract, one's attitude toward an illness, the making up of one's will—it is always necessary to discern what is pivotal in the problem. But a person can make that determination only if he has learned to be objectively realistic and is not drawn aside by what is peripheral or irrelevant, and especially if he is not primarily self-focused but in tune with "that other." Martin Buber tells the story of Rabbi Bunam: "Rabbi Bunam had the keys to all the firmaments. And why not? The man who does not think of himself is the man who is given all the keys."[298] This is the secret of pure discernment: "not to think of oneself"—a love which is rich in knowledge and all discernment.

The pastoral role can be defined, to an important extent, as helping people to arrive at clear discernment. For it is aimed at change in the human condition by the kind of renewal in a person's functioning which leads to his being able to discern God's will. We may also say: pastoral role-fulfilment, as intermediary of God's coming in his word, serves the revelation of the truth, in order that we may live and walk in it. People often live in a dream world; they have an image of themselves, of others, of situations and relationships, which is not true. They often view themselves, others, and "that other" falsely because they do not see it before the face of God. For that reason their self-determinations are inadequate, out of accord with reality and "the object." They allow so many irrelevant factors to blur their judgments: fear, self-protection, the desire to dominate. It is the pastor's job to join with the other-in-the-pastoral-relationship in a search for the freedom of the new man-in-Christ, in which he—liberated from the

---

[295]R. Bultmann, *TDNT*, I, 708, s.v. *ginōskō*.

[296]G. Delling, *TDNT*, I, 187, s.v. *aisthanomai*.

[297]We shall pass by the question whether it is correct to speak of moral nurture as a separate element. In our opinion, the treatment of the ethical in isolation from the total spiritual-mental functioning of a person is not devoid of danger.

[298]M. Buber, *Tales of the Hasidim* (*Later Masters*), pp. 267-68.

powers in and around him—can determine himself with objective realism, asking only for the will of God. In this activity the pastor's focus is agogic, i.e., aimed at the other person's self-based functioning. When it comes to clear discernment, it makes particular sense to stress this focus on self-reliance. To choose, to judge, to make self-determinations are preeminently activities which are a person's own. To judge by what usually happens, pastors have a tendency to overlook this obvious fact. We wish to make three observations at this point.

First, the pastor may not make choices for the other in the relationship. True, in preaching the pastor will not distance himself from the realities of life in which people exist. The word he preaches is aimed at the situation of his hearers—the Kingdom's proclamation comes to them in their present. The teaching he brings is intended to help them, in the context of their own lives, observe all that Christ has commanded. He addresses them in all the contingencies of life with an eye to salvation. So the "arrows" of kerygma, didache, and paraklesis always point to the actualities which form the situation of choice and self-determination for the hearers. In pastoral care his relatedness to that situation is even more direct. Often pastoral care is occasioned by the fact that the other finds himself in a certain precarious situation of transition and self-determination. Every pastor knows from personal experience how tempting it is in such a situation to tell the other what he would do if he were in the other's shoes and how he thinks the other should decide. In his preaching he has a tendency to drop the modesty of the subjective: "This is my opinion . . . this is my advice to you . . . ," and to say instead: "This is what the Lord expects from us." But a focus on the other's self-motivated functioning means to help him confront and sort out the issues in order to leave the self-determination in that situation to him as inalienably his own business. Much of what we said in the section on the preagogic category of "equihuman address" is directly applicable here.

Second, the pastor must bring within reach of the other's experience what true discernment is. A moment's reflection on the enormous significance of contextual influence will make the truth of this observation obvious. The pastor's own way of functioning, spiritually and mentally, belongs to the context of the other person's life the moment she is involved in the pastor's fulfilling his role in preaching, catechesis, or pastoral care. There are few other situations in life—outside of the immediately agogic—in which a person so directly witnesses the way another person functions as in the pastoral situation. In his preaching one senses how he relates to the Bible; how he relates to life-situations; how he relates to people; how he uses language and logic. If a person were to analyze the action of a pastor from the perspective of his way of functioning, then one would view him over and over making choices. The church would then be involved in his activity of self-determination. It is inescapable that, especially for those who are not yet very "self-based" in their spiritual functioning, the way the pastor makes his determinations will have paradigmatic value. In the pastor's modeling they realize that, apparently, this is how you relate to the Bible, this is how you relate to people who are listening to you, this is how you relate to a given problem or doubt, and, more specifically, this is the way to make your self-determinations in matters of faith. If the pastor is aware that his way of functioning spiritually and mentally is a model to the other in the pastoral relationship—a significant factor of influence—he has all the more reason to be very careful. He may well make the objective orientation of his own determinations more explicit and go clearly to the heart of a matter so that the other may get a glimpse of how this is done. In his catechizing work the pastor will pay deliberate and systematic attention to this whole issue of how one makes up his mind in the face of life's problems.

Third, with an eye especially to the need for self-based functioning in true discernment, *the pastor must be aware of the dangers of influence-by-suggestion.* One has to be cautious, of course, even with the concept of suggestion. It belongs to that category of concepts which are easily bandied about but are no more than theoretical constructs. Suggestion, according to Hofstätter, indicates "a psychological process which leads to the uncritical appropriation of ideas conveyed by the words and actions of another."[299]

[A fine example of suggestion surfaced in the research of Sorokin and Boldyreff. On two separate occasions they played the same record, part of Brahms's *First Symphony,* to a group of 1,484 high school and college students. The first time it was introduced as a masterpiece, far superior to a work which was to be played later. The second time it was announced as "an exaggerated imitation of a well-known masterpiece, totally deficient in self-subsistence and beauty." Ninety-six percent of the students accepted the suggestion that the second time a different piece had been played; 59 percent judged the "first" record as superior; 21 percent were undecided; 16 percent had another opinion.[300] Likely, what we have here is the phenomenon that a judgment concerning the credibility of a communication depends on the receiver's perception of the expertise and reliability of the communicator.]

Brown states that research has shown that suggestibility levels increase from the fourth to the eighth year of life and then decrease. From this he infers: "(a) that it originated with the acquiring of language, the ability to communicate and be the object of communication, and (b) that it derives its emotional force from submission to parental authority."[301] Perhaps one may say that what suggestibility reveals is a lack of mental self-reliance. A determination is present but it takes place in direct dependence on the perceived self-determination of another or others: "If he says it, you can depend on it"; "This is the way it is— everyone agrees." The fact that this can happen—also with adults—has a back-

---

[299]P. R. Hofstätter, "Psychologie," in *Das Fischer Lexikon,* VI, 164, s.v. *Hypnose und Suggestion.*

[300]Reported by J. A. C. Brown, *Techniques of Persuasion,* pp. 25ff., without further indications as to source. Cf. C. I. Hovland, I. L. Janis, and H. H. Kelley, *Communication and Persuasion,* p. 21.

[301]Ibid., p. 25.

ground. We become aware of this background when we observe that suggesti-bility levels are very low in people who have clearly found their place in life, live in harmonious relationships, and hold their opinions and convictions without rigidity; and that particularly those who are unsure of themselves and restless, tense and in conflict, and searching for stability and fellowship are easily influ-enced by suggestion. Apparently, a person is inclined to accept that piece of information which suits him and only then to accept information if it helps him gain or hold a desired position. Possibly this tendency is even deeper than the perception of expertise and reliability which would seem to be dependent on it.

Roscam Abbing expresses the opinion that "the suggestive" is a kind of psychological force. "The force which proceeds . . . from the person of the speaker, or from the one who sent him, penetrates the listener, probably at a tender spot, puts pressure on him, or carries him away."[302] It seems to us—but much of what is called suggestion is still unclear—that it is not entirely warranted to speak of "the suggestive" as a force which proceeds from something or someone. Suggestion seems to be much more a force which works in a field of correspondence between a communicant and a communicator and which origi-nates from the properties of that field. Two persons may receive the same com-munication; one accepts it uncritically and with enthusiasm, the other is not even touched by it. The force which affects the one, it would seem, arises from the field of tension existing between the communicant, on the one hand, and the communication and communicator, on the other.

The point which concerns us now is that *the pastor must know that this can happen.* The pastor may say something which to him is relatively insignificant or even unsure, but it may have an enormous impact on the one who hears it; it may become for him a driving force which controls him in making choices. Now if the choices made seem desirable to him, the pastor may believe he is successful, and even speak of "unexpected blessing." It would be wiser for him to ask himself, however, whether or not something had happened which is a danger to the other. Pastoral role-fulfilment is predicated on the hope that "the truth may persuade"—as St. Augustine has it—but then it had better be *the truth* which did the persuading, and not something in his dream world to which he is now more firmly tied or on which he is made even more dependent.

This is not to deny that in some situations a suggestive component in pastoral care is unavoidable and even necessary, as Roscam Abbing concludes. Pastoral speech "may be a speaking with authority, not only externally and formally on the basis of theological expertise, but especially inwardly on the basis of his speaking in God's name." But, as we noted earlier, real authority is life promoting and helps the other achieve self-reliance. The moment a pastor notices that his words and actions have become determining forces for someone, he must critically review his actions in the relationship: Has something happened

---

[302]P. J. Roscam Abbing, "Over het Suggestieve in de Zielzorg," in *Nederlands Theologisch Tijdschrift* 18 (1964): 145ff.

between her, my equal, and me which has robbed her (even though I like the direction in which she is moving) of the possibility of moving *herself* (wherever that may be)? Is she not further removed, by making herself dependent on me, from the ability to *choose* well—meaning self-based self-determination with true discernment—even though she made the right *choice*. The pastor who is concerned, with reference to his public actions, to test what is the right thing to do (*dokimazein ta diapheronta*) needs to ask himself, as a lead question in his self-examination: Am I relating realistically to the other in true discernment? Depending on the answer there will be either an agogic component—promoting the independent life of the other—or a psychagogic component—threatening the independent life of the other—in his actions.

Creativity

We must now address ourselves to a third dimension in relating: *creativity*. A humanly functioning person initially enters a relationship by opening herself receptively to "that other"; she chooses her position in the relationship with discernment; and she performs in and fulfils the relationship in creativity. Should we not speak now of an "activity" and grace it, as with the earlier relational dimensions, with an adjective "pure" or "objectively realistic"? There are two objections to this procedure. The first is formal: In the categories of "receptivity" and "discernment" we were also dealing with activities—all of human functioning is action. From an agogic point of view, too, it is important to remember that a person must learn, and practice, the activity of receiving and making up his mind. The second objection is more important. When a person enters a relationship, he does not fully experience his humanity—the freedom and the responsibility of his existence as spirit or mind; this occurs when he comes to the kind of action which can be called "creating."

But is "creating" not too big a word? Strictly speaking, only one subject goes well with the verb: the Creator. J. B. Charles once said of a poet: "For Achterberg the days of creation did not end with the seventh; there is an eighth in which he too, following his Lord, Soli Deo Gloria, picks up things: felt, uranium, bronze, the lithosphere; gives them a name, and look: there they are; he speaks and it is there."[303] But this is a poet speaking of a poet—perhaps then one can speak in this vein, if at least one does not forget the quotation marks. "The artist's act of creating," says Vander Leeuw, "is in no way parallel to that of the Creator; it is a faint reflection of it, completely overshadowed by the brilliance of the life of God."[304] It is good to remember this: before we say a word about the creativity of man we have to say he is a creature—his activity is "in no way parallel" to the creative action of God. No, not parallel—but God

---

[303]J. B. Charles, "De derde Dichter van de achtste Dag," in F. Sierksma, *Commentaar op Achterberg*, p. 46.

[304]G. vander Leeuw, *Wegen en Grenzen* [On Religion and the Arts, *Tr.*], p. 370.

did come close to making man supernatural (Ps. 8:6); he makes him rule over
the work of his hands and puts all things under his feet. During the original days
of creation man was not there to help as co-creator. But then came the eighth
day and man, almost divine, was called to be "almost a creator." In that sense
we can now speak of human creativity in which his functioning as spirit or mind
attains the apex of his human-creaturely responsibility and freedom.

If we wish to see what is essential in human creativity we must see it as
an extension of God's creating. What does God do when he creates? Make
something out of nothing? Perhaps that is not the most essential feature of it.
The story of creation tells us: "Now the earth was a formless void, there was
darkness over the deep" (Gen. 1:2, *JB*). Jeremiah had the horrifying vision of
a return to the *tōhû wābōhû* of the beginning, the chaos which would follow
after God's judgments.

> *I looked to the earth, to see a formless waste;*
> *to the heavens, and their light had gone.*
> *I looked to the mountains, to see them quaking*
> *and all the heights astir.*
> *I looked, to see no man at all,*
> *the very birds of heaven had fled.* . . . . (Jer. 4:23-25, *JB*)

To create is to introduce the light which overcomes the darkness, to bring
life and form in the place of the *tōhû wābōhû*, to inject order in the place of
chaos.

> *Yes, thus says Yahweh,*
> *Creator of the heavens,*
> *who is God,*
> *who formed the earth and made it,*
> *who set it firm,*
> *created it no chaos,*
> *but a place to be lived in.* . . . . (Isa. 45:18, *JB*)

To create is to introduce order, not in the imperious "Prussian" sense of
Ordnung muss sein. The Latin *ordo* is related to the Greek *ordeō*, to lay the
warp, to set up a loom, to begin to weave. To create means that lines are being
drawn and a design takes shape; a perspective grows; a way opens up, and the
world becomes traversable and inhabitable; life becomes livable. It is this ordering perspective which is also the perspective of human creativity.

["Creativity" has not been a subject of significance in psychology for very
long. It did not get much attention until people in the United States, shocked by
the sudden discovery of a Russian advantage in technological development,
began to ask themselves how they could stimulate and give shape to human
creative potential. In the beginning it was necessary to know more precisely
what creativity is and how a creative process runs. Something else, something
less dramatic, also made this necessary. A typical feature of modernity, as Dippel
puts it, is that we have "the techniques of invention by the tail." "Technics, as
the sphere in which the burden of work shifts increasingly to rationalized work

preparation, has found its own true form in this; even in the birth of new tools the labor of invention has its own rational preparation."[305] Among the many problems associated with this process is that of creativity, its development and its formation. Partially connected with it is a third reason to take notice of creativity, an economic one. In economics it is not enough simply to produce a good product; the idea is to come up with something new: a new product, a new version of an existing product, a new stimulus to buy the product, a new sales argument. For that purpose one needs a constant flow of creative ideas. But one dare not depend on "breaks," the lucky brainstorm; so—especially in the advertising world—people began to develop methods by which to promote the creative flow, methods which provoke and regulate the imagination.[306]]

When creativity is discussed in psychology, the reference is to creativity as a possibility of every human being, and not just the creativity of people with special talents. Says Carl Rogers: "The action of the child inventing a new game with his playmates; Einstein formulating a theory of relativity; the housewife devising a new sauce for the meat; a young author writing his first novel; all of these are . . . creative."[307] Maslow says he discovered "that . . . cooking or parenthood or making a home could be creative whereas poetry need not be; it could be uncreative."[308] The focus is not so much on any product of creativity which others may admire or be induced to buy, but "creativity as an attitude, which is the condition of any creation in the former sense but which can exist even though nothing new is created in the world of things . . . creativity as a character trait."[309]

Some who engage in theoretical research are especially interested in the marks of the creative personality. In one such study the difference between the most and the least creative persons proved to be that the first were marked by "their greater flexibility of thinking, breadth of perspective, openness to experience, freedom of impulse, breadth of interest, autonomy, and integrity."[310] Guilford mentions as the most important elements in creativity flexibility of thinking—originality—sensitivity to problems—the ability of redefinition ("an ability to give up old interpretations of familiar objects in order to use them or their parts in some new way")—elaboration ("the ability to construe a whole from just a few givens").[311] Rogers sees as the most important inner condition required for creativity "openness to experience: extensionality." This is the op-

---

[305]C. J. Dippel, *Verkenning en Verwachting*, p. 20.

[306]Cf. M. Tyson, "Creativity," in B. M. Foss, *New Horizons in Psychology*, pp. 172ff.

[307]C. R. Rogers, "Toward a Theory of Creativity," in H. H. Anderson, *Creativity and Its Cultivation*, p. 72.

[308]A. H. Maslow, "Creativity in Self-Actualizing People," in H. H. Anderson, *Creativity and Its Cultivation*, p. 84.

[309]E. Fromm, "The Creative Attitude," in H. H. Anderson, *Creativity and Its Cultivation*, pp. 44ff.

[310]N. Sanford, *Self and Society*, p. 204.

[311]J. P. Guilford, "Traits of Creativity," in H. H. Anderson, *Creativity and Its Cultivation*, pp. 145ff.

posite of psychological defensiveness, the rejection of stimuli from within or without which could lead to the kind of new experiences which would force him to revise his self-concept. It is very different with the person who is open to his own experiences: ". . . instead of perceiving in predetermined categories (trees are green; college education is good; modern art is silly) the individual is aware of this existential moment as it is, thus being alive to many experiences which fall outside the usual categories (*this* tree is lavender, *this* college education is damaging; *this* modern sculpture has a powerful effect on me)."[312]

[A fine example of "openness to experience" is offered by the child in Andersen's tale *The Emperor's New Clothes*. The emperor, the chamberlains, the people—none is open and everyone strenuously holds up his self-image. Too much is at stake: position, reputation, a whole world. There can be no thought of pure receptivity or discernment; they have to be nonobjective to maintain their own dream world. The result is that nothing can happen; no order can be created. They remain imprisoned in the *tōhû wābōhû* of their self-deception. The deception of the rascally tailors, the mutual deception of the court, self-deception—the evil spell cannot be broken. " 'But he has nothing on!' said a little child. 'Good heavens, listen to the voice of innocence,' said the father, and the child's remark was whispered from one to another." Only perfect love—most profoundly, faith in the forgiveness of our stupidity and unfitness for the positions we hold, sins which none of the others would admit—drives out fear (cf. I John 4:18). The person who knows this consistent love is creative; she has, to quote Fromm, "the ability to *see* (or to *be aware*) and to *respond*."[313] Then chaos is overcome. " 'He has nothing on!' shouted everybody in the end. And the Emperor cringed inside himself, for it seemed to him that they were right."[314] At last "the loom was set up and they began to weave."[315]]

One may question, given the above example, whether it is correct to approach creativity by way of tracing the marks of the creative personality. The really creative moment in the action of the child in the fairy tale springs up in the interaction between the child and "that other." Rollo May is very explicit: "We cannot speak of a 'creative person'; we can only speak of a *creative act*. For what is occuring is always a *process*, a *doing;* specifically, a process interrelating the person and his world."[316] Beets is even more direct: "If creativity

---

[312]C. R. Rogers, "Toward a Theory of Creativity," in H. H. Anderson, *Creativity and Its Cultivation,* p. 75. In another book Rogers has explained that he views "openness to experience" as the most fundamental change in a personality system resulting from a successful therapeutic process; the final effect is that a person's behavior becomes more creative. [The source given is a Dutch translation of Rogers and Kinget, *Psychotherapy and Human Relations,* pp. 213ff. *Tr.*]

[313]E. Fromm, "The Creative Attitude," in H. H. Anderson, *Creativity and Its Cultivation,* p. 44.

[314]Quoted from H. C. Andersen, *The Emperor's New Clothes,* pp. 31-32.

[315]Cf. the etymology of *ordo* (p. 226).

[316]R. May, "The Nature of Creativity," in H. H. Anderson, *Creativity and Its Cultivation,* p. 65.

originates anywhere, it begins not in the slumbering creative powers that lie hidden in me, but in the face-to-face relationships."[317] The sculptor becomes creative when he sees a block of material in front of him, looks deeply into it, and hears its "voice." He knows what to do and what he wants to do with it once he has "heard" from the material what it "wants" of him.

The matter becomes very clear when a person becomes creative in an interhuman relationship. As long as he does not really relate himself to the other, is not open to what the other is all about, he cannot help the other move ahead; then there is no perspective in the relationship, the situation of conflict remains unresolved, and there is no way out of alienation and misunderstanding. But when a person is there for the other and gives the other a chance to be what she is, the creative process begins—the process that leads to order, to the passable road, and to the inhabitable world.

More important than the question of the marks of creativity is that concerning "the nature of the creative interaction between the person and his meaningful environment," or rather, the question of the "how" of the "dialectic" between a person and her world. "Dialectic" is interaction—action in reciprocal challenge and response. Not the dominant person, but the dedicated caring person, is creative. A. B. Dow summarizes the essentials of creativity in one word: "care." "So we might say that, if we are going to be creative, all we need is to develop a deep sense of care."[318]

A clear indication of the divergence between creativity and the sterile, unjust, and nonobjective way of relating is found in the indictment of the ancient prophet: "Trouble for the shepherds of Israel who feed themselves! Shepherds ought to feed their flock, yet you have fed on milk, you have dressed yourself in wool, you have sacrificed the fattest sheep, but failed to feed the flock. You have failed to make weak sheep strong, or to care for the sick ones, or bandage the wounded ones. You have failed to bring back strays or look for the lost. On the contrary, you have ruled them cruelly and violently. For lack of a shepherd they have scattered, to become the prey of any wild animal; they have scattered far. My flock is straying this way and that, on mountains and on high hills; my flock has been scattered all over the country; no one bothers about them and no one looks for them" (Ezek. 34:2-6, *JB*). What these shepherds lack—in the jargon of social psychology they are high scorers on the F Scale—is a sense of caring. The result is chaos.

We can be brief about the significance of all this for agogy. Agogy is "life help."[319] That is, it does not aim at "Enlightenment"—the pedagogical ideal of the eighteenth century; nor at *"Bildung"* (education in a classical sense)—the

---

[317]N. Beets, "Debat en Gesprek," in *Wending* 22 (1967-68): 68ff.

[318]A. B. Dow, "An Architect's View on Creativity," in *Creativity and Its Cultivation*, pp. 42ff.

[319]Cf. the title of Brezinka's book: *Erziehung als Lebenshilfe*. The term is typical for modern pedagogical thought. According to one scholar the term "life help," which is fast becoming an interdisciplinary formula, is a typically European counterpart to the American expression "planning of change."

pedagogical ideal of the nineteenth century; nor at the refinement, adornment, or glorification of existence. Agogy is life-oriented; it aims at the fulness, the multiplicity, the breadth, and the depth of human life—the full functioning of a human being in all the situations which make up a human life. In the final analysis this means that *all agogic intervention aims at the activation of humans as* "creators on the eighth day," *people who are underway and find a home in a traversable and inhabitable world.*

Thus viewed, agogy—life help—is itself a creative process. This means that agogy itself is what it aims at in the end. Agogy can be described with the same words we used to describe what it means to be human: Agogy is the act of functioning, with objective realism, in pure receptivity, discernment, and creativity, of one person in relation to another for whose humanization the agogue bears responsibility, *in order that* the other may learn to function humanly in a similar way. The core of all agogy is life that begets life; being a concrete and relevant human being serving the concretization and actualization of the humanness of another.

This conclusion, following a long and broad-ranging tale about agogy, may sound simplistic. We believe, however, that we could not have said it without the long tale—we would not have known what we were saying. In the following part, in which we take another look at pastoral role-fulfilment—this time as an agogic situation—it will become apparent how the data we have discovered may become functional in practical theology.

IV. Pastoral Role-Fulfilment as an Agogic Situation

1. INTRODUCTION

Pastoral role-fulfilment is intermediary to God's coming in his word—this we have learned well. We have also seen that God's coming entails a dynamic sequence of events: he draws near to a person, reveals his name, makes known the truth, and actualizes salvation. The new aeon is there for the person who has been so visited. The kerygma proclaims for her a new state of affairs—here and now. The didache opens up to her the way of discipleship. The paraklesis addresses her personally in her situation of despair, fear, pain, and sin—offering comfort, admonition, encouragement, the call to renewal, and a reminder of God's grace.

We have said that God comes to a person *in his word*. He does not manipulate human beings as objects; he addresses them. Thus human listening is integral to the process. That process of being addressed and listening—viewed from a certain perspective—is *conversion*. Conversion, in one dimension, is a change in one's spiritual-mental functioning. When God comes to a person in his word and the person listens, she becomes a new person and her life becomes Kingdom life.

God comes through the intermediary of pastoral role-fulfilment. In other words, what God wants to happen will happen in an interhuman relationship. In the field of tension which that relationship constitutes the powers which work conversion, or change, begin to be effective. God's *agoge* actualizes itself in a situation which can be viewed as agogic.

It is of some importance to distinguish properly. Having said what we did about pastoral role-fulfilment as an agogic situation, we do not mean that this description exhausts the subject, nor that in the situation of pastoral role-fulfilment agogy should happen now and then so as to make the situation agogic. We do mean that, for the purpose of research done in the interest of the methodology of pastoral role-fulfilment, the situation of pastoral role-fulfilment *can be viewed* as an agogic situation.

The fact that this can be done and that this is legitimate does not have to be demonstrated: it simply proceeds from the fact that there is an agogic component in pastoral role-fulfilment. Our concern now is to state that for the purpose of research the methodological transposition of the situation of pastoral role-fulfilment into an agogic situation is of some importance.

For its theory of pastoral role-fulfilment practical theology needs to consult with other disciplines. It can take advantage of many data accumulated in the research done in relation to "planning change." It can also use the insights and findings of the research sometimes summarized under the heading "the new 'scientific' rhetoric."[1] But it cannot do this naively. Practical theology cannot simply take over everything that is said about "influencing" on the basis of recent research. It must sharply define its own questions; only then can it hear the answers which are relevant to pastoral role-fulfilment.

[The term "influencing" itself must make us cautious. C. J. Straver wrote a sociological study about religious influence, especially by means of preaching. He tells us that he chose the term "influencing" because in reference to religion it is more easily understandable than "information" and less theologically charged than "proclamation." Straver describes "influencing" as "working on people with the objective of achieving a certain specific effect."[2] For us it is a question, however, whether pastoral role-fulfilment can legitimately aim at "specific effects," and whether one can define these "intentional influences." A. H. S. Stemerding shows "how a process of influencing in seemingly totally different areas can run along comparable lines."[3] Perhaps this can be said following a socio-psychological analysis of the actual course of a process of influencing, e.g., in advertising, in brainwashing, at seminars, or in preaching. But can practical theology, in doing its own methodological research, allow preaching to stand in such a series? In his comparison of political rhetoric and preaching, W. Trillhaas remarks: "It is the genius of political rhetoric to search for the point of least resistance. . . . But preaching should not overpower; it should convince. . . . It should not, as Delilah did to Samson, shear off the hearer's locks while he is sleeping."[4] The pastor will not, or should not, try to "influence" in the manner of a propagandist.]

---

[1] It is under this heading that N. Maccoby describes the research undertaken by a Yale University group; cf. W. Schramm, *The Science of Human Communication*.

[2] C. J. Straver, *Massacommunicatie en godsdienstige Beïnvloeding*, pp. 16ff. According to W. G. Bennis, K. D. Benne, and R. Chin, *The Planning of Change*, it is not possible to offer an all-encompassing definition of the process. "However, in a general way we can say that it implies a relationship between persons or groups where one or the other party (or both) utilizes some form of interpersonal (or intersystem) operation to induce the other to do, or feel, or think that which the influencer believes is desirable" (p. 480).

[3] A. H. S. Stemerding, *Vorming, Voorlichting, Beïnvloeding in de moderne Mattschappij*, p. 25.

[4] W. Trillhaas, *Evangelische Predigtlehre*, p. 136. Trillhaas here pictures a type of political propaganda of which F. C. Bartlett says that it is "an enemy of education" (cf. "The Aims of Political Propaganda," in D. Katz, D. Cartwright, S. Eldersveld, and A. McClung Lee, *Public Opinion and Propaganda*, p. 470).

For the purpose of asking its own questions and making proper use of the research data on "influencing," practical theology can view pastoral role-fulfilment as an agogic situation. When a pastor in fulfilling his role aims at a certain type of influence, then it cannot be one which tries to get a person to "cross a line," so to speak, but one which tries to help her—for that is the typically agogic, as we have seen—arrive at a state of spiritual functioning that is objective and independent, marked by pure receptivity, true discernment, and creativity.

In this part it is our aim to transpose pastoral role-fulfilment methodologically in the terms of an agogic situation. In the sections which follow we shall process some of the data from the research on "influencing" within the framework of an agogic model of pastoral role-fulfilment. And in the final section, on the basis of what we shall have found, we shall comment on the training and forming of those who are preparing themselves for pastoral work.

No one should expect that in this part we will bring a rich harvest of wide-ranging research. We must limit ourselves to showing that there are new possibilities on the horizon for practical theology. One person alone cannot realize those possibilities; nor can this be done within the confines of an exploratory study.

2. DEFINING PASTORAL ROLE-FULFILMENT IN TERMS OF AN AGOGIC SITUATION

[Prior to our attempt at defining pastoral role-fulfilment as an agogic situation we need to say something about two terms we will use frequently in this and subsequent sections. In pastoral role-fulfilment at least two people enter a relationship. The one bears responsibility for the other and is pastorally at the other's disposal. He may do this as a preacher, a catechist, a pastoral worker, or in some other pastorally defined role. We shall simply call him "pastor." The other—the person who hears him, the catechism student, or whoever—is "the other-in-the-relationship." We shall call him, in the absence of a word which is applicable in all situations, the "church member."]

In Part III, section 6, we described the specifically agogic as the change in the mental functioning of persons in virtue of their active involvement in a relationship which is directed toward producing this change. What is striking in this definition, the reader will note, is the fact that it does not mention what is *done* —say, by the nurturer or agogue—but only what *happens* —in the other-in-the-relationship. This means that a situation is not yet agogic when there is a nurturer or agogue who to the best of his knowledge and ability engages in agogic action. Nurture, or agogy, can only be recognized by its effect. To this we immediately need to add that not every situation in which the effect occurs— namely, the change in spiritual functioning—is an agogic situation. Someone must *aim* at this effect, though this does not have to mean that the effect was consciously aimed for at the moment. It is in the connection between the two—

the relationship which aims at change and the effect (the change)—that the specifically agogic is located.

Leaning on this description of the specifically agogic, we can now say that pastoral role-fulfilment is agogic when it creates a situation in which pastor and church member are so related to each other that the church member experiences a change in spiritual functioning in virtue of his being an active participant in the relationship. In other words, pastoral role-fulfilment proves to be agogic when the member ceases to be the person he was, and the process of his becoming human proceeds in the right direction, in functional dependence on what the member and the pastor jointly and mutually experience in the relationship.

The question may arise: But then what in this situation is relevant? On the basis of what we said in the previous part we now must say: everything. In Part III, section 5, we put it like this: Nurture is everything (1) which happens in the field of tension between the nurturer and the growing person, and (2) which was aimed at the independent spiritual functioning of the person in her world. We said this about nurture but, as we saw, it applies to all agogy. There is a field of tension between two people; i.e., they are so interrelated that the existence and behavior of the one influences the existence and behavior of the other and vice versa. Everything which happens in this field of interaction is relevant: what the agogue says to the other with agogic intentionality but also whatever he says within the hearing of the other; what the agogue does in relation to the other from an agogic motive, but also the nondeliberate presence and action of the agogue; what happens between the two while they clearly play their roles as nurturer and nurturee, but also what happens while they simply spend time together as two human beings. When we say, "Everything is relevant," this does not mean that from an agogic perspective everything is positive. Only what is directed toward the independent spiritual functioning of the other in her world is of positive significance, and hence of really agogic significance.

This is of real significance for the methodology of pastoral role-fulfilment and for the training and molding of those who are, or will be, in the pastorate. Often people's attention is focused especially on what the pastor *does* in the performance of kerygma, didache, and paraklesis. And, of course, this is very important. Next to, and in direct association with, an intensive theological schooling process, there should be an intensive training period in learning how to act pastorally. But that action takes place in pastoral *role-fulfilment*, i.e., in concrete relations with others for whom the pastor has to be pastor. To be sure, action does take place in a role-relationship, but in that role the entire person makes an impact. Not just the person in his outward appearance but as he is in his inner being is there. He appears in the way he himself functions spiritually, which in part becomes visible: his own way of relating to that which he tries to communicate to the other in kerygma, didache, and paraklesis; his own way of experiencing and handling an interhuman relationship. He comes across with his faith and his unbelief, his genuineness and his self-deception, his interest and his apathy. He appears simultaneously—it is given as a direct role-concomitant—as representative of a denomination and a parish. He brings his world and his experience in that world with him. And all that is agogically relevant: it all comes along in the field of tension between the pastor and the church member, i.e., in the process which must be directed toward the independent spiritual functioning of the member.

Viewed agogically—it is implied in all that we have seen in Part III—it is primarily the *humanness* of the agogue that counts and, in that context, the agogic *action*. Toward the end of the previous part we put it this way: Agogy is the objectively realistic spiritual functioning, in pure receptivity, discernment, and creativity, of a person in relation to another, for whose becoming human he is responsible, *in order that* the other may function spiritually in that way. Within the agogic model of pastoral role-fulfilment the questions regarding the manner of that role-fulfilment can be reduced to the central one: How does the pastor function spiritually? How does he experience his being human and how does he express his humanness in his role? Is he himself in process? Is he himself objective and realistic—oriented toward the other and "that other" in all openness? Is he "righteous"—aiming for the integrity of the other and "that other"? Is he receptive—attuned to the language of the other and "that other" in true discernment; does his love abound in clear knowledge and all discernment in order to be able to tell in each case where the core of the issue lies? Is he creative in the relationship; can he caringly dedicate himself to the other and "that other" so that a passable road may be discovered and the world is made inhabitable again?

Questions like these provide practical theology with points of departure for its reflection on the theory of pastoral role-fulfilment and can serve to guide it in selectively processing the answers to its questions about communication, influencing, change, etc., which it receives from other disciplines. Questions like these also offer an indication of the nature of the training, forming, and continued education needed for the pastorate, for the subjects one faces, and for the way in which one faces them in the pastorate.

3. CONTEXTUAL INFLUENCE EXERTED BY PASTORAL ROLE-FULFILMENT

Pastoral Role-Fulfilment as Context

We explained in Part III, section 3, how the process of personality formation occurs in a dynamic field in which the growing person is present with everything that is significant for him. In other words, the process of growth takes place in a context which is codeterminative of personality. Nurture begins with a person, responsible for the spiritual development of another, living in the realization of how important contextual influence is for that other. His very existence has a nurturing quality when he lives his own life in that realization and gives to the immediate context of the other the character of a structured field of nurture.

Applying the agogic model to pastoral role-fulfilment, we must face the question whether this role-fulfilment can be viewed as contextual for the church member's human development. Pastoral role-fulfilment encompasses more than pastoral action—we have seen this already—but it is still somewhat incidental. The church member, on the average, spends an hour a week in a church service or in a church classroom, and for the most part sees little of the pastor in pastoral care situations.

How contextually important is the pastor's role-fulfilment then? In the first place, the incidental nature of being in a situation of pastoral role-fulfilment is not very different from that of other situations of influence. A child's development does not occur continuously in one context either; one moment that context is the family, another it is the school, or a group of playmates, or life on the street, or the world which comes to her on television. In the second place, contextual influence is not directly proportionate to the amount of time spent, or to the frequency of spending time, in a specific context. It would not be hard to illustrate this point with many examples. A three-week stay in the atmosphere of a campground may do more for a boy's faith than years of living at home. In the third place, pastoral role-fulfilment—in a church service, in a church classroom, or in pastoral care—does not stand by itself. For the person who is involved in it this role-fulfilment is a typical concretization of a world in which she also knows herself to be outside those regularly recurring moments: the world of the church, "the faith," Christianity.

[We remind the reader that we are now speaking of pastoral role-fulfilment simply as a factor of contextual influence. The world of the church concretizes itself in numerous other ways as well; e.g., in context with other Christians, and in all kinds of manifestations of the church: its broadcasts, its publications, its buildings, etc. At this point we need not enlarge upon them.]

The Ambience of Pastoral Role-Fulfilment

When we discussed the subject of contextual influence it became clear that the *atmosphere* in which a person grows up is of special significance. Referring to the individualized atmosphere, or aura, a person creates or conveys, we are really talking about an expression of a "spirit" which is pervasive in a person's life and which sustains and animates all his conduct. Every behavior, or at least every unit of coherent and concurrent behaviors, represents the person in the totality of his "spirit" and is experienced by the other as such—perhaps mostly unconsciously. The result is that, at least with persons whom we know well or with whom we come into intensive contact, we react not so much to their explicit behavior or to their underlying intentions as to the "spirit" which comes to expression in and around them: the hard-to-put-your-finger-on but clearly perceivable person-specific quality. There are people with whom, no matter what they say or do, you can never be angry, because their "spirit" is not such that you can get angry with them. There are other people whom you can never trust, not because their outward behaviors as such elicit mistrust, but because their "spirit" does not inspire confidence.

It is this "spirit," experienced in the atmosphere someone exudes, which influences the other who stands in an agogic relationship to the influencer. We have already seen this when we discussed the authoritarian personality syndrome. In an atmosphere which is completely conditioned by rejection of what is different, strange, or from "the outside," and by an anxious attachment to the familiar or "one's own," the growing person cannot possibly learn to function as a human being with any objectivity or realism. He never opens himself up to the special language of the other; never learns to tell what is essential in the other. He sees only what threatens his self-concept and proceeds to build his defenses accordingly; he does not become creative but dismisses the other with a ready-made, stereotyped prejudice.

One cannot say that the spiritual identity of the church member is totally determined by the atmosphere surrounding pastoral role-fulfilment. In the first place, pastoral role-fulfilment is not his only context. In the second place, the power of contextual influence is not absolute; many people manage to come to their own terms with whatever affects them through contextual influence. In the third place, pastoral role-fulfilment is only intermediary: the power of God, who comes to people in his word, can overcome the influence of the intermediating role-fulfilment as such. But when it comes to a theory of pastoral role-fulfilment, and the training and forming of pastors, one dare not presume on all this. Whatever qualifications one may have to make, they do not negate the fact that the "spirit" operative in the field of pastoral role-fulfilment codetermines the processes at work in the lives of church members. We now wish to make a few remarks about the "spirit" which emanates from pastoral role-fulfilment.

"Make Me Right Simple, Lord . . ."

"The most important rule . . . for educating people in objectivity is: Be objective!" says Künkel.[5] The kind of "objective realism" at stake here is one which can be observed in a great educator like Pestalozzi—who in another sense was quite "nonobjective." R. Kynast has this to say of him: "In love Pestalozzi discovers a psychological factor of fundamental import. It is, as it were, *the* category for all nurture, *the* principle animating his method."[6] In I Corinthians 13:4-7, Paul offers an operational definition of that love which is objective, and which constitutes the core of all the charismata. If one wishes to avoid the terms "love" and "objectivity" because they may occasion misunderstanding, one could speak of "genuineness." We saw earlier that Carl Rogers

---

[5]F. Künkel, *Einführung in die Charakterkunde*, p. 34.
[6]R. Kynast, *Problemgeschichte der Pädagogik*, p. 165.

regards "genuineness" as the central category for the therapeutic attitude in a counseling relationship.[7] On this quality Vossen remarks: "For the client it is essential that as therapist I am real—therefore authentic and reliable. My words must not serve to create false appearances or excuses; my words should be congruent with my deeds, my entire behavior, and my true intentions. When my words are about sympathy and acceptance but my body language (voice, eyes, hands, or behavior) expresses withdrawal, I am ungenuine, and therefore deceptive for the other." "Ungenuine" is "everything that is artificial, all that is merely exterior, a facade, in me: a facade, for instance, of sympathy and acceptance to which no inner emotions correspond; or putting an excess of emotion in word or gesture while my real feelings do not have this intensity."[8] It seems to us that genuineness is more than just a condition for effectiveness in counseling—though it is that too. It conditions the atmosphere of the field in which the therapeutic process takes place and is itself a factor of influence. In the attitude of the therapist the client encounters a new and liberating possibility of being human, in which he can grow to be genuine toward self and others.

There is still another way in which we can track down the essential disposition so fundamentally significant for pastoral role-fulfilment. Systematic theology discusses "the simplicity of God." The point of that attribute, as H. Bavinck puts it, is that "every property . . . is identical with God's being." God not only exhibits truth, love, etc., but is himself truth, love, etc.[9] Says Karl Barth: "This signifies that in all that He is and does, He is wholly and undividedly Himself. At no time or place is He composed out of what is distinct from Himself."[10] God's simplicity implies his reliability and trustworthiness.[11] It is a reflection of this simplicity which makes a person a man or a woman of God. In Psalm 86 a man calls on the LORD in his affliction. He asks the LORD to teach him his way and then he says: "Unite my heart to fear thy name" (v. 11). What he is asking is that the LORD will bring everything together in him so that his life will display clarity and genuineness; he is saying: "Make me right simple, O Lord"— delivered from inner contradictions and so free from incongruence between the "inner" and the "outer." This is something every human being needs to ask of God, but certainly the pastor who by his role-fulfilment—also by the unintentional elements in it—has so much influence on human growth.

The Self-Image of the Pastor

Objectivity, love, genuineness, simplicity: such words can only hint at the "spirit" or "mind-set" of a person; from this "spirit" an atmosphere emanates

---

[7]See above, p. 163.
[8]A. J. M. Vossen, *Zichzelf Worden in menselijke Relatie*, p. 68.
[9]H. Bavinck, *Gereformeerde Dogmatiek*, II, 144.
[10]K. Barth, *CD*, II/1, p. 445.
[11]Cf. K. H. Miskotte, *De Praktische Zin van de Eeenvoud Gods*, pp. 22, 27.

in which the other can learn to function freely and objectively. We must now try to make these insights useful for our praxis. To that end we shall first consider the self-image of the pastor. In a sense, when we talk of objectivity, love, genuineness, and simplicity, this is the critical point.

K. Crawford, in his essay on the minister's self-image, points out that a person is hardly conscious of his self-image. "It refers to how one in the depths of his being really feels about himself."[12] One could say perhaps that it reflects the total interior organization out of which a person functions as a spiritual-mental being. Crawford distinguishes six self-concepts which are probably an unconscious part of each pastor's self-image: (1) the idea that he is "God's righthand man"; (2) "the savioristic image"; (3) "the Solomonic self-image"— the man who possesses superior wisdom; (4) "God's speaker"; (5) "God's sacrifice"—the one who denies himself all sorts of pleasure, always thinks of others, etc.; and (6) "God's judge." We can leave aside the question how such a self-image comes into being. It is clear that social influences are an important factor. Many elements in the pastoral self-image as Crawford outlines it belong to the pastoral role;[13] one could even say that Crawford's picture is typically a pastoral role-concept, i.e., the picture which a pastor has of his own role. But because pastoral psychology usually speaks of "self-image" in this context, we follow this—not entirely correct—usage.

We are not saying that this self-image is the pastoral self-image—in part it is typical for a certain churchly subculture. But whatever the image, besides the creative elements it always contains frustrating possibilities. Crawford remarks that in the image he has drawn the emphasis is on doing, while for the pastoral relationship it should be on being. One could add that especially 1, 3, 4, and 6 bear a suggestion of inviolability, and 5 a certain amount of alienation from ordinary human life. If we now remember that pastoral role-fulfilment serves as a factor of contextual influence, it becomes evident that this self-image—the total mind-set—may easily generate an atmosphere of activism (with the concomitant danger of denying the restful and receptive); of a simplistic a priori cocksureness (with the concomitant danger of not being open, of not being able to listen, of not being able to penetrate carefully the heart of an issue); of detachment (with the concomitant danger of denying the possibility of being creative in one's own life). It goes without saying that for the growing person for whom pastoral role-fulfilment is an important context, being in such an atmosphere may result in an inability to function spiritually with objective realism.

---

[12]K. Crawford, "The Minister's Self-image and Pastoral Counseling," in *Pastoral Psychology* 18 (1967): 49ff.

[13]"Role" is a concept in social psychology; the term summarizes "the pattern of wants and goals, beliefs, feelings, attitudes, values, and actions which members of a community expect should characterize the typical occupant of a position" (D. Krech, R. S. Crutchfield, and E. L. Ballachey, *The Individual in Society,* p. 338).

Well, what should a pastor do? In the first place, for the effective fulfilment of his pastoral role, a pastor should try to become conscious of his self-image and role-concept; i.e., he should begin to make some discoveries: this is how I see myself as bearer of the pastoral role; this is how I believe I have to be; it is with this mind-set that I believe I have to operate. Second, he should try to discover what kind of atmosphere he generates as a result of living by the dictates of his self-image and how that affects people for whom his role-fulfilment is a context for living as human beings. Third, he must get to the point where he is willing to look at his self-image critically. "Can I be like this? Does that not make me inauthentic? Must I be like this? Is this what people, is this what God, expects of me?" Perhaps if that self-scrutiny should lead him to pray "Make me right simple, Lord," an *image* would fall apart and a *person* would be born—a person who is becoming human and who can thus minister to others in process of becoming human.

The Motivation of the Pastor

This brings us to the pastor's motivation. Lippitt, Watson, and Westley, on the basis of their analysis of processes of planned change, conclude that "an important function of the change agent is an honest self-examination. He needs to think through for himself the reason why he wants to help others."[14] The personal problems of a change agent are diverse. But one generalization can be made, namely, "that the change agent's problems of motivation cannot be safely ignored. No change agent can afford to take himself for granted."[15]

[A. van Kaam is of the opinion that a counselor should examine his motivation after every session. He needs to confront himself and his actions with questions like these: "Does he need to sound like an oracle? Is he in love with his sonorous voice or clever verbalizations? Does he feel that he 'knows' people through and through? Is he authoritarian, domineering? Does he need to be popular? to be liked or exalted as a 'nice chap' by his counselee? Is he afraid of depth in himself and others? Does he repress his own feelings and paralyze his spontaneity? Is he afraid to verbalize or to hear the verbalization of certain experiences?"[16]]

It needs to be said immediately that this matter of examining motivation brings certain difficulties with it. In the first place, the concept of motivation itself is not very clear. Says Gordon Allport: "As for motivation . . . psychologists are in a state of turmoil and disagreement."[17] In general the concept of

---

[14]R. Lippitt, J. Watson, and B. Westley, *The Dynamics of Planned Change*, p. 93.
[15]Ibid., p. 96.
[16]A. van Kaam, "Counseling from the Viewpoint of Existential Psychology," in R. L. Mosher, R. F. Carle, and C. D. Kehas, *Guidance*, p. 71.
[17]G. W. Allport, "Psychological Models for Guidance," in R. L. Mosher, R. F. Carle, and C. D. Kehas, *Guidance*, pp. 21ff.

"motivation" is more inclusive than what we usually have in mind when we speak of "personal motives." A person's motive is a consciously held reason for doing or not doing something; "motivation," on the other hand, is the driving force behind a given behavior, a force which may at times be different from the motive of which a person is conscious.

[Most churches, before admitting a person to candidacy for the office of minister, insist on an examination into his or her reasons for wanting to enter the ministry. This is not motivational research in the true sense. The examiner as a rule discovers only what the candidate is able and willing to say about the motives of which he is aware—even though a wise and competent examiner may sometimes, "reading between the lines," sense a bit more of the real motivation.]

A second and related difficulty is that to a degree it is as true of a "motive" as of what we discovered about "attitude"—namely, that it is an inferred something. In practice this means that motives must be construed from behavior. They cannot be determined with exactness; they can only be supposed.

Third, the mere mention of examining a person's motivation arouses spontaneous opposition: it is considered so much "prying and rummaging in yourself and others." The search for hidden motivation and the unraveling of reasons can of course be very unhealthy. There is not a reason but something else "behind" it; but it is a question whether a person serves his own cause or that of another by attempting to dig up the background of a behavior. Could it not be enough that someone wants to be pastor simply because he or she has found "the way of life" and would love to show it to others?

Fourth, introspection can go too far. Suppose it were possible for a person to get to know himself through and through and to become aware of the backgrounds of all his thinking and willing and doing and speaking. By the time he had accomplished it he would be paralyzed in mind and spirit; he would have lost all confidence in himself.

We mention these objections, not in order to anticipate possible criticism, but as a warning that we are venturing into an area in which the need for caution is imperative. Still, we need to consider the matter. The atmosphere surrounding pastoral role-fulfilment—which is an important factor in contextual influence— is codetermined, not so much by the conscious reasons why a person seeks out the pastorate and displays a certain way of fulfilling the pastoral role, but especially by his motivation for seeking out this profession and acting in it as he does.

A clear description of the concept of "motive" is given by Krech and Crutchfield. "A motive is a need or a desire coupled with the intention to attain an appropriate goal."[18] If a motive is characterized by a "need," then it propels a person in the direction of changing a situation which is experienced as unsatisfactory ("deficiency motivation"). When it is characterized by a "desire," then it propels a person in the direction of enriching life ("abundancy motivation").

---

[18]D. Krech and R. S. Crutchfield, *Elements of Psychology*, p. 272.

In every person both motivations occur, but in some the needs are dominant, in others the desires.[19] Murray, who undertook a far-reaching analysis of the need concept, prepared a list of twenty needs he could identify, a list which is certainly not exhaustive but which conveys an idea of what is involved. By way of example we shall mention a few: the need for accomplishment, the need for aggression, the need to dominate, the need for attaching oneself to others, the need to make an impression, the need to be seen and heard, the need to support, to comfort, to take care of.[20]

As with most behaviors, the motivation which leads to a choice of the pastoral profession will as a rule be very complicated; even in one person different motives can play a role.

[One could say that for the choice and all pastoral behavior which followed, there is but one legitimate motive, namely, the one Paul mentions in II Corinthians 5:14: ". . . the love of Christ constrains us. . . ." This is not a motive in a psychological sense, however. What Paul says here is that the power which moves him in his apostolic work is the love of Christ, i.e., the love which moved Christ to die for all (cf. v. 15). It is that love which took possession of Paul; it grips him—*synechei*—and activates him.

Perhaps one could say: apart from the strictly personal motivation which is dependent on the psychosomatic disposition, the personal history and situation of a man or woman, there is something which transcends a person and grips his or her life with new power and direction. To distinguish this from motivation one could call it *synechia*. This synechia did not arise from within the person; it cannot be explained in terms of the person's history or disposition. It is another power, or the power of the Other who has come over him. As Paul says: "It is no longer I who live, but Christ who lives in me" (Gal. 2:20). This synechia as such is not psychologically ascertainable; it cannot be inferred from a person's behavior. But it need not be any less real for all that—not all reality is open to psychological probing. Psychologically, the best one can do is state that a person has the feeling and conviction that he has been taken up into a transcendent context, and that out of that feeling and conviction desires have been formed which crystallized into real motives. To the extent that such motivation is conscious one could speak of "a sense of calling." More than the "sense" is not ascertainable.]

A pastor will have other motives beside that of synechia. We do not know whether research has ever been done into factors common to the personality structures of pastors,[21] but it seems likely that if it were done points of similarity in motivation would show up. Certain motives are indispensable for assuming and carrying out the pastoral role. Someone not motivated to help others, to

---

[19]Ibid., pp. 278ff.

[20]Cf. C. S. Hall and G. Lindzey, *Theories of Personality,* pp. 172ff.

[21]W. E. Henry did this kind of research in the case of business executives (see T. M. Newcomb, *Social Psychology,* pp. 408ff.).

understand people, to develop bonds with them, is unsuited to essential parts of the role. But there are also motives which interfere with the role or hinder its fulfilment. One thinks, for example, of a motivation which is strongly colored by the need to dominate or by what Murray calls the "exhibition" need.[22] The presence of such motives need not exclude that of the first mentioned. They need not even be an absolute hindrance to an adequate level of professional performance. But when, for example, the desire to help others in their troubles is coupled with the desire to dominate, or the desire to gain insight into complex matters is interwoven with the desire to shine in the eyes of others, the danger exists, to say the least, that the entire role-performance of the pastor is pervasively affected by an air of nonobjectivity and artificiality. A really pastoral relationship will then be hard to form and the situation will fail to be agogic, since an agogic situation is one which, as the context of a life-in-process, helps the other to function spiritually with increasing objectivity. Contextual influence can still take place then, but it is detrimental to the church member involved.

This is not to say that only "the saint" is suited to the pastorate. Lippitt, Watson, and Westley, addressing the motivation of the change agent, are right when they say: "Motivation is complex and involves both altruism and self-interest. This is not bad in itself. The danger comes at the point where the change agent is so busy creating a situation which will satisfy his own needs that he is unable to respond to the needs of the client system."[23] In order to escape this danger zone, in which the pastor is not only not effective but actually destructive, he does not necessarily have to refrain from anything that is self-affirming. Crawford states that the pastor, too, needs to come to terms with his grief, joy, weakness, strength, sin, virtues, love, hate, etc.[24] This is possible only if he possesses "openness to experience" (Rogers); this is an openness in which the pastor does not conceal his emotional problematics from himself but, on the contrary, lives with himself, knows his own motivations, and accepts himself as Christ also accepts us, "to the glory of God" (cf. Rom. 15:7). The conclusion we need to draw is now obvious: The personhood of the pastor needs to be given attention regularly and methodically, by himself and perhaps occasionally by competent others. For the effective functioning of the pastorate as an agogic structure this is indispensable.

The Credibility of the Pastor

Research done in the context of the new "scientific" rhetoric has shown that one of the most important factors in the process of "influencing" is that of

---

[22]Briefly defined as the need to impress, to be seen and heard, to provoke, to amaze, to fascinate, to entertain, to shock, to amuse, or to mislead (for the summary, see C. S. Hall and G. Lindzey, *Theories of Personality*, p. 174).

[23]R. Lippitt, J. Watson, and B. Westley, *The Dynamics of Planned Change*, p. 93.

[24]K. Crawford, in *Pastoral Psychology* 18 (1967): 54.

a person's *credibility*. The concept is complex. Hovland, Janis, and Kelley distinguish two components: (1) the perception of the communicator's competence, and (2) the confidence that he intends to say only the things he believes to be true ("trustworthiness").[25] Research has shown that changing one's opinion as well as one's attitude is related to the perception of credibility; i.e., the more the source was perceived to be credible, the greater the immediate change. In this research something surfaced which had not been suspected, the so-called "sleeper-effect": it turned out that in a time frame of three to four weeks the factor of perceived credibility had lost much of its force. The difference between those who on the basis of the perceived credibility of the source had accepted a communication and those who on the basis of the perceived incredibility of the source had rejected it proved to be almost nonexistent after that period. A tendency to dissociate oneself from the source and to consider the communication on its own merits appears to be at work here.[26]

It is clear that these data are important especially for situations in which there is a concern for "influencing" of a kind that leads to immediate activity, e.g., in advertising or political campaigns.[27] Pastoral role-fulfilment is another matter; the issue here is not immediate and possibly short-term change, nor is it primarily a matter of a change in opinion or attitude but one of learning to change as a way of life. Still, the material adduced is of some importance for the theory of pastoral role-fulfilment. We referred to the function of *perceived* credibility. Says J. T. Klapper: "The source of a communication, or, to be more exact, the source as conceived by the audience, has been shown to influence the persuasive efficacy of the communication itself."[28] The important thing, he says, is "the *audience image* of the source, as opposed to the actual source."[29] The reference in words like "credibility" is not to certain abstract qualities; "credibility and like terms do not represent attributes of communicators; they represent judgments by listeners."[30] Such judgments play an important role: we have been familiar with it in the psychology of learning and perception for years. "The ways we perceive and judge are determined, not by properties of the single objects in isolation, but within the context in which they are found concurrently and in time sequence. They are affected by the structural properties of the situation that set bounds for feasible modes of perceiving and judging in the

---

[25]C. I. Hovland, I. L. Janis, and H. H. Kelley, *Communication and Persuasion*, p. 21; C. Boekestijn, *Sociale Relatie en Zelfbeeld*, describes it more accurately as "perceived disinterestedness" (p. 16).

[26]For the evidence in this paragraph, see C. I. Hovland, I. L. Janis, and H. H. Kelley, *Communication and Persuasion*, pp. 27ff., 31ff., 39ff., 241ff.

[27]Cf. D. F. Cox, "Clues for Advertising Strategists," in L. A. Dexter and D. M. White, *People, Society, and Mass Communications*, pp. 361ff.

[28]J. T. Klapper, *The Effects of Mass Communication*, p. 99.

[29]Ibid., p. 102.

[30]C. W. Sherif, M. Sherif, and R. E. Nebergall, *Attitude and Attitude Change*, p. 201.

situation."[31] One cannot isolate speech from its context any more than a word. A communication does not function in isolation from a communicator and a receiver. In speaking, the communicator is present; in hearing, the receiver. The situation of reception is a world of its own, a complex of relations subjectively ordered and experienced by the receiver. The situation is the dynamic context in which the receiver experiences her humanness. Not the communication itself, but the communication in the context of the receiver's world in which it functions, influences the receiver.

In this perspective, the significance of the credibility of the communicator in pastoral role-fulfilment becomes evident. Pastoral role-fulfilment, as we have observed, is a situation of intermediation: God comes to people in his word; that coming takes place in the mode of an interhuman field of tension which is the pastor doing what he is called to do. In Part II, section 7, we glimpsed something of what it means for God to come in his word. The word of God is the form of his presence; God himself is present, addressively present, in his word; his word is self-communication by means of which he binds himself to people. The word is the revelation of his name; he is actively present in face-to-face contact with his children, who by his good pleasure are discovering his name. The word is revelation of the truth; the truth is the trustworthiness of God; one cannot know it as an objective datum, but must know it in a biblical sense, which includes one's walk of life. The word actualizes salvation: In God's speaking to a person, and in a person's hearing him, a person stands revealed as involved in the history of salvation. Of this process—the coming of salvation—pastoral role-fulfilment is intermediary. In the dynamic field of the relationship between pastor and church member, and vice versa, everything the word does happens. It can also be true that nothing positive happens. This nonoccurrence occurs when a church member has ears but does not hear, i.e., when she refrains from entering the field of dynamic interaction, or when the pastor so refrains: when he utters words but does not allow himself to be involved in the event of God's coming in his word—if he does not receive the Lord who has drawn near to him; does not enter the strong tower which is the name of the Lord; does not believe the truth in order to walk in it; does not let himself be implicated in the history of salvation.

This is the point at which the question of the credibility of the pastor comes up. This question is not primarily that of his perceived competence, trustworthiness, and selflessness, however important it may be. Helmut Thielicke formulates the issue as follows: "Credibility has to do with the relation of the faith to the person. . . . It is not a matter of whether a person 'is' in earnest about it; for who would dare to impugn the seriousness of any earnest witness? . . . No, it is rather a question of whether he himself lives and exists in the house of his teaching and preaching. The question of credibility is therefore a

---

[31]Ibid., p. 223.

question of an existential fact and not of a mental and emotional state."[32] So the point is not whether the pastor is serious about his faith but whether he makes serious work of his faith. We are not saying that in order to be a pastor a person should be "converted"—the expression too strongly suggests a state of spiritual arrival. One would rather say: In the fulfilment of the pastoral role something of the pastor's conversion should manifest itself—in the sense of a process which is ongoing. A sense of his *involvement* in God's coming to people should be present. A church member should be able to experience in the pastor and his work the actuality of the saying that "a Christian is one who is in the making"— as one who listens to the word, is in dialogue with God, lives in God's presence, and strives to enter the Kingdom (Luke 13:24).

The issue of the credibility of the pastor is at bottom *the question of the recognizability,* in the pastor, *of the man of God in process of becoming.* If he is a man who preaches but does not practice (Matt. 23:3); verbalizes the event of salvation he is called to serve but does not live it in his own existence; or conveys the impression of having "had" all that, of being safely on the inside far ahead of the others, his role-fulfilment cannot be intermediary of God's movement toward people. The opposite is also true: when he is *human* in the fullest sense of the word, with objectivity, love, genuineness, and simplicity, then his role-fulfilment becomes an agogic field—a context in which the church member can learn to function as a child of God with objectivity, love, genuineness, and simplicity.

4. PASTORAL ROLE-FULFILMENT AS FIELD OF EQUIHUMAN ADDRESS

The Fundamental Structure of the Agogic Relationship

"All unnecessary reasoning and discussion with youth is to be avoided; the object is that they may soon learn to follow the prescribed laws without contradiction and willingly submit themselves to the existing government." This is part of a piece of Prussian school legislation from the year 1819,[33] but it is really not typically Prussian nor typical for its times; it is an expression, rather, of what many people everywhere in all times regard as the highest wisdom. Research done by Kaufmann showed that between 1900 and 1960 the climate for rearing children in Germany could be described as gradually becoming less "severe, authoritative, and distant from the child," but it still could not be said that there was a totally different climate at the end of that period.[34] Many parents or parent figures still believe that children should be seen and not heard and that obedience is the first and most important thing for them to learn.

---

[32]H. Thielicke, *The Trouble with the Church,* p. 15.
[33]Quoted by H. Heinrichs, *Brennpunkte neuzeitlicher Didaktik,* p. 24.
[34]I. Kaufmann, *Untersuchungen zur Elternrolle,* p. 82.

Still, it is clear that the trend—certainly in the *theory* of nurture—is in another direction. Mollenhauer refers to a shift in emphasis in the area of *goals*. The shift entails moving away *from* stressing "the need to fit into the existing order, to acknowledge authority, to be protected and isolated, to learn to obey, to emulate examples" *to* an emphasis on self-activity, spontaneity, learning roles, and assuming tasks and being responsible for them.[35] This shift is accompanied by a change in the relationship between nurturer and nurturee: "Youth have become partners in the pedagogical process; they are given more space, at least in principle, to be productive participants in the nurturing process."[36] For social pedagogics, according to Mollenhauer, this attitude is unquestionably constitutive.[37] There, says Lattke, the authority figure "becomes the facilitator, the escort on the road, the one who arouses interest, releases power, and helps to set goals. Under this encouragement and enabling influence the ones who are led become partners by involvement, for example, in education."[38] In work groups of that kind the leader is not *on top* but *on tap*.[39] This shift in the nurturing relationship is based on the change which has occurred in our "image of the adult person as a person come of age, to whose coming-of-age the process of nurture is expected to contribute."[40] Or to put it in terms of our own description of "nurture," a focus on the independent spiritual functioning of another is only realistic on condition that one recognizes and treats the other as an equal.

When in the previous part we discussed the category of equihuman address, we called it a preagogic category. We also said that the agogic structure is fundamentally conditioned by this category. Equihuman address is not itself agogic; it occurs in all kinds of nonagogic or potentially agogic situations. It is, to be sure, the presupposition and condition for all agogy: a person learns to function as an independent spiritual being only when she is acknowledged as an equal.

Now that we are viewing pastoral role-fulfilment as an agogic situation we have to state that, in this perspective, equihuman address is definitive for pastoral role-fulfilment. This is not to say that the word "partnership" covers all elements in the pastor–church member relationship. We can only say: Insofar as that relationship is agogic it is characterized by equihumanity; i.e., in this relationship two people relate to each other as equals on the human level.

The Basic Pastoral Posture

Essentially, as we saw, the existence of man-as-spirit is *existence as movement*. This movement cannot be aimless and arbitrary, however; it is movement-

---

[35]K. Mollenhauer, *Einführung in die Sozialpädagogik*, p. 24.
[36]Ibid., p. 34.
[37]Ibid., p. 25.
[38]H. Lattke, *Sozialpädagogische Gruppenarbeit*, p. 119.
[39]A. R. Trecker and H. B. Trecker, *How to Work with Groups*, p. 8.
[40]K. Mollenhauer, *Einführung in die Sozialpädagogik*, pp. 24ff.

in-continuity. Psychologically, this means that a person-in-movement has a sense of the direction of this movement; she experiences the parts of her existence as belonging to a continuum which bears her stamp and her name, so that in the whole she recognizes and experiences herself: this is who I am, this is how I am.

One can refer here to the word "identity." The beginning of a sense of identity, says Erikson, occurs in the encounter between a "perceiving subject"— a child—and a "perceived object"—generally the mother—who recognizes the subject. It is through this experience, confirmed by subsequent experiences, that a person attains to fundamental trust, a basic confidence in her world and in her situation, in which she herself, in distinction from and in relation to the other, can be something and somebody.[41] But what Erikson calls the beginning of a sense of identity is also a continuing condition. A situation in which a person has the feeling that she is not recognized as a fellow subject and an equal makes her unsure of her own identity.

[This is the background against which one must read Vanden Ban on his experience in agricultural education. It became evident that a person will much more readily ask a question of an expert when he has the feeling that the expert can gain insights from his questions.[42] This does not necessarily have anything to do with arrogance or conceit; it must be viewed much more as an expression of a person's desire to maintain a kind of intersubjective balance in his relations, a balance he needs for the preservation of his own identity. Precisely when a person gets into a situation of manifest dependence on another—because he is the party receiving help, counsel, or instruction—he will look for a way to restore some balance in the relationship, at least enough to satisfy his feelings.]

This is of special significance for a situation in which a clear agogic component is present. In certain nonagogic situations one can say that it is simply a smart policy to give the impression that the other, too, is coactive in the situations; he will then be all the more malleable. Think, for example, of advertising, propaganda, commerce, and industry.[43] But in a situation which is intentionally agogic, explicitly or implicitly, the idea is not that the other will open himself up to be influenced or to assume a task. Agogy implies a focus on the independent functioning of a spiritual being and his ability to relate with objectivity, in receptivity, with discernment and creativity. Here the goal is that the other will be a subject or coagent in life with a clear identity of his own.

---

[41]E. H. Erikson, *Young Man Luther,* p. 114; in general, *Identity and the Life Cycle.* Cf. T. M. Newcomb, *Social Psychology,* p. 21.

[42]A. W. vanden Ban, *Boer en Landbouwvoorlichting,* p. 137.

[43]Cf. M. Argyle, *The Psychology of Interpersonal Behavior,* pp. 96ff., on the social skills which a person must have to get along with others. Among the skilled responses which can be used to create rapport he mentions: "Treating the other as an equal. . . . Finding some common interest, experience, or other bond. . . . Showing a keen, sympathetic interest in the other, giving him full attention. . . . Adopting his terminology, conventions, and generally meeting him on his own ground" (p. 97).

But in order to reach it, one will have to do things which encourage the formation of that identity, and that is the way of equihuman relationship.

Especially for that reason—a nonpragmatic but essential one—one has to stress *voluntary* participation in a variety of situations aiming at change. This applies to social work, psychotherapy, reeducation, and spiritual formation. It is also true of pastoral role-fulfilment. Perhaps initially one cannot speak too freely of voluntary participation. Not all young people go to church or to instruction classes because this is what they have chosen; a church member sometimes accommodates herself to a pastoral visit or a sick visit because there is no decent way to refuse. But so long as there is a sense of "having to comply" at work, the situation falls short of being agogic; it is, in fact, the opposite. Pastorally, this means that when a church member is forced to participate in a situation, she must be given an option.

[R. Hostie, S.J., offers an example of such a situation in the area of pastoral care. A father makes an appointment with a priest for his son. When the boy arrives he is sullen. He makes very clear that the idea of seeing the priest is not his own.

Dialogue between priest (P) and boy (B): *B.* "It is a kind of blackmail. My dad has threatened not to let me go on in school and to put me in a lousy job in his business if I did not come to see you." *P.* "I can see that you feel this to be blackmail! . . . But what do you want? It is not my policy to speak with someone unless he wants it. . . ." *B.* "And what happens if I don't?" *P.* "Very simple. We will end the conversation right now and remain good friends." Then the priest tells the boy he is willing to talk but only if the boy wants it. At this point Hostie remarks: "No conversation can get started unless the other takes the initiative—either voluntarily or despite external pressures—to lay his whole situation open for discussion."[44]]

Much more difficult, and more frequent, are the situations in which one cannot speak either of coercion or of voluntary participation. Sometimes it will be desirable and possible to tell the church member she can still make a choice. But more important than this information is the attitude of the pastor and the atmosphere he creates: the church member needs to experience that she is a *free* human being *in* the situation. We will offer a few observations which will help, we hope, to give the reader a glimpse of the basic pastoral posture.

1. First, we need to see that *an equihuman relationship bears the marks of a basic reciprocity.* Say Lippitt, Watson, and Westley: "The client system must willingly accept the influence of the change agent. But this means that the client system must believe that it also possesses influence over the change agent and over the course of the helping process. Change agents seem to agree that the client must never feel that she is the object of a one-way power relationship. . . . The change agent has the job of making the reciprocal-influence situation

---

[44]R. Hostie, S.J., *De pastorale Dialoog*, p. 78.

as clear as possible early in the change relationship."[45] So the idea is this: the change agent helps the client system to change—to that end he influences the client system. But change must be an activity of the client system; it must be willing to assimilate the influence of the change agent and also influence him, so that leadership is a joint one. In other words, leadership is not a one-way activity of the change agent but a reciprocal dialectic between client system and change agent.

Referring to pastoral care, E. Thurneysen points out another dimension of reciprocity. "Content and character of pastoral conversation depend on the fact that *both* men who speak and answer here are or are becoming men confronting the Word of God. . . . Pastoral counselling happens in the form of a conversation—listening to the Word of God and responding to the Word of God. The partners in the conversation become servants of this Word for one another."[46] These words of Thurneysen may lead to misunderstanding, especially because they sound a bit high-flown. Pastoral care situations are conceivable in which the pastor does not "administer the word of God" in so many words; situations in which the church member, in her role as church member vis-à-vis the pastor, administers the word to the pastor, are extremely rare. But we do need to remember that the parakletic mode of pastoral role-fulfilment implies a basic reciprocity, as we saw earlier. In the mode of didache, too, the pastor can be effective only if he is deeply conscious that in the church one is Master and we are all brothers (cf. Matt. 23:8). The pastor has no monopoly on comforting, admonition, or instruction; he shares the rights to them with the church member whom he comforts, admonishes, or instructs.

This means, in the first place, that the situation of pastoral role-fulfilment is basically one of "reciprocal influence," in the sense already indicated. In pastoral care a pastor simply does not tell the other apodictically how it is and how it should be![47] In instruction classes he is not the all-knowing teacher who has the answer to every question and a reply to every objection. In pastoral care and instruction classes he is the fellow listener who not only leads but also follows.[48]

This means, in the second place, that he can never be merely a functionary in a pastoral care situation. He will then always be a human being, the church member, attentive to God's coming to him through the mediating action of the

---

[45]R. Lippitt, J. Watson, and B. Westley, *The Dynamics of Planned Change*, pp. 172-73.

[46]E. Thurneysen, *A Theology of Pastoral Care*, p. 109.

[47][An apodictic statement!]

[48]From this perspective it would seem that, both for pastoral care and for teaching, certain elements of what is known as "the Rogerian method" of conversing are of significance. There is plenty of literature on its application. For its application to teaching, cf. W. A. Smit, *Pastoraal-psigologiese Verkenning van die Client-centered Terapie van Carl R. Rogers*.

other. The person who works from that inner posture will discover that the light often comes from an unexpected direction.

[We have spoken of this basic reciprocity only in the context of pastoral care and catechesis. Preaching is primarily governed by the mode of kerygma, the proclamation of a new state of affairs in the present. The category of basic reciprocity is not inherent in this mode. Something of the recognition of this reciprocity will be present in preaching too, but it is a secondary motif—just as in pastoral care and catechesis the authority motif is secondary.]

2. A second issue is this: *the pastor must take the church member seriously.* To get at this issue we shall pass on remarks which we have heard repeatedly from church members about pastors—especially with reference to their preaching role: "He talks to us as though we were in kindergarten"; "He acts as if he has kids for his audience." One repeatedly hears that pastors—often people speak in a general way about "the clergy"—are not part of the real world, that they know little of what is really going on, that they pay too little attention to what their members know of it. We need not defend "the pastor," or refer to unfair generalizations about him; apparently (but we are going by incidental and subjective impressions) church members—to say nothing of the outsider—are dissatisfied with a perceived tendency on the part of pastors to underestimate the other. We shall mention only one point by way of illustration.

[The Yale research on communication and change has been concerned with a matter which deals directly with the issue of taking others seriously. The intent of the research was to find out what helps to change opinions and attitudes and what doesn't. What type of information will "do the trick"?—the type in which only those arguments are presented which support the recommended conclusion or the type which also adduces arguments on the other side of the issue? It turned out that one cannot speak of "either-or" in this connection. In some situations the greatest effect was achieved by presenting only one side of the issue; but in many cases more is achieved by allowing both sides to be aired. The latter is the case when the receiver tends toward a view which is opposite that of the communicator; when the I.Q. of the receiver is high; and when, after receiving the information, the receiver gets into a situation in which she is confronted with the other side.[49] That is to say, the rule usually posited with reference to propaganda: "Do not admit there is any other side," in many cases does not hold water.[50]

The following is especially significant for our study. In some fashion, explicitly or by implication, a communicator has given reason to expect that he will show both the pro and the con of an issue. His audience, however, gets the feeling that he is ignoring an important counterargument. In that case chances are slim that they will change their minds in the direction favored by the com-

---

[49]See the summary in C. I. Hovland, I. L. Janis, and H. H. Kelley, *Communication and Persuasion*, p. 294.

[50]Cf. C. I. Hovland, et al., *The Order of Presentation in Communication*, p. 154.

municator. It also happens that an audience is relatively well-disposed toward the communicator and the position he has defended. But again they have the uneasy feeling that he is intentionally omitting reference to an important counterargument, although initially he gave the impression that he would give an honest overview of an issue. In that case, the communicator will very likely achieve the opposite of what he intends. The reason is that people suspect the communicator of manipulative intent. This in turn is joined with feelings of being humiliated; of being treated as a puppet or a guinea pig. The perception of manipulative intent arouses powerful resistance to change.[51]]

The focus of this research, as we said, was on changing opinions or attitudes—something in which the agogic is not primarily interested. But the background of resistance to change is here: it is aversion to being handled in a way which is not really equihuman; a way of being treated which gives people a sense of not being taken seriously, of being considered manipulable objects and not free and independently responsible equals.

That is why the thrust of this research is important for our subject. In pastoral role-fulfilment—preaching, catechesis, and pastoral care—one deals with issues which are complex, about which one can have a variety of opinions, with issues, too, which evoke one set of feelings in one person and another set in another. In many cases the pastor has his own point of view, insights, and experience. That is not an objection—the opposite is more so. The situation gets dangerous if he acts with the air of having to speak the last word in all matters and of representing the only worthwhile way of looking at them. Or when he presents the alternatives in a way which gives the impression that his presentation serves only to demonstrate the correctness of his own position.[52] The church member then begins to perceive manipulative intent and is, perhaps, insulted.

A human being, also in her role as church member, wants to be taken seriously. She is receptive to an objective communication, i.e., to a communication which conveys an attitude of pure receptivity, uncluttered discernment, and creativity, both toward the subject of the communication and toward herself, the church member.

3. The third observation, flowing directly from the second, is that *the pastor must be critical of any tendency on his part to engage in psychagogic action.*

In his classic study on the psychology of religion E. D. Starbuck remarks: "It is a significant fact that of the whole number of respondents who expressed an opinion, only two or three of those who had been through revival experiences spoke in unqualified terms of approval of the methods usually employed. There

---

[51]C. I. Hovland, I. L. Janis, and H. H. Kelley, *Communication and Persuasion,* pp. 295ff.

[52]A. Huxley, *Brave New World Revisited,* says: "The nature of oratory is such that there has always been a tendency among clergymen to oversimplify complex issues. From a pulpit or a platform even the most conscientious of speakers find it very difficult to tell the whole truth" (p. 71). Not altogether untrue!

were a few of the number who condemned them severely. There was a general depreciation of the emotional pressure exerted; and this, coming from the converts themselves, should be of value."[53] It is worthy of note that, as Wetter and Green discovered, an especially high percentage of atheists come from Methodist circles in which revival experiences play a significant role.[54] According to J. A. C. Brown, the conduct of the "fundamentalist Christian evangelist" is characterized by three things: "First, he never argues but inculcates belief by affirmation (Jesus is waiting for you!), by repetition (Hallelujah! Praise the Lord!), and by crowd contagion. Secondly, he utters terrible warnings of hell fire. . . . Thirdly, having induced fear and guilt in his audience, the evangelist tells them how they may be saved. . . ."[55] This, then, is the background of what Starbuck, and Wetter and Green, tell us. Revival preaching is characteristically direct in its address to people. O. Riecker, who analyzed the work of a number of great revivalists and evangelists—in a spirit of congeniality in distinction from Brown—says by way of introduction: "The evangelist in action goes on the attack, arouses, shocks, and convinces, lures and invites, demands the act of faith and offers help in surrendering, and opens perspectives in the name of God in which a person's final fate is both illumined and mediated."[56] The most direct and deliberate intervention in the history and life of a person is "the missionary offensive."[57] Riecker believes that the evangelist is justified in his aggressive behavior— even though excesses must be avoided and his behavior must not lead to "emotional rape."[58] From the data cited one may infer that many who were converted under the influence of revivalist preaching suffered something like "emotional rape" or thought of conversion in those terms in retrospect.

In the literature of social psychology Allport's axiom is often quoted: "It is an axiom that people cannot be taught who feel that they are at the same time being attacked."[59] The Yale researchers also canvassed this issue. The research had to do with a certain type of emotional appeal, namely, "the threat" or the "fear-arousing appeals."[60] The findings suggest "that the use of strong fear-appeals will interfere with the overall effectiveness of a persuasive communication if such appeals evoke a high degree of emotional tension without ade-

---

[53]E. D. Starbuck, *The Psychology of Religion*, p. 174.

[54]G. B. Wetter and M. Green, "Personality and Group Factors in the Making of Atheists," in *The Journal of Abnormal and Social Psychology* 27 (1932-33): 179ff.; cited by H. Sundén, *Die Religion und die Rollen*, p. 394.

[55]J. A. C. Brown, *Techniques of Persuasion*, p. 231.

[56]O. Riecker, *Das Evangelistische Wort*, p. 102.

[57]Ibid., p. 103.

[58]Ibid., p. 105.

[59]Cf. J. A. C. Brown, *Techniques of Persuasion*, p. 67; K. Lewin and P. Grabbe, "Principles of Re-education," in W. G. Bennis, K. D. Benne, and R. Chin, *The Planning of Change*, p. 508.

[60]C. I. Hovland, I. L. Janis, and H. H. Kelley, *Communication and Persuasion*, pp. 56ff.

quately providing for reassurance."[61] The evocation of intense fear also arouses strong resistance, which in turn holds back a change of attitude.[62] But, says Brown, this does not always apply to religious conversion. Still, that does not make this way of acting correct. Insofar as pastoral role-fulfilment aims at conversion—and here the evangelist's role is included—it also aims at changing human beings to where they can function spiritually with objectivity, receptivity, discernment, and creativity. To exert strong emotional pressure—as a method which may seem immediately effective—is actually an effort to win a person in a way which tries to prevent a "coming-to-terms-with" reality. The focus of such activity is the very opposite of that of agogy. It is psychagogic; it works on the wrong side of the boundary between authority (*auctoritas*) and emotional superiority, between convincing a person and overpowering her, between equihumanness and "rape."

4. Finally, to describe the basic pastoral posture, we need a fourth point: *pastoral role-fulfilment must be marked by the preservation of distance.*

This statement will not likely evoke contradiction. It is of some importance, however, to realize that accepting it may occasion tension. This is most evident in pastoral conversation. One of the functions of a pastoral conversation is to give the church member an opportunity to unburden herself. As a rule, unburdening occurs when "a mostly younger person feels the need to 'talk things out' with a mostly older, more mature person. She expects help from him in coping with the uncertainties and difficulties which she cannot quite handle alone."[63] When a person unburdens herself, she expects that the other can and will empathize. She trusts, in fact, that the other has been "there" already. The condition for every conversation, says Vanden Berg, is "coexistence"—constituting "a world" together. This is particularly true for the unburdening process; it can happen only in a situation of mutual openness. The person who listens "must enter with his whole soul into the distress and anguish of the other. Listening and letting the other speak is always a serious engagement."[64] "A brotherly bond develops," remarks Rensch.[65]

The situation in which preaching and church instruction occurs is not essentially different from that of pastoral care. Both are forms of a communication process; both are structurally determined by kerygma, didache, and paraklesis, and we have seen that in each of these modes of pastoral role-fulfilment the need for concreteness and relevance is central. Just as in conversation, so for

---

[61]Ibid., p. 271.

[62]N. Maccoby, in W. Schramm, *The Science of Human Communication*, p. 46. It is sometimes called "the boomerang effect" or "the law of reversed effect" (cf. J. A. C. Brown, *Techniques of Persuasion*, p. 78). Sometimes it would appear that some methods used in antismoking advertising operate in terms of this law.

[63]O. Bollnow, *Sprache und Erziehung*, p. 68. Bollnow seems to view "unburdening" as typical for puberty, though not as limited to that stage.

[64]Ibid., p. 71.

[65]A. Rensch, *Das seelsorgerliche Gespräch*, p. 186.

preaching and catechesis, it is essential that pastor and church member "constitute one world" together by faith and in experience.

But then there must be a concomitant: *the preservation of distance*. E. L. Smelik, speaking of pastoral care, puts it even more strongly: the pastorate invites very personal encounters[66] but at times it undergoes "depersonalization." "It acquires a kind of anonymity."[67]

The "preservation of distance" is important for at least three reasons. It is necessary, first, because the pastor—who is in a sense a change agent—must be able, not only to *enter into* the problem situation in which he is to help another, but also to *analyze* it. As a change agent he must be "inside" the situation of the church member but at the same time far enough "outside" of it to discover both the problem points and the possibilities.[68]

It is necessary, in the second place, in his own interest. There are two aspects to this. The issues which arise in preaching, catechesis, and pastoral care are not, in general, peripheral: they concern the highest joy, the final certainty, fear and hope, sin and forgiveness. They deal, not with *concepts*, but with *realities*—very human, very personal realities which belong to the sometimes bitter, sometimes enchanting secret of a person. The pastor, if he wishes to have credibility, cannot speak of them matter-of-factly; in talking about them he discloses himself; in preaching he reveals himself to many. How necessary it is, then, that he guard his own secret. The pastor who guards both against being overly self-disclosing and against artificiality will be sober and restrained in his speech—the little word "I" will rarely cross his lips. There is still another side to the pastor's preservation of distance. In his pastoral relations he often has to come so close to the inner core of another that he can glimpse this person's secret. Sometimes he sees and hears things which only God can understand. In his zeal to help, he may be tempted to try to understand the incomprehensible— to unravel the secret. He then attempts what no human being can do and assumes heavier burdens than a human can carry.

The third motive for preserving distance is the most important in this context. An equihuman treatment of another implies the recognition of her as agent and of the concomitant responsibility she bears for the management of her life. It is precisely this recognition-in-fact which is so important in the kind of nurture which is directly related to the process of humanization, the process in which a person begins to function independently as a spiritual being. In pastoral care situations a church member sometimes "dumps" herself, as it were, onto the pastor and becomes totally self-disclosing. In such a situation he will show

---

[66]E. L. Smelik, "Pastoraat en Masker," in M. A. Beek, *Maskerspel,* p. 155.

[67]Ibid., p. 159.

[68]Cf. R. Lippitt, J. Watson, and B. Westley, *The Dynamics of Planned Change,* p. 134: "What the client system really wants is two change agents in one. It wants an agent who will identify himself with the client system's problems and sympathize with the system's needs and values, but who will at the same time be neutral enough to take a genuinely objective and different view of the system's predicament."

"that he views himself as only an object." But even then, precisely then, says Künkel, in a word which is also applicable to the pastorate, it is crucial "that the therapist will respect the unconditional equality and dignity of the patient and treat her as an independent subject."[69] From the pastor's responses it must be clear that he does not find these intimate unbosomings interesting, or sensational, or shocking. In many instances he will respond, not so much to the revelations themselves, but rather to the reasons for the abject self-disclosure.

Such self-disclosing speech does not always derive from the urge to "surrender" and so to escape one's own responsibility. In some situations a person simply cannot achieve lucidity alone, not even in the way of prayer to God. She simply needs another person who can listen, who will walk with her through the darkness and the anguish. It is to this situation that Vanden Ende refers when he says: "Some problems which believers take to the priest are so intimately personal that it would be intolerable if the priest were to listen to them as an individual."[70] One can feel here the tension between personal engagement and personal distance. The person who cannot come to clarity alone is looking for another *person*—not an agency; not a wall to bounce her voice against; not a mirror to see a reflection of her own problem situation. She is looking for a human being like herself; one who does not understand everything, perhaps, but who knows enough about life and herself to know that sometimes it is chaotic. But it would be intolerable if the other listened and reacted "as an individual." One could say that she must listen and react as the bearer of a role, in this case the pastoral role. That is true enough—as far as it goes. But one must immediately call to mind that this role is determined above all else by the humanness of the bearer. Suppose it were possible to strip away all aspects of the pastoral role and transfer them in one heap to a robot. Then the essence of the role would still be left. For the essence is not a quality you can strip away; it is "humanness" as such and, speaking concretely, the humanness of this particular person at that.

So the fact that the pastor does not listen and react "as an individual" can never mean that as a person he stays outside of a situation; that he is present as an official agent but not as a human being. But a person can be present in a situation in two ways. I can relate to another as an object: view, treat, value him as an object. I can also relate to him as a fellow human being who is my equal in the quality of being human. *He* is there; *I* am there; this is how we relate to each other; this is how I listen to him; this is how I speak to him. In a pastoral situation, or any agogic situation for that matter, the second way of being present is the only appropriate one.

It may seem that at this point we are caught in a contradiction. One would say at first blush that the first way of relating—as subject vis-à-vis an object—

---

[69]F. Künkel, *Die Arbeit am Charakter*, p. 130.

[70]W. M. I. vanden Ende, "The Personal and the Functional Element in Pastoral Care," in *Social Compass* 8 (1961): 35ff.

preserves distance better. Still, this is not the case. When the other is an object to me I can look at him as long and as deeply as I please; I can condemn, mock, and injure him. But when he is a subject to me I cannot do that: then I look him in the eyes, then I address him, then I acknowledge him in his "me-ness."

We are here dealing with a subtle matter which concerns the quintessence of the pastorate. We can perhaps best express it with the following quote from Martin Buber: "Rabbi Mendel of Kotzk once said to his congregation: 'What do I ask of you? Only three things: Not to look furtively outside yourselves, not to look furtively into others, and not to have yourselves in mind.' "[71] This means, according to Buber, "first, that each must keep and consecrate his own soul in its own place, not to envy another person's way and place; second, each one must respect the mystery of the soul of another human being and not enter into it with impertinent curiosity and use it; and, third, each person, in living with himself and the world, should guard against self-centeredness." This is required of every human being, but certainly of that human being whose humanity is the essence of his role, the pastor.

In this context—the preservation of distance—we have spoken especially about pastoral role-fulfilment in the form of pastoral care. That is where the tension between personal engagement and personal distance is most directly felt. This is not to say that in this setting it is most difficult to preserve distance and that here one must be especially on guard. In pastoral care the focus, says Rensch, should be on "chaste listening";[72] but it is easier to listen and to speak "chastely" in relation to another whom one can see and of whose bodily presence one is aware than in relation to an audience of which one cannot look each person in the eyes. In pastoral role-fulfilment, we have stated, our concern is with realities which belong to the deep secrets of a person: fear and hope, despair and certainty, sin and grace. In the anonymous, collective situations especially, it must be borne in mind that these realities may be broached only by persons who stand together on the same ground floor of existence. The flat-footed over-familiar style, the facile use of "we all," speech without hesitation, unmarked by a sense of dealing with profound mysteries, the kind of behavior which does not leave the other the dignity of having a unique secret—all this is unchaste. It *denatures* the pastoral role and turns the agogic situation into its opposite.

We have dealt with our issues under the heading of the basic pastoral posture. (1) Pastoral role-fulfilment creates the freedom in which a person can learn to function independently as a spiritual being when there is a relationship marked by fundamental *reciprocity*. (2) In this relationship, which is an equi-human one, the pastor must take the church member *seriously*; i.e., as one who relates to the issues which come up with receptivity, discernment, and creativity. (3) The pastor must guard against coming on too strong in *psychagogic action*

---

[71]M. Buber, *Tales of the Hasidim* (*Later Masters*), pp. 282-83.
[72]A. Rensch, *Das seelsorgerliche Gespräch*, p. 191.

by which he overwhelms the other and her feelings. (4) He must *preserve distance*, i.e., respect the deep secrets of the other who is his equal.

If we were to characterize the basic pastoral posture in one word, it would be a word which belongs in the series with which we dealt in a previous section: objectivity, love, genuineness, simplicity. It is a word which encompasses all of these: *respect.* To be pastor is to be human. "There is one thing," says Goethe, "which none of us brings into the world, but on which, nevertheless, everything depends if a person is to be an all-around human being: RESPECT!"[73] That which makes a person a human being is for the pastor the *conditio sine qua non. Only that person can be a pastor who respects the other as his fellow human being in equality.*

Interaction and Psychic Resonance

When in an earlier section (II, 4) we discussed the category of equihuman address, we observed that in psychotherapy there is increasing support for the idea that the central factor in the therapeutic process is the interaction between therapist and client.[74] The same thing can be said of pastoral role-fulfilment. It is not exactly what the pastor *does* by itself that is important, but what happens in the field of tension between pastor and church member.

T. M. Newcomb describes interaction as a process "by which an individual notices and responds to others who are noticing and responding to him."[75] In its references to interaction social psychology has in mind that back-and-forth movement which is present in almost all behavior. Of the process in general one cannot say that it goes anywhere or that it can fail or succeed. There are various situations, however, in which people do seek interaction for specific reasons. They simply want to establish a relationship or they have in mind a goal they wish to reach by means of mutual activity. In such a concrete situation it may happen that the interaction process moves in the intended direction and the actions of the partners are appropriate both for each other and for their aim. In that case, one could speak of convergent interaction. It may also happen that in the course of the process the two actors drift apart or away from their common aim; then the interaction process is divergent. These phenomena of convergence and divergence occur over and over in the situation of interaction around pastoral role-fulfilment. In the following paragraphs we wish to deal with this important subject.

An analysis of sexual behavior among humans has shown, not that male and female functioning is parallel, as it is often pictured, but that "there is a functional unity in which the several stages of male sexual behavior depend on

---

[73]Quoted by F. Schulze, *Pädagogische Strömungen der Gegenwart*, p. 105.
[74]See above, pp. 165-66.
[75]T. M. Newcomb, *Social Psychology*, p. 21.

the several stages of female sexual behavior and vice versa."[76] Stokvis and Pflanz, who report this information, compare with it the interaction process which takes place in "suggestion." In earlier studies the practice was to place the "suggestor" with his suggestivity on one side of the page and the "suggerendus"[77] with his suggestibility on the other. In this model, the only really acting person was the suggestor; the "suggerendus" was his "victim," disposed to undergo the process by his suggestibility. But Stokvis and Pflanz view suggestion as a process of convergent interaction. In suggestion "the behavior of one person . . . is primarily attuned to that of the other. It is not a simple linear back-and-forth operation between two individuals . . . but a duet, an expression of two-sided resonance. It is not just that something proceeds from suggestor to suggerendus; the roles are so divided that both are partners in a single unified field of action." In the case of suggestion we observe that the condition for convergent interaction is the presence of psychic or affective resonance.

This model is of some importance for the understanding of other phenomena as well. Suggestion, far from being in a category by itself, is one type of "influence." Says Van Parreren: "Who among us does not remember . . . that the substitute teacher was not successful in the classroom because the students, though they might dutifully take note of what 'that man' said, did not assimilate it the way they do with their own teacher with whom they relate positively, if all is well?"[78] Something needs to be added here. Many a person will remember the regular teacher—no substitute—from whom you did not learn anything even "though he was a nice man"; it just did not get through to you. Something like that can have many causes, but in general psychic resonance is lacking: the teacher is operating on a different wavelength from that of his pupils. One observes the same phenomenon at work in the context of pastoral role-fulfilment. "His sermons mean nothing to me," one hears. "He is a good fellow and he means well, but his visits are a farce," says the sick person.

Viewed against this background, it is not so strange that in the pastoral situation the partners need a period of time in which they get used to each other—discover each other and become attuned to each other, not just as people but as bearers of a role. An older church member remarked to a pastor who had been in a congregation for three years: "When you came I thought: 'Must this youngster come and tell me the truth!?' " This church member went to church regularly and had no difficulty addressing the minister as "pastor." But he did experience a degree of inner resistance against fitting himself into a specific role-relationship. Probably, this inner "static" would have remained if the pastor had immediately started to be "the pastor" and to lay down "the truth."

---

[76]B. Stokvis and M. Pflanz, *Suggestion,* p. 27, in a reproduction by P. Matussek.
[77][Meaning "the person who is intended to be changed by suggestion." *Tr.*]
[78]C. F. van Parreren, *Psychologie van het Leren,* I, 246.

Interaction and Selective Processes

When there is psychic resonance between the actors in a process of inter-action, this does not mean the interaction will "come off" as the initiator of it expected. The process of interaction starts with an action of the initiator—an action which may be viewed as a communication. One person (the sender) does something in relation to another—by means of an action, an attitude, a glance, or a word—and so conveys a message to another (the receiver). This message is brought in the form of a code: a word, a gesture, a glance. In order to understand the message, the receiver has to decode it. This sounds simple enough. One almost involuntarily thinks of a telegraphic message. The wire services operate with a clear code to which both the sender and the receiver have the key; an apparatus in one place sends the signals and an apparatus in another place records them exactly. But that is not what happens between persons. Here a word, a gesture, or a glance may mean something different to different persons. A consciously intended word may be accompanied by an unconscious gesture which changes the meaning of the word for the receiver. There are no machines on the side of the sender or receiver which work apart from the content of the communication.

The "history" of a communication is not unlike what happens with a newborn person. This person appears, as we saw, within a specific social struc-ture and a given culture. What that person is in fact, and eventually becomes, is not just a matter of temperament; it depends on how he acts in that socio-cultural context. Similarly, a message sent by one person and received by another does not arrive in virginal territory but in a world that is somewhat structured. That other person was there before the communication arrived. He has his own psychosomatic makeup; he has experienced a process of personality formation for who knows how many years; probably he has his own set of ideas, feelings, and attitudes toward the communicator and the content of the communication. If one remembers this, it will be clear that the message will not be received with the same understanding the sender had when he transmitted it; the decoding of the message will be determined by numerous factors in the complex world of the receiver.

Three partially connected processes tend to come into play. J. T. Klapper speaks of (1) *selective exposure*—people allow themselves to be open to those messages which they expect will reinforce what they already believe; (2) *selective perception*—people receive only those elements which fit their own opinion or so interpret a message that it will confirm their own opinion; and (3) *selective retention*—people remember best what agrees with the prevailing opinion. These effects are not universally present in all situations, "but the selective processes do occur extremely frequently, and when they do, they function as a protective net in the service of existing predispositions."[79]

---

[79]J. T. Klapper, *The Effects of Mass Communication*, p. 25. Says J. A. M. Meerloo, *Het Web*, p. 13: "In every person the reception and absorption of new information may be hindered by the 'eavesdropping' influence of earlier information."

The fact that a human being spreads a like protective net over herself has also surfaced in the research into forcible indoctrination known as "thought reform" or, more popularly, "brainwashing." Chinese Communist "thought reform" is a fairly long process aiming at a total change of a person's value system—including his self-image—and his view of life in general. In the process of "thought reform" there is intensive interaction between the leaders of the process on the one hand and the candidate for indoctrination on the other.[80] According to Holt, forcible indoctrination is not very effective in producing lasting conversion. His conclusion is: "To alter personality and behavior lastingly and to any great extent . . . you must have the person's willing cooperation; the new behavior must be meaningfully related to important preexisting aspects of the person's identity. . . ."[81]

These same phenomena crop up in one's experience as a pastor.

[Item: A preacher has been inwardly accepted by his church member as pastor; there is psychic resonance. He preaches a sermon in which he clearly expresses a point of view differing from what the church member has always held. "That was a fine sermon, pastor . . . ," says the church member. "It certainly makes clear again that . . ."—and then, to the amazement of the pastor, the church member explains how *he* has always thought about that subject.

Item: At the request of the attending physician a pastor informs a sick church member of her condition. Very carefully but clearly he tells her about the nature of the disease and that, humanly speaking, she will not get better. After the short conversation which follows, the pastor has the impression that she has understood what he has told her. When they say their good-byes, however, she thanks him for his encouraging words: "It is just as you said, pastor. We must not be anxious before the time. If only we trust in God, all will be well."

Item: In his catechism classes the minister talks to the students about the formation of the Bible or about the miracles in the Gospels. He explains what it means that human beings have written the Bible, or that the miracles are signs of the Kingdom. The next time the class meets it turns out that most of the students remember only those words which fit the very ideas from which he tried to deliver them.]

Such experiences can be very discouraging. A pastor may ask himself: "Do I express myself so badly?" Sometimes he begins to feel that the members of his congregation are stupid or hard to teach. So he begins to talk in even simpler language; he may even express himself in rock-hard language bordering on the offensive. The effect is usually still less satisfactory and he risks disturbing

---

[80]For a description of the process, see R. Lifton, "Thought Reform of Chinese Intellectuals" in M. Jahoda and N. Warren, *Attitudes*; E. H. Schein, "The Chinese Indoctrination Program for Prisoners of War" in E. E. Maccoby, T. M. Newcomb, and E. L. Hartley, *Readings in Social Psychology*; R. R. Holt, "Forcible Indoctrination and Personality Change," in P. Worchel and D. Byrne, *Personality Change*, pp. 300ff.

[81]R. R. Holt, ibid., p. 315.

his relationship with the people to the point where all affective resonance is gone. In such situations, the reason why things go wrong is usually not the pastor's lack of clarity or the ignorance of the church people; in other words, the situation is not that the interaction goes off in divergent directions because the receiver is lost in the process and bows out. The interaction goes wrong at the point where the receiver begins to occupy himself with the content of the communication; paradoxically, it goes wrong where it starts to go right.

To understand this disappointing outcome we need to remember that the process of learning, as Prins put it, "is an active, creative, expressive, and intentional procedure by which the student selects from the potential elements of his environment those which fit into his developmental structure, are compatible with his developmental level, and agree with his needs."[82] To learn is to select; and certainly this selective activity of the receiver is not contrary to the aim of the agogic situation. The agogic situation in fact comes into its own when the other begins to function independently as a spiritual being and the activity of selection belongs to such functioning. Says Bradford: "Learning is not a matter of filling a void with information. It is a process of internal organization of a complex of thought patterns, perceptions, assumptions, feelings and skills and of successfully testing this reorganization in relation to problems of living."[83] So where the receiver is actively making her selections, that process of organization is evidently at work and the learning potential is present; but were she simply to "swallow" everything which is said, one must doubt that learning is taking place.

Now in the examples we offered a few paragraphs above the act of selection meant the elimination of the core of the message. The reason is, as Klapper has said, that the selective processes function as a net to protect existing predispositions; a person tends to protect herself against everything which is incongruent with the structure of her needs and expectations.[84] Spokesmen for revolutionary movements and revival preachers—hence precisely those communicators who, superficially speaking, have something new to say—know this. So they accommodate themselves directly to the structures of need and expectation they find among their listeners. In their words, but often even more in their platform manners, they offer people something which sounds like an answer to questions vaguely present in their minds, something which promises to fulfil wishes of which they are hardly aware. They sweep people along with them because they know how to find them where they really are.

This is not to suggest that the pastor could use some of that demagogic talent. On the contrary: especially when the most momentous matters are at issue the pastor should treat the church member as fully his equal. He should

---

[82]See above, pp. 194-95.

[83]L. P. Bradford, "The Teaching-Learning Transaction," in W. G. Bennis, K. D. Benne, and R. Chin, *The Planning of Change*, p. 499.

[84]Cf. H. H. Hyman and P. B. Sheatsly, "Some Reasons Why Information Campaigns Fail," in E. E. Maccoby, et al., *Readings in Social Psychology*, pp. 164ff.

search him out where he really is. He should invite the church member to join him in taking a look at the fortifications he has built around himself and then lead him to the questions why he thinks he needs them. Together with the church member he must try to understand the reasons why he clings to a certain point of view, a certain idea, a certain attitude. Only after he has begun to understand the church member's attitudinal "idiom," so to speak, can the process of inter-action begin and new insights, new ideas, and reasons for a new attitude be transmitted and received. Only then is there a chance that the other can open himself up to what is new, and only then can the message be decoded in terms which are intelligible within the framework of the receiver.

[One may wonder whether it is practicable for the pastor to be so deeply involved with a church member. We can only respond that pastoring-on-the-run or the pastoral quick-fix is a contradiction in terms. The pastor who, when he preaches, or teaches, or offers pastoral care, only deposits his message on the church member's doorstep, in many cases not only fails to achieve his goal but brings about the opposite of what he intends. Klapper argues plausibly that the typical effect of the mass media—from which the element of intensive inter-action must necessarily be absent—is reinforcement: "In general, mass com-munication reinforces the existing attitudes, tastes, predispositions, and behavioral tendencies toward change."[85] In the communication situation of the pastor the same thing tends to happen—as one can tell for himself—when the process of interaction is not marked by objectivity, i.e., by pure receptivity, fine discern-ment, and creativity, first of all on the side of the pastor.]

Active Participation

We have surveyed the relationship between the actors in a process of interaction as well as the activity of the receiver in a process of communication. This leads us to a third issue which is important in this context. We can sum-marize what we have to say about it with the term "active participation."[86]

One of the most common dualities is the relationship in which the role of one person is subordinated, to a degree, to that of the other; think, for instance, of the relationship between the role of follower and leader, laborer and foreman, employee and boss. We sense a similar subordination between the role of a child and that of the parent, pupil and teacher, church member and pastor. One may say that, although there is back-and-forth communication in these relation-ships, yet one—e.g., the preacher—is typically the communicator and the other—

---

[85]J. T. Klapper, "The Social Effects of Mass Communication," in W. Schramm, *The Science of Communication,* p. 75.

[86]C. I. Hovland, I. L. Janis, and H. H. Kelley, *Communication and Persuasion,* use the term to indicate a situation in which "a person is induced to assert what has been said in a communication as if it represented his own opinion." The semantic radius of this concept is much longer, however.

e.g., the church member—is typically the receiver. It is not hard to see, moreover, that the role of the one who is typically the communicator must contain a double element: he must be able, to use G. H. Mead's expression, "to take the role of the other";[87] i.e., he must be able to anticipate the way the other will receive his communication. The process of communication between a teacher and a pupil, for instance, is intended to serve the process of learning which the pupil must undergo. The idea is not that the teacher may "unburden" himself of his knowledge, but that the pupil may learn. In the whole process of interaction the focus is on the activity of the pupil, and all the actions of the teacher are related to that activity. One may suppose that the effect of the teacher's activity will be greater to the degree that he, the communicator, is skilled in anticipating the reception of his communication and appropriate in dealing with that anticipated reaction. In the same breath it can be said that the learning dividend of instruction is bigger to the extent that the pupil is involved in the activity of the teaching agent; one can also say: a person learns more and better if he is not only a learner but at the same time, in conjunction with his teacher, *his own teacher*. This participation of the receiver in the activity of the transmitting agent is what we call "active participation."

[A fair amount of attention has been paid to active participation in social psychology. We wish to refer to researches done in industrial enterprises. It was demonstrated that resistance to change in production methods and associated job definitions was least in a group which took part *en bloc* in the deliberations leading to the change.[88] An increase in productivity could be noted for a work group which had regular consultations with a supervisor about proposed changes. Productivity went down for a group which simply had changes imposed on it.[89] In mass production industries management often believes that older women are less suited for the work than younger ones. This stereotype is hard to change. But that change proved possible when the people involved had a chance to discover the facts for themselves. Marrow and French, in their report on the experiment, conclude that "through a process of guided experiences which are equally his own, a person may be reoriented so that he gradually takes on within himself the attitudes which he could not accept from others."[90]

Studies have been done on what happens in *role playing*, which is typically intended to lead people to active participation in training situations. Role playing has proven to be an effective means in training persons who have to deal, in a

---

[87]Quoted by T. M. Newcomb, *Social Psychology*, p. 307. Newcomb explains the expression in these words: "A person who is speaking to another is also, so to speak, informing himself as to what the other is hearing."

[88]L. Coch and J. R. P. French, Jr., "Overcoming Resistance to Change," in E. E. Maccoby et al., *Readings in Social Psychology*, pp. 233f.

[89]G. C. Homans, "Group Factors in Worker Productivity," in E. E. Maccoby et al., *Readings in Social Psychology*, pp. 585ff.

[90]A. J. Marrow and J. R. P. French, Jr., "Changing a Stereotype in Industry," in W. G. Bennis, K. D. Benne, and R. Chin, *The Planning of Change*, p. 586.

variety of roles, with other people. It is used, for instance, in training social workers, pastors, salespeople, and managers. Role playing offers trainees an opportunity to *experiment,* in an "as-if" situation, with the social role they have to fulfil. It offers a special opportunity "to take the role of the other," not by anticipating his expected behavior, but by playing that role oneself. In the situation of play one can walk in the shoes of another person who in ordinary life plays the counterrole. A manager may assume the role of a "boss" and vice versa. A social worker can experience what it means to be a welfare recipient in conversation with a social worker. Role playing can be quite effective in certain situations, as Janis and King have demonstrated. A group of test persons were given information about a controversial subject; the information embodied a certain point of view on that subject. A part of the group only *received* the information (passive participation); another part were told to act as advocates of the point of view embodied in the information. At the outset there were no significant differences regarding the issue itself. But at the close of the experiment it was clear that the active participants were more influenced than the passive.[91] According to Hovland et al., especially the element of improvisation determines the effectiveness of role playing in bringing about change in opinion. "Improvised role playing could be viewed as a technique whereby the communicatee is stimulated to help make the communication as effective as possible, to think up exactly the kinds of arguments, illustrations and motivating appeals that he regards as being most convincing. In effect, the communicatee is induced to 'hand-tailor' the content so as to take account of the unique motives and predispositions of one particular person—namely, himself.[92]]

Although it is not altogether clear what psychic mechanisms determine the effectiveness of active participation, the material we have referred to supports our thesis that the learning dividend is larger to the extent that the learner is involved in the activity of the teaching agent. This effect does not concern only the matter at hand. In the context of "planned change," Lippitt, Watson, and Westley assert: ". . . in most cases the involvement of the client in the processes of diagnosis affords a training in the general methodology of problem solving which will serve in the future to help the client meet the problems which will continue to arise as long as the client . . . exists."[93] In more general terms, active participation means that from the beginning the learner is so involved in the content of the information that he himself must try to discern what the core of the issue is, and he himself must begin to relate creatively to it. And precisely this is the focus and aim of the agogic.

The question now comes up: How can the church member participate

---

[91]I. L. Janis and B. T. King, "The Influence of Role Playing on Opinion Change," in E. E. Maccoby et al., *Readings in Social Psychology,* pp. 472ff.

[92]C. I. Hovland, I. L. Janis, and H. H. Kelley, *Communication and Persuasion,* p. 237.

[93]R. Lippitt, J. Watson, and B. Westley, *The Dynamics of Planned Change,* p. 236.

actively in pastoral role-fulfilment so as to maximize her own spiritual growth? Perhaps, with a view to this question, it would be desirable to create new forms of pastoral role-fulfilment.[94] But this is not to say that the existing forms do not have room for it.

This is most clearly the case in *catechesis*. The central mode of catechesis as a form of pastoral role-fulfilment is didache. We dealt with it in Part II, section 10. In the Old Testament it is a transfer of consecration; the didache initiates the child into the story of Yahweh and his people; it draws the child into the story in such personal terms that the child understands the story as his own. Didache in the Old Testament is also a companion on the road and instruction in the way of wisdom, so that the child gains personal understanding and insight. New Testament didache is initiation into the life of discipleship. Earlier we saw, as Marrow and French discovered, that people may be led to independent, objective functioning as psycho-spiritual beings by "a process of guided experiences." That is also typical for the didache which appears in the Bible: people themselves incur experiences when the Master goes with them.

R. Bijlsma tells this story of Andreas Althamer, one of Luther's contemporaries. Althamer's ideal in catechesis was that the students be able to repeat the words "as the valley and the forest repeat an echo." Behind this ideal lay a view of what it is to learn, a view which was expressed in the methodical pattern of the various catechisms, a pattern which for centuries determined the way it was taught. To learn was to know the answers to questions which to the mind of the teacher were worth asking. In terms of the pattern of the catechism, to learn is to find out the answer of another to the question of another. We have seen that to learn is, first of all, to begin to ask questions of your own. All knowing begins in wonder, which takes the form of asking questions. To learn, in the second place, is to walk from the home base of the question and go, provisionally, in the direction of an answer. The question how this insight can be implemented in the classroom, the question of method, we can leave aside here. But if we view pastoral role-fulfilment as an agogic situation, it is clear that what must determine method—a given both of the biblical concept of didache and of modern concepts of learning—is that catechesis is a situation in which the learner is involved in "a process of guided experiences." If the catechist tells a story, he will tell the story in a way that allows the learner to begin to sense the relevance of the story for her own life. If he asks questions, they do not take him, the knower, into his own familiar territory; he asks questions in equihuman fashion, i.e., as someone who himself feels the pain of the question; he does not so much confront the learner with his questions as refer to a question which may induce the learner to join him on the road to an answer.

In *pastoral care*, too, it must be possible for the church member to be able to participate actively in pastoral role-fulfilment. It is precisely in pastoral care,

---

[94]We cannot, in this study, enter upon a discussion of those possible forms. See above, p. 91.

whose central mode is paraklesis, that the contingent situation—"the now and thusness"—of a particular person is at stake. Says H. O. Wölber: "The two coordinates of pastoral care are: address to a person's lostness and personal communication. . . . Its entire concern is the lost person who is 'you'—not some repair work inside the world of the soul or some religious enhancement of the inner world. . . ."[95] Perhaps it is somewhat one-sided to speak only of what is lost[96]—pastoral care is aimed at the person in the concreteness of her personal situation, however that may be. In that situation pastoral action occurs as an address—perhaps an inarticulate one—aimed directly at that person in that situation: "The concern is . . . you."

Pastoral care is more than attention to a fellow human being; it is first of all address to an equal. With a slight change in Wölber's exclamation one could say: "The concern is You." Perhaps this person has lost her way; she is flooded by a sense of inadequacy. But pastoral care means that she is addressed in the language of respect and dignity. However undignified and worthless she seems, pastoral care is primarily an acknowledgment of her in her dignity. However irresponsibly he may have lived, pastoral care is an acknowledgment of him in his freedom and responsibility, an acknowledgment which must often assume the form of helping him regain acceptance and experience of that freedom and responsibility.

To that end it is necessary that, in pastoral care situations, too, the church member be involved in "a process of guided experiences." The pastor does not read him the riot act about his sinful attitude; rather he tries, through interactions with him, to discover a line of continuity in the complexities of a self-willed existence, leading him to ask: What is propelling me in this direction and what am I looking for? The pastor does not address a few words of encouragement in his direction; instead, he tries to join this battered person in a search for a perspective of hope that has its origin in the gospel. The pastor offers no solutions for a problem situation, gives no advice ("if I were you, I'd . . ."); on the contrary, he attempts to trace with this church member how something became a problem for him. We are aware that these indications are extremely vague; we could make our intent more clear and concrete only by analyzing a set of verbatim reports. But the thrust of what we are saying is this: the pastor cannot and must not exercise pastoral care with a know-it-all, meddlesome, or facile attitude. Pastoral care, above all, aims at the independent, objective functioning of the church member as a psycho-spiritual being. It is he who has to go on in a rocky marriage. It is he who must struggle out of the hole he got into. It is he who

---

[95]H. O. Wölber, *Das Gewissen der Kirche*, p. 33.

[96]J. H. vanden Berg tells an anecdote in the Foreword of E. vander Schoot's *Hoofdstukken uit de pastorale Psychologie*. At a conference on psychotherapy and pastoral care the need to define "pastoral care" arose. A German rose to speak and said that pastoral care is "to be with a person in his anguish." A Frenchman protested: "No—definitely not; pastoral care is much more to be with another in his joy."

must endure his illness and die his own death. Naturally, the pastor is aware of all this and so he often ends a conversation by saying: "In the final analysis, of course, it is up to you. . . ." Pastoral role-fulfilment is agogic only when this acknowledgment constitutes the systematic point of departure for every pastoral encounter.

In addressing the subject of the church member's active participation in *preaching,* one encounters the difficulty that preaching, in form at least, is an address *to,* and not *with,* others. Its stock, as a means of influencing, has gone down. Cartwright, thinking of monologic address, remarks: "It is no exaggeration to say that all of the research and experience of generations has not improved the efficiency of lectures . . . to any noticeable degree."[97] We may assume that it was not Cartwright's intention to say that the efficiency of the lecture was well established, only that research and experience have not increased it. His opinion is obviously that for the purpose of influencing behavior public address is of virtually no significance. This again is related to the fact that a listener to a public address is only a passive participant—if the word "participation" can still be used here.

We are prepared to grant that in general the change-producing dividend of public addresses, orations, lectures, and sermons is not impressive. "In one ear and out the other" is a verdict more often applied to this kind of communication situation than to any other. But even without research we dare to state that numerous addresses and sermons have been given which not only made a deep impression on the listener but also essentially influenced him—influenced him in an agogic sense, so that they were a means of helping him function as a more objective, independent person in a given relationship or in general. In those cases the participation *was* active. The listener was not swept along; he was led by the speaker on a road he himself could travel. He was active—though all he did was listen. But listening can be activity of the highest sort.

The question how a public speaker can induce his hearers to be active participants—in other words, which elements would make this situation one in which the hearers were involved in "a process of guided experiences"—is not one we can answer—at least we know of no researches which provide data of a quantity and a quality that they could serve as a base for the formation of a theory.[98] We therefore have to limit ourselves to a few observations.

Aristotle, in a well-known definition, tells us that, by its evocation of pity and fear, tragedy produces a catharsis of these emotions. H. J. Heering, observing that few classic texts are as embattled as this one, remarks that Aristotle

---

[97]D. Cartwright, "Achieving Change in People," in W. G. Bennis, K. D. Benne, and R. Chin, *The Planning of Change,* p. 701.

[98]Very little empirical research has been done in homiletics. We can mention E. Lerle, *Arbeiten mit Gedankenimpulsen;* E. Altmann, *Sprechen und Sprache im Kontaktgeschehen der Predigt;* and C. J. Straver, *Massacommunicatie en godsdienstige Beïnvloeding.* For a variety of reasons none of these studies is very conclusive for the questions we are considering.

fails to elaborate on his definition precisely at the crucial points: pity, fear, and catharsis. "If we have understood him we believe that we may view this catharsis as something grand: as a purification of all human pettiness in thought and deed. It is everyman—the ordinary person, the Athenian trader, everyone else who in later ages saw and heard these tragedies—who is drawn into this grandeur."[99] Whatever Aristotle may have had in mind when he spoke of catharsis, it is clear from his description that he is speaking of a far-reaching mode of influence which brings about a change in psycho-spiritual functioning. He obviously derived his view from experience; he had seen the effect of tragedy on the public. We are aware that a play is not a speech. An important difference is that in general a play offers more possibilities for identification than a speech. The play brings into view people like oneself and human life-situations like one's own. Here opportunities for listening in a posture of active participation are more numerous than when listening to a speech delivered by one person, which as a rule does not picture a human situation, though it may offer commentary on it. This suggests that the sermon may take a cue from drama—even though the two genres are ineradicably different. The sermon too—rather, the event of preaching—must bring into the listeners' world an existential human situation. For that purpose the preacher does not necessarily have to possess a powerful talent for portrayal, nor exceptional storytelling abilities.[100] The fundamental condition for communication is that the preacher be present in his preaching as a human being. For his hearers, for the congregation to which he belongs, he should be there himself. The sermon must not be a "scene," but a "presence." A preacher cannot say on a Saturday evening: "My sermon is finished." The sermon must come alive in the confrontational setting of Sunday morning in the place where pastor and congregation are *epi to auto*.

[It would take us too far into the field of homiletics to consider the important question in how far this situation can be anticipated in the process of preparing a sermon. We only wish to refer to Altmann's study, in which he offers an array of arguments against the homiletics which "has made the verbally articulated concept a fundamental condition for preaching." A consequence is "a far-reaching loss of directness in homiletic communication."[101]]

In the context of considering how listeners to sermons may be led to participate actively, we wish to say something about the sermon application.

[The theological problems which come up at this point cannot be dealt with here. Hoekstra's idea is that the application is the most typically *agogic* moment in preaching. The preacher, says he, "must risk an effort to get inside

---

[99]H. J. Heering, *Tragiek*, pp. 14ff.

[100]Not that we wish to dismiss the story in preaching. In fact, in our opinion the possibilities for story-as-sermon are rich indeed.

[101]E. Altmann, *Sprechen und Sprache im Kontaktgeschehen der Predigt*, p. 140. Altmann's understanding is in complete agreement with that of modern rhetoric; cf. M. Weller, *Das Buch der Redekunst*, pp. 85ff.

the hearers with the message of his text and there he must leave it to do its work in renewing their lives. Scripture is 'profitable for teaching, for reproof, for correction, and for training in righteousness' (II Tim. 3:16-17), and this usefulness shows especially in the application of the Word."[102] In our opinion the issue of the application must come up primarily under the aspect of the *hermeneutic* moment. Says W. Trillhaas: ". . . what must happen is a melting of horizons. What happened, and was valid then and there, has suddenly become our own affair; we recognize ourselves and our own concerns in the text. Gadamer has alerted us that, generally, there is no understanding in the full sense without 'application,' that is to say, unless the person who seeks understanding enters into vigorous dialogue with the text. . . . There is no understanding by the reader unless he reads the text in his own life-context."[103] Preaching, says H. Urner, is "interpreting a Bible-text with one's face and mind and mouth turned toward the congregation."[104] We prefer to put it this way: pastoral role-fulfilment is intermediary for God's coming in his word, by which he causes us to understand him and ourselves. This is not just an isolable element in preaching; it is a constantly present component in everything that is said.]

Here we are interested in another set of questions which come up in the communication situation present in preaching. This question, for instance: Must the preacher tell the church member in so many words what the practical significance of his message is or must he let her draw it out herself? In other words, must he make the conclusion explicit or leave it implicit?

Communication research has devoted much attention to the issue of the explicitness and implicitness of the conclusions to be drawn. The issue is always relevant when it comes to persuasive communications, i.e., those communications which aim at changing opinions and attitudes. Klapper summarizes the findings of a number of studies in these words: ". . . the great weight of evidence to date favors explicitness over implicitness in attempts at attitude conversion."[105]

So it would seem obvious that in the sermon, too, the central message—what the congregation has to take home and work with—should be clearly presented in memorable form. One should, however, remember something else as well. According to Straver's research, "There is a clear need for a manner of preaching that makes people think and leaves perspectives open. . . . People want to *work* with the material themselves; it must not all be neatly packaged."[106] Hovland, *cum suis*, points out that in the matter of explicitness and implicitness a number of factors play a role. One important factor is "the degree of sophistication of members of the audience concerning the issue presented." An intelligent audience, familiar with the problems broached, is probably less receptive

---

[102]T. Hoekstra, *Gereformeerde Homiletiek*, p. 300.
[103]W. Trillhaas, *Evangelische Predigtlehre*, p. 78.
[104]H. Urner, *Gottes Wort und unsere Predigt*, p. 74.
[105]J. T. Klapper, *The Effects of Mass Communication*, p. 88.
[106]C. J. Straver, *Massacommunicatie en godsdienstige Beïnvloeding*, pp. 47ff.

toward explicit conclusions. Another important factor is probably "the degree to which the issue is of primary concern to the individual." People will want to form their own opinions and shape their own attitudes when it comes to communication dealing with "strong 'ego-involving' issues." A third factor concerns the relative complexity of a subject. "If it is easy to see the implications, it is not to be expected that the communicator's drawing the conclusion will make much difference." All this constitutes a ground for positing a general hypothesis: "In persuasive communications which present a complicated series of arguments on impersonal topics, it is generally more effective to state the conclusion *explicitly* than to allow the audience to draw its own conclusions."[107] On balance, however, when the argumentation is not complex and the communication relates to matters of personal concern, it is more effective if people are given the opportunity to draw their own conclusions. One could say that the sermon bears most resemblance to the latter type of communication.

Something must be added, however. Hoekstra's dictum that "the great majority of people are not able rightly to apply the word of God explicated" sounds too pessimistic; but it would not be correct either to view the average congregation as "an audience composed of highly intelligent individuals," one that as a rule had little need of explicit conclusions.[108] One might be inclined to search for a middle way: conclusions, yes, but not too many and none too emphatic. But in our opinion we need to strike out on a different path.

The agogic process, we recall, is not primarily aimed at a change of opinion or attitude, but at change as a constant process—at open, objective, psycho-spiritual functioning. This means that preaching, viewed as an agogic situation, does not aim so much at getting the church member to accept a certain conclusion as at his becoming a person who can draw his own conclusions, i.e., who is able so to relate himself to God's coming in his word that he himself begins to live by its power and in its perspective. The ideal effect of a sermon is not that people "get something out of it" but that people start to work with it and work in terms of it. That activity must begin with the act of preaching— in the dynamic field of pastoral role-fulfilment in which the pastor's activity and that of the listening church member operate in mutual orientation. One can understand church members who say: "I have to work hard all week long, in church I want to take it easy." But "to participate actively in the event of preaching" does not mean to engage in mental gymnastics. It means that as one follows the sermon one discovers essential questions, sees new perspectives open up, senses a possibility of living. A sermon which is abstract or very theological or far-ranging offers little opportunity for this; and a sermon which is a sentimental story or a chain of simplisms or a summation of "truths" which no one ever doubts offers even less. Nothing is more deadly for preaching than the feeling:

---

[107]C. I. Hovland, I. L. Janis, and H. H. Kelley, *Communication and Persuasion*, pp. 102ff.

[108]Ibid., p. 103.

"It's all true but I knew it already." Equally noninvolving is the sermon which is all "application," which darts off in a dozen "concrete" directions. Few will want to wait till their particular problem situation has its turn.

Active participation for the church member is possible only if the sermon is fully a human-to-human address; then it will be an acknowledgment in deed that the church member is a human being whose own life lies open before God, who has to find and go his own way, and who has to offer his own act of obedience to the word of the Lord.

In summary: In this section we have viewed pastoral role-fulfilment as a field of human-to-human address. This point of view certainly does not reveal everything there is to know about the pastoral role. But if it is true, as we put it, that the structure of the agogic is determined by this category of equihuman address, then, with reference to the agogic moment in pastoral role-fulfilment, we have been looking at some matters which are very basic for that role. If practical theology is to serve pastoral praxis, then it will have to occupy itself intensely with the issues we could only touch superficially here.

5. THE CONTRAPUNTAL ASPECT OF PASTORAL ROLE-FULFILMENT

In Part III, section 5 we explained that nurture relates dialectically to what people experience and undergo as they grow up in a specific context; nurture functions as counterpoint in the process of personality formation. We are aware of the danger of reasoning by analogy, but it seems that it is justified here because the agogic and the contrapuntal are analogous. In polyphonic music the tones of the countermelody, though directly related to the primary melody, do form an independent melody of their own. Something similar must be said of nurture. Nurture presupposes the existence of someone and something: a human being and his world, a person and her context. Nurture is attuned to both. But it does not simply follow whatever is or happens; nurture constitutes a counter-voice—*punctum contra punctum*; it can transcend or oppose the given situation.

Now that we are viewing pastoral role-fulfilment as an agogic situation, we must attend to the contrapuntal aspect of pastoral role-fulfilment. In the following paragraphs we shall consider, successively, how pastoral role-fulfilment relates to a person in her world, and what pastoral role-fulfilment specifically and uniquely contributes to the church member's process of becoming fully human.

Empathy

There is a well-known anecdote about a French queen who, when informed that the people of Paris lacked bread, responded in all seriousness: "Then why

don't they eat cake?" This reaction was "wild": there was absolutely no correspondence between these words and the situation to which they had reference.
This type of thing happens in all kinds of situations—also in the pastorate. The
reason why this is so horrible is that pastoral role-fulfilment must be intermediary
for God's coming in his word—and God wants to enter human existence in
reality.

At this point it is often said—especially in the context of pastoral care—
that the pastor must *listen*. One cannot compose the countermelody if one does
not know the primary melody. In pastoral psychology, which picked up the word
from psychotherapy, this intense act of listening is called "empathy." The concept
is not very clear, but because it refers to a matter of great importance to the
pastoral role, we shall try to get a feel for it.

The concept of empathy plays a significant role in the counseling method
of Carl Rogers. "To sense the client's inner world of private personal meanings
as if it were your own, but without ever losing the 'as if' quality, this is empathy,
and this seems essential to a growth-promoting relationship. To sense his confusion or his timidity or his anger or his feeling of being treated unfairly as if
it were your own, yet without your own uncertainty or fear or anger or suspicion
getting bound up in it, this is the condition I am endeavoring to describe."[109]
The significance of empathy, as viewed from the side of the client, is described
by Rogers in these words: "When someone understands how it feels and seems
to be me, without wanting to analyze me or judge me, then I can blossom and
grow in that climate."[110] Empathy, as Rogers points out in a number of publications, is not so much a matter of understanding the client as of standing and
understanding *with* the client: "The therapist is thinking and feeling and ex-
ploring with the client."[111] The therapist must continually ask empathically: What
does this mean for this other person? How does he experience it? How does
what he is talking about function in the whole of his existence? As the client
picks his way through the darkness of his existence, the therapist walks with
him. "The therapist's responses are . . . in the nature of calls through the darkness: 'Am I with you? . . . Is this the direction you are heading?' " Patterson
puts it nicely: ". . . the counselor is not a Sergeant Friday trying to get 'the
facts,' but is trying to see things as the client sees them."[112]

This issue itself is not so new. The concept of empathy is akin to concepts
like *Einfühlung* and *Verstehen* which had long been around in Continental psychology. Wise people who cared about others have always been aware of **it**.
Years before the views of Carl Rogers became known, the concept was already

---

[109]C. R. Rogers, "The Interpersonal Relationship: The Core of Guidance," in
R. L. Mosher, R. F. Carle, and C. O. Kehas, *Guidance*, p. 53.
[110]Ibid., p. 54.
[111]C. R. Rogers, *Client-Centered Therapy*, p. 31.
[112]C. H. Patterson, *Counseling and Guidance in Schools*, p. 117.

available in fairly clear formulations.[113] But now we are able to say a bit more about its implications—and about the problems associated with it.

Empathy—this in the first place—is not in any way related to telepathy or the like: it is not a special gift which only a few possess. Nor is it an "autonomous activity of the therapist with regard to the experience of the client. . . . Empathy . . . has reference to interactional relations."[114] Empathy is really a process between two people in a relationship. Empathic understanding arises in an empathic process in which therapist and client, or pastor and church member, are both involved through their interactions. This is an important datum for the training of pastors. The capacity to understand another seems hardly transferable as such; but it is probably not impossible to train people to relate to others in a way which prompts an empathic process.

This is not to say that empathic understanding is a function of the ability to interact. There are distinct differences in empathic ability between different persons.[115] Different personality types score at different levels on the scale. Hare summarizes the findings succinctly: ". . . high-empathy persons appear to be outgoing, optimistic, warm, emotionally secure, and interested in others. Low empathy is associated with rigidity, introversion, emotionality, self-centeredness and interpersonal incompetence."[116] The difference is not absolute, however. Some people, as we all know, at first have a hard time placing themselves in the situation of others or relating to their experiences, but later change—usually as a result of deep experiences in their own lives. Of importance, it seems to us, is the question where a person's horizon of interest lies. Someone whose real interest does not extend beyond the boundaries of his own existence will not be able to be empathic. Someone who cares and aims to promote the well-being of another will often be able to understand another. This, too, is important for pastoral training. It will not be enough simply to provide technical exercise in the process of interaction. Attention needs to be given to the humanness of the pastor or the pastor-in-training. He needs to be aided in learning to function objectively, receptively, discerningly, and creatively, as a psycho-spiritual being himself.

It is generally agreed that empathy has something to do with self-knowledge. Says Dijkhuis: "The therapist understands the experience of the client because it is congruent with his own experience-potential." Gruhle, speaking of understanding criminals, even remarks: "Anyone can transpose himself into the inner life of most criminals for the simple reason that the motives of the criminal

---

[113]S. F. H. J. Berkelbach vander Sprenkel, *Over de Verkondiging*, said in 1935, for instance, "The pastor, as man among men, must be able to 'sense' where people are. Not by forcing his way, or dominating, or teaching, but simply by accepting the person as he is—that is the beginning of the pastoral tasks."

[114]J. J. Dijkhuis, *De Proces-Theorie van C. R. Rogers*, p. 290.

[115]R. F. Dymond, "A Scale for the Measurement of Empathic Ability," in P. Hare, E. F. Borgatta, and R. F. Bales, *Small Groups: Studies in Social Interaction*, pp. 197ff.

[116]P. Hare, *Handbook of Small Group Research*, pp. 82ff.

are the same as those of all the rest of mankind."[117] Everyone knows the desire for the possessions of another, for the forbidden sexual act, for vengeance, for returning the insult. "Everyone . . . understands revenge or else the word would have no meaning to him." This sounds convincing; still, caution is in order here. Everyone will know these desires in the sense that they will sometimes occur to him. But it is a question whether everyone *knows* them: whether everyone recognizes them when they occur; whether everyone is sufficiently open to himself to experience them and then to work through them. This is true not only of desires. Everyone comes into situations in which there is a chance to experience "a taste" of death. How many people, however, allow the experience of death to come close? How many people have the courage to become familiar with the "feel" of death? And is that not necessary to gain empathic understanding of the dying, of their fears, of their "anticipation"? Surely, the training of pastors must include attention to the way pastors-in-training function in relation to others, but also in relation to themselves and to what touches and moves their own existence!

Empathic understanding arises, we said, in a process of interaction between pastor and church member. We can also express this somewhat differently: empathic understanding depends on what happens in back-and-forth communication. There are two sides to that. The concept is determined both by the activity of the communicator and by the perception of the receiver. As far as the first is concerned, one can observe that a person may say something other than he means or say it in a way that differs from what he intends to say. It also happens that misunderstanding arises because the verbal communication is accompanied by an unintentional nonverbal communication. We have already dealt with these matters. More important here is the interference of alien elements in the reception. Says M. Mulder: "The picture of the 'personal encounter,' in which Person and Other relate to each other in complete openness, proves, upon examination, to be more ideal than real."[118] A study by Murray shows that children who had been exposed to fear-arousing activities saw something very different in pictures of adults shown to them afterward than children who took part in pleasant experiences. In all his observations of others a person is himself present, with his own specific experiences, his own expectations, his individual selectivity. Says Meerloo: "In the well-known television debates between Nixon and Kennedy . . . the verbal differences were not very great. But every time Nixon spoke, Kennedy moved toward him, and when Kennedy began to speak Nixon involuntarily shrank back a little. The public understands such body language better than one thinks."[119] In our opinion this is putting it too simply. True, most people can recognize certain fundamental themes in such motor expressions, but they may differ widely in their interpretations. There must have

---

[117]H. W. Gruhle, *Verstehen und Einfühlen*, p. 283.
[118]M. Mulder, *Mensen, Groepen, Organisaties*, I, 234.
[119]J. A. M. Meerloo, *Het Web*, p. 26.

been people who when they watched the television debates thought: "That man Kennedy is not afraid"; others saw the same thing but thought: "What an aggressive fellow—that Kennedy." The pastoral profession calls for an understanding of others in which subjective elements do not too strongly color one's observations. For the training of pastors this business of "purifying" one's observation is an important matter.

[The question whether empathy can be learned is one we have dealt with by implication in the preceding. Empirical research has not yet proven anything in this regard, but according to Carl Rogers empathic ability can certainly be developed through training.[120] We are inclined to share that opinion. In such training special attention will have to be given to the interactions which lead into an empathic process and to the degree of objectivity in the way the trainee functions in relation to others and himself.]

The issue of empathy, as we said, comes up especially in pastoral care. But it seems of fundamental significance also for preaching and catechesis. For in these contexts, too, the pastor is not speaking to an anonymous mass but is addressing *people,* and what he says makes sense only if he really addresses those particular people. For that purpose he will need more than familiarity with the general situation of the congregation: the socio-economic, the socio-cultural, and the religious situation. He must also understand how people relate to, and live in, that situation—what it means to them. With regard to catechetical instruction, the pastor must not only know what a preteen is, what pubescence means, and what the world in which his students operate is like. Over and over, through his interactions with the students, he must try to understand how they are experimenting with adulthood and creating and living in their own world. At present we cannot delve into these matters further. To sum up the point we are making: To be a pastor is *to listen,* to be open in transparency to the other. To be a pastor is to be willing to "sing the countermelody"—to be the voice which makes sounds of its own but harmonizes well with the speech of the other.

Disclosure of the New Reality

Martinus Nijhoff once gave a review of a volume of poems in the form of an open letter to the poet. In this letter he said—and we quote: "I want to tell you something. Something of interest to you because it concerns something in you: your *seriousness.* It is a remarkable all-or-nothing, I dare say absolute, seriousness. It is not a firm tone in the face of an issue; not a solemn tone that goes with a specific attitude; no, it is a seriousness that presents itself as vacant intensity; attention *without any object.* You are not thinking of anything specific, and still you continue to think. For that reason, the formlessness of your verses still has a sonorous effect; and for that reason, the emptiness of your thoughts

---

[120]C. R. Rogers, "The Interpersonal Relationship: The Core of Guidance," in R. L. Mosher, R. F. Carle, and C. O. Kehas, *Guidance,* p. 54.

still rises from you with a heavy, enthralling sound."[121] Nijhoff here touches on a pitfall into which any lover of words or any professional wordmonger may drop. Few regular church attenders will find it hard to relate the poet's words to the picture of the preacher. Pastoral role-fulfilment—in preaching, catechesis, or pastoral care—may have a true and worthy pastoral exterior and be no more than a facade; it is "a vacant intensity; attention without any object." What appears to be kerygma is only exclamation, not proclamation. What appears to be didache is an equally impressive but quickly dissipated sound, not a voice which points the way. What appears to be paraklesis is a concatenation of words—think of Job's indictment of his "windy" friends (Job 16:2-4)—not speech that addresses people in their own situation. Possibly some church members are "edified" by such a performance; but an agogic situation, one in which life has been promoted, it is not.

A situation can only then be agogic, we have said, when from the side of the agogue a counterpoint is posited to the influence which affects the other in his process of personality formation from the side of his world. That contrapuntal action is marked by relatedness to what the other really experiences. What is needed is empathy: understanding the other in his situation and in his process. But that cannot be the only thing; something materially new needs to be introduced into that situation. The second melody must not only harmonize with the primary one: it must also be a melody in its own right.

When we discussed the false dilemma of formal versus material nurture we offered two quotations which are relevant. The one was from Klafki: "Nurture is the embodiment of processes in which the contents of a material and spiritual reality disclose themselves" (cf. p. 191). The other was from Buber: "The education of men by men means the selection of the effective world by a person and in him" (*Between Man and Man*, p. 101). It is certainly not Buber's intention to have the nurturee continue his life with a selection of influences provided by the nurturer as though it were the whole of relevant reality. Picture the following situation: Someone enters an enormous factory which is totally foreign to him. From now on he will work and live in that complex of buildings, but first he is given time to get used to it. If he should now wander around in it on his own, chances are that after a time the place would be even more bewildering and therefore more threatening than it was at first. For that reason someone who is familiar with business, who knows how one department dovetails with another and how the system of communication runs, goes with him. This guide does not show him everything, does not tell him everything he knows—he makes a choice, and by making a representative selection he offers a mental picture of the whole, which the neophyte can now discover for himself in terms of his own needs.

Buber's definition has still another element. The "selection of the effective

---

[121]M. Nijhoff, "Johan Huyts' *Aan de Ondergang*," in A. Marja, *Over de Kling*, pp. 111ff.

world" influences a person through the mediation of another. The nurturing person is himself a digest of selected materials; in his own person he represents a certain ordering of reality and by association with him this ordered reality may become significant for the nurturee. This ordered reality, embodied in the nurturer, must be such that through it, in Klafki's words, "the contents of a material and spiritual reality disclose themselves" to the other. That is to say, one cannot yet speak of nurture simply because the nurturer has heart and empathy for the nurturee and knows how to relate and act nurturingly. If this were all, it would have an air of "vacant intensity." One can speak of nurture only if the nurturer has something to offer the other.

If from this perspective we now look at pastoral role-fulfilment, we encounter the questions of *hermeneia*; for the agogic and the hermeneutic moment can no longer be kept separate. We shall limit ourselves to a few observations which accord with a strictly agogic perspective.

So what can the pastor offer that is significantly helpful? In popular adult education there is a strong emphasis on the need to be "practical." The concern here is to offer help to people in their life-situations—occupation and family. This principle of "closeness-to-life," as we have stressed throughout this study, applies also to the pastoral role. But one had better have a clear sense of what this principle entails. In the eyes of the people involved much of what is assumed to be "practical" bears the common stamp of triviality. "It may impress him as necessarily belonging to his life, but it does not *feel* close since it offers no enrichment. . . . Paradoxically enough, for many people today, that is 'real' and 'close-to-life' which stands out in relief from their everyday existence. 'A certain distance from life is a condition for being educationally effective.' "[122] These last words seem to be in conflict with the fundamental principle of "closeness-to-life." Actually, they are an interpretation of it: closeness to life, which is more than existence, is what causes people to breathe again, what breaks out of the banality of their everyday existence and opens new perspectives. It turns out that only that seems life-related and "practical" which is life-enhancing. "Practical" is what makes a difference where people are.

In that sense, what is offered to people in pastoral role-fulfilment must be life-related. Congregations expect "practical" sermons; catechumens want to learn something they can work with in their lives; church members in pastoral care settings hope to receive from their pastors something directly relevant to their situation. But the pastor must not misunderstand this yearning. The demand for the practical, the manageable, the actual and concrete, is only one aspect of the demand for the unexpected, the unimagined, the really illuminating. What people are really asking for is what expands their life spaces and opens doors to new possibilities.

This leads us to this rule-of-thumb concerning preaching: the preacher dare not open his mouth before he has found something in his text which he

---

[122]W. Schulenberg, *Ansatz und Wirksamkeit der Erwachsenenbildung*, p. 192.

had never seen before. There is a style of preaching one could call stupefying. There are sermons which remind a person of the verses of Nijhoff's review: sonorous and full of a vacant intensity. Seriousness, pathos, conviction: it is all there, but the effect is always the same; there is never anything new. It is all true and devout, but it only produces a yawn.

Similar rules-of-thumb can be formulated for catechesis and pastoral care. These situations cannot be agogic if in one way or another the new or the unexpected is not present. Again, this must not be misunderstood. We are not making a plea for the bizarre, the farfetched, or the affectatious. But the pastor must be profoundly aware that his work does not mean a thing if he merely does the expected, the usual, and the conventional. His role is to provide a significant countermelody to the usual. In him—in what he says and is—another reality must disclose itself or new aspects of reality must become visible.

At the end of the part in which we dealt with the agogic, we made the statement: "All agogic intervention aims at the activation of humans as 'creators on the eighth day,' people who are underway and find a home in a traversable and inhabitable world."[123] Agogy is authentic only when it helps persons to become creative in functioning objectively and independently as psycho-spiritual beings. It is not the pastor's job to bring this about. In the pastoral role, it is *truth* which must persuade (Augustine); i.e., truth which is the disclosure of the new reality of God. But that truth, which comes to people in kerygma, didache, and paraklesis, becomes manifest in words spoken by a human being and in the human being who is pastor. His words and his existence constitute a "selection" from the world; they are the living, breathing presentation of the new reality. The thought of it may at times terrify a pastor. But through this intermediary— the activity of a puny man "risen from the dust" (Calvin)—God is pleased to come to people. Knowing this, the pastor can breathe again. In order that ordinary people might be at his disposal, God poured out his Spirit—the breath of life.

6. TRAINING AND FORMATION WITH A VIEW TO PASTORAL ROLE-FULFILMENT

We concluded our survey of pastoral role-fulfilment with a reference to the outpouring of the Holy Spirit. But that cannot be the last word on the subject. Faith in the Holy Spirit is not something we finally fall back on, or, as we said earlier: "The Spirit does not make conscious and planned action *superfluous*; he makes it *possible*."

This means, among other things, that in the study of pastoral role-fulfilment attention must be given to education, to training and formation with a view to the pastorate. This can be done only in fragmentary fashion within the bounds of the present study: we have not here developed a theory of pastoral role-

---

[123]See above, p. 230.

fulfilment but have only tried to make an initial contribution relative to one focal point, namely, the agogic moment. For that reason we shall limit ourselves to a few observations which can be made from that perspective.

Theological Training

To study theology is not identical with studying to be a pastor, although studying to be a pastor is indeed, in the first instance, to study theology. This is true in a general sense; it is also, in our opinion, practically and in principle necessary. If a pastor-by-profession is no longer a theologian, the pastoral profession has lost its identity. With respect to the pastoral calling, this being a theologian must be understood in the strictest sense of the term. The pastor who has learned something about theology by hearsay but is not himself able to discern a theological issue and to occupy himself with it, cannot meet the demands of his calling. Not only the making of a sermon but also, in many instances, conducting a pastoral conversation requires then-and-there, extemporaneous theologizing.

When we view pastoral role-fulfilment from the agogic perspective, we are led to offer a contribution, be it mostly in the form of questions, to reflection on the entire process of theological education. In our study of "the agogic" we came to the conclusion that agogy is the objective functioning, psycho-spiritually—with pure receptivity, clear discernment, and creativity—of one human being in relation to another, for whose becoming he bears responsibility, *in order that* the other may similarly function independently. One could say that the agogic quality of a person's action depends in part on the quality of his humanness. With reference to pastoral role-fulfilment this includes the quality of his effectiveness as a theologian, which is something other, of course, than the quantity of his theological knowledge. When the pastor cannot function independently in theological matters, when he is unable to grasp a theological issue, to discern the heart of the matter at hand, and to occupy himself creatively with it, then his action at a very specific point is without agogic value—a lack which can be compensated for only in part by the very fine human qualities he may possess.

For that reason the practitioners of theological education must be asked constantly to bear in mind that instruction is *helping in the learning process.* In other words, instruction makes sense only if it serves the learning processes of the student. Whatever a person has learned by personal observation is more real to him than what another reports to him or his observations. Making a personal choice is a more existential experience for a person in process of becoming than conforming himself to the choices of another. To be personally creative in a given context requires and produces more involvement than the passive acceptance of the products of another person's creativity. This means that instruction helps the learning process only when there is optimal active participation on the part of the student in the teaching process. In our opinion, this insight need not lead to the abolition of lectures in the university in general or in theological departments in particular; but it should lead to reflection on the question how the student can be actively involved at the earliest possible stages in the process of acquiring and assimilating knowledge. The primary problem to be discussed, then, is not that of the organization and methodology of the instruction given; attention will have to be given, first of all, to the questions by what criteria and in what manner the material to be learned must be selected.

[Here we should discuss the significance of the didactic principle of "the exemplary." This principle was first clearly formulated at a conference on "University and School" in 1951, from which the "Tübingen Resolutions" emerged. These resolutions concluded, among other things, that "the penetration of the essence of what is taught has absolute priority over every expansion of the scope of the material." The resolutions called for "a freer shaping of the curriculum for the purpose of allowing deeper involvement in that which is essential."

One can speak of the exemplary in two senses of the term. With respect to the formation of the person, that is exemplary "which is history-making— which once and for all opens up a new way of behaving and a new range of reality, value, or experience." In teaching, such an event can occur when in a quite incidental part of the study material the entire field of the subject in question is suddenly illumined for the student.

Second, the exemplary may be a representative part of the whole. Thus "exemplary," in the first instance, is what causes the subject to open up for this particular person, but probably not for another. In the second sense of the word, the exemplary is a part in which, objectively considered, the fundamental structure of the whole can be clearly recognized. "Exemplary presentation of material allows what is actually absent to be potentially present. It makes the course lighter by limiting the mass of material to be learned while at the same time it enriches it by suggesting a system of relations consisting of lines, parallels, and analogies which can be extended." This liberating restriction of material can concentrate on two foci: on the fundamental structure of a field of knowledge or on the fundamental methods of intellectual operations; if someone discovers how he must get hold of *this*, he can manage by himself the rest of the way.[124]]

A very conscious selection of subject matter which is offered to the student as material on which, with the help of a guide, he must work himself will possibly limit for theologians the extensive quantity of material to be covered in examinations and—this is the important point—lead him to independent psycho-spiritual functioning.

Perhaps this will also mean that the student will have to produce more units of work than is presently the case. One must not, however, think just of individual assignments. From the perspective in which we here view pastoral functioning it is very desirable that the prospective pastor learns to work with

---

[124]The quotations are from H. Scheuerl, *Die exemplarische Lehre*, p. 9.

others, to listen to others, to think cooperatively along with others, not only in more or less artificial practical situations as part of his training in practical theology, but also in ordinary work situations—where, presumably, he will not have the feeling that there is a concern to improve his social functioning. Uhsadel notes that "current theological training favors dogmatically opinionated discussion and neglects objective dialogue." In his opinion, one of the most important tasks of the university is "to foster a culture of dialogue." The concern here is not simply for dialogue but for a person's learning to function psycho-spiritually in an objective way when relating to and cooperating with others. If theological education offers something of this gift for dialogue as a bonus, then it has given the pastor-in-training something which is indispensable for the pastorate.

Training and Formation within the Framework of Practical-Theological Education

In the preceding paragraph we spoke about theological education in general and disregarded practical theology. As we begin the discussion of this part of theological education we reject the idea that only now, at last, real theological education has come into view. For the prospective pastor *the whole* of theological education is education for his calling. We reject with equal firmness the notion that education in practical theology is purely professional education. Practical theology is part of theology as a whole; even a person who studies theology without intending to be a pastor cannot afford to skip this division.

It is true that within the framework of education in practical theology, special attention needs to be given to the training and formation of prospective pastors specifically with a focus on their calling. This training usually works best in rather small work groups. Practice in preaching, catechesis, and pastoral conversation is proper, respectively, to homiletics, catechetics, and poimenics. We shall not go into the specific didactic issues which arise in training persons for various forms of pastoral role-fulfilment. In the context of our study another question comes up: How can the prospective pastor be helped in learning to function in such a way that his role-fulfilment becomes agogic for those to whom he must be pastor?

With this formulation of the question an answer-in-general has already been given: the training and formation must be such that again and again an appeal is made to a person as mind-and-spirit, to one who orients himself and enters into relationships. We shall look at this more closely from the perspective of the three relational dimensions we have already distinguished.

1. Objective functioning begins with pure receptivity. We have noted repeatedly how difficult it is to observe and perceive things objectively and "justly." Often we think that we can tell at a glance what is going on; and that as intelligent persons we need no more than a word or a phrase to understand a situation. We know so much; and without any effort we see in the new situations what we have experienced before. Sometimes we hardly dare open our eyes to a new situation;

it is so threatening to our favorite view of the world and our self-image that we bestow only a furtive glance on it.

It is a matter of professional integrity for the pastor to keep himself in a posture of pure receptivity toward all issues and people that come his way. Now practice in observation is an important part of his training. But this exercise needs to be systematic. It is desirable that he begin early on in his studies with "finger exercises," for example, reading a piece of prose or poetry, scrutinizing photographs, or observing typical street scenes. Practice may also be gained by observing a discussion, a role play, or a one-to-one group in a practical setting, as well as by listening to a tape-recorded address. (Some concerns are: What information was offered; at what points was there a discernible change in tone; which questions were left open; when did the speaker hesitate, etc.?) In a similar way, stage performances and movies can serve as material for observation. Through these and similar preparatory exercises a certain amount of theoretical clarification pertaining to perception-phenomena can then be given.

In training directly focused on pastoral role-fulfilment specific attention to issues of perception is also in order. In preaching exercises—which are first of all exercises in the *making* of a sermon—questions come in a certain sequence. "How do you put it?" does not come first; but "What does the text say and, hence, what needs to be said?" In practicing pastoral dialogue, the analysis of a verbatim report or a role play needs to be brought back again and again to the actual words spoken.

All that is already more than merely technical training, though it is that too. Still, it is necessary in training to bear down harder on the perceiving person—on the person who frequently neglects to take the trouble to observe carefully, who in new situations so easily encounters only the familiar, who is sometimes afraid to do justice to specific aspects of reality. If we do not wish to sidestep such matters in the training process, it is clear that we must operate with the utmost caution. Many things cannot be discussed in the group setting; such matters will have to be taken up in conference between teacher and student, a process in which the teacher must be duly conscious of the limits of his competence.

When we discussed the relational dimension of pure receptivity we stated that Fortmann has called attention to the need to "know in the first person"; and that Buytendijk posited humility as a prerequisite for pure receptivity. To achieve meekness, said Buytendijk, "a certain practice, a soul-technique" is needed. Such practice does not seem to belong typically to the domain of higher education; at any rate, it is virtually unknown there. But if it is established that the university may properly educate people for a profession in which knowing in the first person and perception-in-meekness are essential requirements, then in our judgment the university has a task to fulfil here.

[This practice may have the character of exercises in meditation. In the culture of Reformed Protestantism—we dare say almost universally—this practice is virtually unknown. Otto Haendler, in his *Grundriss der praktischen Theo-*

logie, devotes several pages to the subject. We shall offer a few quotations.
Meditation and meditative posture must define the basic life stance of the pastor
as a person. "Meditation is not a vocation but a life practice. It does not aim
to find ideas but to recognize realities; it does not wish to accomplish anything
but to experience what is essential. It is designed to off-set the mind which races
toward everything that happens, and to recall each event, in order to grasp not
merely the superficial but the essential; not only to register it but really to
encompass and experience it." "At all events, meditation is a way of getting into
the nature of things. . . ."[125] In his section on liturgics Haendler makes the point
that "to maintain the meditative posture (in worship) means to be totally open
to a reality, so that it can be apprehended, received, and experienced in its
totality. A perceptible sign of this posture occurs when the deeper layers of
consciousness open themselves—layers which ordinarily keep themselves largely
shut, lest they absorb all the unrest, the poison, the overwhelming threats to
one's own existence. . . ."[126] With regard to sermon preparation he stresses the
importance of a meditative penetration of the text: "Meditation on the text flows
from a nonutilitarian, total inner openness to the text, prior to any focus on the
sermon."[127] Meditation, in the sense in which Haendler speaks of it, is the same
as what Guardini calls "concentration": "concentration is the inbreathing of the
spiritual man. By it he pulls himself back out of dissipation into the inward part,
the depth, and the center of himself. Only the 'centered' person is actually
somebody. Only he can really be addressed and is able to answer."[128] Meditation,
concentration, is not simply introspection; it is a person's retreat from the complexity and business of *existence* to the simplicity of *life,* a return to the fundamental pastoral posture of respect, where a person can again be attentive to
the other and that other.]

We do not wish to be misunderstood. We do not believe that a class lecture
or practicum session is the appropriate setting for such meditation. The pastor-
in-training must, however, somehow realize that meditation is a necessary element in his work. In all honesty we have to say that it is not entirely clear to us
how this can be actualized. It is too easy to say that the most important factor
is the spiritual and mental atmosphere in which a group cooperatively reflects
on a preaching text or a person prepares himself for a role-played pastoral
dialogue. The concept of "atmosphere" would then at least require an operational
definition. Thus the question here remains an open one but one which, in our
opinion, has great significance for the pastoral calling.

2. Discernment, as we have seen, concerns the specific act of relating to
some matter or person. It is very important, therefore, that a person continually

[125]O. Haendler, *Grundriss der praktischen Theologie,* pp. 119ff.
[126]Ibid., p. 154.
[127]Ibid., p. 253.
[128]R. Guardini, *Besinnung vor der Feier der heiligen Messe,* pp. 33ff.; quoted by
A. Rensch, *Das seelsorgerliche Gespräch,* p. 184.

makes his choices and decisions with clear discernment. In fact, the whole of human conduct consists in making choices: I do one thing, not another; I say this, not that; I go here, not there. Sometimes the choices a pastor makes in the line of his calling have very significant results. What he says in a sermon can influence a person for life; a specific way of dealing with a subject in a catechism class can be the reason why someone makes a final break with the church and the faith; a given action in a pastoral care setting can result in someone's finding definitive reassurance—or the opposite. It would be crippling if the pastor had to bear this constantly in mind, but the awareness of it must always be present somewhere near the surface: a decision of mine can make or break another person. Out of this awareness the pastor must regularly set aside time to examine his activities in retrospect—e.g., by critically listening to a recording of one of his sermons or by writing and analyzing a verbatim report of a pastoral conversation.

In training persons for pastoral role-fulfilment, systematic attention must be given to the issue of discernment. Because role-fulfilment is here "enacted" in an imagined situation, the element of choice can be made explicit if necessary. For example, when in role playing a pastoral care situation the person playing pastor is stuck, he can request a break to discuss his alternatives with the group or the group leader; or he may ask for permission to go back to an earlier phase in order to get a better overall view of, or insight into, the situation. In discussing sermons he can at some point ask for feedback from his fellow students: "I said this. . . . How do you react to it?" "How would you react if I said that instead?"

Here, too, a technical approach to training is not enough. Often the real issue is not the choice made but the person who makes the choices. We have already referred to the *self-image* or *role-concept* of the pastor because it is such a strong factor in the decisions made. For instance, when in a sermon "talk-down" a person is asked: "Why did you speak so forcefully to your hearers at that moment?" the answer is often given along these lines: "As a preacher you have a prophetic task—you have to shake people up, don't you?" When in a pastoral conversation the question is asked: "Why did you not at that moment react more forcefully?" the answer may be: "As a minister one has to remain patient and cool, right?" Such answers are not necessarily incorrect; they may be correct; the point is: in any case they unmask something of a pastoral self-image, and a discussion which focuses on that self-image can help the group to come to greater clarity on the matter of self-image and on how it affects discernment.

In such concrete choices something surfaces of the personal motivation which helps to shape a person's conduct. From our earlier discussion on motivation we know it entails both needs and desires. Instructors will have to be exceptionally on their guard here. From time to time the instructor may have to intervene to change the course of a group discussion of a sermon or role play, e.g., when analysis no longer centers on a project but concerns the person. But that does not end the matter for him. Sometimes he may have to follow up the group discussion with a private interview to discuss the deeper issues underlying a person's behavior. In any case, the fact that motivation is a factor in discernment and colors it needs to be a topic of conversation in the group. The effect of a certain motivation can be demonstrated by role playing in which a kind of role behavior is prescribed. Exercises in observation and in empathic understanding may then be combined with the role playing.

3. The person-as-spirit or man-as-mind effects relations in *creativity*. The meaning of creativity in pastoral role-fulfilment may easily be inferred from what we said about the concept earlier. We will recall that though one can distinguish among creative personalities, creativity remains a possibility for every person; and that, as Beets puts it, the creative process begins "in face-to-face relationships." We remember Dow saying: "All we need is to develop a deep sense of care."

In general it is not likely that a creative process will occur in the training period which is similar to creative processes in pastoral role-fulfilment;[129] pastoral role-fulfilment in the training period has an "as if" character: the audience for a class sermon is not present as a congregation; a "sick" person in a role play is not a sick parishioner. Specifically, the element of care for and commitment to another person—the heart of creativity—must necessarily be lacking. This is not to say that in the context of training there are no possibilities for creativity. In the analysis of reports on or tapes of instruction sessions, an effort can be made to check whether a creative process is in evidence; and in this way students can develop a sense for the factors which play a role in it. Even in simulating a pastoral situation a creative process can occur, namely, the creativity of game playing. The experience may be conducive to sensitivity to the creative in general. We shall not pursue the matter now; rather, we shall focus on one more issue which is of great importance for training pastors.

A pastor has to do a lot of speaking. This is not the only way he is active, and in numerous situations some kind of action or even silence is more appropriate. But this does not alter the fact that speaking is a very important activity in pastoral role-fulfilment. Some schooling in speech technique and rhetoric is not superfluous for the pastor-in-training. In addition to this training in speech, which has a more or less technical character, he needs what Bollnow calls "language-education."[130] Bollnow calls attention to a number of defects in the use of language: "a person can be too sparing of words or overly talkative; say too little or brag; be too vague or too rigid." The word can fulfil its function only when it is intensely related to life in the world, to the whole "underground" of the unspoken.[131] Bollnow says of "language education": "It appears to me that this whole complex of questions—the significance of language for a person's own development and the formation of his own world—is of great educational

---

[129]Something like that applies also, to a degree, to receptivity, discernment, and empathy.

[130]O. F. Bollnow, *Sprache und Erziehung*.

[131]Ibid., pp. 92ff.

significance."[132] Language is more than an aid to communication; it is a way of being human. For that reason the defects mentioned by Bollnow are other than mere mistakes in the use of language. A person not only declares or—unwittingly—*expresses* his pride, selfishness, or intransigence; he can, in his speech, *be* proud, self-seeking, or intransigent. In his language, in short, he can be a creative or an uncreative human being.

There is a good possibility that the words a pastor speaks are not intensely related to life in the world and to the whole "underground" of the unspoken. What he says must in many cases relate, on the one hand, to "what no eye has seen, nor ear heard, nor the heart of man conceived" (I Cor. 2:9); and, on the other, to what may be called the human existentials: hope, fear, exaltation, loathing, joy, grief, love, hate, life, death—that beyond which nothing exists but the outer darkness of hell or the highest bliss of heaven. It is to these things— those of God's revealed reality and those of human existence—that the words of the pastor must be intensely related. Bloated words, facile words, banal words, hackneyed words, cold words, and words that sound like formulas are not able to bear an authentic relation to those realities. In the use of those words a pastor is uncreative; he brings no order, blazes no trail, builds no home. He leaves the people to whom he is speaking "out in the cold"—the cold of the *tōhû wābōhû*.

So it is clear that education in the use of appropriate language must be a significant element in pastoral training. The purpose of this education is not to make language artists—this is neither possible nor necessary. But in the entire program of pastoral training and formation constant attention must be paid, not only to speech and the use of language, but to the challenge of being authentically human in one's speech. The pastor-in-training must be confronted over and over with the question: "In my words, am I what a pastor and a human being should be—objective, genuine, 'simple,' trustworthy?" "In my language am I a person who can be creative in that which is the essence of an agogic relationship—a growth-producing relationship?"

In this section we did not offer a program for pastoral training and formation within the framework of practical-theological education. In the construction of such a program various matters need to be noted which fall outside the scope of this study. Yet the indications we have given here point, in our judgment, to a basic blueprint for a program. In whatever way the training is structured it must, in whole and in part, aim at a capacity for independent spiritual functioning in pastoral role-fulfilment—in pure receptivity, clear discernment, and caring creativity.

Initiation into the Pastoral Calling and Supervision (Mentorship)

In speaking of the beginning social worker, Charlotte Towle asserts that postponement of adequate orientation tends to encourage undue absorption in

---

[132]Ibid., p. 114.

routine activity. In her own words: "When the individual is insecure, when he is unable to master his environment, when he is not equipped to meet the changing demands of a situation, he falls back on automatic behavior as a source of security. Therefore, as the individual gains basic security in a work situation, he will have less dependence on *habitual ways* and should move into a more flexible meeting of the varying aspects of the complex total of his job."[133] Note the connection: inadequate orientation—insecurity—automatic behavior (the opposite of "objective functioning"). One may not read this sequence in reverse: if a social worker is deficient in objectivity, that is the result of insecurity, which was caused by a lack of adequate orientation. Many factors may play a role here. But the lack of a well-prepared, systematically structured orientation, with adequate supervision, may result in insecurity, which in turn makes for an automatic style of behavior.

The same thing can be said of the pastor. In fact, the situation, especially in Protestant churches, is even less favorable. A starting *social worker* enters the service of an agency in which as a rule he has one or more supervisors who assign him tasks usually suited to his status as a beginner. A beginning *pastor* all at once bears full responsibility for the pastorate in its varied forms and, with the church council in which he presides, assumes the leadership of a congregation or parish. A few experienced elders or wardens often alert him to the ways of the church but there is no carefully considered task distribution, to say nothing of adequate supervision.

Some churches, reacting to this problem, have instituted a pastoral internship to provide a bridge between the theological school and the pastorate. The arrangements vary but the main features are a period of orientation (in a church other than the one in which he will be a minister); performing a selected number of pastoral activities; and being directed by an experienced pastor who gives him specific assignments, discusses his performance, and observes the candidate's attitude in and to the work. Such an internship has already proven itself in pastoral education. Through it the intern gains the opportunity to learn from experience about the church as well as the pastoral role and himself as the bearer of that role. All this occurs in a somewhat protected situation in which a mentor and possibly an on-the-job "coach" assist him.

Valuable as this is, however, it is not enough. When someone first enters a situation in which the pastoral role is thrust upon him, he must have help, both individualized and systematic. Sometimes this help can come to him only in the form of regular supervision.

[We use the concept of supervision here in the sense it has acquired in the area of social work. According to V. P. Robinson, supervision is "the most original and characteristic process that the field of social casework has developed."[134] *Supervision* literally means "to oversee, to watch the work of another with responsibility for its quality," but in practice the word is further weighted

---

[133]C. Towle, *Common Human Needs*, p. 105.
[134]V. P. Robinson, *The Dynamics of Supervision under Functional Controls*, p. VIII.

with the idea of the responsibility one has for bringing a learner up to the level of knowledge and skill required for an occupation. In social work the supervisor initially was the experienced social worker who had a beginning social worker under his care. The only necessary qualification for a supervisor, says Young, is "that she should be reasonably competent and knowledgeable in her own field of practice."[135] In those days, according to Williamson, the caseworker was especially "occupied with making over the client"; i.e., social work meant to fashion the client into the person the social worker thought he had to be. In the same period, the supervisor's aim was "to make over the worker—usually in his own image, seeming to say, 'Do as I do and you will be right,' or possibly, 'Do it this way, because I say so.' "[136] As a result of the improvement of training and the expansion in depth and scope of methodological reflection on social work, supervision was approached more systematically. First it became "casework done on the caseworker." But with growing clarity the insight prevailed that it has to be an "education . . . process."[137] The person under supervision is not a client seeking help in dealing with his personal problems; he is a student–social worker and the intent of supervision is "to help him in the doing of a job."[138] Heywood expresses it clearly: "The supervisor's correction and guidance of the student is directed toward his functioning as a social worker and enabling him to use the personality which he has in a professional way to help other people. Supervision is, therefore, a highly individualized form of teaching, adapted to each individual student." "The focus . . . is on professional practice, knowledge, and behavior."[139] W. F. van Stegeren, who is specifically concerned with the supervision of students-in-training in social pedagogy, affirms "that supervision is designed to help the student experience consciously his own process of learning during its practical stage . . . ; via supervising the integration of theoretical/practical knowledge and practical experience is promoted and a bridge built to the society in which the student must soon function as a graduate."[140]

Thus, three issues are in focus in the supervision of trainees, each in direct relation to the others: (a) the student as bearer of a professional role; (b) the knowledge he has gained in his education; (c) the practice he experiences in his work. In supervisory discussion one proceeds from the concrete experiences of the student. A line of contact with the experiences is usually sought by way of a student-formulated report of, say, a conversation or a group session he has led. Such a report is never a pure reproduction, but it can generally be employed as "an abridged version of the original event."[141] In any case it is indispensable: "The improvement of skill must come from analyzing one's own work, not

---

[135]P. H. Young, *The Student and Supervision in Social Work Education*, p. 12; V. P. Robinson, *The Dynamics of Supervision*, pp. 30ff.

[136]M. Williamson, *Supervision: New Patterns and Processes*, p. 41.

[137]C. Towle, *Common Human Needs*, p. 95.

[138]M. Williamson, *Supervision*, p. 102.

[139]J. S. Heywood, *An Introduction to Teaching Casework Skills*, p. 67.

[140]W. F. van Stegeren, *Groepssupervisie*, p. 9.

[141]P. H. Young, *The Student and Supervision*, p. 67.

another's."[142] Supervisory conferences are held regularly, usually once a week or once every two weeks. Regularity and frequency are of great significance; the nature of supervision is decidedly not the incidental provision of help; it has in view a systematically guided process.

The most common form of supervision is individual supervision; in addition, group supervision is given in some situations, but this can never altogether replace individual supervision.]

From this survey of the concept of supervision we return to the question of training and molding as it relates to pastoral role-fulfilment. It seems altogether unacceptable that a form of assistance deemed not just valuable but indispensable for a beginning functionary in social work should not be necessary for the beginning pastor. His work situation is generally less easy to oversee; monitoring it tends to be less systematic; his responsibilities and competencies are greater from the very start; his tasks are more diverse and opportunities for asking for help or advice are more limited. Superior professional training does not compensate for this; sadly enough, this division of theological training generally cannot stand comparison with the corresponding part of a student's training in a school of social work.

When we talk of supervision with a view to pastoral role-fulfilment, we have in mind primarily supervision of the trainee, a continuation of the training which is focused on an individual's functioning in practice. This supervision thus intends, as Van Stegeren puts it, "to help the student to experience consciously his own process of learning at this stage." It seems of some importance that this supervision—possibly with lesser frequency—be continued at least during the first year of a pastorate.

We stated that the tasks of the pastor are more diverse than those, say, of a social worker or of a functionary in some socio-cultural setting. Supervision there means a continuation of the training given earlier in casework or group work. Apart from the important roles the pastor fulfils in leading and organizing a congregation and shaping its policies, at least three very diverse kinds of work remain to which the supervisor needs to address himself: (a) speaking to large, heterogeneous audiences in preaching; (b) giving instruction in church classes; and (c) conducting private or small-group meetings in pastoral care settings. In each of these forms of activity a distinction must be made between the hermeneutic moment (in which the more typically theological issues may be on the agenda) and the agogic moment (in which the focus is on the spiritual functioning of the church member). Regrettably, we can say nothing from our own practical experience in supervision or that of others concerning the problems which arise here. We stand at the borders of virgin territory; all we can do is attempt to arrive at a preliminary point of departure on the basis of theory developed in this study.

In sum, we have seen that for methodological reflection it is of importance

---

[142]Ibid., p. 77.

that one should not simply assume the validity of the historically developed forms of pastoral role-fulfilment. The basic form underlying pastoral role-fulfilment is the coming and being together of the congregation. This basic form is defined by three structural modes: kerygma, didache, and paraklesis. Within this complex structure, which is intermediary for God's coming to people, something happens: there is a "motivating movement" which brings a person to understanding (the *hermeneutic* moment) and change (the *agogic* moment). This change, which cannot be separated from understanding, is a never completed process of renewal of the human-being-as-spirit, a process whose aim is independent, objective, spiritual functioning in the relational dimensions of pure receptivity, clear discernment, and caring creativity. This process occurs in a field of tension constituted by the relation between pastor and church member. The "magnetic" field of pastoral role-fulfilment may be viewed as an agogic situation. The fundamental structure of an agogic situation is defined by the category of human-to-human (equihuman) address. The actual role-fulfilment of the pastor, viewed from an agogic perspective, is the *context* of the other person's becoming a human being; it has agogic quality if it relates dialectically, as counterpoint, to the other in his world of experience.

On the basis of the preceding summary, in which we repeated the broad lines of our argument, we now believe we can say the following with reference to pastoral supervision. The crucial point in pastoral role-fulfilment, viewed methodologically, *is the independent objective spiritual functioning of the pastor.* He needs to be a theologian; he needs to know the world and human life; he must be able to "move"; he must be able to speak; and so on. But if the meaning of his role-fulfilment is that it serve as intermediary for God's coming to man in his word, then the central prerequisite of his calling is that he be able to relate to the person to whom God decides to come—in pure receptivity, clear discernment, and caring creativity. This, then, is the focus of pastoral supervision.

It is not immaterial whether one proceeds in this context from a sermon, a catechism report, or a counseling verbatim—attention must be given to each of these forms of pastoral role-fulfilment with a respectively different emphasis. But the focus remains the same: the spiritual functioning of this person in his role-fulfilment. Automatically, all the other matters we discussed in this part will come up, such as the mind-set of this person, his genuineness, his self-image, his motivation; reciprocity and seriousness in his relations with others; the preservation of distance and respect; inducing the other to participate actively, empathic understanding, and material "input" selectively mediated into the change process.

Having received such systematic supervision, is the pastor "all set to go"? With a variation of a saying of Luther to which we referred a number of times, we can only say: *pastor est in fieri* ("to be a pastor is to be in the making")! His training and spiritual forming are never finished.

Every ending is a beginning.

List of Works Cited

C. Aalders, *Terug naar de Medicina Sacra*. Den Haag, n.d.

T. K. Abbott, *A Critical and Exegetical Commentary on the Epistles to the Ephesians and the Colossians*. Edinburgh and New York, 1946.

K. Abraham, *Der Betrieb als Erziehungsfaktor.* Freiburg, 1957².

R. Abramowski, *Das Buch des betenden Gottesknechts*. Stuttgart, 1939.

J. E. Adams, *Competent to Counsel*. Grand Rapids, n.d.

T. W. Adorno, E. Frenkel-Brunswik, D. J. Levinson, and R. N. Sanford, *The Authoritarian Personality*. New York, 1950.

M. Albinski, *De Onderwijzer en de Cultuuroverdracht*. Assen, 1959.

G. W. Allport, *Personality*. n.p., 1937.

————, "Psychological Models for Guidance," in R. L. Mosher, R. F. Carle, and C. D. Kehas, *Guidance*. New York-Chicago-Burlingame, 1965.

————, "Attitudes in the History of Social Psychology," in M. Jahoda and N. Warren, *Attitudes*. Harmondsworth, 1966, pp. 15ff.

G. W. Allport and L. J. Postman, "The Basic Psychology of Rumor," in E. E. Maccoby, T. M. Newcomb, and E. L. Hartley, *Readings in Social Psychology*. New York, 1958³, pp. 54ff.

E. Altmann, *Sprechen und Sprache im Kontaktgeschehen der Predigt*. Halle, 1966.

G. Anders, *Burning Conscience*, London, 1962.

M. Argyle, *Religious Behaviour*. London, 1958.

————, *The Psychology of Interpersonal Behaviour*. Harmondsworth, 1967.

H. Asmussen, *Die Seelsorge*. München, 1937.

Augustine, *De Doctrina Christiana* (Corpus Christianorum, Series Latina XXXII). Turnhout, 1962.

J. T. Bakker, *Kerygma en Prediking*. Kampen, 1957.

A. W. vanden Ban, *Boer en Landbouwvoorlichting*. Assen, 1963.

A. Bandura and R. H. Walters, *Social Learning and Personality Development*. New York, 1963.

W. Barclay, *Turning to God*. London, 1963.

J. Barr, Review of *The Authority of Scripture*, by J. K. S. Reid in *Scottish Journal of Theology* 11 (1958): 86ff.

K. Barth, *Das Wort Gottes und die Theologie*, München, 1929.

————, *Der Dienst am Wort Gottes*. München, 1934.

————, *Church Dogmatics* I/1-IV/3 (*CD*). ET Edinburgh, 1936.

————, *Evangelium und Gesetz*. Zollikon-Zürich, 1940[2].

————, *Auslegung von Matthäus 28, 16-20*. Basel, 1945.

————, *Dogmatics in Outline*. ET New York, 1959.

————, *Evangelical Theology: An Introduction.* ET New York, 1963.

F. C. Bartlett, "The Aims of Political Propaganda," in D. Katz, D. Cartwright, S. Eldersveld, and A. McClung Lee. *Public Opinion and Propaganda*. New York, 1956[2], pp. 463ff.

H. O. Bastion, "Vom Wort zu den Wörtern," in *Evangelische Theologie* 28 (1968): 25ff.

H. Bavinck, *Gereformeerde Dogmatiek*, I-IV. Kampen, 1928-1930[4].

J. H. Bavinck, *An Introduction to the Science of Missions*. ET Philadelphia, 1960.

————, *Alzo wies het Woord*. Baarn, 1960[2].

M. A. Beek, "De Prediking der bijbelse Wijsheid," in C. W. Mönnich and F. J. Pop, *Wegen der Prediking*. Amsterdam, 1959, pp. 351ff.

N. Beets, *Volwassen worden*. Utrecht, 1960.

————, "Debat en Gesprek," in *Wending* 22 (1967-68): 68ff.

R. Benedict, *Patterns of Culture*. New York, 1957[17].

W. G. Bennis, K. D. Benne, and R. Chin, *The Planning of Change*. New York, 1962.

P. H. Benson, *Religion in Contemporary Culture*. New York, 1960.

J. H. vanden Berg, *Psychologie en theologische Anthropologie*. Utrecht, 1952[3].

————, "Het Gesprek," in J. H. vanden Berg and J. Linschoten, *Persoon en Wereld*. Utrecht, 1956[2], pp. 136ff.

————, *Het Ziekbed*. Nijkerk, 1957[6].

————, *Metabletica*. Nijkerk, 1957.

————, *Psychologie en Geloof.* Nijkerk, 1958.

W. J. Berger, *Op Weg naar empirische Zielzorg*. Utrecht-Nijmegen, 1965.

S. F. H. J. Berkelbach vander Sprenkel, *Over de Verkondiging*. Utrecht, 1935.

————, *Catechetiek*. Nijkerk, 1956.

H. Berkhof, *De Mens onderweg*. 's-Gravenhage, 1960.

————, *The Doctrine of the Holy Spirit*. ET Richmond, 1964.

G. C. Berkouwer, *Faith and Sanctification*. ET Grand Rapids, 1952.

————, *Faith and Justification*. ET Grand Rapids, 1954.

————, *Faith and Perseverance*. ET Grand Rapids, 1958.

————, *Man: The Image of God*. ET Grand Rapids, 1962.

————, *The Work of Christ*. ET Grand Rapids, 1965.

————, *The Sacraments*. ET Grand Rapids, 1969.

————, *Holy Scripture*. ET Grand Rapids, 1975.

J. H. Bernard, *A Critical and Exegetical Commentary on the Gospel according to St. John*, I, II. Edinburgh, 1942[2].

Biblisch-historisches Handwörterbuch, I, II. Göttingen, 1962.

R. Bijlsma, *Kleine Catechetiek*, Nijkerk, 1962.

W. Birnbaum, *Theologische Wandlungen von Schleiermacher bis Karl Barth*. Tübingen, 1963.

W. Bitter, *Die Wandlung des Menschen in Seelsorge und Psychotherapie*. Göttingen, 1956.

F. Blättner, *Geschichte der Pädagogik*. Heidelberg, 1961[8].

C. Boekestijn, *Sociale Relatie en Zelfbeeld*. Amsterdam, 1963.

H. R. Boer, *Pentecost and Missions*. London and Grand Rapids, 1961.

C. W. du Boeuff and P. C. Kuiper, *Psychotherapie en Zielzorg*. Utrecht, 1950.

G. Bohne, *Das Wort Gottes und der Unterricht*. n.p., 1962.

M. H. Bolkestein, "Het Terrein der Praktische Theologie," in *Nederlands Theologisch Tijdschrift* 15 (1960-61): 282ff.

O. F. Bollnow, "Das veränderte Bild vom Menschen und sein Einfluss auf das pädagogische Denken," in O. F. Bollnow, *Erziehung wozu?* Stuttgart, 1956.

————, "Die Ermahnung," in *Erziehung zur Menschlichkeit: Festschrift für Eduard Spranger*. Tübingen, 1957.

————, *Existenzphilosophie und Pädagogik*. Stuttgart, 1962².

————, *Die pädagogische Atmosphäre*. Heidelberg, 1964.

————, *Pädagogische Forschung und philosophisches Denken*. n.p., n.d.

————, *Sprache und Erziehung*. Stuttgart-Berlin-Köln-Mainz, 1966.

D. Bonhoeffer, *Ethics*. ET London, 1955.

————, *The Cost of Discipleship*. ET New York, 1959.

————, *The Communion of the Saints*. ET New York, 1963.

————, *Letters and Papers from Prison*. ET London, 1971.

L. P. Bradford, "The Teaching-Learning Transaction," in W. G. Bennis, K. D. Benne, and R. Chin, *The Planning of Change*. New York, 1962, pp. 493ff.

W. Brezinka, *Erziehung als Lebenshilfe*. Wien, 1963³.

C. A. Briggs and E. G. Briggs, *A Critical and Exegetical Commentary on the Book of Psalms*, I, II. Edinburgh, 1927⁴.

A. M. Brouwer, *De Gelijkenissen*. Leiden, 1946.

C. Brown, trans., *New International Dictionary of New Testament Theology*, I. ET Grand Rapids, 1975.

J. A. C. Brown, *Techniques of Persuasion*. Harmondsworth, 1963.

N. Brox, *Zeuge und Märtyrer*. München, 1961.

E. Brunner, *Das Gebot und die Ordnungen*. Zürich, 1939³; ET *The Divine Imperative*. ET Philadelphia, 1979.

————, *The Christian Doctrine of the Church, Faith, and the Consummation*. ET Philadelphia, 1950.

M. Buber, *I and Thou*. ET Edinburgh, 1937.

————, *Tales of the Hasidim (The Later Masters)*. ET New York, 1947.

————, *Between Man and Man*. ET New York, 1948.

————, *Two Types of Faith*. ET London, 1951.

R. Bultmann, *Theology of the New Testament*. ET New York, 1951.

————, *Jesus Christ and Mythology*. ET New York, 1958.

————, *Jesus*. München-Hamburg, 1964.

F. J. J. Buytendijk, *Erziehung zur Demut*. Ratingen, 1962.

J. Calvin, *Institutes of the Christian Religion*. ET Philadelphia, 1960.

D. Cartwright, "Achieving Change in People," in W. G. Bennis, K. D. Benne, and R. Chin, *The Planning of Change*. New York, 1962, pp. 698ff.

H. Carrier, S.J., *Psycho-sociologie de l'Appartenance religieuse*. Rome, 1960.

J. B. Charles, "De derde Dichter van de achtste Dag," in F. Sierksma, *Commentaar op Achterberg*. 's-Gravenhage, 1948.

I. L. Child, "Socialization," in G. Lindzey, *Handbook of Social Psychology*, II. Cambridge, Mass., 1954, pp. 655ff.

Christelijke Encyclopaedie, I-VI. Kampen, 1956-61.
L. Coch and J. R. P. French, Jr., "Overcoming Resistance to Change," in E. E. Maccoby, T. M. Newcomb, and E. L. Hartley, *Readings in Social Psychology*. New York, 1958[3], pp. 233ff.
D. F. Cox, "Clues for Advertising Strategists," in L. A. Dexter and D. M. White, *People, Society and Mass Communications*. Glencoe, Ill., 1964, pp. 359ff.
K. Crawford, "The Minister's Self-Image and Pastoral Counseling," in *Pastoral Psychology* 18 (1967): 49ff.
H. Cremer and J. Kögel, *Biblisch-theologisches Wörterbuch der neutestamentlichen Gräzität*. Gotha, 1915[10].
O. Cullmann, *Christ and Time*. ET Philadelphia, 1950.

E. E. Davis, *Attitude Change*. Paris, 1965.
H. Diem, *Dogmatics*. ET Edinburgh, 1959.
————, *Die Kirche und ihre Praxis*. München, 1963.
J. H. Dijkhuis, *Het Proces van de Interactie tussen Psycholoog en Cliënt*. Utrecht, 1963.
J. J. Dijkhuis, *De Proces-Theorie van C. R. Rogers*. Hilversum-Antwerpen, 1964.
C. J. Dippel, *Verkenning en Verwachting*. 's-Gravenhage, 1962.
C. H. Dodd, *The Apostolic Preaching*. ET Chicago, 1937.
A. B. Dow, "An Architect's View on Creativity," in H. H. Anderson, *Creativity and Its Cultivation*. New York, 1959.
N. Drazin, *History of Jewish Education from 515 B. C. E. to 220 C. E.* Baltimore, 1940.
J. von den Driesch and J. Esterhues, *Geschichte der Erziehung und Bildung*, I, II. Paderborn, 1960[5].
R. F. Dymond, "A Scale for the Measurement of Empathic Ability," in P. Hare, E. F. Borgatta, and R. F. Bales, *Small Groups*. New York, 1966, pp. 197ff.

G. Ebeling, *The Nature of Faith*. ET Philadelphia, 1961.
————, *Word and Faith*. ET Philadelphia, 1963.
————, *Theology and Proclamation*. ET Philadelphia, 1966.
H. Ellis, *The Transfer of Learning*. New York and London, 1965.
W. M. I. vanden Ende, "The Personal and the Functional Element in Pastoral Care," in *Social Compass* 8 (1961): 35ff.
E. H. Erikson, *Young Man Luther*. London, 1958.
————, *Identity and the Life Cycle*. New York, 1959.

H. Faber, *Pastorale Verkenning*. 's-Gravenhage, 1958.
————, *Leren voor Dominee*. Leiden, 1964.
J. Fangmeier, *Theologische Anthropologie des Kindes*. Zürich, 1964.
R. O. Ferm, *The Psychology of Christian Conversion*. Westwood, N.J., 1959.
K. Fezer, *Das Wort Gottes und die Predigt*. Stuttgart, 1925.
Fischer, *Erziehung als Beruf*. Leipzig, 1921.
H. M. M. Fortmann, *Aan de Mens nabij*. Nijmegen, 1957.
————, *Wat is er met de Mens gebeurd?* Utrecht-Antwerpen, 1961[2].
————, *Opdat zij Gezond zijn in het Geloof*. Utrecht-Antwerpen, 1963.

————, *Als ziende de Onzienlijke,* I-IIIa. Hilversum-Antwerpen, 1964-65.

L. K. Frank, "Fragmentation in the Helping Professions," in W. G. Bennis, K. D. Benne, and R. Chin, *The Planning of Change.* New York, 1962, pp. 43ff.

V. E. Frankl, *Homo Patiens.* Wien, 1950.

————, *Medische Zielzorg.* Utrecht, 1959.

G. Friedrich, "Geist und Amt," in *Wort und Dienst* (Jahrbuch der Theologischen Schule Bethel). Bethel bei Bielefeld, 1952, pp. 61ff.

K. Frör, "Die theologische Lehre von Gesetz und Evangelium und ihre Bedeutung für die Pädagogik," in *Glauben und Erziehen: eine Festgabe für Gerhard Bohne.* Neumünster, 1960, pp. 97ff.

————, *Biblische Hermeneutik.* München, 1961.

E. Fromm, "The Creative Attitude," in H. H. Anderson, *Creativity and Its Cultivation.* New York, 1959, pp. 44ff.

E. Fuchs, "Das hermeneutische Problem," in E. Dinkler, *Zeit und Geschichte.* Tübingen, 1964, pp. 357ff.

————, "The New Testament and the Hermeneutical Problem," in J. M. Robinson and John B. Cobb, Jr., *The New Hermeneutic.* New York-Evanston-London, 1964, pp. 111ff.

R. Füglister, *Die Pastoraltheologie als Universitätsdisziplin.* Basel, 1951.

E. Gaugler, *Der Römerbrief,* I, II. Zürich, 1945-52.

H. Gerth and C. Wright Mills, *Character and Social Structure.* New York-Chicago-Burlingame, 1953.

G. Giese, *Erziehung und Bildung in der mündigen Welt.* Göttingen, 1957.

W. H. Gispen, *Israëls "Verhaaldwang."* Assen, 1947.

————, *De Wijze in Israël.* Amsterdam, 1956.

A. Godin, S.J., *De menselijke Relatie in de pastorale Dialoog.* Brugge-Utrecht, 1964.

J. Goldbrunner, *Realisation.* Freiburg, 1966.

E. P. Gould, *A Critical and Exegetical Commentary on the Gospel according to St. Mark.* Edinburgh, 1932[7].

J. H. de Groot and A. R. Hulst, *Macht en Wil.* Nijkerk, n.d.

F. W. Grosheide, *Commentary on the First Epistle to the Corinthians.* ET Grand Rapids, 1953.

————, *Het heilig Evangelie volgens Johannes,* I, II. Amsterdam, 1950.

W. K. M. Grossouw, *Sint Paulus en de Beschaving van zijn Tijd.* Nijmegen, 1947.

H. W. Gruhle, *Verstehen und Einfühlen.* Berlin-Göttingen-Heidelberg, 1953.

R. Guardini, *Grundlegung der Bildungslehre.* Würzburg, 1957[4].

J. P. Guilford, "Traits of Creativity," in H. H. Anderson, *Creativity and Its Cultivation.* New York, 1959, pp. 142ff.

O. Haendler, *Grundriss der praktischen Theologie.* Berlin, 1957.

C. S. Hall, *A Primer of Freudian Psychology.* New York, n.d.

C. S. Hall and G. Lindzey, *Theories of Personality.* New York, 1962[8].

O. Hammelsbeck, *Evangelische Lehre von der Erziehung.* München, 1958[2].

H. Hanselmann, *Andragogik.* Zürich, 1951.

P. Hare, *Handbook of Small Group Research.* New York, 1962.

P. A. Harlé, "Le Saint-Esprit et l'Eglise chez saint Paul," in *Verbum caro* 19, No. 74 (1965): 13ff.

K. Hauschildt, "Wachstum im Glauben," in *Glauben und Verstehen: eine Festgabe für Gerhard Bohne*. Neumünster, 1960, pp. 236ff.

T. T. ten Have, *Vorming*. Groningen, 1959.

H. J. Heering, *Tragiek*. 's-Gravehage, 1961.

H. Heinrichs, *Brennpunkte neuzeitlicher Didaktik*. Bochum, n.d.

A. J. M. Hely, *New Trends in Adult Education*. Paris, 1962.

J. S. Heywood, *An Introduction to Teaching Casework Skills*. London, 1964.

M. J. Hillebrand, *Psychologie des Lernens und des Lehrens*. Bern-Stuttgart, 1962[2].

J. C. Hoekendijk, *Kerk en Volk in de Duitse Zendingswetenschap*. Amsterdam, 1948.

T. Hoekstra, *Gereformeerde Homiletiek*. Wageningen, n.d.

P. J. A. ter Hoeven, *Houdingen in Beweging*. 's-Gravenhage, 1962.

P. R. Hofstätter, "Psychologie," in *Das Fischer Lexikon*, VI. Frankfurt am Main, 1957.

L. J. van Holk, *Encyclopaedie der Theologie*. Assen, 1938.

R. R. Holt, "Forcible Indoctrination and Personality Change," in P. Worchel and D. Byrne, *Personality Change*. New York-London-Sydney, 1964, pp. 289ff.

D. E. Holwerda, *The Holy Spirit and Eschatology in the Gospel of John*. Kampen, 1959.

G. C. Homans, "Group Factors in Worker Productivity," in E. E. Maccoby, T. M. Newcomb, and E. L. Hartley, *Readings in Social Psychology*. New York, 1958[3], pp. 583ff.

L. vander Horst, *Anthropologische Psychiatrie*, I, II. Amsterdam, 1952[2].

R. Hostie, S.J., *De pastorale Dialoog*. Brugge-Utrecht, 1963

C. I. Hovland, I. L. Janis, and H. H. Kelley, *Communication and Persuasion*. New Haven, 1953.

C. I. Hovland et al., *The Order of Presentation in Communication*. New Haven, 1961[2].

P. T. Hugenholtz, *De Psychagogie of reëducatieve Behandelingsmethode*. Lochem, 1946.

A. R. Hulst, *Het heilige Volk*. Baarn, n.d.

J. W. van Hulst, *De Beginselleer van Hoogvelds Pedagogiek*. Groningen, 1962.

A. Huxley, *Brave New World Revisited*. New York, 1958.

P. J. Huyser, *De Paraenese in de Prediking*. Franeker, 1941.

H. H. Hyman and P. B. Sheatsly, "Some Reasons Why Information Campaigns Fail," in E. E. Maccoby, T. M. Newcomb, and E. L. Hartley, *Readings in Social Psychology*. New York, 1958[3], pp. 164ff.

P. J. Idenburg, "Op het Keerpunt der Onderwijsgeschiedenis," in *Gedenkboek voor Prof. Dr. Ph. A. Kohnstamm*. Groningen-Djakarta, 1957, pp. 60ff.

W. Jaeger, *Early Christianity and Greek Paideia*. Cambridge, Mass., 1961.

M. Jahoda, *Current Concepts of Positive Mental Health*. New York, 1958.

M. Jahoda and N. Warren, *Attitudes*. Harmondsworth, 1966.

W. James, *The Varieties of Religious Experience*. New York, 1902.

I. L. Janis and B. T. King, "The Influence of Role Playing on Opinion Change," in E. E. Maccoby, T. M. Newcomb, and E. L. Hartley, *Readings in Social Psychology.* New York, 1958[3], pp. 472ff.

A. L. Janse de Jonge, *De Mens in zijn Verhoudingen.* Utrecht, 1956.

W. Jentsch, *Urchristliches Erziehungsdenken.* Gütersloh, 1951.

————, *Handbuch der Jugendseelsorge,* I, II. Gütersloh, 1963-65.

H. Jonker, *Woord en Existentie als Probleem der Praktische Theologie.* Utrecht, 1959.

————, *Actuele Prediking.* Nijkerk, n.d.

C. G. Jung, *Psychological Types.* New York, 1933.

A. van Kaam, "Counseling from the Viewpoint of Existential Psychology," in R. L. Mosher, R. F. Carle, and C. D. Kehas, *Guidance.* New York-Chicago-Burlingame, 1965.

D. Katz, "The Functional Approach to the Study of Attitudes," in E. P. Hollander and R. G. Hunt, *Current Perspectives in Social Psychology.* New York, 1963.

I. Kaufmann, *Untersuchungen zur Elternrolle.* Bonn, 1963.

W. Klafki, *Studien zur Bildungstheorie und Didaktik.* Weinheim, 1967[3].

J. T. Klapper, *The Effects of Mass Communication.* Glencoe, Ill., 1960.

L. de Klerk, *Beginnende Volwassenheid.* Haarlem, n.d.

C. Kluckhohn, *Mirror for Man.* Greenwich, Conn., 1963[5].

A. F. J. Klijn, *Wat weten wij van Jezus van Nazareth.* 's-Gravenhage, 1962.

A. L. Knutson, *The Individual, Society and Health Behavior.* New York, 1965.

H. Köhler, *Theologie der Erziehung.* München-Salzburg, 1965.

P. Kohnstamm, *Persoonlijkheid in Wording.* Haarlem, 1929.

J. L. Koole, *De tien Geboden.* Baarn, 1964.

H. Kraemer, *A Theology of the Laity.* ET Philadelphia, 1958.

D. Krech and R. S. Crutchfield, *Elements of Psychology.* New York, 1961.

D. Krech, R. S. Crutchfield, and E. L. Ballachey, *Individual in Society.* New York-San Francisco-Toronto-London, 1962.

F. Künkel, *Die Arbeit am Charakter.* Schwerin, 1939[2].

————, *Einführung in die Charakterkunde.* Zürich, 1950[11].

H. M. Kuitert, *De Mensvormigheid Gods.* Kampen, 1962.

A. Kuyper, *Encyclopaedie der heilige Godgeleerdheid,* I-III. Kampen, 1908-1909[2].

————, *Calvinism.* The Stone Lectures. ET New York, n.d.

————, *The Work of the Holy Spirit.* ET Grand Rapids, 1941.

R. C. Kwant, *Sociale Filosofie.* Utrecht-Antwerpen, 1963.

R. Kynast, *Problemgeschichte der Pädagogik.* Berlin, 1932.

M. J. Langeveld, *Studien zur Anthropologie des Kindes.* Tübingen, 1956.

————, " 'Humanisering' mede in verband met 'Opvoeding'-'Kultuur,' " in *Gedenkboek voor Prof. Dr. Ph. A. Kohnstamm.* Groningen-Djakarta, 1957, pp. 153ff.

————, *Beknopte theoretische Paedagogiek.* Groningen, 1963[9].

————, *Kind en Religie.* Groningen, 1963[3].

H. Lattke, *Sozialpädagogische Gruppenarbeit.* Freiburg, 1962.

G. vander Leeuw, *Wegen en Grenzen.* Amsterdam, 1955[3].

E. Lerle, *Arbeiten mit Gedankenimpulsen*. Berlin, 1965.

K. Lewin, *Resolving Social Conflicts*. New York, 1948.

K. Lewin and P. Grabbe, "Principles of Re-education," in W. G. Bennis, K. D. Benne, and R. Chin, *The Planning of Change*. New York, 1962, pp. 503ff.

R. Lifton, "Thought Reform of Chinese Intellectuals," in M. Jahoda and N. Warren, *Attitudes*. Harmondsworth, 1966, pp. 196ff.

W. Linke, "Grundformen erzieherischen Verhaltens," in *Erziehung zur Menschlichkeit: Festschrift für Eduard Spranger*. Tübingen, 1957, pp. 291ff.

J. Linschoten, "Nawoord," in J. H. vanden Berg and J. Linschoten, *Persoon en Wereld*. Utrecht, 1956², pp. 244ff.

O. Linton, *Das Problem der Urkirche in der neueren Forschung*. Uppsala, 1932.

R. Lippitt, J. Watson, and B. Westley, *The Dynamics of Planned Change*. New York-Burlingame, 1958.

T. Litt, *Führen oder Wachsenlassen*. Stuttgart, 1962¹⁰.

S. O. Los, *Moderne Paedagogen en Richtingen*. Amsterdam, 1938.

N. Maccoby, "The New 'Scientific' Rhetoric," in W. Schramm, *The Science of Human Communication*. New York, 1963.

R. M. MacIver and C. H. Page, *Society*. London, 1961⁷.

A. J. Marrow and J. R. P. French, Jr., "Changing a Stereotype in Industry," in W. G. Bennis, K. D. Benne, and R. Chin, *The Planning of Change*. New York, 1962, pp. 583ff.

M. E. Marty, *The Improper Opinion: Mass Media and the Christian Faith*. Philadelphia, n.d.

A. H. Maslow, "Creativity in Self-Actualizing People," in H. H. Anderson, *Creativity and Its Cultivation*. New York, 1959, pp. 83ff.

R. May, "The Nature of Creativity," in H. H. Anderson, *Creativity and Its Cultivation*. New York, 1959, pp. 55ff.

J. A. M. Meerloo, *Het Web*. Den Haag, n.d.

F. Melzer, *Der Guru als Seelenführer*. Wuppertal, 1963.

O. Michel, "Der Abschluss des Matthäusevangeliums," in *Evangelische Theologie* 10 (1950-51): 16ff.

P. S. Minear, *Images of the Church in the New Testament*. Philadelphia, 1960.

K. H. Miskotte, *De praktische Zin van de Eenvoud Gods*. Leiden, 1945.

————, *Om het levende Woord*. 's-Gravenhage, 1948.

————, *When the Gods Are Silent*. ET London, 1967.

K. Mollenhauer, *Einführung in die Sozialpädagogik*. Weinheim, 1965³.

B. Morgan, G. E. Holmes, and C. E. Bundy, *Methods in Adult Education*. Danville, Ill., 1960.

C. F. D. Moule, *Worship in the New Testament*. London, 1964³.

O. H. Mowrer, *The Crisis in Psychiatry and Religion*. Princeton, 1961.

A. D. Müller, *Grundriss der praktischen Theologie*. Gütersloh, 1950.

M. Mulder, *Mensen, Groepen, Organisaties*, I, II. Assen, 1963.

T. M. Newcomb, *Social Psychology*. London, 1955².

————, "An Approach to the Study of Communicative Acts," in A. P. Hare, E. F. Borgatta, and R. F. Bales, *Small Groups*. New York, repr. 1966, pp. 132ff.

H. Nieuwenhuis, *De Taak van de Opvoeder in deze Tijd*. Groningen, 1954.
O. Noordmans, *Dingen, die verborgen waren*. Zeist, 1935.
M. Noth, "Die Vergegenwärtigung des Alten Testaments in der Verkündigung," in *Evangelische Theologie* 12 (1952-53), pp. 6ff.

W. E. Oates, *The Religious Dimensions of Personality*. New York, 1957.
Over de onderlinge Verhouding van Psychotherapie en Zielzorg. 's-Gravenhage, 1957[2].

J. Paillard, "Les Attitudes dans la Motricité," in H. C. J. Duyker, *Les Attitudes*. Paris, 1960, pp. 7ff.
W. Pannenberg, *What Is Man?* ET Philadelphia, 1970.
C. F. van Parreren, *Psychologie van het Leren*, I. Zeist-Arnhem, 1963[2].
C. H. Patterson, *Counseling and Guidance in Schools*. New York, 1962.
M. L. Peel, "Theological Education in America," in *Vox Theologica* 33 (1962-63): 85ff.
N. Perquin, *Algemene Didaktiek*. Roermond-Maaseik, 1961.
————, *Pedagogiek*. Roermond-Maaseik, 1962[6].
C. A. van Peursen, *Filosofische Oriëntatie*. Kampen, 1958.
————, "Communicatie," in M. Kamphuis, *Om de Leefbaarheid van het Bestaan*. Lochem, 1959.
————, *Body, Soul, Spirit: A Survey of the Body-Mind Problem*. New York: 1966.
A. Plummer, *A Critical and Exegetical Commentary on the Second Epistle of St. Paul to the Corinthians*. Edinburgh, 1925[2].
F. Pöggeler, *Der Mensch in Mündigkeit und Reife*. Paderborn, 1964.
H. Pohlmann, *Die Metanoia als Zentralbegriff der christlichen Frömmigkeit*. Leipzig, 1938.
K. J. Popma, "Psychagogia," in *Christelijk Middelbaar Onderwijs* 22 (1941-42): 83ff.
J. M. Price, J. H. Chapman, L. L. Carpenter, and W. Forbes Yarborough, *A Survey of Religious Education*. New York, 1959[2].
D. Price-Williams, "Cross-cultural Studies," in B. M. Foss, *New Horizons in Psychology*. Harmondsworth, 1966, pp. 396ff.
F. W. Prins, *Wisselende Aspecten in de Didaktiek*. Rotterdam, 1957.

Die Religion in Geschichte und Gegenwart, I-IV (*RGG*). Tübingen, 1957-62[3].
H. Renckens, S.J., *De Godsdienst van Israël*. Roermond-Maaseik, 1963[2].
A. Rensch, *Das seelsorgerliche Gespräch*. Göttingen, 1963.
H. N. Ridderbos, *Het Evangelie naar Mattheüs*, I, II. Kampen, 1952[2].
————, "De Apostoliciteit van de Kerk volgens het Nieuwe Testament," in J. Ridderbos, *De apostolische Kerk*. Kampen, 1954.
————, *Paul and Jesus*. ET Philadelphia, 1957.
————, *Aan de Romeinen*. Kampen, 1959.
————, *Aan de Kolossenzen*. Kampen, 1960.
————, *The Coming of the Kingdom*. ET Philadelphia, 1962.
————, *The Authority of the New Testament Scriptures*. ET Philadelphia, 1963.
————, *Paul: An Outline of His Theology*. ET Grand Rapids, 1975.

N. H. Ridderbos, *De Psalmen*, I. Kampen, 1962.

O. Riecker, *Das Evangelistische Wort.* Gütersloh, 1953[2].

D. Riesman, N. Glazer, and R. Denney, *The Lonely Crowd.* New York, 1960[4].

D. Ritschl, *Die homiletische Funktion der Gemeinde.* Zollikon, 1959.

A. Robertson and A. Plummer, *A Critical and Exegetical Commentary on the First Epistle of St. Paul to the Corinthians.* Edinburgh, 1929[2].

J. M. Robinson, "Hermeneutic since Barth," in J. M. Robinson and John B. Cobb, Jr., *The New Hermeneutic.* New York-Evanston-London, 1964, pp. 1ff.

V. P. Robinson, *The Dynamics of Supervision under Functional Control.* Philadelphia, 1949.

C. R. Rogers, *Client-centered Therapy.* Chicago, 1951.

————, "Toward a Theory of Creativity," in H. H. Anderson, *Creativity and Its Cultivation.* New York, 1959, pp. 69ff.

————, "A Process Conception of Psychotherapy," in W. G. Bennis, K. D. Benne, and R. Chin, *The Planning of Change.* New York, 1962, pp. 361ff.

————, "The Interpersonal Relationship: The Core of Guidance," in R. L. Mosher, R. F. Carle, and C. O. Kehas, *Guidance.* New York-Chicago-Burlingame, 1965.

C. R. Rogers and M. Kinget, *Psychotherapy and Human Relations.* n.p., n.d.

M. Rokeach, *The Open and Closed Mind.* New York, 1960[4].

J. Romein, "Duur en Verandering in de Geschiedenis," in *De Nieuwe Stem* 17 (1962): 615ff.

P. J. Roscam Abbing, *Diakonia.* 's-Gravenhage, 1950.

————, "De Kerk en haar Dienst in de Wereld," in N. vander Linde and F. Thijsen, *Geloofsinhoud en Geloofsbeleving.* Utrecht-Antwerpen, 1951, pp. 281ff.

————, "Over het Suggestieve in de Zielzorg," in *Nederlands Theologisch Tijdschrift* 18 (1964): 143ff.

H. W. Rossouw, *Klaarheid en Interpretasie.* Amsterdam, 1963.

J. Rudert, "Die unkontrollierte Erziehung," in *Erziehung Wozu?* Stuttgart, 1956, pp. 81ff.

H. C. Rümke, *Levenstijdperken van de Man.* Amsterdam, 1963[7].

A. A. van Ruler, *Reformatorische Opmerkingen in de Ontmoeting met Rome.* Hilversum-Antwerpen, 1965.

G. Ryle, *The Concept of Mind.* London, repr. 1962.

W. Sanday and A. C. Headlam, *A Critical and Exegetical Commentary on the Epistle to the Romans.* Edinburgh, 1945[2].

N. Sanford, *Self and Society.* New York, 1966.

H. Schaal, *Erziehung bei Kierkegaard.* Heidelberg, 1958.

E. H. Schein, "The Chinese Indoctrination Program," in E. E. Maccoby, T. M. Newcomb, and E. L. Hartley, *Readings in Social Psychology.* New York, 1958[3], pp. 311ff.

H. Scheuerl, *Die exemplarische Lehre.* Tübingen, 1964.

R. Schippers, *Getuigen van Jezus Christus in het Nieuwe Testament.* Franeker, 1938.

————, "De Dienst des Woords en het Woord Gods," in *Van den Dienst des Woords*. Goes, 1944.

————, *Gelijkenissen van Jezus*. Kampen, 1962.

————, *De Geschiedenis van Jezus en de Apokalyptiek*. Amsterdam, 1964.

A. Schlatter, *Das Evangelium nach Johannes (Erläuterungen zum Neuen Testament)*, I-III. Stuttgart, 1928⁴.

F. D. E. Schleiermacher, *Pädagogische Schriften*. Langensalza, 1902³.

H. Schlier, *Het Woord Gods*. Bussum, 1959.

J. Schniewind, *Die Freude der Busse*. Göttingen, 1956.

E. vander Schoot, *Hoofdstukken uit de pastorale Psychologie*. Utrecht, 1959.

W. Schramm, *The Science of Human Communication*. New York, 1963.

H. Schreiner, *Die Verkündigung des Wortes Gottes*. Hamburg, 1949⁵.

————, *Evangelische Pädagogik und Katechetik*. Gütersloh, 1959.

W. Schulenberg, *Ansatz und Wirksamkeit der Erwachsenenbildung*. Stuttgart, 1957.

F. Schulze, *Pädagogische Strömungen der Gegenwart*. Heidelberg, 1958.

E. Schweizer, "Die neutestamentliche Gemeindeordnung," in *Evangelische Theologie* 6 (1946-47): 338ff.

————, *Gemeinde und Gemeindeordnung im Neuen Testament*. Zürich, 1962².

C. W. Sherif, M. Sherif, and R. E. Nebergall, *Attitude and Attitude Change*. Philadelphia-London, 1965.

L. Smedes, *Mere Morality: What God Expects from Ordinary People*. Grand Rapids, 1983.

E. L. Smelik, "Pastoraat en Masker," in M. A. Beek, *Maskerspel*. Bussum, 1950, pp. 154ff.

W. A. Smit, *Pastoraal-psigologiese Verkenning van die Client-centered Terapie van Carl R. Rogers*. Kampen, 1960.

H. N. Snaith, *The Distinctive Ideas of the Old Testament*. London, 1947³.

R. Stählin, "Die Geschichte des christlichen Gottesdienstes von der Urkirche bis zur Gegenwart," in K. F. Müller and W. Blankenburg, *Leiturgia: Handbuch des evangelischen Gottesdienstes*, I. Kassel, 1954, pp. 1ff.

J. A. Stalpers, *Zelfbehoud, Aanpassing, en Cultuur*. Arnhem-Zeist, 1964.

J. J. Stam, *Rondom de Preek*. Amsterdam, 1946.

E. D. Starbuck, *The Psychology of Religion*. London, 1901².

W. F. van Stegeren, *Groepssupervisie*. Amsterdam, 1967.

A. H. S. Stemerding, *Vorming, Voorlichting, Beïnvloeding in de moderne Maatschappij*. Utrecht-Antwerpen, 1967.

F. J. Stendenbach, *Soziale Interaktion und Lernprozesse*. Köln-Berlin, 1963.

D. Stewart and T. Hoult, "A Social-Psychological Theory of the Authoritarian Personality," in *The American Journal of Sociology* 65 (1959-60), pp. 274ff.

B. Stokvis and M. Pflanz, *Suggestion*. Basel-New York, 1961.

S. Strasser, *Opvoedingswetenschap en Opvoedingswijsheid*. 's-Hertogenbosch, 1962.

C. J. Straver, *Massacommunicatie en godsdienstige Beïnvloeding*. Hilversum-Antwerpen, 1967.

H. Sundén, *Die Religion und die Rollen*. Berlin, 1966.

Theological Dictionary of the New Testament, I-IX (*TDNT*). ET Grand Rapids, 1964-74.

H. Thielicke, *The Trouble with the Church*. ET New York, 1965.

E. Thurneysen, "Rechtfertigung und Seelsorge," in *Zwischen den Zeiten* 6 (1928): 197ff.
————, *A Theology of Pastoral Care*. ET Richmond, 1962.
————, *Der Mensch von heute und das Evangelium*. Zürich, 1964.
P. Tillich, *Die verlorene Dimension*. Hamburg, 1962.
T. F. Torrance, "The Epistemological Relevance of the Holy Spirit," in *Ex Auditu Verbi*. Kampen, 1965, pp. 272ff.
C. Towle, *Common Human Needs*. Silver Springs, Md., 1973.
A. R. Trecker and H. B. Trecker, *How to Work with Groups*. New York, 1958[4].
W. Trillhaas, *Evangelische Predigtlehre*. München, 1964[5].
M. Tyson, "Creativity," in B. M. Foss, *New Horizons in Psychology*. Harmondsworth, 1966, pp. 167ff.

W. Uhsadel, *Evangelische Seelsorge*. Heidelberg, 1966.
A. D. Ullmann, *Sociocultural Foundations of Personality*. Boston, 1965.
UNESCO, *Attitude Change in Intergroup Relations*. Gauting/Munich, 1962.
H. Urner, *Gottes Wort und unsere Predigt*. Göttingen, 1961.

J. W. Vander Zanden, "The Klan Revival," in *The American Journal of Sociology*, 65 (1959-60): 456ff.
J. T. van Veenen, "De profetische Prediking," in C. W. Mönnich and F. J. Pop, *Wegen der Prediking*. Amsterdam, 1959, pp. 195ff.
G. M. van Veldhoven, *Attitudes van Meisjes in Militaire Vrouwenafdelingen*. Nijmegen, 1963.
W. Vischer, "Alttestamentliche Vorbilder unseres Pfarramts," in *Gottesdienst-Menschendienst: Eduard Thurneysen zum 70. Geburtstag*. Zollikon, 1958, pp. 251ff.
H. Vogel, "Rundfunk und Fernsehen als Kommunikationsmittel der christlichen Wahrheit," in *Evangelische Theologie* 18 (1958): 158ff.
A. J. M. Vossen, *Zichzelf worden in menselijke Relatie*. Haarlem, 1967.
J. H. Vrielink, *Het Waarheidsbegrip*. Nijkerk, 1956.
T. C. Vriezen, *An Outline of Old Testament Theology*. ET Oxford, 1958[2].
————, *The Religion of Ancient Israel*. ET Philadelphia, 1967.

J. Waterink, *Plaats en Methode van de Ambtelijke Vakken*. Zutphen, 1923.
————, *Theorie der Opvoeding*. Kampen, 1951.
O. Weber, *Foundations of Dogmatics*, II. ET Grand Rapids, 1983.
M. Weller, *Das Buch der Redekunst*. Düsseldorf, 1954.
E. Weniger, "Zur Geistesgeschichte und Soziologie der pädagogischen Fragestellung," in H. Röhrs, *Erziehungswissenschaft und Erziehungswirklichkeit*. Frankfurt, 1964, pp. 346ff.
J. Weima, *Psychologie van het Antipapisme*. Hilversum-Antwerpen, 1963.
J. A. M. Weterman, "De Verkondiging van het Woord Gods," in H. Boelaars, *Levende Zielzorg*. Utrecht-Antwerpen, 1954, pp. 174ff.
H. R. Wijngaarden, "Gesprekstherapie," in *Nederlands Tijdschrift voor de Psychologie en haar Grensgebieden*. N.S. 16 (1961): 421ff.
————, *Hoofdproblemen der Volwassenheid*. Utrecht, 1963[5].
A. de Wilde, *De Persoon*. Assen, 1951.

T. Wilhelm, "Sozialisation und soziale Erziehung," in G. Wurzbacher, *Der Mensch als soziales und personales Wesen*. Stuttgart, 1963, pp. 120ff.

M. Williamson, *Supervision*. New York, 1961.

G. Wingren, *The Living Word*. ET Philadelphia, 1960.

H. O. Wölber, *Religion ohne Entscheidung*. Göttingen, 1959.

————, *Das Gewissen der Kirche*. Göttingen, 1963.

————, *Tröste mich wieder*. Metzingen, 1964.

N. Wolterstorff, *Educating for Responsible Action*. Grand Rapids, 1980.

P. H. Young, *The Student and Supervision in Social Work Education*. London, 1967.

G. K. Zollschan and W. Hirsch, *Explorations in Social Change*. New York, 1964.

Index of Subjects

307

Index of Authors

Index of Scripture References